THE STRUGGLE AND THE DARING

THE STRUGGLE AND THE DARING

The Remaking of
French Rugby League

Mike Rylance

Scratching Shed Publishing Ltd

First published by Scratching Shed Publishing Ltd in 2018
Registered in England & Wales No. 6588772.
Registered office:
47 Street Lane, Leeds, West Yorkshire. LS8 1AP
www.scratchingshedpublishing.co.uk
ISBN 978-1999333904

Images sourced as per the acknowledgements
and courtesy of www.rlphotos.com

Cover: Christian Duplé of Bordeaux and France, *left*;
and Tony Gigot of Catalan Dragons and France

Page xiii: 'The France XIII remain world champions' announces *Miroir-Sprint,* following the victory over Australia at Lyon on 25 January 1953. Gabriel Genoud is tackled by Brian Davies, as Louis Mazon, Edouard Ponsinet and Roy Bull look on

Back (central image) and page v: Artwork for Albi Calendrier-revue by Francisco Bajén, a former Spanish Civil War refugee who settled in Albi

A catalogue record for this book is available
from the British Library.

Typeset in Oriya MN Bold and Palatino
Printed and bound in the United Kingdom by
Short Run Press Ltd
Bittern Road, Sowton Industrial Estate, Exeter. EX2 7LW
Tel: 01392 211909 Fax: 01392 444134

F.BAJÉN

Contents

The Albi forward and ex-*résistant* Gabriel Berthomieu in action for France

Preface

•

FRENCH RUGBY LEAGUE has often confounded expectation. Unpredictable, skilfully improvised, it stunned Australia with virtuoso attacking displays and defensive rigour on the tour of 1951, backing up in 1955 and again in 1960. These remain magnificent illustrations of *le rugby à treize à la française*, echoed in a home series victory over the Kangaroos in 1978.

But at the heart of these remarkable exploits there lies a paradox, in fact two paradoxes. The first revolves around the equally remarkable revival of the French game after it had been stifled by the Vichy regime. The second appears later and asks why, after a period of undoubted success, both internationally and on the domestic front, the game entered a period of slow decline from which it found it hard to re-emerge. Only relatively recently, first with Paris Saint-Germain, then, more successfully, with the Catalan Dragons and Toulouse Olympique, has rugby league in France found its way into modern professional sport.

The Forbidden Game, first published in 1999, threw up questions about the postwar consequences of the Vichy ban: the astounding rise of rugby league in the decade after the war, the difficulties it was forced to face and the continuing strife between the two rugby federations. While chasing down some answers, I wanted to give prominence to the world-class players France has produced but who are too little known on this side of the Channel. To pay homage, in fact, to those who wrote 'some of the most glorious pages in the history of French sport', as one former French Rugby League Federation president put it.

No one expects historical research to be straightforward. Far from it. But the lack of official archives was a major hurdle in establishing basic historical fact. The Federation's pre-war archives appear to have been destroyed and those from the period immediately after the war have been largely lost, either in the various changes of headquarters, or in the flood which damaged the Paris offices in the mid-seventies. No one seems absolutely sure. Frustratingly, that goes for much of French rugby league. Until relatively recently its past has remained largely unexamined, except by a dedicated few. As a minor example of the issues facing those who look for accurate details, official attendances can prove unreliable, even for finals or internationals, unless the figure given is for 'paying entries', leaving out the hundreds, sometimes thousands of spectators who had the right to free tickets. Also missing are players' first names, which were rarely used until recent times, either in team lists or in articles.

In the absence of official records, I was fortunate to be able to call on the assistance of many treizistes who went out of their way to provide information, documents or photographs. Over many years, Laurent Roldos has answered my numerous queries, provided valuable material and, as chairman of the Past International Players' Association, acted as a link to many ex-players. Two of the very greatest, Elie Brousse and Jacques Merquey, stars of the 1951 touring team, left an unforgettable impression when I interviewed them at length. Invariably it was gratifying and informative to speak to a whole cast of former players and coaches, who gave freely of their time. They are Georges Aillères, Jean-Marie Bez, Jean-Marc Bourret, Jean Cabrol,

Irénée Carrère, Pierre Chamorin, Honoré Conti, Serge Costals, Gilles Dumas, Edouard Duseigneur, André Ferren, Bernard Guasch, Antoine Jimenez, Jacques Jorda, Guy Laforgue, Patrick Pedrazzani, René Rouanet, Gilbert Verdié, Carlos Zalduendo; and players' relatives: Madame Jeannine Cabrol, daughter of Félix Bergèse; Madame Solange Berthomieu, wife of Gabriel 'Hugues' Berthomieu; Madame Jacqueline Carrère, daughter of Irénée Carrère; the late Madame Marcelle Mathon, wife of Charles Mathon. Some of those ex-players have also, of course, had important roles as club chairmen or officers of the Federation.

I am also indebted to the following journalists, officials and enthusiasts, some of whom have held high office within the Federation. Many are friends and colleagues. Jérôme Cavalli, who assisted with my earlier book, tracked down important evidence while also making useful suggestions. I also relied on Raymond Roussennac to provide elusive information. No less helpful were André Allouche, Eric Berger, Edmond Bouffil, Bernard Bru, Jacques Cavezzan, André Cros, Francis Desplats, Laurent Garrigues, Hervé Girette, Christian Jacob, Jean Larronde, Didier Navarre, Henri Planel, Pierre Rayssac, Yannick Rey, Jean Roques, Nicolas Rouzaud, Thomas Sartorel, Fernand Soubie, Jean-Louis Toulouse, Bernard Tranier.

Robert Fassolette, whose standing among historians of French rugby league is undisputed, has offered precious advice over the many years we have worked on similar projects. I am equally grateful to Louis Bonnery, a man of many roles over decades of involvement in rugby league, and whose book *Le Rugby à XIII le plus français du monde* became an indispensable reference point, along with André Passamar's *Encyclopédie*.

Not all treizistes are French by nationality. Harry Edgar, a pioneer in rugby league publishing, with whom I have also had the pleasure of working for several decades, not only read the manuscript and gave support to the project but provided important material from his own collection. Rugby league's most respected historians, Tony Collins and Robert Gate, offered valuable help and suggestions. I have also benefited from the wide historical knowledge and expertise of Neal Rigby, with whom I also worked alongside over a long period.

I should declare my gratitude to the many journalists who covered rugby league in the postwar era. Their reports and accounts are acknowledged in the endnotes, though many wrote without a byline. The source of some material, taken from cuttings, has unfortunately not always been possible to identify. Similarly, I am thankful to numerous photographers whose pictures have been passed on to me from private collections and to the artist Francisco Bajén. I apologise to copyright holders for any infringement but hope that they will appreciate that the main purpose of this book is not a commercial one.

I wish to acknowledge the assistance given by the staff of the archives of *La Dépêche* and *Midi-Olympique* newspapers and especially Carole Cosson; and of *Tarn Libre*; of the departmental archives of the Aude, the Gironde, the Haute Garonne and the Tarn; the municipal archives of Villeneuve-sur-Lot; the Bibliothèque Nationale; the RFL archives at the University of Huddersfield and the former staff of the FFRXIII in Paris. I wish to record my thanks to my colleagues at Scratching Shed Publishing and *Forty20*, Phil Caplan and Tony Hannan (who also designed *The Forbidden Game*), for seeing the project through to fruition.

I thank Laura, Dan, William and Florence for their encouragement and particularly my wife Judy for her unfailing support, patience and timely advice.

A final note of gratitude to the great American poet Walt Whitman, a half-line of whose work provided the title. An admirer of the French revolutionary spirit, Whitman wrote *O Star of France* in response to the defeat of the uprising known as the Paris Commune of 1871. The words I have borrowed for the title equally suggest the difficulties French rugby league has encountered for most of its existence, especially during and in the aftermath of the Vichy regime. They evoke the boldness of confronting those problems with an adventurous style forever associated with the French way of playing this game.

MIROIR-SPRINT

LE XIII DE FRANCE RESTE CHAMPION DU MONDE

... grâce à Puig-Aubert (10 points) et à ses avants. Les adversaires se marquèrent de près, comme sur notre cliché. De g. à dr. : Mazon Genoud, « tenu » par Davies, Poncinet (serre-tête) et Bull.
(Phot. de n. env. spécial G. Le Bihan.)

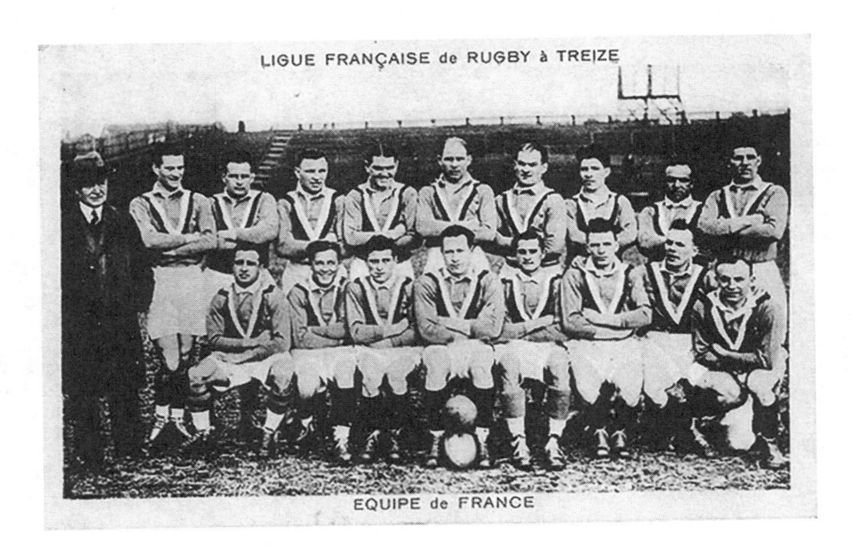

The men who started it all: Jean Galia's pioneers, March 1934

Chapter 1

•

Liberation: 1944-45

THE BIGGEST CROWD of the season turned out on the fifth of May 1941 to see Toulouse Olympique clash with Stade Toulousain in the final of the Coupe des Pyrénées, a regional cup competition. In a match played according to the rules of rugby union, the only form of rugby permitted in wartime France, twenty thousand spectators watched Olympique, the rugby league club founded by Jean Galia in 1937, defeat the famous Stade, pride of French rugby union and six-time national champion since its creation in 1907. The prestigious Stade could not compete with the upstart Olympique, whose fans cheered from the terraces as their pack tore into their red-shirted opponents. Those forwards more than made up for the absence of no fewer than five key players, while full-back Teychenné, with his accurate kicking, pinned the Stade back in their own 22 metres. Stand-off Duprat intercepted to score the first try before winger Sarris twice found his way to the line in the 14-0 victory.

It was a match, said one prominent observer, which recalled the fervour of times past, and, though a *Stadiste* himself, he had to admit the dominance of TO, based on 'the superiority of their infantry'.[i]

Toulouse Olympique was one of those clubs which continued to keep the spirit of rugby league alive despite playing with fifteen men. The victory over Stade Toulousain was no flash in the pan. Three seasons later, Olympique reached the semi-finals of the national championship, going down to another long-established club, Aviron Bayonnais, led by the former Roanne XIII and France centre, Jean Dauger. In May of the same year they won the Coupe de France by beating Stade Bordelais, one of France's oldest clubs, by 19-3 in their own city. The Toulouse Olympique captain, Robert Barran, was outstanding in a powerful set of forwards, as was, once more, full-back Marcel Teychenné.[ii]

In another derby with Stade Toulousain, the ex-rugby league team again beat their neighbours, winning 19-0. It was the final game between the two rivals. The Allied landings in Normandy, precipitating the Liberation of France, were just a month away on 6 June 1944. American and French landings in Provence, which helped seal victory over the Nazis, were to follow two months later on 15 August. Active resistance against the German occupying forces had been growing fast. The Vichy government was starting to lose its grip. But in May 1944 you could still watch one of the regime's favoured sports, rugby union, and be unaware of the impending dénouement of an occupation that had lasted four long years. At such times it might be possible to agree with the writer and Resistance activist Albert Camus that 'matches on Sundays, in a stadium full to bursting' might be one of the rare places where one felt 'innocent'.[iii]

As the Nobel Prize-winner indicated, one of the pleasures of sport is its abstraction from everyday concerns. Participation in sport was increasingly appreciated during the war years, as was noted, though with a specific reservation, by journalist Henri Garcia. 'To our society's shame,' he wrote, 'the only period when young people really occupied the stadiums was during the Nazi occupation.'[iv]

At that time the Vichy government had set about trying to

reverse what it saw as the moral and physical degeneracy of French youth by encouraging sporting activity both in schools and clubs. Measured in numbers of new participants, the plan had remarkable success, with all the traditional sports showing increased uptake in a very short period.[v]

Rugby union, apparently in terminal decline as the number of its clubs plunged by almost forty per cent in the decade up to 1940,[vi] was stabilised. Rugby league, in the six years before France's military defeat, had gone from zero to 225 clubs[vii] and looked set to overtake its older rival. Within weeks of the swiftest rout in France's history, and the installation of the puppet regime at the spa town of Vichy, the open conflict between the two codes of rugby was settled by a stroke of the pen in the offices of the Ministry of Education and Sport.[viii] As if bad for the nation's moral health, rugby league was prohibited and, crucially, was unable to take advantage of the French public's new enthusiasm.[ix]

The writer of the comments on the Stade Toulousain-Toulouse Olympique final was one of those who had paved the way for the so-called reunification of French rugby, based on the disappearance of rugby league. Dr Paul Voivenel, president of the Pyrenees Rugby Union, honorary president of the French Rugby Federation, was charged by Jean Borotra, the former tennis champion now in effect Vichy's minister of sport, with producing a report on the state of rugby. The wheels had already been set in motion to crush the treizistes; Voivenel's report helped to provide the 'evidence' to confirm a conclusion already reached in an unforgivable abuse of power.[x]

Raymond Roussennac witnessed at first hand the outcome of the quinzistes' insidious new monopoly. 'It must have been towards the end of 1943,' he recalled. 'I was ten years old. My teacher, Monsieur Arribaut, who played on the wing for TO before the ban, had to take us for a half-day of sport, which was called gymnastics – running, climbing ropes, high jump and long jump, etc – and for the last half-hour a team sport of our choice. Obviously I suggested rugby league, sure that he would agree, since I was a supporter of his. It was then that he took me aside and told me that I must not say that name again and that he risked sanctions if he allowed it to be played, but we could, if I wished, enjoy ourselves playing rugby union, which of course was not my choice.'[xi]

By the summer of 1944, however, the Vichy regime, headed by Marshal Philippe Pétain, was on its last legs. In occupied France in July and August, the balance of power tipped in favour of the Allied forces, who were making the final breakthrough in the struggle to rid France of the German army. As control of French towns and cities began to be given back to their citizens and the Germans driven out, local Resistance units played a significant role throughout the country and importantly in the south-west.

Bitter struggles and vicious reprisals accompanied the German withdrawal as the battle to liberate France reached its climax. Two young men who were to become key players in the Racing Club Albi XIII team were among those who took part in Resistance action. Gabriel Berthomieu and René Rouanet had deserted from the youth work camps which had replaced military service after France's defeat. Rouanet had been stationed in Haute Savoie in the Alps but had found his way back home despite a warrant being put out for his arrest. Berthomieu had taken leave of a camp nearer to home. They both joined a maquis group hiding out in a barn in a wooded area close to Albi.

On the night of 17 August 1944, they and two dozen others set out on the back of a truck with the aim of attacking the thousand-strong German garrison at Albi the next morning. Two other groups each comprising around thirty *maquisards* were due to fight alongside them but did not appear. Not discouraged, they took up position at dawn the next morning. When the Germans appeared, they opened fire. A second German section attempted to encircle the *maquisards*, which provoked furious fighting that lasted over three hours[xii]. As the *résistants* tried to fall back, Rouanet was forced to run between the machine-gun fire of his own men and the bullets of the Germans. Berthomieu had been positioned in a field of maize which lay outside the garrison, where fierce combat took place, with the *résistants* heavily outnumbered. The future international second rower made his escape by following a stream that was little more than an open sewer, but not before he had saved a comrade from enemy fire by throwing him to the ground. He would later call it 'the best tackle I ever made'.[xiii] Of the sub-group of ten men, only Berthomieu, who arrived back home in Graulhet on foot at four the next morning, Rouanet and one other survived. The Germans lost 72 men and quit Albi the following day after 21 months of occupation. Rouanet did not talk of bravery, even less of glory. 'We were twenty years old. We were a bit crazy,' he said.[xiv]

In the southern half of France, which, apart from the Atlantic coastline and its hinterland, was at first free from enemy command, resistance had grown after the Germans had taken control of almost all French territory in November 1942. Active defiance became stronger still when, from that same period onwards, the Nazis began to demand that young Frenchmen be sent to Germany to serve the war effort there. A number went on the run, joining maquis groups, hiding and setting up base in the depths of the countryside.

Charles Mathon, a member of Jean Galia's pioneering team of 1934 and captain-coach of Lyon-Villeurbanne in its inaugural season, founded a resistance movement in France's second city which helped young men escape to the maquis stronghold of the Vercors. With his former team-mate René Barnoud, Mathon created the Sport-Libre group which, from the autumn of 1943 onwards, channelled future *résistants* via Grenoble to the vast wooded and mountainous area of the Vercors, which sheltered some 4,000 *maquisards*.[xv] But despite his commitment to the Resistance, Mathon was to become, absurdly, one of its victims in the chaotic, turbulent spring-summer of 1944.

The first player to lift the Lord Derby trophy in 1935, when Lyon-Villeurbanne beat XIII Catalan in the Cup final at Toulouse, Mathon had temporarily left Lyon to live with his family in the country near Bourg-en-Bresse, where food was less desperately scarce than in the big city. On the morning of 9 June 1944 – three days after the Allied landings in Normandy – he went out fishing with three friends and came to a road-block manned by a maquis group. The four men showed their papers and were allowed to pass but almost immediately afterwards Mathon and one of his friends, Louis Chauvin, were called back. A local man, apparently drunk, arrived on the scene and denounced the pair as members of the collaborationist Milice. Nothing could have been further from the truth, but the maquis leader, without a word of explanation, ordered both of them to be put up against a wall and shot. Chauvin, amazingly, survived to tell what had happened; Mathon died there.[xvi]

Though a relatively small proportion of sportsmen were actively involved in the fight against the Germans, rugby players figured prominently in resistance groups in the Aude *département*, around Carcassonne, Lézignan and Limoux. Among them two men who would later come together at AS Carcassonne XIII: Louis 'Lolo' Mazon, a future France front row forward, and second rower Henri Moutou. A third, Paul Barrière, was to become president of the French Rugby League.

'The affinity that comes from rugby … leads, on the most serious matters, to secret, complicit communication which only the initiated can grasp,' wrote the leader of the resistance group in which all three took part, himself a rugby player. 'Rugby is a sect. It seems as if, through the smell of lemons and embrocation, the clatter of studs on the dressing-room floor, the accursed whistle of the unfortunate referee and the clamour of the often partisan crowd, there is a silent bond between players which breaks down all barriers, whether intellectual, social or political. [Players] know they agree: "We're not going to let them walk over us" – a reaction of human dignity and revolt against anything imposed by force, a desire to respond to the force of the occupier by a more intelligent, clandestine force, a sense of community, of team spirit and battle which rugby produces. There is no need for big words to explain the patriotism of these men… It is on the field that everything is played out.'[xvii]

Mazon, who was to make a unique reputation for himself

at ASC XIII, had been sent to a forced labour camp in Germany but had escaped and joined a resistance group.[xviii] One of his duties was to ensure food supplies to the 350 *maquisards* hiding out in the forest around Picaussel.[xix] On one fateful day, Mazon and two others were captured by the Germans and locked up in a hut. In the night he made a hole in the roof and fled. The next day his two companions were taken out and shot.[xx]

Robert Barran, former Albi and Toulouse Olympique rugby league player, and future journalist and captain of Stade Toulousain, recalled that perilous time: 'I was among those who had the luck to slip through the net, while still pursuing their sporting activity, even having the good fortune to win, with Toulouse Olympique, the last Coupe de France, before returning to clandestine life. And still there was rugby! I was able to organise the most unlikely match, to celebrate the fourteenth of July with a makeshift ball in the middle of the fir trees of the Haute Ariège. What enthusiasm, due in part to the fortuitous distribution of as much wine as we wanted, thanks to the interception of a few barrels destined for the Nazi troops. It was only a brief respite. A few days later, three of our men died on a mission and the maquis of Picaussel, in the neighbouring upper valley of the Aude, was pulling back after a hard day of battling against the SS. Charged with meeting one of their columns at the Col de Pailhères, a mountain path, now a tourist route linking Ax-les-Thermes and Quérigut, I came across my old friend, the Carcassonne … international Lolo Mazon.'[xxi]

If much of France had been freed from the occupying forces by the end of August 1944, fighting still went on in the east of the country. While some of his former team-mates had begun the new rugby season, the Paris XIII and France forward Roger Claudel was still on active service in Alsace. Joining the Free French Forces in 1943, he was later posted to an armoured division of General de Lattre de Tassigny's army and died in the turret of his tank during an offensive at Thann, in the Vosges, in December 1944.[xxii]

Even for those who were not personally harmed, the

The Struggle and the Daring

Occupation had produced stresses barely imaginable today. 'By 1944 we had slowly become used to everything, to the hunger, to the strange absences,' wrote André Amila, nephew of Gaston, another of Galia's pioneers from ten years earlier. 'It was a dangerous year and we had to watch out for the Germans' random roundups. It only needed one individual to make the wrong decision and the Nazis would have gone and raided the maquis in the upper valley [of the Aude] and everything would have got even worse. It's impossible to forget the end of that regime. In the changing rooms, hatred made its appearance. Tension was at its height. Following insults and death threats, training stopped...'[xxiii]

As the Germans withdrew, local populations often suffered acts of vengeance, ruthlessly carried out. At Carcassonne, the retreating Nazis killed 26 people and set fire to houses.[xxiv] In their evacuation of Albi, they took with them any form of transport they could lay their hands on, going from door to door, taking what they wanted and not hesitating to shoot the occupants at the slightest sign of refusal.[xxv] 'Our city, our *département* have suffered less than other localities,' reported *Le Tarn Libre*, making its first appearance on the very day the Germans left. 'But they have, particularly in the final days of the occupation, suffered enough ... for everyone to celebrate the liberation with indescribable enthusiasm.'[xxvi]

After the euphoria which followed the German withdrawal from most of France, life was slow to return to normal. The Nazis had bled the country. Food remained scarce, as did fuel. Transport was unreliable and communication often difficult. The shortage of paper reduced newspapers to a few pages or even a single sheet, though that was not the only problem to affect the press. Those newspapers which had continued to publish throughout the war suddenly stopped appearing after the Liberation, suspected rightly or wrongly of collaboration. Thus the major sporting publication, *L'Auto*, closed down and did not reappear until nearly two years later as *L'Equipe*.

When the Vichy regime collapsed as the Germans were

ousted, revolution was in the air. It was due to the political vision and rigour of General Charles de Gaulle, leader of the Free French in exile, now the head of the provisional French government, that none of the disparate forces involved in the Liberation gained control. In Toulouse, for example, 'this city of trigger-happy guerrillas'[xxvii], local resistance groups and liberation committees had seized power in the absence of a more legitimate authority until the General imposed order.

Those suspected of collaboration with the Nazis were punished, often by mob rule. Food rationing gave rise to a rampant black market. In places, industry and transport infrastructures lay literally in ruins. Inflation was running at thirty per cent. Such was the situation confronted by the two million or so French men and women returning from prisoner-of-war camps or from forced labour in Germany.

It had been four long years since the German invasion of France, since the government had fled to Vichy and since Pétain had been granted full powers. Four years too since rugby union had been resuscitated, while its perceived rival, rugby league, had been banned from French soil. At senior level, rugby league had come to a stop after the weekend of 12-13 October 1940. The last recorded game was played between the students of La Rochelle and Royan on 15 December of the same year.

In those euphoric, if materially deprived days which followed Liberation, French men and women, having shaken off the long period of repression, were at last free to express themselves without fear of censure. The collaborationists, Pétain, his prime minister Pierre Laval and other notable Vichy ministers, were taken off to Germany by the retreating Nazis. A year later Pétain, after being returned to France, was sentenced to death by the High Court of Justice, but was reprieved by de Gaulle and spent the rest of his life in permanent detention. Laval, who had tried to commit suicide, was executed by firing squad.

The task of reinstating democratic government, at both central and local level, while maintaining a common sense of purpose between all interested parties, was an immense one. The turmoil was reflected in the less complex world of rugby, but the former players and officials of the Ligue Française de Rugby à XIII who had been obliged by Jean Borotra's government department to turn to rugby union lost no time in re-establishing their game. Just three weeks after Paris, Toulouse and Marseille had been liberated, officials of the Ligue met in Toulouse on Sunday, 17 September 1944 and decided unanimously that 'on the principle that all the decrees made by Vichy are [now] abolished, and that the unjust action taken against them by Jean Borotra [is] null and void, the Ligue [will] return to its life as it was in the past.'[xxviii]

Before competition resumed, the Ligue set out certain principles. All players registered with a given club in 1939 would remain qualified to play for that club and any request to switch clubs would have to go before the transfers committee. Recalling an earlier decision from 1938 which took its example from the English Northern Union, the Ligue insisted that all players should have a regular job and that rugby league should not be their only source of income. While waiting for replies from Bordeaux, Lyon, Paris and Roanne, eight clubs were to play a series of friendly matches. Each club in the national (first) division would be required to field a reserve team and junior team. Marcel Laborde, the pre-war chairman of the Ligue who in 1940 had been summoned by Borotra to be told of rugby league's demise, was re-elected.

By Sunday 24 September, Racing Club Catalan, who had not yet ditched their wartime rugby union name in favour of their original title of XIII Catalan, were winning at Lézignan by 30 points to two. The Perpignan side had got into their stride quicker than most. Le Racing provided essential continuity by keeping team members (and officials) together, even when playing to 15-a-side rules. From the XIII Catalan Cup-winning team of 1939, key players such as full-back François Noguères, prop André Bruzy and three-quarter or stand-off Jep Maso were joined in the victorious 1945 side by future international stars such as centre or stand-off Paul Déjean, scrum-half Irénée Carrère, centre Gaston Comes and prop or second row Ambroise Ulma, all of whom had emerged from RC Catalan. 'We weren't professionals,' said Carrère, who came from the outlying village of St Féliu d'Aval. 'We just played for match bonuses, like in rugby union. We were all from the Roussillon [département], more or less. The USAP players who joined us were not given much money to sign. They enjoyed playing league more than union.'[xxix]

On the morning before that match at Lézignan, referee Vignals gave a talk to players and officials about the rules of rugby league in case some things had been forgotten. During the match, the crowd showed little reaction. Rugby league had only been adopted by Lézignan in 1939, and their supporters did not show much understanding of the game.[xxx]

The following weekend, Toulouse Olympique, without two young stars, Robert Barran and Yves Bergougnan, who were to be attracted by the aura of Stade Toulousain, were defeating Carcassonne 11-3 despite the best efforts of ASC's Félix Bergèse. This was the same Toulouse Olympique which, only four months earlier, had eclipsed the famous Stade in that final fifteen-a-side local derby.

When rugby league sprang back to life in that month of September 1944, the passion which had propelled the game forward between 1934, the year of its launch, and 1940, remained just as strong, if not greater. But in the war years the immense changes had inevitably affected sporting life and particularly rugby. The name of Colonel Joseph ('Jep') Pascot first came to the attention of a wider public in October 1940. A rugby union international who had played most of his career with the Perpignan club USAP, Pascot gained notoriety as Jean Borotra's right-hand man at Vichy's equivalent of the Ministry of Sport, since it was he who had effectively signed rugby league's death warrant.[xxxi] When it was first announced that a committee was to be set up to integrate rugby league clubs into rugby union, it was Pascot, as chairman, who saw through to completion what he had helped to instigate. His appointment, commented the Toulouse newspaper, *La Dépêche du Midi*, 'has met with unanimous approval among sportsmen and players of the oval ball game …

His fine career as a player is both proof of his authority and a guarantee of impartiality.'[xxxii] If, in 1940, rugby league players did not find that statement derisory, they would certainly have agreed with the more critical comments which appeared four years later. One article in the *Midi Libre* newspaper – also founded at the time of Liberation, as the name suggests – recalled Pascot's achievements, when he acted as Borotra's Director of Sports and when, from 1942, he replaced the former tennis player as head of the department.

'[Pascot] worked by wielding the cosh…Pascot and his acolytes knew quite well what they were doing, pursuing acts of revenge or shady schemes. Pascot was all for rugby union; rugby league, which had made an excellent start, was a nuisance to him. So he banned it! What meanness! What childishness! [But] the Sun King[xxxiii] is no sooner locked up than the Ligue de XIII re-forms and grows. Everything he did is undone and everything he demolished….is rebuilt.'[xxxiv]

The mood had now swung back, just as Pétain himself and the collaborationist Vichy regime had been dismantled and discredited. The same journalist commented, two days later, on the French Rugby Union's ambitious or perhaps foolhardy announcement of a national championship, which seemed to take no account of the severe travel restrictions in place. Soon after, the Fédération Française de Rugby backed down and instead confirmed a series of friendly matches. 'The FFR, which had powerful friends at Vichy, relied too much on them to manage its business. Thanks to those who suspected nothing, [the Rugby Union Federation] found jobs for its own … Rugby union was decreed a State sport. Benito Mussolini had discovered it long before Pascot[xxxv] … Rugby union was made compulsory in educational establishments… As for rugby league … it had been excommunicated, which has not prevented it, in a few weeks, and fairly, from putting a few spokes in its elder's wheel. The elite of rugby [union] is melting away towards [rugby league] like snow in the sun.'[xxxvi]

The writer is overstating the case but a number of clubs,

as well as high-profile players, had joined the ranks of the Ligue, even though its championship had not been completely organised. In those exceptional circumstances, it is not surprising that there were false starts, late additions and even later withdrawals. But after several clubs had played a month of friendly matches, the rugby league championship officially restarted on 5 November.

The difficulties involved in getting the clubs back into action were greater than is sometimes imagined. The wave of enthusiasm which carried treizistes along in the late summer and early autumn of 1944, the burning desire to right the wrongs of the previous four years, the excitement at finally throwing off the rugby union yoke compensated for a lack of financial investment. When rugby league was banned in 1940, the game also lost every material asset which it had gained, right down to the last jersey. The Ligue's bank account had been raided and clubs lost all their equipment, and, if they owned it, the ground they played on. One exception to the general rule was FC Lézignan, which had competed in just the one, obviously restricted season of 1939-40. In the autumn of 1940, the club secretary, who had been tipped off, withdrew all funds from the bank account while another official hid all the kit, so that when the bailiff turned up, the cupboard was bare.[xxxvii] Other clubs which could not be quite so canny had to rely on directors to guarantee their restart costs, as was the case, for example, at Carcassonne, where Messrs Noubel and Ramond underwrote the club's early expenses, possibly expecting to recover the funds confiscated under Vichy, which of course never materialised.[xxxviii] At Albi, the pre-war chairman, Dr Simon Bonpunt, and fellow-directors took charge of the expense of reviving the club, although with players being recruited largely from the local area those costs were not considerable. Apart from match bonuses, players were usually satisfied if they could be found employment at, say, the *mairie*.[xxxix] Louis Sabarthès, who joined Toulouse from Narbonne rugby union, described typical playing terms. 'When I started at Toulouse in 1945,' he said, 'we only had one training session a week, on Thursdays, but it lasted from two o'clock in the afternoon till six. Jean Galia wanted to see the ball burn our fingers. France was coming out of wartime and our match bonuses were not great. Fifty francs for a win, twenty-five francs for a draw and ten francs for a training session. At the beginning of the season we signed on for a made-to-measure suit and a pair of shoes.'[xl]

The misconception about full-time professionalism, which had provided the pretext for Vichy to get rid of rugby league, carried over from pre-war days. An article in the sports magazine *But*, which appeared two years later, was one which attempted to dispel the myth. Under the heading 'These rugby players do not earn their living from sport', the journalist Géo Villetan wrote: 'It is claimed everywhere, as a way of combating the Ligue de rugby à treize, that all its players are professionals and that they have no other job. That is perfectly incorrect ... At Carcassonne, as at Roanne, Paris or elsewhere, rugby league players work throughout the week. And the match bonuses they receive on a Sunday simply complement their wages.' The article was accompanied by pictures of four Carcassonne players: Puig-Aubert, described as a commercial inspector for a firm at Banyuls, Jean Poch, a dyer, and Roger Guilhem and Germain Calbète, both butchers.[xli]

The four clubs which finished at the bottom of the league table in the last full season of 1938-9 failed to make the starting line in 1944. Brive and Narbonne returned to rugby union; Dax, who had withdrawn in '38-39 and did not reappear in '39-40, were absent again, while Pau, who had been present in every pre-war season, could not now find a ground to play on.

As it was envisaged in October, the 1944-45 championship was to consist of twelve clubs: the majority from the pre-war period, plus Montpellier; AS Béziers, who had switched from rugby union (not to be confused with SO Béziers who played only in the '34-35 season); and Stadoceste Toulousain, a second Toulouse club formed by Jean Galia, who left the Toulouse Olympique club which he had formed in 1937. The other clubs from the pre-war era, apart from Toulouse Olympique, were Albi (established in 1934), Bordeaux (1934), Carcassonne (1938), XIII

Catalan (1934), Côte Basque (1934), Lézignan (1939) and Villeneuve (1934). AS Béziers was a potentially important addition to the Ligue, having been prompted by the Communist local council to make the switch, short-lived though it turned out. By the time the championship started on 5 November, Tarbes had also enlisted, to be joined later by Sporting Olympique Avignon, who had decided to throw their weight behind the Ligue, much to union's disadvantage. With the continuing transport problems, however, it was decided to split the division into two pools, south-west and south-east, while distant Paris, Lyon and Roanne were left out for the time being.

Just like the earliest days of rugby league in France, the Ligue's cohort of clubs remained far from fixed. The comings and goings meant that the officials who were responsible for fixtures had to improvise regularly. Jean Galia's new side, Stadoceste Toulousain, for which he had had high hopes, was forced to merge with Toulouse Olympique on 15 December, unable to secure a ground after playing only a handful of matches. Montpellier, more than half of whose team had been recruited from the Toulouse rugby union club, TOEC, quit five days later. AS Béziers, again at the local council's behest, had a change of heart and reverted to union at the beginning of March 1945. Tarbes would last no longer than the end of the season.

Below the national division, changes had also taken place. Amateur clubs came and went but it was noticeable that the region around Bordeaux had lost several teams. Bordeaux was a hub of the pre-war game where representative matches had drawn large crowds. The city remained the headquarters of the Ligue. But some of the smaller clubs along the Atlantic coast and its hinterland fell by the wayside. In Béarn, whose main city is Pau, only one club out of nine survived. Four amateur clubs in Bordeaux itself folded, along with those at Royan and La Rochelle.[xlii]

The Ligue's ambitions were signalled by the decision to play the final of the Coupe de France in Paris at the Parc des Princes. The same venue had already been used in February to celebrate rugby league's comeback. That game served both as a charity event for the armed forces still fighting in the east of the country and as a promotional vehicle for the eventual return of a Paris club to the national division, as well as to let the general public know, through the Parisian media, that rugby league was making a glorious return, liberated just as the capital itself had been six months earlier.

Carcassonne took part in both matches, facing Villeneuve in February and losing 27-18 to XIII Catalan in the final of the Cup, where centre Paul Déjean scored three tries for the Catalans and winger Frédo Trescazes achieved the same feat for the ASC, who went on, a week later, to beat Toulouse 13-12 in the Championship final at Perpignan. It was Carcassonne's first trophy of many.

The journalist Maurice Blein, who had been involved in French rugby league from the start, serving Galia's pioneers on their first tour of England as interpreter, wrote comparing the English Cup final (the second leg of which he had witnessed at Odsal) and the French. Full of praise for the Huddersfield and Bradford teams, and acknowledging the spectacle provided by the Catalans and Carcassonne, he could find few parallels, so different were the concepts of play and refereeing. The brief brawl which had erupted in the Paris final – the only one in the five matches which the two sides had played that season – was at least minor in comparison with rugby union's Championship final, also played in Paris and described as 'a sad spectacle'. Blein concluded: 'We have an enormous amount of work to do just to reach the standard of 1939. But isn't all French sport in the same situation?[xliii]

A similar point was made by the dual international Antoine Blain, who had been part of the France rugby league team which had registered its first victory in England in 1939. In an article headed 'Quinze et Treize', Blain maintained that the salient event of the 1944-45 rugby season was the rebirth of rugby league. He remarked that ever since league had reappeared on the French sporting scene there had been considerable debate about which form of rugby was the better and which one would eventually triumph over the other. In a well-argued piece, the man they called

'The Lawyer' expressed the hope that, as in England, both forms could exist side by side. Blain made the point, as the Côte Basque chairman, Georges Déjeant, had done before him in 1940, that the fundamental mistake and cause of all the friction lay in considering the men who had brought rugby league into France as dissidents, when they should have been regarded as innovators. The reasons why rugby league found new territory in France, he stated, were the same as when the game was born in England: shamateurism and distortion of the spirit of the game. Rugby league exists and will continue to exist in France, he continued, because it is clearer, more comprehensible and better suited to the individualist French temperament. Like everyone else, Blain was well aware that it would take time before France could reach the level of the team which had won the European Championship in 1939. Rugby officials of both codes, he concluded, had a great deal of work on their hands and should not waste their time on petty squabbles when more urgent matters lay ahead. He blamed particularly the rugby union officials for their intransigence and lack of comprehension and reminded them of the recent 'disaster of Richmond', when the French were routed by an English side with several rugby league players in its ranks.[xliv]

That match, played at Richmond because Twickenham was unavailable, involved a British Empire team and France. The British side, which featured rugby league stars such as Gus Risman, Stan Brogden, Willie Davies, Ike Owens and Doug Phillips, beat France 27-6 on 28 April 1945. In the France team Jean Dauger lined up at centre and on the wing the future Prime Minister, General Jacques Chaban-Delmas. It was not the first time that rugby league players – or ex-rugby league players in Dauger's case, since he had returned to union with Aviron Bayonnais – had been permitted to play union. On New Year's Day of the same year a British Army side containing Ernest Ward, Gus Risman, Doug Phillips and Trevor Foster was beaten 21-9 at the Parc des Princes by a France team in which Dauger, who scored two tries, and two other former league players, Jep

Desclaux and Yves Bergougnan, played starring roles. The usual strict demarcation between the two codes imposed by the Rugby Football Union was suspended as a gesture towards the brotherhood of arms. During wartime, rugby union players were not to be regarded as having been 'professionalised' by playing alongside rugby league men.

The links between the British rugby union authorities and their French counterparts were reconnected in the aftermath of the war and had a very significant effect in reviving French rugby union's fortunes. Cast out from the Five Nations tournament in 1931 for failing to uphold the spirit of the game on several counts, the troublesome French were thrown a lifeline in 1939. The lack of top-flight international competition in French rugby union had helped rugby league make its first, spectacular appearance on the French stage. By 1939 rugby league had gathered such a following that rugby union's governing bodies, on both sides of the Channel, were desperate to try to reverse the situation. In March of that year, with war against Germany on the horizon, the British began to reconsider the ban on the nation which was their ally both against the Germans and rugby league. Though the British, in their magisterial way, regarded the game across the Channel as still unsatisfactory, the French eventually agreed to do away with their domestic championship, regarded as the breeding ground for the shamateurism and violence which the British condemned. That move paved the way for the resumption of matches between the two nations. The future British Prime Minister Sir Anthony Eden may have played a role in the decision to bring the French back into the fold, which, if true, provides further evidence that rugby union had access to the highest authority, which rugby league simply could not match.[xlv]

In 1940 France was to be allowed back into the Five Nations championship, which, however, was cancelled at the outbreak of war. But one match between British and French representative sides – the first since the 1931 ban – did take place in February 1940 in Paris, three months before France was invaded by Germany. For the French, the match had a special significance.

It was not only symbolic of France's reintegration, but went down in the annals as the hundredth match of the France XV and could be considered as the only international match ever played in Europe during wartime. The British regarded it as a game between the British and French Armies. In any event, it ended in a humiliating 36-3 defeat for the French, who had lost many of their outstanding players to rugby league. That situation was rectified when the Vichy government came into power four months later.

At the Liberation, however, the movement of players between one Federation and the other was unprecedented. Captained by ex-Bordeaux XIII star Jep Desclaux, the Perpignan club USAP, which won rugby union's Championship final in 1944, beating an Aviron Bayonnais side with the former Roanne XIII centre Jean Dauger in its ranks, lost nine of its team to league. Was it merely coincidence that USAP had been the club of Jep Pascot?

Three of those Perpignan players were signed by Carcassonne, whose appearance in both the Championship and Cup final in 1945 marked the beginning of a historic run in which the club featured in no fewer than fifteen finals over the next nine years. They coped easily with the loss of players to the rival code, as when scrum-half François Labazuy signed for Lourdes, who won union's Championship in 1952 and '53, and prop Yves Noé, who went to 1947 Championship winners Stade Toulousain.

The Association Sportive Carcassonnaise XIII, which had switched to rugby league only in 1938, quickly achieved a fearsome reputation in the post-war period. It started up again with just two experienced players. Front rower Jean Poch led the forwards and stand-off Félix Bergèse the backs. A Basque from Le Boucau, near Bayonne, Bergèse had represented France six times at union and would undoubtedly have achieved similar honours at league if the war had not interrupted his career.

He had been made a prisoner of war but escaped from Germany back to France. With a fellow soldier he managed to free himself from the Stalag camp and set off on the long trek home. At a fork in the road at one point, he and his friend decided to split up. 'He was always lucky,' his daughter recalled. 'His friend ran into German troops and was shot; my father was able to make his way back to Carcassonne via Paris.' Once back home he was playing rugby again the very next day. Not long after his return he came across a German officer who recognised him – not as an escaped prisoner of war, but as an opponent on the rugby field when Bergèse had played for France against Germany. The German officer told Bergèse that he would be leaving Carcassonne for the eastern front in Russia and hoped that they would meet again. They never did.[xlvi]

Bergèse brought two players from his home town of Le Boucau into the ASC team – the ball-handling loose forward Germain Calbète and a back rower who quickly converted to become one of France's most accomplished hookers, the wonderfully named Martin Martin. The outstanding athlete Edouard Ponsinet, a junior triathlon champion capable of running the 100 metres in eleven seconds, came through the junior ranks and, with Roanne's Elie Brousse, formed, in the opinion of many, the world's best second row partnership. Alongside him in the ASC forwards were the two former members of the Picaussel maquis, Henri Moutou and the unstoppable Louis Mazon, often described as a 'force of nature' who never took a backward step. The Carcassonne forwards were collectively dubbed by the Villeneuve director Dr Pierre Mourgues 'la famille Taillefer' after a dynasty of fearsome warrior princes whose power extended throughout Languedoc from the tenth century onwards.

In the backs, centre Jep Maso and winger Frédo Trescazes made an exciting combination, both of them going on to become internationals. Trescazes, with prop Louis Carrère, had come from USAP, but it was the third signing from that source who was to make all the headlines from the very start. Nineteen-year old Aubert Puig, to become known throughout the world of rugby as Puig-Aubert, had, in 1944, managed to slip through the net cast by the Germans, who were rounding up young Frenchmen of his age to work in the labour camps in Germany. His team-mate Jo Crespo had not been so lucky, having been caught in a round-up and sent off to dig coal in the Ruhr, but Puig-Aubert had escaped to the depths of the Pyrenees, to the disused mines of Sahorre, where he and a few friends holed up.[xlvii]

After returning to Perpignan, the talented young full-back had been targeted by three other rugby league clubs before Carcassonne made him an offer of 150,000 francs plus a bonus of 800 francs per match and a job as a sales representative in wines and spirits. The ASC chairman Ramond, secretary Noubel and treasurer Bousquet (who would become his father-in-law) turned up at his house to make this final offer. Puig-Aubert's father, a loyal follower of USAP, was out hunting when the deal was made. When he returned, he was furious and complained to the police, pressing charges for abduction of a minor. But his anger did not last long, particularly when he discovered that a good job went with the contract. His mother, much more favourable to the move, was given the responsibility of returning the 50,000 francs which the USAP chairman had offered in order to try to persuade him to remain in this supposedly amateur sport.[xlviii]

Over the course of rugby league's dazzling revival during the coming decade, it was Puig-Aubert who embodied more than any other the game's spectacular style. The pleasure that he and so many others took in playing this game which, like France itself, had come back from the depths, was reflected by a growing public. As Puig-Aubert's team-mate, Edouard Ponsinet, remarked, 'We were happy to be alive. We were emerging from the war and we had the tough attitude of motivated winners.'[xlix]

A capacity crowd at Toulouse's Stade Chapou for the Carcassonne-XIII Catalan Cup final, May 1946

Chapter 2
•
Revival: 1945-48

SINCE THE AUTUMN of 1944, the RFL had re-established contact with key figures from the pre-war era. Marcel Laborde, continuing as chairman of XIII Catalan and president of the Ligue, requested, 'in the interest of Franco-British friendship', that a match should be played in Toulouse or Perpignan or both. Jean Galia, the great pioneer of rugby league in France, wrote asking permission to bring his Toulouse team on a short tour. At that stage – Easter 1945 – an exchange of that kind was considered impossible. 'The Committee confirmed their willingness to take a team to the South of France as soon as circumstances would permit,' it was recorded, 'but considered that at present such a journey could not be undertaken. It was pointed out by members, who had information from first hand, that travelling, accommodation, food, money, etc. were difficulties that seemed too great to be overcome, even if permission could be obtained from the Foreign Office.'[i]

By November 1945, however, Castleford, undaunted, responded to an invitation to make a brief tour in the south-west, becoming the first English club side to visit France since pre-war days. An 8-all draw was recorded at Bordeaux against a Bordeaux-Villeneuve selection and Côte Basque were defeated 11-8 at Bayonne. A crowd estimated at 20,000 watched at Bordeaux, where Castleford's tactical superiority was matched by French energy and determination, especially in defence. Already Villeneuve loose forward Gaston Calixte, by far the best player on the French side, stood out as a star in the making.[ii]

Australian journalist Harry Sunderland, who had been involved in the birth of rugby league in France, was among those who made that first post-war trip. He recalled a visit to what had been the Federation's headquarters in Bordeaux. 'It was at Bordeaux that those of us who were there were taken to the League's offices which then were just as they had been left after the last of the Vichy Government's police raids. There was, I recall, destruction and confusion everywhere; in fact, by one of those freaks, little had escaped complete damage except a coloured photograph of the Hunslet team which, as Northern RL champions, had toured in France just before the war.'[iii]

The potential problems raised by the RFL Council were as nothing in comparison to the bureaucratic wrangling over the game's future across the Channel. Fortunately the Ligue found a dynamic and tenacious new leader who was equal to the task. Paul Barrière emerged from the war as an important figure in the Resistance in the Aude.[iv] He was the nephew of Jean Bourrel, the businessman who backed Quillan rugby union club's rise to three consecutive championship finals between 1928 and 1930 and whose name is recorded as a vice-president of the Ligue when it was first constituted in 1934. But Barrière had less interest in rugby than in cycling and horse-racing – until a chance meeting with Marcel Laborde triggered an involvement which was to mark both the man and the game.

In the immediate aftermath of the Liberation, Resistance groups took on responsibility for aspects of local administration. Barrière was operating in that role at provisional headquarters at the Hotel Terminus in Carcassonne (where the proprietor had earlier allowed Allied pilots to find refuge at considerable risk to himself).[v] There he met Laborde, who had come to request a permit to travel to Paris, where he was to lodge the papers relating to rugby league's reconstitution. Laborde was impressed with Barrière and set about persuading him to become involved in the Ligue. Not only that, the Ligue's president asked the young Resistance captain to go to Paris in his place and present the dossier to the authorities.

Once arrived in Paris, waiting in the corridors of government offices, Barrière suddenly became aware of the obstacles which rugby league was going to face when he heard a civil servant mutter that rugby league would never start up again. That reactionary, disdainful attitude which harked back to Pétain and Vichy immediately sparked Barrière's sense of injustice.

The idea that rugby league would not return to the French sporting scene seemed to fly in the face of the declaration made by General de Gaulle from Algiers in October 1943. That declaration, issued by the French National Liberation Committee, the self-styled provisional government of France, was intended to reverse the legislature put in place by Vichy. As far as the Ligue was concerned, the essential factors were that any legislation forcing mergers between clubs would be annulled and that any club in existence before 16 June 1940 would have the right to be reconstituted. Furthermore the property of any dissolved association (though this did not include federations, e.g. the Ligue) would be restored. Rugby league ought, therefore, to have been allowed to return to the situation it had enjoyed before the war.

Barrière would soon find himself with a different kind of struggle on his hands. For one thing, the Algiers declaration fell a long way short of providing rugby league with a guarantee for its future. Although preventing anyone who had collaborated with the enemy from being involved in the running of a club or federation, the new legislation appeared to concur with Vichy in the way in which it upheld amateurism. First of all, the governing body of a sport had to be approved by the state, while federations with 'a commercial or profit-making aim' could be dissolved. The policy was far from what might have been expected. As one historian put it: 'This government, despite its roots in the Resistance, driven by the desire for social reform, was closely akin to the English bourgeoisie at the end of the [nineteenth] century.'[vi] Faced with such proposed legislation, Barrière might well have found himself in agreement with the view, later expressed by other historians, that 'the Liberation was a restoration, not a revolution'.[vii] Consequently, rugby league was unable to gain anything more than provisional approval, as was made clear by a government pronouncement of 25 November 1946.

The Comité National des Sports presented another high hurdle, just as it had done before the war. Membership of this autonomous organisation, which acted as an interface between sports federations and the government, not least in the distribution of grants, had always been denied to rugby league. Rugby union had seen to that by instigating a pact with other federations to keep rugby league out. Their attitude, it almost goes without saying, had not altered in the intervening period. Nevertheless, access to this institution was finally opened up, thanks entirely to Barrière. His connections in the cycling federation and his ability to convince the federations of two minor sports, archery and real tennis, were sufficient to see rugby league voted in. Not only that, but Barrière managed to get the media on rugby league's side too. 'The Parisian press gave a very warm reception to the presentation which Lieutenant Barrière[viii] gave concerning his interviews [with Ministry and CNS officials] and the outcome obtained by him in Paris,' it was reported in a newspaper article headed 'Rugby league officially recognised'.[ix] That statement would turn out to be more than a little premature.

Whatever the obstacles with which the Ligue was confronted, a wave of public support carried the game forward. As a victim of Vichy, rugby league found popular opinion on its side, especially amid the euphoria which followed the Liberation. To support rugby league was, in a sense, to support the backlash against the now vilified regime. The *sport-résistant*, as it has been called, looked forward whereas the defeated collaborationists had based their policies on a distinctly unmodern thesis.

But it is easy to gloss over the difficulties which accompanied rugby league's revival. As Robert Fassolette states: 'To emphasise the undoubted success of rugby league after 1945 makes us think, by magnifying the achievement, that its resurgence was natural and expected, even made easy – thus conferring a mythical aspect on the dazzling success of the only sport banned by Vichy – and on the other hand skirts round, by "forgetting" them historically, the many obstacles constantly placed in its path within the various sporting, educational, military and political institutions.'[x]

Because of their roles in the Vichy government, Jean Borotra, the Commissioner for Sport, and Joseph Pascot, who assisted and then succeeded him, came under examination at the Liberation. Borotra, though a faithful supporter of Pétain, had been openly defiant towards the Germans. He was arrested and interrogated by the Gestapo in Paris in November 1942 on his way to joining the Free French in Algiers and was then deported, spending a period of time in the notorious Sachsenhausen concentration camp. No action was taken against him and indeed he received the *légion d'honneur*. When he reappeared at Wimbledon after the war, it was feared that his association with Vichy might provoke a reaction. In an attempt to forestall untoward comments, his old team-mate René Lacoste wrote to *The Times*: 'All those who knew what Jean Borotra had done are proud of him. First because of his conduct in the Field, as an officer in the French Army, twice mentioned in despatches in the First World War, and again at the start of the Second. Then for his action since 1940 at the head of the "General Education and Sports Commissariat" which, under his leadership, became a stronghold of the spirit of Resistance [sic], preparing French youth for the battles of the Liberation. Finally for what he did after his dismissal from that appointment on German demand, when he tried to join the Free French to resume the armed fight and was arrested by the Gestapo and imprisoned for 30 months in Germany.[xi] He tried three times to escape, and, on the last day, took an active part in the battle against the SS. I am sure that those facts deserve to be put in front of the British public, whose sense of justice is so great.'[xii]

But Pascot – he who had persuaded Borotra of the necessity for rugby league's disappearance in 1940 – had a more ambiguous case to answer. The Führer of French sport, as he had been referred to, had openly applauded, on occasion, the occupying forces.[xiii] Certain left-wing and Resistance elements saw no good in either Pascot or Borotra. For the Committee of Liberation of the Administration of Sports, the aim of the Sports Commissariat had been to 'Nazify [French] youth in order to drive them into military participation against the Allies'.[xiv] 'The place of this traitor [Borotra], like Pascot, is in prison, to wait for their baseness and cowardice to receive exemplary punishment. That is the opinion of French sportsmen who do not forget their dead [...] Those sacrifices will never forgive treason.[xv] These views represent one extreme of the spectrum. The actual verdicts did not confirm that judgement. Pascot, like Borotra, was not seen as a political figure. The national interest had been his sole concern, he claimed, declaring, 'I lived for my work. I believed that it would endure.'[xvi] The former rugby union international got off with ten years' loss of civil rights and exile from France.

Rugby league people could certainly testify to the enduring nature of Pascot's work. From 1940 to 1944, more than one thousand million francs was invested in French sport, whereas the Front Populaire, which came to power in 1936, had only spent 63 million in two years.[xvii] In many respects, Pascot could point to an impressive legacy, with more French people than ever taking up sport, as evidenced by the substantial figures recorded by individual federations. Among the team sports, soccer's rise was nothing short of phenomenal. The figure of 7,000 clubs and 300,000 players registered in 1943 was three times higher than in 1939 and eight times greater than in 1935.[xviii] Basketball saw numbers grow from 23,000 in 1939 to 60,000 five years later. The eighteen volleyball clubs which existed in 1938 grew to over four hundred by 1944. As for rugby, the measures which Pascot had instigated in 1940 - to force rugby players to play fifteen-a-side or not at all - successfully halted rugby union's slide. In the 1943-44 season, there were 482 rugby union clubs in existence,[xix] a slight improvement on the figure of 473 in 1940. Compared with other team sports, the figures are unexceptional, but the important thing was that the trend towards catastrophe had been stopped: in 1930 there had been 784 rugby union clubs.[xx]

The war was over, the Vichy regime discredited and disgraced, but the conflict between league and union continued. Rugby union's antagonistic attitude remained unchanged. After those happy years from 1940 to 1944, when the FFR was untroubled by a rival, the union game once again had to cope with the challenge it thought it had overcome. In view of their association with the Vichy regime, it might have been expected that the union men, embarrassed by the outrage they had caused league to suffer, might make some accommodation towards league for its recent fate, possibly even reparation for all that was taken from the game, including a healthy bank account and property. Far from it.

The chairman of the Comité de l'Aude de Rugby à XV launched a typical attack in the press, using a familiar term to call rugby league's governing body a 'dissident' or breakaway federation, and comparing those involved with the sport with common traffickers on the black market – a stinging accusation given that black marketeers were seen as the lowest of the low. The same official ended by making a familiar threat – that clubs who dallied with rugby league would be excommunicated. His counterparts of the Comité Languedoc-Roussillon de Rugby à XIII Amateurs expressed their astonishment at 'the attempt to revive, in the here and now of the Fourth Republic, the methods of a past regime characteristic of Pascot and Borotra. Dissolved by Vichy, the Ligue adheres to the declaration of the Official Journal giving back to all associations abolished by the French State the right to exist.'[xxi]

Except that the rugby union authorities had no desire to see rugby league spring back to life. Until 1940, rugby union had been engaged in a bitter fight for survival. It is not fanciful to suggest that, without the Second World War and the arrival of the Vichy government, rugby union in France would have dwindled to the point where it would have given way to rugby league as the dominant code. Even a loyal supporter such as Adolphe Jauréguy, captain of the France XV in the 1920s and a legendary figure, could write, in 1939, 'The public is turning away from rugby union, dreaming of rugby league.'[xxii] The officials of the FFR were not likely to forget the predicament which the 'neo-rugby' had forced them into.

This time rugby union clubs, it was claimed, were forced to take matters into their own hands. In an article with the sub-heading 'The noxious effects of competition' (i.e. the renewed rivalry between codes), one writer expressed the view that 'the return to activity of rugby league clubs threatens to create a malaise for which the oval ball game will pay the price.' He referred to the 'violent assaults' on rugby union as league clubs went on a 'massive' recruitment drive, forcing union clubs to 'protect themselves from being stripped' by offering 'princely emoluments and fabulous positions' to certain players. The clubs responsible for all this 'poaching' were alleged to be supported by wealthy patrons 'of doubtful morality who had accumulated scandalous amounts of money' on the black market during the Nazi Occupation.[xxiii]

Any argument was put forward to present rugby union, ironically, as the victim. With views such as those in common currency, it was no surprise that, despite Barrière's skilful manoeuvrings, it would take rugby league almost four years to become a recognised sport in the eyes of the authorities.

On the field of play, rugby league was making quick progress. In this first full season of 1945-6 (the 1944-5 season had only begun in November), the championship was contested by thirteen clubs operating in a single pool. Libourne, a town near Bordeaux, was a new addition, while Cavaillon, drawing on local players, joined Avignon in representing the south-east. Despite the loss of Tarbes, Béziers and Montpellier, the Ligue was considerably strengthened by the relaunch of two established clubs from the pre-war era, Roanne, champions in the last full pre-war campaign, and Lyon. Together these two clubs would make a significant impact over the coming years.

Roanne was and is a small town but achieved success far greater than its size might suggest. Much of the credit for that was due to its chairman, Claudius (Claude) Devernois, who had led the club since 1936 and had recruited stars such as Max Rousié and Jean Dauger. In the post-war period, Devernois was one of several successful businessmen associated with rugby league clubs. The hat and knitwear company which he founded and which exists to this day, with an extensive chain of ladies' fashion shops throughout France and other countries, was based in Roanne, situated on the Loire, 50 miles from Lyon. Devernois was not only a successful club chairman. He and Paul Barrière, whom he succeeded as president of the Federation in 1955, formed a dynamic combination which took French rugby league to new heights. The club's ambition was shown when, with the former international prop and one of Galia's original pioneers, Jean Duhau, returning as coach, the Roanne directors brought in a number of top young players. Three of them, all Catalans – second rower Elie Brousse, centre Gaston Comes from XIII Catalan's 1945 Cup-winning team, and scrum-half Jo Crespo – were to figure among France's greatest players. Even in their first season back, Roanne and chairman Devernois were already looking to help rugby league's development and expansion. To boost interest for the first post-war international match in January 1946, as well as the return of a Paris club to the first division, Roanne played a league fixture against Côte Basque at the Parc des Princes, where the 1945 Cup final and the Carcassonne-Villeneuve charity match had been staged.[xxiv]

Lyon and Roanne provided stiff competition for the likes of Carcassonne, XIII Catalan and Toulouse at the top of the elite division. The ASC appeared in both Championship and Cup finals in 1945 and 1946, winning the Championship twice against Toulouse and the Cup once out of the two finals played against the Catalans. At the beginning of November 1946, Carcassonne, as champions the previous season, faced their English counterparts, Wigan. In the sunshine, after a closely contested first half, Wigan had to use all their tactical experience before pulling ahead in the second to win 26-14. Typically, the match was followed by a reception at the town hall, where the mayor of Carcassonne spoke of the wider value of such matches and of Anglo-French friendship, praising the valour of the British effort in the world conflict that had not long ended. Two days earlier, Wigan had beaten Cup finalists XIII Catalan by 37-8, scoring 29 points in the second half after the teams had gone in level at half-time. At the match, Wigan coach Jim Sullivan met up again with his old international adversary, Jean Galia, who had been in Perpignan to sign a player for his Toulouse Olympique team.

Carcassonne took note of the lessons that Wigan handed out. Five months later the ASC undertook their own short tour. In March 1947, they lost 7-2 on a heavy pitch at Swinton, but in snow at Central Park, watched by an 11,000 crowd, they defeated Wigan 11-8.

For that 1946-47 season, Bordeaux and Côte Basque merged, after both clubs discovered that their council-owned stadiums would not be available as often as needed to fulfil their fixtures. The Bordeaux chairman, Mr Calamel, stated that the merger was also driven by a desire to put together a top team capable of competing with the best, and to restore to rugby league the aura it had had in the region before the war.[xxv] The Ligue was further strengthened by the revival of Paris and the creation of a new club at Marseille. Thus the game could boast a top-level team in five of France's greatest cities.

The people of Marseille have always been known for their passion for the round ball game, but, following an exhibition match between Roanne and Paris XIII in April 1946, the famous Stade Vélodrome began to welcome rugby league on a regular basis as well. The game had first been on show there in 1938, when France played Australia. The 24,000 spectators (more than twice as many as the crowd for the first test in Paris) who turned up to see Australia win 16-11 showed that there was a future for rugby league in this important city. That match also produced record receipts for the stadium, beating Olympique de Marseille's best, which was for a football match against Sète.[xxvi] Soon after the Roanne-Paris exhibition game, another demonstration, this time given by champions Carcassonne against a Provence select XIII, was put on as part of a multi-sports gala in the stadium. It was attended by 35,000 and the decision was quickly taken, initially by four enthusiasts, to form a rugby league club to compete in the first division.[xxvii]

Typical of a period when the game could attract major industrialists, the club's great sponsor and honorary president was Paul Ricard, the founder in 1932 of the pastis company, whose yellow and blue colours were replicated in the team jerseys. A future chairman, Albin Rougier, was a director of the Saint Louis sugar refinery, for which some of the newly-recruited players worked on the docks. Many of those players were Basques, signed up and coached by Jean Duhau, who had moved from Roanne. Rugby league soon took hold – to the extent that it was said that the Olympique de Marseille football team played curtain-raisers to the rugby league. In truth, when both teams played on the same afternoon, the rugby league followed the soccer to protect the pitch, but big crowds came for the rugby, even if there was no football first – and far in excess of anything the longer-established rugby union club, playing under the OM banner, had ever managed to achieve.

Paris had competed, though with mixed success, in the first four seasons since the inception of the game in 1934, but had withdrawn before the start of the 1938-9 campaign. Ever since the very first rugby league match was played in France at the Stade Pershing on 31 December 1933, the presence of a first division club in the capital had been an objective of the Ligue. It had become a priority again in the immediate post-war period. Top-level rugby league reappeared in the capital in the form of Rugby Club Paris XIII, launched by two Basques, Maurice and Marcel Mentèche, under the chairmanship of Mr Abadie, who together recruited almost a whole team of their compatriots.[xxviii] But the new club got off to an inauspicious start from which it struggled to recover. On the opening weekend of the 1946-7 season, Paris were due to play Lyon at the Parc des Princes, but, in an echo of a pre-war pattern which led to the demise of the original Paris club, the stadium became unavailable. The match was moved not to Lyon but to Roanne. To make matters worse, four of the team's best players left before a ball was passed. The Hatchondo brothers and Bichendarritz joined the other new club, Marseille, while scrum-half Jean Dop opted to play rugby union with Agen before also signing for Marseille.[xxix] That first season was tough but the club survived to win five matches and draw one out of 23, finishing the season third from bottom, just behind Cavaillon and above Avignon and Libourne.

In their second season since re-forming, league leaders Roanne met Carcassonne in the Championship final in Lyon. Now coached by another of Galia's pioneers, Bob Samatan, Roanne put on a convincing display in sweltering heat and, with centre Gaston Comes outstanding, beat the title-holders by 19-0. Carcassonne, who had appeared in all six finals so far, Championship and Cup combined, carried off the Lord Derby trophy instead. Winger Frédo Trescazes scored three tries as Avignon, surprise finalists after finishing bottom of the league, revealed their limitations and were beaten 24-5.

After three seasons, the Ligue had been able to achieve a degree of stability, reflected in the fact that the same fourteen clubs contested the first division championship in 1947-48 as the previous year. Carcassonne, Roanne and XIII Catalan were leading the way, with Bordeaux also in contention, and the game had, as expected, found strong support in Albi, Lézignan and Villeneuve. In the south-east, Cavaillon and Avignon appeared to be on the turn, while a major force, Marseille, was about to challenge the hierarchy. Further up the Rhone valley, Lyon was soon to come into its own.

At the end of the 1947-48 season, Marseille and Carcassonne met in the first of two consecutive Cup finals. At Toulouse, the Mediterranean club beat the holders and favourites

5-4 thanks to a magnificent try two minutes from the end when scrum-half Jean Dop broke from his own line and centre André Hatchondo burst through in support for loose forward Raoul Pérez to race fifty metres for the match-winner.

For the first and only time Marseille hosted the Championship final, when a 20,000 crowd saw Roanne take the trophy by beating Carcassonne for the second year in a row. For long periods Carcassonne had the upper hand but Devernois' team retained their title by the slender margin of 3-2 thanks to a solitary try from stand-off Pierre Taillantou against a 45-metre Puig-Aubert drop goal. Champions Roanne proved worthy ambassadors for French rugby league. Ten days after beating Carcassonne, they travelled to Wigan in the first leg of a contest between champion clubs and ran the 1947 English title-holders close, losing by the narrow margin of 17-15 in front of a 24,300 Central Park crowd. In the return fixture Wigan took a tighter grip on the game as they won 24-5.

The enthusiasm of the city of Marseille for rugby league was remarkable. Despite having no great tradition of rugby, the Marseillais had taken to the game quickly. The great Mediterranean port had suffered from a mafioso reputation – the first chairman of Lyon-Villeurbanne, Joseph Pansera, was believed to have been a victim of a settling of scores carried out by Marseille gangsters – but equally, in the Vichy period, the city became home to a large number of artists, writers and intellectuals, either as a point of departure or refuge. A sense of openness and tolerance allowed a cultural life to develop even in straitened circumstances.[xxx] It was fitting that rugby league should be so openly embraced there. The early backer of Marseille XIII, Paul Ricard, had seen his own product, just like rugby league, banned by the Vichy government in 1940. The pastis which his company produced fell foul of the ban on alcohol over 16 degrees proof.

Not only in Marseille but elsewhere in the south-east rugby league was making great strides to the extent that one observer called the game 'Provence's adopted child, soon to become the spoilt child'.[xxxi] In just two years 'a tiny number' of clubs had risen to 27. By the start of the following season it was expected that no fewer than 80 teams, drawing on two thousand players, would be competing regularly.[xxxii]

But Marseille's rise contrasted with the misfortune of Paris XIII, who had rejoined the Ligue at the same time. Midway through their second season, in January 1948, the warning signs were all too visible. 'What is certain,' reported *Midi-Olympique*'s correspondent in the capital, 'is that in Paris rugby league doesn't bring in the crowds.' The team needed star players, the writer argued. Its position in the league table was modest. The public remained indifferent, although the crowds would have returned to watch a 'class' team.[xxxiii] The club folded at the end of the 1947-48 season, leaving rugby league, for the moment at least, without a first division presence in the capital.

Chapter 3

•

A New International Era: 1946-49

BEFORE THEY SET out for the first representative rugby league match to be played in France since the war, the English players received a letter from the RFL's secretary, John Wilson. The match was due to take place at the Parc des Princes on 6 January 1946, when the French would face, at their own request, an England Select team. Wilson wrote: 'The way to the Continent these days is strewn with difficulties and edged with red tape so it is of the utmost importance that all instructions be complied with to the letter [...] Paris will probably be cold and your hotel unheated, so wear warm clothing and be prepared.'[i]

Wilson's concern was justified. Paris had been liberated from the occupying German forces less than eighteen months earlier and life was a long way from returning to normal. Chronic shortages of fuel meant that many buildings could not be heated, even in the capital, where the weather was bitterly cold in a winter regarded as the most severe in living memory. Food had been strictly rationed, as in Britain, and there were regular power cuts. Nevertheless the English team arrived at St Lazare station some time after eight in the evening, having left Leeds at mid-day the day before and crossed the Channel by the Newhaven-Dieppe ferry. Watched by a crowd estimated at 10,000, the match was won 19-6 by the English XIII against the French Selection, composed of Carcassonne and XIII Catalan players, on a frost-hardened pitch. 'It was the football lesson we have been waiting for,' a French official was quoted as saying. 'Our players, who are badly in need of coaching, have learned a lot. It was just the kind of match we were hoping for and it will do the game over here a great deal of good.'[ii] The legacy of wartime was apparent. 'While the English truly played rugby league,' it was reported in *Midi Libre*, 'our players seemed essentially to play a kind of rugby curiously similar to rugby union.'[iii]

The first official international match between England and France for seven years took place at Swinton the following month, on 23 February 1946, and was won by the home side by 16-6. Of the France team which had won the famous victories against England at St Helens in 1939 and Wales at Bordeaux, only loose forward Maurice Bruneteaud and prop Henri Gibert survived. New stars who would shape the France XIII's future made their first appearance and included full-back Puig-Aubert, centre Gaston Comes, loose forward Gaston Calixte and second rower Gabriel 'Hugues' Berthomieu, who, a year and a half before, had been fighting German soldiers in the liberation of Albi. As they began their defence of the championship they had won seven years earlier, the French showed that they had a good deal to catch up on. Watched by 20,000 spectators, England went 16-0 ahead by half-time and although France narrowed the margin with three Comes penalty goals, the home country was not often troubled. A *Yorkshire Post* report pointed out 'several glaring faults' in their play – their attacks were too often predictable and their support play was lacking. In addition, 'they showed a most un-Gallic lack of thrift in the price they paid for the dummies so freely offered for sale by Ryan and McCue.'[iv] The same report did however praise the handling of both backs and forwards, which was superior to England's and 'neither [English] centre was as thrustful as Comes, a gallant and elusive runner as well as the kicker of three good goals.' Despite the efforts of loose forward Bruneteaud, the French were unable to unlock the English defence. In all, the writer thought it would be 'some time' before France regained the title.

On their own soil at Bordeaux, however, the French were more than a match for a weakened Wales side. Full-back Puig-Aubert revealed not only his goal-kicking prowess but also his counter-attacking instincts when he launched a move deep in his own half which resulted in a sparkling length-of the-field try for Paul Déjean. The outstanding forward at Swinton, Bruneteaud, a loose forward said to most closely follow the English style of play, scored another of France's tries in the 19-7 victory. A new international era had begun, which was confirmed when it was agreed in principle that France should play both England and Wales, home and away, each season.[v]

Despite their lack of competition at this level, the French were learning fast and closing the gap on England. In the opening international match of the 1946-7 season, they lost by the only try of the game, again at Bordeaux, where a 24,000 crowd watched as centre Ernest Ward crossed the line seven minutes from the end. In January the French again defeated Wales, winning 14-5 at Marseille in front of a similar-sized crowd, with Elie Brousse outstanding but well supported by fellow back-rowers Gabriel Berthomieu and Gaston Calixte. It was said of the French forwards that they gave their talented backs more opportunities than they had been used to getting against British sides, while the Welsh backs 'were surprised by the handling ability and speed of the young French threequarters.'[vi] At Headingley in the final match of the 1946-47 season, a weary England had difficulty in overcoming a French side which, if they had played with their usual verve in passing the ball, rather than go-it-alone tactics, could easily have won. In the event England triumphed 5-2, though once again Comes was singled out as the best back on the field.

By the end of 1947, France had not yet managed to beat England in four encounters but had come frustratingly close. At

Huddersfield on 25 October, the French were defeated 20-15 despite being 'livelier, better together and incomparably more attractive in their handling than a disappointing England side. The Frenchmen had all the bad luck that was going.'[vii] For the first time a French referee, Monsieur Guidicelli, officiated in an international match and the experiment was considered a great success.

However, the French got the better of the Welsh in three out of four, only losing by a slim margin at Swansea in April, when they went down by 17-15. In November, playing at Bordeaux, they won 29-21 in front of a capacity 26,000 crowd. The match was sold out two days before. 'A queue as long as at the height of the famine [during the Occupation] filled the pavement outside the Ligue's offices,' it was reported.[viii] The crowd was not disappointed. In fact they were treated to 'some great rugby'[ix] as each side scored five tries, centre Paul Déjean touching down three times for France and full-back Puig-Aubert providing, with his seven goals, the difference between the two teams.

The match served as sound preparation for the first-ever meeting with New Zealand a month later. The Kiwis had just ended the British leg of their tour, in which they had lost the Test series 2-1. The first of two matches against France was played in Paris at the Parc des Princes, where a crowd of 15,000 spectators might have been bigger had it not been for the incessant rain which had fallen all day. Despite the conditions, the play was spectacular, particularly in the second half, when the French tried to get back on terms but eventually went down 11-7. The second match, played a month later at Bordeaux, was a triumph. France beat New Zealand for the first time, winning by the emphatic score of 25-7 in front of 22,000 spectators to square the two-match series. With hooker Henri Durand – the last survivor from pre-war days – shovelling the ball out of the scrums, France's backs took full advantage. Local stand-off Robert Caillou, who scored two tries, was the pick. The Kiwis, at the end of an exhausting tour, were a pale imitation of the side which had won in Paris, but there was no doubt that the French were now breathing down the necks of the other three nations.

Towards the end of the season, in April, France took another tilt at England. Without Puig-Aubert, Durand, Caillou and Duffort, they could not contain a powerful English team, who won 25-10, and with it a second successive European championship. Nevertheless the huge 32,000 crowd at Marseille showed once more the enthusiasm of the people of that city and beyond for rugby league.

In October 1948, a France team which included six Marseille players and three from Carcassonne recorded another victory over Wales, winning 12-9. One of those ASC representatives, Puig-Aubert, who captained the side from full-back, was the outstanding player on the Swansea field. That performance was followed, a month later, by a very creditable showing against England at Bordeaux, where another capacity crowd saw a narrow English victory. France were 5-2 ahead and seemed set for a historic win until England scored ten points in the final two minutes in a surprising turnaround. But France had been impressive. 'England played well together but were upset by the individual brilliance of the Frenchmen,' it was reported.[x]

Those two matches set the France team up to receive the Australians for the first time since 1938 and only the second time in their history. In England the Australians had lost two hard-fought tests and had agreed to play the postponed third clash after their French tour, which began in December of 1948. The following month the tourists defeated France twice. Their first victory came against a side weakened by the absence of Puig-Aubert, Maso, Trescazes, Pérez and Berthomieu when they won 29-10 in front of 18,000 spectators at Marseille. France found it hard to adapt to the pace set by the Aussies and were not helped by an early injury to front rower André Béraud, followed by three others, but they were well served by forwards Calixte, Brousse, Négrier and Martin. Gaston Comes, who played full-back that day, observed: 'The Australians' game was based on a professional level of physical fitness ... on strength and particularly on the fact that the team as a whole followed the plan and obeyed to a man what the coaches asked of them... On the other hand you could say that they lacked imagination and were a little naïve, which allowed us to fool them more often than they fooled us.'[xi]

The French narrowed the gap in the second at Bordeaux, losing by 10-0. Once again the backs were not at full strength but great spirit was shown up front. 'The forwards who were called on to withstand the might of the Australian heavy tanks are due full praise,' wrote Roger Bastide in *L'Equipe*, singling out the captain, Gaston Calixte, for his 'magnificent' distribution, the excellent play of hooker Martin Martin and the line-breaking runs of second row Ulysse Négrier and prop Paul Bartoletti. In the centre, Robert Caillou and Paul Déjean put up 'impeccable' defence.[xii]

But Clive Churchill's men did not make a clean sweep of the French leg of their tour. Before those two matches, on Boxing Day 1948, after a full programme of league matches had taken place on Christmas Day, the Australians came up against the Catalans de France. This select side, made up of players born in the Roussillon region, had first played against the visiting Kiwis the previous January and had only just lost 10-7. In a bid for Catalan autonomy – a political aim long held, especially on the Spanish side of the Pyrenees – it had been suggested by their captain Paul Déjean and Federation president Paul Barrière that the Catalans de France should enter international tournaments as a team in their own right. But the RFL demurred and the 'separatist plot' was stifled.[xiii]

The Catalans started badly against the Australians and a 15,000 crowd at the Jean Laffon stadium in Perpignan saw them go 5-0 down within minutes. But even without internationals Puig-Aubert, Jo Crespo and Raoul Pérez, the Catalans were strong enough to take a grip on the game and scored tries through loose forward Marcel Blanc (Albi), stand-off André Rouzaud (Marseille), centre Jep Maso (Carcassonne) and second row Ulysse Négrier (Marseille), with Gaston Comes (XIII Catalan) adding two conversions and Paul Déjean (XIII Catalan) a drop goal. The Catalans won comfortably by 20-5 and accounted for the Australians' only defeat in ten matches, a feat which has become woven into the folklore of Catalan rugby league.

Paul Déjean recalled: 'I am convinced that everyone who played had their finest hour, and everyone who witnessed it certainly experienced the greatest joy that a spectacle of this kind can bring… No one who was there will forget it. Such empathy between the crowd and the team I never felt again. The match was quite simply brilliant, with the high points being the Trescazes-Maso try in the second half and the one scored by brave Ulysse Négrier, who went between the Australian posts with a huge blood-stained bandage around his head. And then those last twenty minutes when, like men possessed, the Australians did everything to get past us and we, just as crazy, did everything to stop them. In those last moments everyone was heroic, particularly my friend Gaston Comes. … The clamour which greeted our victory will ring in my ears as long as I live.'[xiv]

In this, the fourth season since their reappearance on the international scene, France had not yet managed to beat Australia or England. But that was about to change. On 12 March 1949, France faced England at Wembley in front of 12,500 spectators – 7,500 fewer than the RFL would have regarded as acceptable for this 'missionary' match in London, though the receipts of £2,500 (about the same as had been produced by 20,000 crowds in the north) were regarded as more than satisfactory. As it turned out, the venue suited the French more than the English. The England team was criticised for being 'stale' and 'slow-footed by the side of the sprightly Frenchmen.'[xv] Winger Odé Lespès touched down from 19-year old debutant stand-off Charles Galaup's kick to the corner for France's first try, Puig-Aubert moved up to take Jo Crespo's pass from the scrum base to drop a goal and then added a long-range, angled penalty goal for a 7-3 half-time lead. When England captain Ernest Ward countered with a similar effort with under half an hour remaining, France used all their defensive resources to keep their opponents out. It was the French who finished the stronger as loose forward Gaston Calixte, a model of intelligent play, went over and Puig-Aubert added another drop goal so that England returned home 'chastened'. The full-back's return had given a boost to France's morale. As journalist Gaston

Bénac pointed out, 'Pipette', in addition to his acrobatic performances, 'always brought with him a minimum of four points in his luggage among the packets of cigarettes.'[xvi] Six French players were nominated by the press for the inaugural man of the match trophy named in honour of Jean Galia, who had died two months earlier. The trophy was awarded to the young Bordeaux front-rower Paul Bartoletti, who did so much to disrupt the progress of the English forwards.

France's victory was given due praise in the French press. Remarkably, Pierre About wrote in glowing terms in *L'Equipe*. Remarkably, because this same writer, eleven years earlier, in a publication dedicated to condemning rugby league, wrote of how the newer form of rugby lacked subtlety alongside the 'harmonious whole' offered by union, which demanded of its players a certain 'intellectual culture'. About ended his article with a prediction. 'In a few years, perhaps less, the true rugby will find favour again with the public, because France teams will play it as it should be played, by respecting all its rules. And the spectacle it will provide, by not being artificial [i.e. by not being like rugby league], will be all the purer.'[xvii]

Now he wrote: 'From Twickenham to Wembley, what a contrast! And how we regret that 70,000 enthusiasts two weeks ago should have had to watch a disjointed French XV, short of breath, imagination and willpower, whereas on Saturday no more than 25,000 [sic] spectators who had come out of curiosity, lost in the immensity of the greyer than ever Olympic stadium, got to their feet and yelled in admiration, enthused by the courage, the vigour, the athletic and even acrobatic qualities of the France XIII repeating the feat of St Helens ten years ago!'[xviii]

Gaston Bénac made a similar point, writing of 'this cohesive, committed team which made us forget Twickenham and achieve the feat which for years we had been waiting for: to win at rugby in London!'[xix]

It was the first defeat of an England side in any sport by a foreign team at Wembley and the French were rightly proud of their exploit. Only the Welsh now stood between France and their first European championship win since 1939. With 30,000 spectators in attendance at Marseille on April 10, in the final international match of the season, France duly overcame Wales 11-0 and took the title of champions from the English, who had held it since the war. The French owed their historic victory, achieved after just four seasons, to the more adventurous play of their backs. The Tricolore wingers in particular stood out. Vincent Cantoni, in his first international season, scored the only try of the first half and added a second after the break, with Odé Lespès, regarded as the top winger in France, also touching down. The French completed their season by scoring five tries to claim a 23-10 victory over an Empire XIII (also known as Other Nationalities), a match in which, incidentally, Huddersfield's Australian full-back Johnny Hunter broke a collar bone and his compatriot, Workington second row forward Johnny Mudge, broke an arm.

The 1948-49 international season produced immense satisfaction. It gave the confidence of knowing that the rugby league nation that had come back from the dead was, on this evidence, equal to the best on this side of the globe. Just as important, it filled the France team with the self-belief that was crucial as they prepared to undertake their most ambitious international venture yet.

A caricature depicting Jep Desclaux and Yves Bergougnan, who both switched from league to union after the war

Chapter 4

•

The Bergougnan Affair: 1947-48

IN CONTRAST TO rugby league, the transition of rugby union from wartime to peacetime was relatively seamless, at least at club level. Even before the Liberation, the fifteen-a-side code's 1944 Championship final, contested by Bayonne (who had beaten Toulouse Olympique in the semis) and Perpignan, drew 35,000 spectators to the Parc des Princes. Two years later, the Pau-Lourdes final was seen by a crowd of 30,000 at the same stadium. At international level, though, France's position was more precarious.

Since being kicked out of the Five Nations tournament in 1931, the French were anxious, a decade and a half later, to get back on good terms with the British Unions. The breaking-off of relations had severely dented French rugby union's self-esteem, as well as its bank balance, and had left the door ajar for rugby league to seize the public imagination. The French had been walking a thin line. In 1939, as a means of appeasing the Home Unions, they had agreed to sacrifice their Championship, though in effect it was simply put on hold for three seasons. Not only that but a Cup competition was introduced as well (won by Toulouse Olympique in 1944), which did nothing to calm the frenzied state of the game as it was perceived across the Channel.

Top-level international competition was vital. It restarted, hesitantly, with the two matches between France and the British Army before the Welsh, whose conception of rugby was closer to the French than the English or Scottish, were first to extend an invitation, the two nations meeting at Swansea in December 1945. The Irish followed a month later, but readmission to the Five Nations championship did not take place until twelve months after, in January 1947. Even then the Scots took some persuading to travel to Paris for the opening encounter. It was said, though not verified, that it was none other than Winston Churchill who had had a word in the Scots' collective ear.[i]

After finally being reinstated in the Five Nations, the France XV was about to embark on the second season of matches against the Home Unions when the game was shaken by a huge scandal. On the eve of the opening match of the 1948 series, against Ireland in Paris, scrum-half Yves Bergougnan, the former rugby league player who had since become the undisputed star of French rugby union, was removed from the side amid allegations of professionalism.

As early as 1939, the Ligue had proposed an agreement on the movement of players between the two codes. As war broke out, the Ligue suggested at its meeting of 1 September 1939 that, considering that the country should unite in the face of the threat of war, it should not accept any rugby union player without authorisation provided that the FFR agree to do the same.[ii] At the Liberation, with peace restored between nations but not between rugby codes, it was the Ligue, once more, which took the first steps towards establishing a protocol with the FFR, despite the damage inflicted as a result of the ban imposed by Vichy's rugby union sympathisers. One of Paul Barrière's first moves, on seeking to put rugby league's case to the Minister in Paris, was to try to arrange a meeting with FFR president Alfred Eluère: 'The Ligue would like to reach the widest possible understanding with the

Federation. Mr Barrière has insisted on this point,' said the agency report. 'The two codes of rugby can live apart, he said, without making war.'[iii]

But the agreement was short-lived, with the FFR revoking the arbitration made on 10 July 1947 by Colonel Gaston Roux, the government's Director-General of Sports. Certain rugby union clubs refused to cooperate. Castres called the protocol 'an attack on individual liberty' and demanded 'a free choice for players'. The Carcassonne rugby union club claimed that there was 'only one solution: freedom for all'. The vociferous Languedoc Committee went even further, declaring, 'Languedoc demands total liberty and refuses all links or obligations towards the Ligue à Treize.'[iv]

That refusal had brought the Rugby Football League to the aid of their French counterparts. The matter had caused the RFL 'deep concern', stated the governing body's secretary, Bill Fallowfield, in a letter addressed to each of the four Home Unions, with copies sent to the sports editors of the national and regional press.

'This arbitration was made at the request of the French Rugby League to prevent the "poaching" of players by the French Rugby Union,' wrote Fallowfield. 'There is no doubt whatsoever that professionalism is being actively practised by the French Rugby Union [...]

'My Council are well aware of your Bye Laws on "professionalism" and have recently witnessed with some regret the severity with which they can sometimes be applied. I am referring to the decision not to grant the Ilkley RUFC permission to offer its ground to the New Zealand Rugby League Tourists for training purposes. [...] Our many Rugby Union friends have expressed their dissatisfaction with the English Rugby Union's ruling and are considering how such action is compatible with that of condoning the activities of the French Rugby Union. Professionalism in France is not of recent origin and for many years could be observed by those who wished to see.'

Fallowfield appended to the letter a long list of former

rugby league players who were playing rugby union in France and went on: 'As your Bye Laws might preclude the possibility of your Committee replying officially to an organisation which embraces both professionalism and amateurism, I am taking the liberty of sending copies of this letter to representatives of the Press in order that my Council may determine what steps are being taken to regularise the position.'[v]

The list referred to by Fallowfield had been drawn up by the Ligue's headquarters in Bordeaux and consisted of over one hundred names of players who had switched from league to union since the Liberation. The player at the eye of the storm, Bergougnan, who had moved from playing league with Toulouse Olympique to union with Stade Toulousain, was first on the list, but there were other well-known names who had changed codes, some of them former TO team-mates such as Jean Labadie and André Mellet and stars from the pre-war period such as Antonin Delqué and Louis Brané. According to the list, Stade Toulousain alone had recruited no fewer than eleven former rugby league players, including their future captain Robert Barran, the outstanding centre and future club chairman André Brouat from Villeneuve and the great forward Yves Noé from Carcassonne. Two star players from pre-war rugby league, Jean Dauger and Jep Desclaux, were both allowed to return to rugby union, with Aviron Bayonnais and Perpignan respectively. Before the war, the FFR, in its attempt to halt league's progress, had intimidated players by saying that there would be no return. Now there was. Among the hardest-hit rugby league clubs were Villeneuve, who lost eleven players, Bordeaux, who saw fourteen players leave, while another dozen quit Carcassonne. Côte Basque came under so much pressure that it ultimately failed to survive. On the other hand rugby league clubs wasted no time in signing up rugby union players. It is a commonly quoted fact that half of USAP's 1944 Championship-winning team converted to league, including the future international stars Puig-Aubert, Jo Crespo and Frédo Trescazes. Many other rugby union players were to follow.

Players who switched from league to union, such as

Barran and Brouat, would never have the chance to represent the France XV, despite their obvious talents, because of a slim connection with league: Barran because he had accepted an offer from Albi in order to finance his studies in the last season before war broke out and Brouat because he had played with Villeneuve immediately after the war. For Barran the switch to union came about because, as he said, 'I no longer had the rugby league mentality or physique'.[vi] It was absurd that the former *résistant*, who had made the personal commitment to combat the Nazis, could not make the much simpler choice, in peacetime, of which type of rugby to play without that option being compromised.

In contrast to the prevailing attitude in the thirties, French rugby union clubs attracted and embraced former league players. Before the war, any rugby league player or official, whether professional or amateur, was immediately blacklisted by the FFR. Now, the traffic was no longer one-way. Ex-league players, even those who had played for money, were back in favour with the professedly amateur union game. Rugby union's double standards in claiming to be an amateur sport while condoning underhand payments was at the root of the complaint expressed by Fallowfield, speaking for all of rugby league.

Yet rugby union officials up and down the land complained of having their players taken by the 'dissident' code, of having their game 'despoiled'. As the future secretary of the Ligue, Antoine Blain, argued, 'If anyone was despoiled, was it not the Ligue, when, in 1940, with a single stroke of the pen, its capital, its archives, its clubs and its players were removed at the same time as the right to play a sport which, in spite of its short history, had already earned its share of glory in the pantheon of French rugby?

'It will be alleged no doubt that in 1934 the first rugby league players were former rugby union players. But, from the earliest days, the Ligue had its juniors, of whom one of the most glorious, Bergougnan, is today a senior member of the Tricolore XV. And if you take such an argument to its logical conclusion, the first rugby players who, in 1892, contested the first championship between Stade and Racing, didn't they come from other sports?'[vii]

In any case, there was hardly a rugby union club which did not have its player or players with a rugby league background, claimed a contemporary witness, Jean Roques, the press officer of Albi rugby league club. 'This was a magnificent testimony to the dissident rugby, which produced players better than the orthodox rugby,' he wrote. 'But also the union plan was clear: no treaty with rugby league, but outright war.'[viii] Roques quoted an official of the rival Albi rugby union club, who told *L'Equipe*: 'Let the two rugbys fight it out and the one which survives will put the house in order.'[ix]

Roques asserted that rugby union clubs regularly creamed off the best rugby league juniors. 'Rugby league teams were not so numerous that one could not, after a short while, by continual bleeding, weaken, stifle and smother the [...] clubs which appeared in the Ligue's national division,' he wrote. 'The freedom which the rugby union clubs were demanding was the freedom to suppress rugby league by strangulation.'[x]

The RFL's concerns were elaborated by Bill Fallowfield in an article which appeared in the programme for the Wales v England match in December 1947. Discussing French rugby league's post-war position, Fallowfield explained: 'The recovery has not been smooth. Many of the star Rugby League players have been attracted into the French Rugby Union by enticing financial offers [...] The effect on the Rugby League was so serious that an approach was made to the Ministry of Sport, and the Chief Director of Sports, M Gaston Roux, drew up an agreement regularising the transfer of players from one code to the other.

'One hesitates to forecast how the present position in France will be viewed by the Home Unions, but no doubt there is a possibility that the splendid example set by a former British Admiral will be emulated and the telescope will be raised to the "blind eye". The evidence that some Rugby Union players in France receive remuneration for their athletic prowess is irrefutable and this evidence will be given sufficient publicity to ensure that the matter will not be conveniently ignored.

'Many Rugby Union supporters will be of the opinion that Rugby League in England has from time immemorial been poaching ready-made Rugby Union stars, and that now when the boot is on the other foot there seems to be a lot of unnecessary squealing. This is not the cause of complaint. Rugby League is offered to the public for what it is worth. It embraces both Amateurism and Professionalism, and those players who wish to receive money for their efforts sign the requisite form and openly become professional players.

'In open competition Rugby League has nothing to fear, but when the actions of our opponents are masked with duplicity, it is time for the public who support both games to know the full facts and be the ultimate judges.'[xi]

The arbitration overseen by the Director General of Sports, Gaston Roux, and put into effect in July 1947, laid down conditions for the transfer of players from one code of rugby to the other, and even allowed for clubs to have both thirteen-a-side and fifteen-a-side rugby teams. But the agreement, signed by Alfred Eluère for the FFR and Paul Barrière for the Ligue, was doomed from the start. At an extraordinary meeting of the FFR's council in Paris on 24 November, it was decided to tear it up. That in itself created uproar at all levels. The sports newspaper produced by the students of Bordeaux University highlighted the FFR's double standards, quoting Eluère, who claimed that the governing body had been busy persuading club officials of their moral duty in ensuring due observation of the rules on amateurism.

'No kidding!' exclaimed the student reporter. 'Who would ever have doubted it, even if it is public knowledge that almost all the Federation's big clubs practise shamateurism with impunity. Yes, *Messieurs les Britanniques*, the French Rugby Federation is having you on.' The writer went on: 'As for us who remain faithful to the fifteen-a-side code [...] we do not hesitate to declare, in spite of everything, that the open attitude of the rugby league is much more elegant than the ugly hypocrisy of the rugby union.'[xii]

The RFU took a very dim view of the un-British arrangement enshrined in the Roux protocol. Behind closed doors the French were given a ticking-off, so that when the official explanation came out it was said that the protocol, by allowing the passage of players from one code to another, contravened the FFR's rules on amateurism. Furthermore, it could not be accepted that the two rugby codes could co-exist within the same club because of their 'divergence of purpose'. To put the protocol into practice would be to abandon the FFR's essential aim: the playing of strictly amateur rugby. It would mean that French rugby union would 'fail to meet its international commitments, which it intends to respect'.[xiii]

There were many 'strictly amateur' rugby league players in France. The terms in which the FFR's renunciation was couched were vague on this point, referring only to the impossibility of reintegrating players who had 'manifestly or implicitly contravened the FFR's rules on amateurism'.[xiv]

If the Bergougnan affair produced a seismic shock in the French rugby world, it was preceded by the bombshell of this rejection of the Roux arbitration. The FFR had acted as it had because, as one writer put it, experience had shown the usefulness, the necessity even, of maintaining constant relations with the British.[xv] But the consequences of the rejection might be that the movement of players would become one-way only – from union to league, with no possibility of return, in other words a repeat of the pre-war situation. With the British looking on with interest, those who had crossed over from league to union were likely to be banned. The consequences for clubs such as Stade Toulousain, however, with their numerous ex-league players, would be serious. And so the Federation simply announced that those players who had taken advantage of the protocol to transfer during the close season of 1947 from league to union would now be excluded. Those who had transferred before then were largely overlooked.

Under pressure to come clean on the state of affairs in French rugby union, the FFR refuted Fallowfield's accusations that professionalism was rife in their game. Aware that the RFL secretary was drawing up a list of former league players now playing union, the FFR stated that it would take immediate action against any player found guilty of 'acts of professionalism'.[xvi] Fallowfield, aided by key information supplied by the French, quickly produced the material which would test the FFR's resolve.

The Ligue duly provided the list of players who had gone over to union, while Maurice Blein was sending other incendiary evidence. Blein informed Fallowfield that the pre-war rugby league international Jean Dauger had recently represented his union club Aviron Bayonnais against Oxford University in Paris. Dauger had also played for France against the British Army and the British Empire two years earlier. The centre had returned to Bayonne from Roanne when the Vichy ban took hold and had opted to remain there after the war. He was appointed manager of a café belonging to none other than Alfred Eluère, who was not only the FFR president but also a committee member of Aviron Bayonnais.[xvii]

But Blein also produced copies of receipts which would incriminate Bergougnan and Jean Labadie. Both had signed contracts with Toulouse Olympique at the start of the 1944-45 season. Labadie received a 30,000 franc signing-on fee but went on to play union with Lavelanet. The document concerning Bergougnan, hand-written by the player himself and countersigned by his father, was dated 8 November 1944 and addressed to the TO club treasurer, confirming that he was returning 10,000 francs of his signing-on fee and that he would return the remaining 15,000 by 30 May 1945. In the final paragraph, Bergougnan appended a reminder that the treasurer had promised to observe total silence concerning the contract made with the club on 26 October. In under two weeks therefore he had had a change of heart.

The scrum-half played for Toulouse Olympique in the 11-8 defeat of Lézignan on 29 October and proved his 'exceptional qualities'.[xviii] It was his only post-war appearance in TO's colours. The following week, instead of turning out against Villeneuve, the

20-year old half-back watched Stade Toulousain play USAP and signed for the rugby union club shortly after. 'People were surprised to see me sign for Stade when everyone thought I would stay loyal to Toulouse Olympique,' he admitted. 'The only reason is … that I prefer rugby union.'[xix] Bergougnan's partner behind the Stade Toulousain scrum was Catalan stand-off Jep Maso, soon to move in the opposite direction, signing for Carcassonne, and, completing the midfield trio of influence, was ex-league international back-rower Louis Brané.

More than three years later, on the eve of France's opening Five Nations match against Ireland in Paris on New Year's Day 1948, the news broke in all the papers that the French had left out Yves Bergougnan, their match-winner. It was a hurried decision, made in the wake of a press report in which Fallowfield, without naming names, declared that he had seen a contract signed by a member of the France XV. It quickly became clear that Bergougnan, by virtue of having played rugby league with Toulouse Olympique, was the player in question. The FFR had therefore taken the precautionary measure of dropping their star scrum-half for fear of a second spell of international exclusion. The FFR insisted that no evidence for the accusation had been given and that the player in question had signed a declaration that he had never been guilty of the charge levelled against him.[xx]

An RFU official who did not wish to be identified, when questioned by a French journalist a few days after the match, which France lost, explained that the British were now prepared to put the past behind them, as Fallowfield had predicted. They would forget the mistakes (their word), and even the rewards received or given, provided that, from a specified time, the French would return to the norm, namely the rules of amateurism.

The anonymous spokesman went further. Bergougnan would not be classed as undesirable by the simple fact of having played rugby league. Astonishingly, the official declared that it was understood that Bergougnan had returned the cheques which he had received, but even if he had kept the money, the British would still accept him as a member of the France national team.

Could it really be that the RFU was sanctioning professionalism at the heart of rugby union's most prestigious tournament, when previously any player who had, even unwittingly, turned out for a club fourth XV alongside a former rugby league player, whether amateur or not, was immediately professionalised? If the French would inform the British when they were in a position to put their house in order, the game's rulers would pass over what happened during the 'confused period'.[xxi] The period referred to was not made clear; either it indicated the Occupation, when no one played rugby league and no one played for money; or, more likely, the Liberation, when players were making quick decisions about whether to pick up rugby league again or stick with union. In any event, it revealed the RFU's unexpected capacity for forgiveness. Or, as Fallowfield expressed it: 'It is an extremely fortunate organisation which has Bye Laws, the co-efficients of elasticity of which range from nil to infinity.'[xxii]

It was unfortunate that the player in question was the sensitive Bergougnan, one of the most enigmatic figures in French rugby of either code. He appeared traumatised by the affair.[xxiii] This tall, elegant, virtuoso half-back is regarded as one of the greatest ever in his position, despite a short career which ended two years later at the age of 25 when he suffered a recurring shoulder injury. A gifted artist and pianist, he was seen as a romantic and conformed to no preconceived view of a rugby player. He became a recluse in later life, which he lived entirely in the shadow of the Stade des Minimes, then as now the home of Toulouse Olympique. That was not his first club: he first played as a young schoolboy with Gallia Club Toulousain, which switched to rugby league in March 1935, a year after the game was introduced in France. At just twelve years old, he played against the touring Leeds and Hunslet schoolboys on 17 May 1936, winning 23-8, and when the Gallia Club juniors merged with Toulouse Olympique two years later, he became captain of the junior side. When rugby league was prohibited by Vichy, he made his first team debut playing union in March 1943 and won the Coupe de France at Bordeaux the following year, alongside the former league stars Jean-Marie Vignals, another of Jean Galia's original pioneers, and his hero, Sylvain Bès, as well as his future Stade Toulousain team-mate, Robert Barran.

In a city which still calls itself the capital of rugby, Stade Toulousain was the premier sporting institution, with a history which could be traced back to the end of the nineteenth century. Though Toulouse Olympique, founded by Galia in 1937, was the superior side during the war years, it was the cachet of Stade Toulousain and the persuasive powers of its officials which lured Bergougnan to switch codes and line up alongside other former league stars. After making his first team debut on 19 November 1944, he was soon selected for his first international match, that historic game against the British Army on 1 January 1945, with Jean Dauger and Jep Desclaux. He may not have been a professional, but the club set him up as the proprietor of a high-class shirt shop in the city centre. By 1946 he was a front cover star.[xxiv] When Stade Toulousain regained some of their former glory by winning the Championship, doing the double by winning the Cup, Bergougnan was described as the best man on the field.[xxv]

After he had been omitted from the France XV to face Ireland, the FFR decided, after consulting government departments, that there was no evidence for the allegations and therefore no case to answer. More important, the International Board was satisfied that the rules on amateurism had not been infringed and a letter was received by the FFR authorising Bergougnan's re-selection.[xxvi] He returned for the match against Scotland three weeks later, when he was described as 'the soul of the France team'.[xxvii]

The whole of French rugby had been watching developments in the Bergougnan case. The Villeneuve rugby league club threatened to make public the professional contract signed by Stade Toulousain's André Brouat, regarded as an international class centre, and more would follow.[xxviii] On the other hand, once the Bergougnan matter had been clarified, other former league players, suspended by the FFR from playing with the union clubs for which they had signed, demanded the same sympathetic treatment. The ex-Villeneuve centre Jean Bellan and Lyon's former back-rower Marcel Lhoste both asked to be allowed to play again with Tarbes. The ex-Carcassonne scrum-half, François Labazuy, asked for clearance to resume playing with Lourdes. In practice what happened was that such ex-treizistes would be allowed to play union at club level, but however good they might be, they would not be selected for the national side, even at a time when the standing of the France team was at a low ebb.

The agreement signed by Barrière and Eluère had a second – and, as it turned out, much more lasting – purpose. The document was not only intended to regulate the passage of players from one code to the other, although that was certainly the major reason why its title appeared as 'Arbitration on the conflict between the French Rugby Union and the French Rugby League'. It was also intended to direct rugby league towards official recognition. It bears the mark of hard negotiation: Barrière on the one hand seeking the approval of the CNS and the state; Eluère refusing to accept that the authorities could agree to another federation being responsible for the sport of 'rugby'. The first clause of the first chapter of the arbitration stated that a new federation of amateur rugby league clubs was to be constituted, bearing the name of the Fédération Française de *Jeu* à Treize. Tucked away within this governing body would be a section dealing with 'independent', i.e. semi-professional players, called the Ligue de Rugby à Treize, the name by which rugby league had been originally constituted in 1934. In practice all of rugby league became known as *jeu à treize*, the thirteen-a-side game.

At the 1947 congress of the French Rugby League at Bayonne, the first presided by Paul Barrière, delegates agreed to their governing body's new name. In their bid to become officially recognised, treizistes had to give up the right to use the term 'rugby' in their sport's name, despite the law of 1901 allowing any sports federation to use whatever name it wanted. The quinzistes were claiming exclusive rights, even though, elsewhere in the world, both codes used the word 'rugby' in their names. The implication was that the fifteen-a-side code was and would remain the only true rugby. That was the price rugby league had to pay in order to gain official authorisation, which was an essential requirement for receiving both central and local funding. Approval would be granted by the Minister after consultation with the Comité National des Sports, the quango which had proved so intractable in the pre-war period, when it stalled tactically over admitting rugby league into its midst; an organisation which, it has been suggested, made the law of sport take precedence over the law of the State.[xxix] The attitude of the CNS was no different now, in this post-war period, due in no small measure to the fact that key members of the committee remained in place. The one significant change saw the chairmanship of the organisation pass, of all people, to Alfred Eluère, whom Pascot had first confirmed as president of the FFR in 1942. But the FFR could no longer keep rugby league out. This relative newcomer to the French sporting scene had fulfilled all the obligations, making a huge concession along the way, and was conditionally accepted on 12 May 1948.

It was understandable, after eight years spent in either complete or partial wilderness, that the mood at rugby league's 1948 congress at Arcachon should be one of 'total confidence'[xxx] in reaching legitimacy in the eyes of the French state. But there were still complications to overcome, with elements within the CNS refusing to acknowledge the candidate's case. The business rumbled on until the autumn, with neutral observers fearing a breakdown between the two parties. Even after rugby league's governing body had done everything to satisfy the requirements of the CNS, there were still those members of the organisation who favoured keeping the door closed to the treizistes. The rugby union hierarchy continued to agitate in the background, with the secretary of the FFR, Edouard Laurent, managing to convince previously favourable members against league's case. 'Like his president [Eluère], Monsieur Laurent thinks he will wear the treizistes down. Any argument is used to kill off the rival...'[xxxi]

Paul Méricamp, vice-president of the CNS and president of the Athletics Federation which supported the FFR's stance, had directed athletes not to run in an event staged at half-time in a rugby league match at Lyon. The Athletics Federation declared that, whether rugby league was admitted to the CNS or not, it wanted its amateur athletes to have nothing to do with league's 'non-amateurs'.[xxxii] Explicit examples involved the international winger Robert Joanblanq, who also represented France at athletics, and Carcassonne's international forward Edouard Ponsinet, another renowned athlete. The Athletics Federation had been approached by those with rugby union interests to ban both of them.[xxxiii]

But the anti-rugby league strategists ultimately failed to bar the sport from achieving recognition. A vote in favour of the new federation was carried. Not that the hostilities ceased against the sport obliged to carry its indeterminate new name for more than four decades. It was the first stage of what Robert Fassolette has called the 'institutional ghettoisation' of rugby league.[xxxiv]

The argument of professionalism, which, for certain elite administrators, destroyed sport's moral worth, never lost its appeal in the eyes of rugby league's detractors. That attitude persisted beyond the Second World War, with only association football, among the major team sports, achieving official recognition as a professional sport, as it did in 1932. Professionalism existed at the highest level in cycling, boxing, wrestling, tennis and the Basque sport of pelota, but concerned only individuals. The value of the collective sport of rugby, with its perceived qualities of character-building and team spirit, would be severely compromised by the exchange of money, it was suggested by officials of the fifteen-a-side code and their acolytes. Through all its brief pre-war existence, rugby league had been diabolised as a professional sport by the rugby union hierarchy, despite the obvious fact that only a dozen or so clubs paid their players, who could only ever be classed as semi-professional. It has been suggested that an anti-professional mood could be traced back beyond Vichy to the Third Republic. But Prime Minister

Camille Chautemps, the radical politician and former Stade Français rugby union player, had not been deterred from granting the Ligue recognition in 1938, even if the CNS had continually blocked rugby league's way. Politicians, of course, as well as sports federation officials, do not always reflect in their thinking and actions what happens on the ground. In the case of FFR officials, the dichotomy was particularly marked.

As Dr Mourgues of Villeneuve put it: 'All bridges between union and league appear broken. Bewildered by the sight of their teams being dismembered, the unionists have answered by paying their players more and engaging in outbidding us. President Eluère does not defend the cause of a sport but of his own shop. It should be for him to put order in his house... We could come to an agreement with him and there would be plenty of room for both rugbys. But would the unionists really want amateurism? That is the crux.'[xxxv]

Gaston Roux was fully aware of the situation at grass-roots level. His sense of frustration was palpable as he confided, 'I will be going shortly to the south to make investigations in the towns where the crisis has reached its most acute phase: Toulouse, Agen, Castres, Béziers, Carcassonne, Narbonne, Perpignan ... I know that it will lead to nothing. All rugby union players, like in rugby league, are paid... People will assure me everywhere that the FFR rules on the definition of the amateur are rigorously observed, that no one has accepted or expected a job, a share in a business or management of a business just to play rugby. People will swear that all rugby players are as unblemished as ermine. I will return to Paris with my head full and my briefcase stuffed with "proof" that our players are totally amateur. I will write my report ... which will be filed with others in a green box and will never come out again.'[xxxvi]

Chapter 5

•

From Marseille to Sydney: 1948-51

IN THE PREVIOUS two seasons, the top division had remained stable, but 1948-49 began without Paris, who had defaulted. Still it seemed there was no shortage of clubs which could be called on to join the core of ten or twelve, as happened when Béziers made a reappearance. This was not the same Béziers as in 1945, or indeed pre-war, but a club known as Aviron Biterrois, which the Ligue admitted more on strategic grounds than on the basis of a viable club. Composed largely of former union players, the newcomers found it hard to compete. Marseille, for example, beat them at a canter by over fifty points, a very big score in those days. There were changes too at existing clubs. The Bordeaux-Côte Basque merger finally came apart at the seams. Bordeaux continued alone, while Bayonne (Côte Basque) picked up the threads, except that this was a different outfit, Nautique de Bayonne. They soon went under. The team was not strong enough, the best players having remained at Bordeaux, and the support dwindled to a point which was unsustainable.

The fifteen teams in the division played each other once in

the first part of the season before the leading ten split off for the second phase, leaving the remainder to play out the rest of the season, which began in January-February. Bayonne didn't make the cut and folded in February 1949, to be replaced by Pamiers from the amateur division. RC Carpentras joined them to make a six-team competition. Carpentras was one of the leading teams in the Provence region, which now counted 27 clubs at various levels. Marseille, Avignon and Cavaillon set a lead, eagerly followed by teams at places such as Antibes, Cannes and Toulon.

Not all teams in the top division were thriving. Unthinkably, Toulouse, Championship finalists in 1945 and 1946, and Lyon, as well as Lézignan, had hit difficult times. None of these clubs made the play-offs but saw the season out as members of the lower group of six. Toulouse officials admitted having made some poor decisions in recruiting players at the start of the season, but asked: 'Is that sufficient reason to allow a club to perish which has contributed so much to the marvellous rise of rugby league in a city where it seemed an impossible task?'[i] It was suggested that a huge investment of capital was needed to sign star players who would bring back the crowds to the Stade des Minimes.

A month later, Jean Galia, the founder of Toulouse Olympique in 1937 and the great pioneer of French rugby league, was dead at the age of 43 from a heart condition. From being chairman of the club before the war and again in peacetime, Galia, a dual international of the highest order, had continued to coach the team after handing over the chairmanship, as well as carrying on his various business interests in the entertainment world. At his death he was on the point of opening Toulouse's first casino, having previously established a chain of cinemas. Many were the tributes paid to him. Referring to his role in establishing rugby league in France when he was just 29, it was said that 'he showed exceptional qualities as an organiser and leader of men' and that this 'born winner … always confronted danger head on.'[ii]

Galia's achievement was immense. Fifteen years on from its launch, despite the exceptional injustice of being totally prohibited for four of those years, rugby league now rivalled the major team sports in terms of public enthusiasm. The 'impossible task' of raising a rugby league club in Toulouse, the capital of rugby (union), was comparatively small compared with the enormous gamble of introducing the game throughout the country.

Two years after Galia's death, one of his original seventeen, François Récaborde, was killed in a road accident on the way back from a rugby union match. Récaborde had been instrumental in setting up the Pau rugby league club in 1934 although it did not restart, ten years on, owing to the lack of a ground. At the time of his death, in January 1951, there had been talk of relaunching the club, with Récaborde, a local councillor, at the helm. He had a distinguished war record. He was taken prisoner in 1940 after Dunkirk but escaped from a German convoy and made his way back to Pau, playing an 'extremely active' role in the resistance. He was arrested by the Gestapo and sent to Buchenwald concentration camp, but once more returned to Pau where he was voted on to the town council in the first elections after the war.[iii]

Galia's original focus had been the big centres of population and if Paris and now Toulouse were faltering, Marseille was proving the embodiment of his dream. Victors over Carcassonne in the 1948 Cup final, the Mediterranean club was now set to appear, in May 1949, in both the final of the Cup and the Championship against those same opponents.

At the end of second phase of the season, the top four teams in the ten-strong elite pool – Carcassonne, Marseille, Roanne and Albi - contested the semi-finals. League leaders ASC duly resisted Albi's challenge by winning at Toulouse, while Marseille overcame Roanne at Lyon.

Since the same two teams had also reached the final of the Lord Derby trophy, the Ligue decided that the Cup final should be hosted by Marseille and that Carcassonne should be the venue for the Championship final. At the Stade Vélodrome, where 25,000 spectators had arrived, Marseille, the Cup-holders, got the better of the ASC, just as they had done the previous season. Although

Carcassonne scored three tries, through wingers Vaslin, who touched down twice, and Thomas, Puig-Aubert was off-form with his kicking. Marseille crossed the ASC line just twice, when Pérez and Dop went over, but Dehaye's two conversions and a penalty made the difference as the 'home' side reclaimed the trophy by 12-9.

Carcassonne were confident of revenge on their own ground, where 23,500 fans watched as the locals took a 5-0 lead from a try scored by second rower Py, converted by Puig-Aubert. But towards the half-hour mark, winger Vaslin took a knock on the thigh and was a passenger for the remainder of the match. Marseille rallied and wingers Costa and Albert André both touched down. Two conversions and a penalty goal from full-back Fachan took the score to 12-5, sufficient to deprive the ASC of victory. Marseille had thus done the double in only the third year of their existence, testimony to the quality of their team under the astute coaching of Jean Duhau. The forwards were all internationals: loose forward Raoul Pérez, the Catalan second row of Ulysse Négrier and Elie Brousse, props André Béraud and François Rinaldi, and hooker Henri Durand made a powerful pack which could also handle the ball with skill. At scrum-half the inimitable Jean Dop constantly had opposition defences guessing.

The rivalry between Marseille and Carcassonne is a feature of the late forties and early fifties. With appearances in all ten finals since 1945, the Canaries were a model of consistency. An already fearsome set of forwards was boosted with the arrival, in that 1948-49 season, of Henri Vaslin, who had signed from Tarbes rugby union. A tough-as-they-come prop or second row, Vaslin had pace enough, like Edouard Ponsinet, to play on the wing, from where he scored his two tries in the Cup final.

Among that Carcassonne pack figured Louis 'Lolo' Mazon, the former *résistant* from Le Chalabre. A particularly fierce rivalry existed between Mazon and his XIII Catalan opposite number, Ambroise Ulma. Matches between Carcassonne and the Catalans were always intense, none more so than the fixture at Stade Jean Laffon, Perpignan, that season. ASC coach René

Carrasco recalled an altercation between the two front rowers after Ulma's charge had been stopped by Mazon, who reportedly put his knee in his opponent's face. As the two grappled on the ground, there followed 'a riot on the terraces and an all-in brawl on the pitch. Since the victim [Ulma] was a member of the local constabulary, the service of law and order entered the pitch armed with their truncheons and proceeded to avenge their fallen comrade. A forceful intervention by Ponsinet flung one of these gentlemen a good two metres. The crowd invaded the pitch... Martung, the referee, a police inspector in Bordeaux, calmed everyone by dismissing Mazon, who refused to leave the field. Martin managed to persuade him and accompanied him to the dressing-room.' But when Mazon emerged, an angry crowd was waiting for him and the front rower was forced to make his escape over adjoining gardens, climbing over fences as the mob pursued him. Somehow or other the team bus picked him up from a café at Sigean on the way back to Carcassonne. It was then that he learned that, in his absence, his team-mates had scored four tries in the last ten minutes to win 24-18.[iv]

During the close season the Federation's annual congress took place at Vichy. Though no one said so at the time, the choice of venue had more than a touch of revanchism about it. Symbolism too, in that the game which had been killed off in the name of the regime which sat in this spa town had gloriously returned to defy its persecutors. If only the delegates could have shown similar unity in determining their immediate future. Stormy exchanges ensued between the council and officials who 'did nothing to hide their displeasure.'[v] The two main points at dispute were whether to have a single national division at the top level or regional pools. President Barrière and vice-president Devernois, both of whom were adamant that rugby league should have the highest profile, saw to it that a single division was maintained, but the composition of that group also brought about fierce debate. In the event, Béziers, who had struggled throughout the season just ended, were demoted to the newly-created second division. Much more controversial was the fate of Roanne,

Championship winners in 1939 and again as recently as 1947 and 1948.

As Roanne chairman, Devernois had become frustrated at the limitations imposed on the club. A lock-out crowd of 8,000 for a home match against Carcassonne in 1948 had convinced him that the future lay elsewhere. Despite Devernois' pleas, the local mayor, reputedly a quinziste sympathiser, had refused to sanction improvements to the council-owned stadium which would allow its capacity to be increased. Meanwhile, some fifty miles away, Lyon rugby league club – not the pre-war Lyon-Villeurbanne but FC Lyon which had switched from union after the war – was floundering. Mindful of the need to maintain a strong rugby league presence in the city, and aware that, among the big city clubs, Paris had already gone and Toulouse was fading, Devernois solved a problem by taking Roanne's best players and moving them to Lyon, where they had a rapid and salutary effect on that club's fortunes.[vi] The by-product was Roanne's demotion to the second tier, where they remained for several years before returning to the elite.

In the newly-created second division, Roanne joined Carpentras and three other clubs from the Provence region – Orange, Salon and Cannes. To these were added Pamiers, Cahors and Arcachon and a second club in Lyon.

At the following year's congress at Aix-en-Provence further discussion took place about the status of players in the top division. 'Professional' was not a description that found favour, despite the fact that all players were paid. But since those same players also had a full-time job and played for match fees, the term 'professional' was rejected and it was decided to retain the pre-war epithet of 'independent' to distinguish them from the amateurs. Their status was actually semi-professional and it was not always the rugby which took precedence over the day job. Lézignan, for example, asked that their first fixture of the 1949-50 season, to be played at Bordeaux, should be postponed since players were fully occupied with the grape harvest.[vii]

Villeneuve's *éminence grise*, Dr Mourgues, who had been

involved with the club since its early years, made cutting comments about perceived ideas of professionalism and amateurism. Writing in October 1944, almost as soon as rugby league became re-established, he pointed out that club officials were not managers or impresarios making big profits 'by the sweat of our players.' Yet the term 'professional' had become an automatic label attached to players in the national division. Mourgues emphasised the educational values promoted by clubs, whose juniors would follow the first team by playing against similar teams of the same age. 'Can anyone show me a rugby union club which does the same for its juniors?' he asked, before adding: 'Those who insinuate that we gorge on huge profits would do well to come and see for themselves what our commitment costs financially. Why not ask what a rugby union club does ... which has taken more than 500,000 francs in receipts from a single match? Where does the money go from these receipts, *Messieurs les Amateurs*? Not to your players, I suppose, since you made them take the Athletes' Oath? [A reference to the Vichy practice of making sportsmen take an oath of amateurism.] Does it then go into your pockets? Tell us then where it goes.'[viii]

The point made by Dr Mourgues about fostering junior teams was echoed in an editorial in *Rugby Treize*, the game's official bulletin The writer claimed that before rugby league arrived in France in 1934, it was unusual, with the possible exception of basketball, to see teams of youngsters giving their all on the sports ground. But thanks to the Ligue's 'enlightened' officials, junior teams had been formed wherever rugby league had taken root. The nature of the game – the necessity for speed, agility, quick decision-making, self-discipline and a healthy régime – made it an ideal sport. 'The Ligue which administers [rugby league], though it deals with adults, does not neglect its young teams either since, barely risen from the ashes in which Vichyites and Hitlerites aimed to bury it, it put back on its calendar, after barely a season, the French junior championship.'[ix]

The label of professionalism could also have proved costly as the government sought to levy a tax on professional sport, which *Rugby Treize* pointed out as early as 1946. 'A plan has been drawn up by which [all rugby league] will be considered professional. We can hardly believe it … Truly we wonder what could make those in power act in this way. Everything leads us to believe that they are again pandering to the dearest wishes of a federation powerless to manage its own affairs and which seeks the death of rugby league, treacherously, by stealth, by forcing its clubs to pay a very heavy tax, i.e. almost 40 per cent of receipts, if they are declared professional. […] If this plan is adopted it will not only be an injustice but once more a veritable scandal.'[x]

The Rugby League Federation was indeed pursued by the state's collector of taxes. As Robert Fassolette has pointed out, the fact that the state did not succeed in its demands was due largely to the brilliance of the lawyer Max Juvenal, a member of the Federation's executive council. In fact it is doubtful whether rugby league in France has ever been better served than by the men who made up the council of the FFJ XIII (as it was now known) in those immediate post-war years. Alongside Juvenal sat three members whose experience dated from the earliest days of French rugby league: Marcel Laborde, the former president and XIII Catalan chairman, who was forced to accept rugby league's fate in 1940, but who persuaded Paul Barrière to take over soon after the end of the war; Emile Pelot, the treasurer, and Marcel Rosemblat, both of Bordeaux. Only Barrière had not held a position within the game before the war, for secretary-general Fernand Quéheillard and vice-president Claudius Devernois had also been committed to rugby league from the start.

At the Aix-en-Provence congress of 1950, Barrière had, however, intimated that he would be ready to step down, a move which would have been unpopular. 'No one disputes the brilliant results of the unbounded activity of M Barrière,' it was reported.[xi] The president admitted that for reasons of health, family losses and personal preoccupations he had thought of withdrawing. In the end, 'We must fight on,' he said. 'I have accepted again to be at your head if there are blows to suffer.'[xii]

Blows there were, from inside and outside the game.

Within rugby league's semi-professional ranks, Toulouse Olympique continued to give cause for concern. The club had suffered a close-season crisis and only managed to survive into the 1949-50 season thanks to loans of players from other clubs. But when a number of those players were recalled, Toulouse found itself in an impossible situation and on 11 March, when Libourne were due to play at Les Minimes, the club folded, though it kept its junior team and played friendlies until the end of the season.[xiii]

Over the Easter period, Bordeaux undertook a short tour of England, as French clubs often did. They had a tough time, losing at Wakefield, Oldham and Halifax. Marseille, champions and cup-winners the previous season, proved more robust opponents when they travelled to Workington in May. In front of a 14,000 crowd, Gus Risman's Workington set up a 15-point half-time lead only to see it overtaken by a revitalised Marseille. Winger Casse scored three of Marseille's four tries, all converted by Fachan, as the Frenchmen won 20-18.

The injection of new players from Roanne resulted in Lyon's first Cup final appearance since Lyon-Villeurbanne took the inaugural trophy in 1935. Lyon XIII now had the likes of internationals Jo Crespo, who played centre in the final, loose forward René Duffort and stand-off Pierre Taillantou in their side. The most sensational signing, even among these stars, was that of second row Elie Brousse, once their team-mate at Roanne, whose move from Marseille caused uproar there. Brousse had two Cup-winners' medals with Marseille, and had won the Championship with both his previous clubs. But neither he nor the other new signings could help win Lyon's first post-war trophy.

Their opponents, XIII Catalan, had welcomed back to Perpignan players who had also won medals elsewhere. In their threequarter line, Frédo Trescazes and Jep Maso had starred for Carcassonne, and Gaston Comes for Roanne, from where second row Lucien Barris also returned. In front of a 13,500 crowd at Carcassonne, Comes scored a try and kicked three goals, second rower Gazé also touching down in the Catalans' 12-5 victory, while Lyon's only points came from a try scored by future international forward François Montrucolis and a goal by Duffort.

In the Championship final, played at Perpignan in front of 18,000 fans, Carcassonne and Marseille fought out another duel. The ASC were seeking to redeem themselves after the double defeat in the 1949 finals, as well as the 1947 and 1948 losses to Roanne. They got off to a slow start. Dominated in the forwards, they saw Marseille score seven points from a Maurice André try and two Poncet goals in the opening sixteen minutes. It was second row Ponsinet, described as the 'crystallising element of Carcassonne's morale'[xiv] who led the fightback. Equally prominent in defence, he launched the first wave of attacks with a break over forty metres, which led to the first ASC try. When Marseille centre Hatchondo was injured, the balance tipped. Nothing Marseille scrum-half Dop tried came off and Carcassonne led 11-7 at half-time, adding ten more points after the break.

Their 21-7 triumph was their third victory in six successive Championship finals. Ponsinet was unstoppable and a new stand-off, 18-year old Claude Teisseire, emerged from the shadow of Félix Bergèse. Centre Bertrand scored three tries (though some match reports credit Teisseire with the first try) Vaslin on the wing another and second row Gacia the fifth, Puig-Aubert adding three conversions.

The growing strength of rugby league in Provence was reflected in the inclusion of Carpentras and Toulon in the 1950-51 elite division. With Marseille, Avignon and Cavaillon also featuring, five first division clubs now operated in the south-east, but whereas Carpentras proved durable, Toulon dropped out at the end of the season after winning just one game despite having persuaded France coach Jean Duhau to join them from Marseille.

From the embers of Toulouse Olympique, which had given up in March, emerged a new club, Toulouse XIII. But the syndrome which appeared to afflict big city clubs now struck Bordeaux.

In February, only 510 paying spectators turned up for the match against Avignon. It was true that the game took place on a

Saturday instead of the usual Sunday, but the low attendance sent out a warning.

'...The impartial observer cannot fail to notice the disaffection of the Bordeaux public for rugby league,' it was reported. 'But the great Atlantic port is officially the capital [i.e. headquarters] of the Ligue. It is serious because not so long ago the game was a big success in Bordeaux.'[xv]

Meanwhile rugby union was making strides again, and not only in Aquitaine, which accounted to some extent for league's decline in the region. In February 1951 the France XV beat England at Twickenham after more than forty years of trying and exactly twelve years after the France XIII first won on English soil. It was not just that defeat which made the RFU unhappy. For the same reasons that led to France's excommunication in 1931 – veiled professionalism, brutality, over-excited crowds, all of which were primed by the championship – the British Unions were once again considering France's future in international competition. Warnings were issued.

'The transfers which had allowed Castres [champions of France in 1949 and 1950] to build their super-team,' Henri Garcia observed, 'the bidding [for players] which the big French clubs indulged in, the reappearance of dirty play, the profusion of decisive matches, with the Coupe de France added to the championship, increasingly worried the British.'[xvi] The French were warned, informally, of British concerns for the game as played across the Channel, although another exclusion was not yet on the agenda, since there was no desire to repeat 'a certain disastrous experience'[xvii] – a clear reference to the ban of 1931 which eased rugby league's passage into France. To show their acquiescence, the French, as they had done with Jean Galia two decades earlier, offered a number of players as sacrificial victims on the altar of amateurism. Chief among them was the France and Castres winger Maurice Siman, who had been offered a substantial sum to join Carcassonne.[xviii] Interestingly, no fewer than four members of that Castres Championship-winning team appeared on the list of players who had switched to union after being registered with the French Rugby League. Their coach was none other than Antonin Barbazanges, yet another of Galia's pioneers, who returned to league with Albi in 1950.

The attitude of the RFU toward the French had not shifted. The president told French officials at a dinner given before the match at Twickenham that it was the duty of the RFU to defend the original concept of rugby, by which it was understood that the first principle was amateurism. France, as the only European nation to whom the responsibility of nurturing rugby had been entrusted, had the difficult mission of ensuring that first principles were adhered to.[xix] Consequently the French barred a number of players from international selection, with Siman heading the list. The Coupe de France, perceived as a seed-bed for ignoble passions, was also dropped.

That was not quite enough to satisfy the British, but although they confessed that they were deeply concerned by certain French clubs' actions, which they regarded as incompatible with the spirit of amateur rugby, they put off suspending France from the Five Nations while the FFR came up with a plan to clean up their game. So it was that the French governing body decided to do away with the championship, just as had happened in 1939 before war intervened.

There was another twist. A deputation of officials from five clubs – and it was perhaps no coincidence that three of them, Perpignan, Albi and Toulouse, had rugby league clubs on their doorstep – put forward at a special meeting of clubs that the championship should be maintained. The FFR president, Alfred Eluère, admitted to club delegates that in his dealings with the British he had lied on their behalf in order to save Franco-British competition. Not because of Eluère's duplicity, but because they did not support the abolition of the championship, the clubs turned against their president, who did not present himself for re-election. His successor, René Crabos, a former international captain who enjoyed excellent relations with the British hierarchy, told the Federation's annual congress that a new era of amateurism had dawned and that club chairmen had sworn a solemn oath to maintain that ideal. On that basis were negotiations with the British Unions successful: the championship and international competition went ahead as before. After all, no one wished to provoke another crisis that would be to the advantage of rugby league. Or one which, by depriving the FFR of international matches, would leave the governing body almost penniless and therefore powerless.

But there were victims and the greatest of these was Jean Dauger, the finest centre of his era. After playing for Roanne and being part of the history-making France rugby league team that won for the first time in England, Dauger remained in rugby union with Aviron Bayonnais after the war. He was nineteen when he last played rugby league, but such was his talent that it was accepted that he had played as a minor and was therefore eligible to return to the fifteen-a-side game, even if not at international level. In January 1953, at the age of 33, Dauger was selected to play for representative sides on two occasions. His performances were superlative, so much so that the French decided to push their luck and select him to play for the full France team against Scotland. The punctilious Scots were outraged and threatened to boycott the match. But public expectation in France was running high for Dauger's return. The French in turn swore to cancel if he did not play. The Scots backed down. The match turned out to be a turgid affair, enlivened only by a French try sparked by Dauger. After that the French selectors decided not to press the British authorities and this brilliant player ended his career with just five rugby league caps and one full international selection at rugby union.

Against this background of sham and skulduggery, created by an authoritarian, archaic view of sport, rugby league carried on in its unpretentious way. The championship of 1950-51, to no one's great surprise, was dominated by Carcassonne, XIII Catalan, Marseille and now Lyon. Yet even these star-studded sides fell on occasion to lesser teams, as did Carcassonne at Avignon, the Catalans at Libourne, Lyon at Cavaillon, and so on. With the exception of Toulon, each of the thirteen teams was capable of beating any other. Villeneuve, the cradle of the French game in 1934, continued to produce fine players and finished the season tucked in behind the top four. As they had done before the war, Dr Vinson and Dr Mourgues presided over the organisation and showed that it was possible for a club which ended the campaign in fifth place to show a slight profit, in this case 61,000 francs on receipts of 4,750,000 francs. Newcomers Carpentras finished tenth, neighbours Avignon two places above, which added to the growing enthusiasm for the game in the south-east.

'You need to go to Provence to see how profitable to rugby league has been the season achieved by these two clubs,' said one report. 'Everywhere clubs are springing up and this region is poised to become the citadel of rugby league.'[xx]

At the top of the table, Claude Devernois' earlier initiative in transferring the best Roanne players to Lyon paid dividends as France's second city club reached the final of both Cup and Championship.

In the Championship final, played at the end of April at Toulouse's Stade Chapou and watched by 22,000 fans, Lyon met XIII Catalan, who had beaten them in the Cup final the year before. The Catalans started promisingly and scored tries through full back Malafosse and winger Thubert, both converted by Comes for a 10-0 half-time lead. But Lyon were far from finished. Opening up the game at each opportunity but without over-elaboration they finally broke down the Catalan defence and went on to score five tries in the last half-hour against opponents reeling from injuries to scrum-half Irénée Carrère, prop Ambroise Ulma and winger Frédo Trescazes. Lyon stand-off René Duffort pulled the strings while up front second rowers François Montrucolis and Elie Brousse went on the rampage. Brousse created three tries as winger Maurice Voron touched down twice, the other tries coming from centre Bellan, full back Lhoste and winger Lecuyer. The exhortations to open up play, coming from coach Bob Samatan, another of Galia's pioneers, were vindicated by a 15-10 victory. It was, recalled André Passamar, 'the queen of finals, the final of kings' in which rugby had been elevated to the level of art.[xxi]

Two weeks later and for the second year running, Lyon appeared in the final of the Coupe de France, which was played at Marseille in front of a 20,000 crowd. Their opponents, Carcassonne, were appearing in their sixth Cup final since the war. After almost 70 minutes of play, a single point separated the teams as Lyon, with tries from Brousse and Lecuyer and two goals, led by ten points to Carcassonne's nine, accumulated from two tries from winger Lassègue and another from Vaslin, this time playing prop. But when the ASC's loose forward Germain Calbète touched down in the 69th minute, it proved the turning point of the match. In an exciting game, full of classy play, Carcassonne took the lead and hammered home their advantage, scoring two further tries through winger Lassalle and second rower Gacia, Puig-Aubert adding two goals in the 22-10 triumph.

At international level too, French rugby league's second coming was confirmed. With their first post-war victory over England, followed by wins against Wales and Other Nationalities, France had ended the 1948-49 international season on a high note. The following season produced further signs of progress, even if the results were not as portentous.

A 16-8 defeat by Wales at a wet and windy Swansea in November 1949 came after France had been reduced to twelve men at the end of the first half when Paul Déjean had left the field with a broken nose, then eleven when Ulysse Négrier was also injured against a team which played a style of rugby of 'unusual violence'.[xxii] That match preceded England's 13-5 victory at Bordeaux, and in the third and final match of the international calendar, played in January 1950 and watched by a 25,000 crowd, two tries from winger Raymond Contrastin helped France to an 8-3 victory over Other Nationalities at Marseille.

The 1950-51 international campaign began with a defeat as England sneaked a 14-9 win at Headingley. But, wrote Alfred Drewry in the *Yorkshire Post*, 'France have made a habit since the war of bringing the worst out of England teams and this game was no exception.' He went on: 'It was an upside-down match altogether. The team that deserved to win lost, and the man who deserved to win it actually lost it. Puig-Aubert's goal, dropped with his left foot after he had measured up for a shot with his right and then been forced to sidestep like lightning, was a superb stroke, but his failure to make the ball dead before Broome scored England's winning try in the last minute was a sad error of judgment.'[xxiii] Puig-Aubert kicked three goals in all and front rower André Béraud was France's try-scorer.

En route from King's Cross to Leeds, Paul Barrière revealed to his players the Federation's most ambitious plan so far. A first-ever tour to Australia was in the pipeline and Barrière wanted the players to back the project by agreeing to take part, which they lost no time in doing. At this stage it was not thought that the planned tour would make a profit – in fact a modest loss was expected – but it was seen as a means of promoting rugby league. The possibly prohibitive cost of transport was pointed out by officials of the Rugby Football League, with whom discussions were held during the weekend. At the back of their minds must have been the thought that a French touring team might not prove much of a draw for the Australian public.

A tour of Australia had been mooted in 1948 and again in 1949, but conditions within France had been considered unfavourable. The unstable economic and political situation made players reluctant to participate in an overseas tour. More specifically the Federation was not yet ready for such an enterprise. '[The Federation] is young and inexperienced and, in the opinion of the leading French officials, the country is not sufficiently organised from a rugby league point of view at present to undertake a major tour in the immediate future,' wrote the secretary of the Australian Board of Control, JK Sharp, following a meeting with British and French officials in 1948.[xxiv] 'Our code is making rapid strides in popularity with the French sporting public,' he continued, 'and is expanding remarkably. ... It is only to be expected that a certain measure of confusion and inefficiency is present.' The timing of the proposed tour was also problematic. If the tour departed before the end of the domestic season, clubs would not be happy if they were without their leading players.

'The French officials were also concerned at possible activity by the French Rugby Union if any disaffection occurs among rugby league clubs and players,' it was noted. 'They state that the French rugby union clubs paid their players much more than the French rugby league clubs could afford to pay, and therefore they cannot run the risk of weakening their position in any way while the French Rugby Union is as strong as it is at present.' No tour could be envisaged before 1950, it was concluded.

A month after the match at Headingley, France met Other Nationalities at Bordeaux on 10 December in a controversial clash which also happened to be the first international rugby league match to be televised in France.[xxv] Puig-Aubert put in an outstanding all-round performance, landing five goals. Centre Jo Crespo scored the only try of the first half, at the end of which France led 7-0. With a typically dazzling 50-yard run, Brian Bevan responded soon after the break. But Louis Mazon went over for the French and Puig-Aubert kicked three more goals to ensure a 16-3 victory, the foundations of which were laid by the forwards, among whom second row Elie Brousse, prop André Béraud and loose forward Gaston Calixte stood out.

But it was not so much for France's victory that the game is remembered as for the first instalment of a feud between Edouard Ponsinet and his opposite number, Arthur Clues, one of nine Australians in the Other Nationalities XIII. The match was played with a physical intensity right at the limit of what was acceptable. 'Never have we seen such a will to score on one side and a will to defend on the other,' reported Jean Boudey in *Midi-Olympique*.[xxvi] But when Clues clattered Ponsinet, a mass brawl was only just averted. Ponsinet staggered from the field, propped up by Mazon, as Federation president Paul Barrière rushed on to the field to help. The second rower needed six stitches in a forehead wound. It was later reported that he almost lost his sight in one eye and in subsequent matches he always wore protective headgear. He was unlikely to forget Clues's actions.

The major reasons put forward for France's superiority in this match were the physical condition of their forwards and the defence of the team as a whole. Certainly France played in a more coherent manner than the team fashioned from Australians, New Zealanders and a Scot, who nevertheless played their part in a convincing four-team international competition.

At club level, international friendly matches proliferated, though it is hard to draw conclusions about the respective merits of the clubs involved. In that 1950-51 season, champions Carcassonne, who frequently competed in these matches, travelled to England in October and met St Helens, who earned a narrow victory by 24-22. Two days later the Frenchmen were overrun by Challenge Cup holders Warrington in a 46-3 defeat.

In these exchanges, much depended on the composition of the sides and availability of players, the seriousness with which they approached the game and the fact that the away side often played on consecutive days. In December, champions Wigan, another club regularly taking part in such matches, travelled to Perpignan and outplayed XIII Catalan, winners of the 1950 Lord Derby trophy, in a 39-2 triumph. On the following day, in summer-like weather, they were run close by Albi, who went down by 23-18. In April 1951, Hunslet were beaten 23-6 by a France Select XIII at Tarascon before travelling to the capital to face Paris Celtic in a promotional match before the Parisians returned to the top division. Welsh international Jack Evans scored five tries in Hunslet's 35-15 victory.

In the final match of the European championship, France met Wales, again at Marseille. Several players had been carrying injuries and with the impending Antipodean tour it was decided to bring in three newcomers, the Marseille pair of prop François Rinaldi and centre Jacques Merquey, and second rower Michel Lopez of Cavaillon. Merquey was a recent acquisition from Toulon rugby union and, at just 20 years of age, had played in all of France's Five Nations matches in 1950. He made an immediate impact, playing alongside Jo Crespo. France dominated the Welsh and led from the seventh minute, when loose forward Pérez went under the posts for the first of his three tries. His Carcassonne team-mate, Puig-Aubert, kicked seven goals in the 28-13 victory, which gave France a total of four championship points from the three matches – the same as Other Nationalities and England, but France's superior points-scoring difference gave them their third European championship title.

In that last match the French had shown their ability to score freely, with a combination of flowing attacking play and Puig-Aubert's goal-kicking ability. It put them in the right frame of mind to approach the tour of Australia and New Zealand on which they would depart from Marseille six weeks later.

As a further warm-up, the RFL sent a team called United Kingdom (though it was captained by Huddersfield's Australian centre, Pat Devery) to face a French Selection in Paris on 3 May. Though the French side, wearing red, lacked a handful of players who would have been first choice, Puig-Aubert and Brousse among them, the match was useful practice. Winger Raymond Contrastin scored two tries and Lopez kicked two goals for a 10-0 lead, but the British, wearing green jerseys, hit back as stand-off Ron Rylance cut through for a try and made another for the full-back, New Zealander Joe Phillips, to set the UK team on the path to a 13-10 win, watched by a Parc des Princes crowd of 12,000.

The match served another purpose, as Paris Celtic prepared to enter the national division. Leading sports journalist Gaston Bénac pointed out: 'The officials of the Ligue de rugby à treize and the dynamic Maurice Tardy were making a trial run, or I might say were taking off on an adventure – to introduce the romantic oval-ball game to the capital. They succeeded in part. Boldness always pays. The Parisian public, who know almost nothing about rugby league, welcomed it sympathetically.'[xxvii] The following month, the French would know if the Australian public would be equally receptive.

The returning heroes receive a ticker-tape welcome in Marseille

Chapter 6
•
The Making of Legends: 1951

AT THE AUSTRALIANS' invitation, the French undertook one of the most audacious ventures in their history, second only to Jean Galia's initiative of 1934 which started the whole thing off. Never had a French team in any sport toured the Antipodes before. On behalf of the Federation, Paul Barrière and Claude Devernois had given a huge commitment – not to say an enormous gamble – by agreeing to tour Australia and New Zealand and picking up the tab for all travel, accommodation and players' expenses. The tour was to be financed by a percentage of receipts.

Five years earlier, Great Britain had made a famous, financially successful tour and had done so again in 1950. The Australian public had a long-established appetite for matches against the old country. But there was no guarantee that the unknown French would be anywhere near as popular.

France had never beaten the Aussies. Did they not say, after a recent defeat: 'We were beaten by a team who were superior in all departments and to whom we can only say, as true sportsmen, "Thank you". Because you don't often find such masters of rugby who can offer such serious and interesting lessons.'?[i]

Neither Barrière nor Devernois accompanied the tour, unable to give up their business interests for five months to do so. The party was led by tour manager Antoine Blain, an imposing figure from France's first triumph in England, twelve years earlier. He was described by Henri Garcia, in his unforgettably vivid description of the tour, as 'a kind of superman, an unusual mixture of animal strength, humour…, lively intelligence, overwhelming dynamism and an incredible capacity for work.'[ii]

Two coaches, of equal standing, were in charge of the group of twenty-seven players. Bob Samatan and Jean Duhau, both members of the 1934 tour of England, headed two of the French championship's outstanding sides. Samatan had guided Lyon to victory in that glorious final and Duhau had overseen the rise of Marseille. The touring team was captained, not by Puig-Aubert who had led the team in recent matches, but by Robert Caillou of Toulouse, his senior by some six years. It had been expected that after France had beaten England at Wembley two years earlier, Caillou would step back from international football. He had said on that occasion, 'It's the best day of my life. I'm 31 and now I can retire. When you've beaten the English on their own ground, you can hardly wish for a more sensational performance.'[iii] A defensively strong stand-off or centre originally from Bayonne, Caillou found his representative rugby league career unexpectedly extended.

The group consisted of Puig-Aubert (Carcassonne), Maurice André (Marseille), full-backs; Vincent Cantoni (Toulouse), Raymond Contrastin (Bordeaux), Odé Lespès (Bordeaux), wingers; Robert Caillou (Toulouse, captain), Gaston Comes (XIII Catalan), Joseph Crespo (Lyon), Jacques Merquey (Marseille), centres; Maurice Bellan (Lyon), Charles Galaup (Albi), stand-offs; Jean Dop (Marseille), René Duffort (Lyon), scrum-halves; Paul Bartoletti (Bordeaux), André Béraud (Marseille), Louis Mazon (Carcassonne), François Rinaldi (Marseille), props; Jean Audoubert (Lyon), Gabriel Genoud (Villeneuve), Martin Martin

(Carcassonne), hookers; Elie Brousse (Lyon), Guy Delaye (Marseille), François Montrucolis (Lyon), Edouard Ponsinet (Carcassonne) second row; Gaston Calixte (Villeneuve), Michel Lopez (Cavaillon), Raoul Perez (Toulon), loose forwards.

There was versatility in the squad, essential for a touring team. Among the centres, Jo Crespo could just as well play scrum-half, while the other three were all capable of taking the stand-off role. At scrum-half Jean Dop could fill in at full back, while René Duffort could be called on to play centre, stand-off or loose forward.

The financial arrangements were, to say the least, loose. 'We didn't know what to expect down there,' said Puig-Aubert. 'Before we left we were told, "If we make money, we'll give you some. If not, well, too bad!" We would get by and make the best of it… For a month it was like being in barracks. We washed our own clothes, we cut each others' hair, with some striking results.'[iv]

Almost unnoticed, the party set off from Marseille's Marignane airport at midday on 14 May on board a Constellation, a British Overseas Airways plane. Because at that time aircraft could not fly long distances without refuelling, there were several stops. Rome was first, followed by the longest halt at Cairo while one of the plane's engines was repaired, which gave the party the chance of a camel ride around the pyramids; then onwards via Karachi and Calcutta, to Singapore, where they stayed overnight at the famous Raffles Hotel. After a final stopover at Jakarta, the group landed, five days after departure, in Australia, at Darwin, before they reached Sydney at 7.15 a.m. the next day.[v] Almost as soon as they got off the plane, the team became the focus of attention. Not surprisingly, since this was the first French football team of any code to play on Australian soil.

The first contact the party had with rugby league in Australia came when they went to watch the New South Wales-Queensland clash at Sydney Cricket Ground. 'It took our breath away,' recalled Gaston Comes. 'It was an absolutely fantastic game … with magnificent attacks, collisions where nothing was spared, played in a highly charged atmosphere… We returned to the hotel quite depressed and despite the efforts of Samatan, Duhau and Blain – who themselves were very impressed – to fire us up, we didn't give much for our chances.'[vi]

Eight days after leaving home, the French team played their first match when they took on Monaro Division in the capital, Canberra, where they were received by the Governor-General. 'The Frenchmen worked up to their match against Monaro,' it was reported, 'with the greatest fanfare of publicity that has ever greeted any team to Australia. The publicity quickly reduced interest in the touring English soccer team to insignificance in the public's mind.'[vii]

As Henri Garcia put it, the arrival of the French in Australia was akin to the appearance of Persians at the court of Versailles in the eighteenth century, as imagined by Montesquieu. It is unlikely that many among the 5,500 crowd, with the possible exception of the French ambassador, were familiar with the work of the French philosopher, but they certainly appreciated the French brand of rugby league. The Monaro side was stiffened by the inclusion of four top-level outsiders including a Kangaroo centre, but the French made an excellent start to the tour as Villeneuve hooker Gabriel Genoud, winger Raymond Contrastin and Gaston Comes scored first-half tries and Puig-Aubert kicked four goals. Comes, it was said, 'played a blinder. [His] brilliant side-stepping and change of pace … brought back refreshing memories to Australians of an art of centre play we have lost. Australia in recent years has cultivated big, hard bumping centres, who go through with their strength.'[viii] France ran in twenty points in the final seventeen minutes to win 37-12, bringing a huge ovation for Robert Caillou and his men as the crowd surged on to the pitch to acclaim the first ever French victory.[ix] It was an almost identical score to the Lions' a year earlier, bringing inevitable comparisons. 'The French backs are certainly more spectacular than England's,' it was observed, 'but there is not the same toughness and method among the forwards.'[x] The team had set out by plane for the match at six in the morning, returning to base at one o'clock the following morning, many of them covered in bumps and bruises as a result of the tactics of their opponents. Despite the score, it was a hard match, said Comes.[xi]

Harder matches were to follow. At Newcastle, graveyard of many a touring team, the French overcame a 26-5 penalty count against them to win 12-8 though the locals succeeded with only one of twelve attempts at goal. At Forbes, facing a New South Wales Western Division side, the tourists were also heavily penalised and went 24-16 down before rallying in the last fifteen minutes to score two late tries, both converted by Puig-Aubert for a 26-24 win.

What was rightly expected to be the most demanding game of the tour so far was scheduled for Sydney Cricket Ground, where the French were to face a Combined Sydney selection. It was a virtual test side, containing nine of the thirteen who would turn out for Australia just over a week later, including captain Clive Churchill and half-backs Frank Stanmore and Keith Holman. One observer went so far as to say that the success or failure of the tour hinged on the result of this match.[xii] The same writer reckoned that France hadn't a hundred to one chance of winning the test series.

A crowd of 44,522, the biggest a French team had ever played in front of, saw this first indication of what would become an extraordinary tour. In the opening twenty minutes the Sydney team pounded the French line. It seemed only a matter of time before the home team took control, but instead the French seized the initiative, with centres Jacques Merquey and Gaston Comes revealing their skill and Edouard Ponsinet – considered by some to be the best second rower to visit Australia for over twenty years – and Elie Brousse crashing through. France's first try ended with the Sydney players 'standing aghast.' 'Gaston Comes who sometimes looks like the Scarlet Pimpernel – and plays like one – completely befuddled the two Sydney centres, Willoughby and Thomas, with a swift serpentine run and change of pace, passed to Jo Crespo, who came from the clouds on the inside to take the pass and rush 30 yards to score.'[xiii] By the time Brousse went over, after demolishing the Sydney defence, France held a 15-4 lead. The

French thought they had done enough to win, but were visibly tiring. The Aussies hit back, with centre Gordon Willoughby helping himself to two tries, and levelled the scores at 17-all before taking the lead with a penalty goal as the match neared its conclusion. At the very end, in fact after the bell for full time had rung, France were awarded a penalty. Nonchalantly, as was his style, Puig-Aubert stepped up and sent the ball between the posts to earn the 19-19 draw. The Sydney public were astounded. It was 'a stirring game which evoked full-throated roars at the Frenchmen's fast, open and daring attack.'[xiv]

The France team was making its reputation and was the subject of intense curiosity wherever they went. Prime Minister Menzies invited them to lunch. But they had not yet played a test match. And, despite their unbeaten record, they had not yet played at their best for the full eighty minutes. They suffered their first reverse at Albury against Riverina Division (NSW), who won 20-10 against a side which included only a couple of players who would represent the France team to face Australia four days later.

It was not unknown for touring teams to experience defeat against country sides. But after securing only a draw against Sydney in the dying moments of the game – spectacular though it was – general opinion found that these unpredictable Frenchmen, who had never beaten Australia in the four matches the two nations had played since 1938, would crumble. After all, the Australians had won the Ashes just a year earlier for the first time in thirty years. Home fans thought their national side simply too strong. From legendary full-back and captain Clive Churchill to a fine half-back pairing of Stanmore and Holman, through to big no-nonsense forwards like Duncan Hall, the Aussies fielded a typically tough, solid team.

From their base at the Olympic Hotel, opposite the SCG, the French players were able to see spectators making their way to the turnstiles while they themselves were still having breakfast. Not many would have given the 'Flying Frenchmen' much of a chance, but, eager to see Australia take on France for the first time on home soil, 60,160 fans entered the stadium on Monday, 11 June

1951 (a national holiday) in the first all-ticket international staged there.

Puig-Aubert at full-back had taken over the captaincy. The threequarter line of Contrastin, Merquey, Comes and Cantoni picked itself, as did the second row of Ponsinet and Brousse. Stand-off Charles Galaup, just turned 22 and a product of Albi rugby league, though he had had a brief spell with Mazamet rugby union club that same season, was brought in for René Duffort, who was switched to loose forward, since both Calixte and Perez were injured. Galaup, who had been in the army on national service, had joined the party three weeks late and was pitched straight in. Replacing the injured Jo Crespo, the firecracker of a scrum-half Jean Dop upped the level of unpredictability. In the front row, the in-form hooker Gabriel Genoud joined the fearsome Mazon and the lively Bartoletti.

There was one Aussie who was confident of a French victory. Bill Moore, who had joined the French camp as masseur, was heard to say in the dressing-room, 'France is going to win, I can feel it. And it will be my finest hour.'[xv]

Coaches Duhau and Samatan had warned the team not to try to take the Aussies on down the middle. In this first test, the style of play already sketched out in the preceding games was to be perfected. Without trying to force the pass, the plan was to move the ball at speed to the wings, where Cantoni and Contrastin, with their blend of pace of power, would be given the best chance to head for the line. 'Our plan was to open out, keep the ball away from the pack and respect the referee's decisions,' recalled Comes.[xvi] Not only that, but they had planned to keep the ball away from full-back Churchill 'and to harass him when he had it. Puig-Aubert and emergency lock forward René Duffort kicked strongly to the opposite wing, or else deep beyond Churchill, with front row forwards moving up to him.'[xvii]

It all worked. On a sticky pitch, Puig-Aubert gave his side confidence with the unexpected bonus of a 4-0 lead after kicking two penalty goals in the opening five minutes. As hooker Genoud heeled the ball from the scrum twice as effectively as his opposite number and with the other five French forwards dominating the Australian pack, France unleashed some dazzling attacks. Two of them led to tries for Contrastin and Cantoni, though there was doubt over whether the Toulouse winger had hit the corner flag in Churchill's tackle before touching down. A subsequent kerfuffle resulted in a penalty for Australia, which Graves converted for Australia's only score of the first half, at the end of which France led 16-2, Puig-Aubert contributing three more goals, two of them from the touchline.

But as Jean Duhau was supposed to have said, you have to kill the Aussies three times over before they're dead. Inevitably the hosts hit back in what appeared to be a reprise of the match against Sydney. Too soon the French thought they had won. In the third quarter of the game, centre Willoughby, second row 'Mick' Crocker and winger Johnny Graves punched holes in the French defence, Graves adding two goals to come within a point of their tiring opponents. The match had been scattered with occasional incidents. Prop Duncan Hall had been cautioned and penalised for hitting Bartoletti in a scrum. Louis Mazon, described in the Aussie press as 'France's wild man prop of the Maquis'[xviii], but also as a non-stop worker, became embroiled in a personal altercation with forward Brian Davies.

It looked like the forecasts were right. Australia was on the path to another victory over these entertaining but insubstantial Frenchmen. Yet it was they who showed the greater resilience, normally such a typically Australian virtue. Scrum-half Jean Dop came into his own as a destroyer of defences, weaving this way and that, throwing out one-arm lobs and switching the point of attack. The French flew at the Aussies from all angles. Tested and tested again the Australian defence finally cracked with just over ten minutes remaining. Genoud went over and, from Comes' break, Cantoni raced in for his second try. Puig-Aubert provided two more goals and France, by 26-15, had won their first international match against Australia.

No wonder the French team were ecstatic, running around the pitch in their excitement before standing together and singing the 'Marseillaise'. The Australians were gracious in defeat. The SCG crowd, after seeing this new, adventurous style of rugby league, cheered the winners wholeheartedly. 'The longer the match had gone, the further the Frenchmen would have gone ahead,' said winger and goalkicker Graves.[xix] 'Australia was outclassed,' wrote George Crawford in the *Sydney Morning Telegraph*. 'France thrashed Australia ... as soundly as a team could be thrashed. The score does not fully indicate France's vast superiority.'[xx]

'The Frenchmen carried the day with the speed and daring of their passing bursts which left the opposition standing like shags on a rock, hopeless and helpless,' wrote Jim Mathers, who was quick to condemn Australian inadequacies. 'Our forwards were about as potent as cold tea... Australia's tackling was for the most part anaemic,' he added, before lashing one of the three-quarters for his 'spineless attempt [to tackle Cantoni, who scored between the posts] with his around-the-neck caress... [which] must have sounded the Death March for ever on his chance of selection in any future Test team.'[xxi]

Former Australian test players were as impressed with the French as they were critical of their own team. 'As a combination, the Frenchmen were the most brilliant thirteen I have seen,' said Frank Burge. In the same newspaper, Tom Gorman declared, 'This was the greatest tonic the League game has had.' 'The Frenchmen have brought back to Australia the very ethics of the game – superb backing-up in both defence and attack,' said Duncan Thompson. Arthur Justice thought that 'Australia should accept the lesson given today and forget caveman tactics.'[xxii]

Reputations were being forged. Ponsinet and Brousse, with their powerful running, were already being spoken of as the best second row in world rugby league. Comes ('one of the most artistic centres ever to come to Australia'[xxiii]) and Merquey (the author of some 'brilliant bursts'), though dwarfed by their opposite numbers, were handing out lessons in the art of centre play. Scrum-half Dop was a master of improvisation. And then there was Puig-Aubert, whose nickname 'Pipette' (slang for a thin roll-up) derived from his attachment to cigarettes; who excelled as an attacking full-back; who preferred a pastis to training; whose approach to goal-kicking was so casual that he turned his back on the ball after placing it for goal. It was he who symbolised the unclassifiable, impromptu yet glorious way of playing rugby league.

With the second test at Brisbane three weeks away, the French increasingly piled up big scores in the country matches. But all was not so simple. The match against Northern Division, played at Armidale two days after the first test victory, was full of controversial incidents. The locals had clearly taken it upon themselves to make up for the national team's defeat. Their play was, to say the least, robust. At the end of the first half, front rower Jean Audoubert was sent off following a fracas and in the second, Robert Caillou momentarily went off injured, leaving France with only eleven men, who were soon reduced to ten when Jean Dop was also sent to the touchline along with an Australian. Two minutes from the end, in another forward exchange, Guy Delaye was sent off, leading to a mass brawl, which the police were called on to stop. Brousse scored two tries in France's 29-12 win. There was, recorded Crespo, a cool atmosphere at the post-match reception.

If the victory was surprising in view of the handicaps they suffered, the match against Queensland in Brisbane proved an even more searching examination of the way in which the tourists had adapted to Australian conditions. Queensland had beaten Great Britain 15-14 the year before and by a single point in 1946 as well. At the end of the first half, France were 20-0 down. The second half was a different matter. Queensland added just a penalty goal to their score. France scored four fine tries through Crespo, Cantoni, Genoud – supplying plenty of ball from the scrums and proving able in the loose – and Contrastin, all converted by Puig-Aubert, who added a penalty goal in securing the 22-all draw.

The tourists continued to train rigorously, sometimes in two groups, since the dozen or so players not chosen for the country matches would stay behind in Sydney or Brisbane to be put through their paces by Bob Samatan, who also imposed a strict timetable and curfews. On more than one occasion the management turned down invitations to receptions that had been laid on for them before matches so that players should not be distracted from their objective. As Gaston Comes wrote home, 'Believe me, the training sessions are serious. There's no messing with Samatan and Duhau. But it's good work and we like it.'[xxiv] One evening in Queensland, the players were all set to go out to a dance hall, but came across Samatan , 'playing the policeman' at the hotel door. 'Even Dop and Pipette, as crafty as monkeys, had to respect orders and go to bed,' said Comes.[xxv] 'You didn't fool around with Samatan,' echoed Brousse. 'If you turned up late you got fined.'[xxvi]

Three more rough matches followed at Rockhampton, Townsville and Bundaberg and although France won easily and the local crowds applauded the tourists enthusiastically, manager Antoine Blain let it be known through the press that these country matches in Queensland and New South Wales did not cover the considerable travel expenses.[xxvii] It was a punishing schedule too. The party got up at 4.30 a.m. to fly to Rockhampton from Brisbane, played the match in the afternoon and then boarded a flight to Townsville.[xxviii] But it was becoming clear that the French players had become more and more adapted to the conditions, the opposition and the refereeing. In the 38-14 win over Central Queensland at Rockhampton, Gaston Calixte made his return from injury, André Béraud found his form again, while two of the biggest successes of the tour went from strength to strength. Vincent Cantoni scored a sensational try over 80 metres and Puig-Aubert, who moved to centre after Odé Lespès went off injured, touched down in stylish fashion.

The tour showed Puig-Aubert at his best. Everyone knew of his virtuoso goal-kicking skill. His favourite trick was to land goals side-footed from the corner-flag.[xxix] Right at the end of his career, the annual *Cahiers de l'Equipe* presented a photo-feature showing the star kicking the ball from the corner and landing it between the posts on seven out of the ten attempts witnessed.[xxx]

With his habitual Gauloises rationed and pastis unavailable, apart from what the French consul in Sydney later managed to procure for him, the Carcassonne full-back got into a healthy regime. Often disinclined to do anything above the minimum in training back home, in Australia he had little choice and emerged a svelte figure who had lost fifteen kilos. At the age of 26, he was, he admitted, 'in the best shape of my life'.[xxxi]

France claimed two more easy victories, despite intense heat, as they ran in big scores over North Queensland (50-17) and Wide Bay-Burnett (44-19). Following the match at Townsville, in which Cantoni, Contrastin and Comes each scored two tries, it was noted: 'The Australian press reports that the French team is playing better and better with every match… All the Australian journalists say that this France team is by a long way the best team seen on the Australian continent since English teams first visited these shores.'[xxxii] In the Bundaberg game, in which winger Maurice André touched down three times and recovering hooker Martin Martin, making his first appearance of the tour, twice, the French thrilled the crowd with their sweeping movements which covered the field with fast, accurate passing.[xxxiii]

The world's best rugby league team was the unofficial title awaiting France if they could follow up their first test success with a second. A 35,000 crowd, producing record receipts for a football match in Queensland, piled into the Brisbane Cricket Ground, otherwise known as the Gabba, on 30 June to see if they were as good as everyone appeared to think. Samatan, Duhau and Blain kept the same set of forwards but switched Merquey to stand-off for Galaup with Crespo moving into the centre. The Australians had other thoughts about the claims being made for France.

Thanks to three penalty goals from Puig-Aubert, France led 6-4 but were overhauled before a converted Merquey try brought the score to 12-11 in favour of the hosts. Australia, of course, were giving nothing away. Rough tactics, offside, late tackles and punches abounded in a bad-tempered game in which, alleged Puig-Aubert, Churchill's 'bad charging of Cantoni early in the game had a lot to do with the troubles in the match.'[xxxiv]

Among various incidents, Ponsinet laid out Davies and Contrastin had a similar effect on Geelan. France went close several times but Australia had tightened their defence and, with Crespo groggy from early on and Dop carrying a leg strain, Brousse was sent off along with Hazzard nine minutes from the end of a bruising match. It was the home side who ended with three tries to one. Merquey, at stand-off, had an excellent game, however. As Antoine Blain pointed out, the numerous openings he made could have been better exploited.[xxxv] To seal the 23-11 victory, a long-range drop goal came from the boot of Churchill, who had earlier spent seven minutes sidelined after being knocked out, but showed in this match that he did not intend to be overshadowed by his opposite number, Puig-Aubert. 'We played a poor match,' said Crespo. 'The Australians won without panache.'[xxxvi]

In fact each side criticised the other for the violent play. 'Out on the field it was just punch, punch, punch,' said Australian hooker Ernie Hammerton. 'When the Frenchmen realised they were beaten they took it very badly.'[xxxvii] Puig-Aubert answered the accusation: 'The Australians didn't want to play football. They wanted to fight.'[xxxviii] 'The first time I've ever been sent off and it has to be in Australia,' recorded Brousse in his journal. 'Revenge in Sydney,' he promised.[xxxix]

A more balanced view came from Ross McKinnon in the *Sydney Sunday Telegraph*. 'If anything the visitors proved more tough and rugged than Australia,' he wrote, comparing the French forwards' harrying of Churchill to being set upon by a pack of starving hounds. 'Although Australia scored three tries to one,' he went on, 'I thought France was superior in attack and defence. Its defence has improved beyond recognition since its Sydney debut. Speed in defence in the three-quarter line made the Australian backs look like cart-horses by comparison. I am not belittling the Australian team's performance. But we would be fooling ourselves if we thought that we had found the answer to this brilliant team.'[xl]

The tourists had the consolation of being invited on board the French vessel, the Bir-Hakeim, where for once the cuisine was just like at home. Crespo noted the list of aperitifs and the various courses in detail. 'It was,' he said, 'our best day in Australia. We felt as if we were in France.'[xli]

The French stayed in Queensland to face Brisbane three days later. With six members of the test side missing, France were heading for another defeat as they trailed 16-15. Once more Puig-Aubert, who had played almost all the matches so far, came to the rescue with a huge 50-metre drop goal with two minutes remaining to salvage a valuable win.

Controversy also surrounded the match at Toowoomba, where France managed a 20-17 win against a local side reinforced with internationals. Ten minutes from the end of the first half, a Toowoomba player was concussed in a tackle. The international forward Duncan Hall then set about Elie Brousse, which sparked a brawl resulting in another home player being knocked out. The referee decided to dismiss Brousse and Hall but the French forward stood his ground, claiming he had done nothing wrong. The rest of the France team agreed and walked off. Discussions ensued before finally Puig-Aubert, as captain, persuaded Brousse to leave the field and, after several minutes' hold-up, play restarted.

'It is undeniable that the matches in Australia are becoming more and more difficult,' it was observed. 'In every game the Australian teams are absolutely raging to see the French beaten.'[xlii]

Jean Duhau, in an open letter to Paul Barrière, wrote of the 'kindness and truly exceptional cordiality' with which the France team was received everywhere they travelled. But he also remarked on the conditions in which the team played, particularly in the country matches. 'The referees we came across in the small towns revealed an odd understanding [of the rules], which disconcerted and often irritated us... In the country teams we found few players with a sound technique and on a tactical level it was always the France XIII which proved superior, showing a brio which all the crowds admired. And this in spite of the violence shown by our opponents...' He continued, 'In each of our matches we give a very flattering insight into the value of French rugby league and I can't help thinking of that emotional match at Headingley [the previous November] when, against England, our team forced the admiration of the crowd. Truly, what a long way we have come since the revival [of 1944] and especially what happy development has taken place this season.'[xliii]

In an otherwise commonplace victory by 33-9 at Lismore, New South Wales, Puig-Aubert scored thirteen points from a try and five goals, which, with a total of 133 points for the tour so far, broke Jim Sullivan's record haul of 132, set on the 1932 tour. That personal landmark was achieved in the context of a collective phenomenon. No less a figure than Harry 'Jersey' Flegg, chairman of the Australian Rugby League, pointed it out at the post-match reception, predicting that France would win the third test. Not only that but, he continued, 'by their superior technique, their speed and will to win, the French have revolutionised the Australian game.'[xliv]

Another sending-off came in the match against New South Wales, watched by a 47,000 crowd. Though Louis Mazon complained to the referee that he had been struck first, he was dismissed for retaliation despite his protests. With six goals and a drop goal, Puig-Aubert scored all France's points in the 14-all draw a week before the third test.

Though some had tried to dissuade them, France fulfilled their fixture at Wollongong, their last before the test. Those with French interests at heart had tried to convince the party that no good would come of playing at this town situated a hundred miles from Sydney. The local team had a deplorable reputation, it was said, and neither the 1946 Great Britain team nor its successors of 1950 had managed to win there. France put out a team made up of players unlikely to feature in the test and, although the police had to be called on to deal with crowd disturbances and though the game was described as 'animated', the tourists won 24-13.[xlv]

None of this was ideal preparation for the third and final test. Crespo recorded that, at their Sydney base, the team was 'confident', and, as a preparation which is now commonplace but was rare at the time, the squad watched film of parts of the second test and the NSW match.[xlvi] But few outside that hotel expected France to stand up to the close scrutiny to which Australia would be bound to subject them, just as they had done to Great Britain the year before. As Crespo said, the team was not lacking in self-belief. Edouard Ponsinet wrote to Paul Barrière: 'We assure you that [the Australians] have nothing to teach us, apart from the art of preventing us from playing, in which they succeeded in the second test, but which is likely to be less successful in the third, whatever happens, because we know that rugby league needs this victory…'[xlvii]

There were fears also that in this crucial decider violence might ruin the event. The second test in Brisbane had, after all, been labelled the dirtiest test match since the infamous 'Battle of Brisbane' in 1932. The Australian Board of Control stepped in and issued a warning to both teams that they must not bring discredit on the game. The vastly experienced Tom McMahon, who had officiated in the first two tests, was retained to referee what would be his farewell international.

On Saturday 21 July, just as before, the Sydney Cricket Ground began to fill up with fans from an early hour. By kick-off there were 67,009 of them – 20,000 more than for the decider against Great Britain the year before. The attendance was the SCG's second-highest, after the 1932 Australia-GB clash which had established a world record of 70,204. The crowd, who paid record receipts for a test match in Australia of £A11,439 and 9 shillings, were not to be disappointed.

The only newcomer in the France team was Gaston Calixte, who, with the help of a pain-killing injection, was brought back to the loose forward role in place of René Duffort, who moved to stand-off, allowing Merquey to resume at centre. Jo Crespo moved from centre to scrum-half to replace Jean Dop. In three tests, therefore, three different half-back combinations had been used, with the Lyon duo of Duffort and Crespo now combining for the first time.

France won the toss and had the wind at their backs in the

first half. It was Australia, though, who dominated the early play. The green and gold forwards tried in vain to drive a wedge through the opposition, but Brousse, Ponsinet and the rest were having none of it. Whereas Puig-Aubert landed two penalties to build a 4-0 lead, Australia fluffed two try-scoring chances on the wings. In the last twenty minutes of the first half, France let rip. Their first try came from a brilliant movement. From a scrum just inside the Australian half, Puig-Aubert linked with the threequarters. 'Puig-Aubert got the ball, straightened the attack and cut out two Australians. He slipped the ball inside to front-rower Paul Bartoletti as Australian winger Flannery knocked him out. As Puig-Aubert lay unconscious on the ground, Bartoletti and Louis Mazon went through to send Jo Crespo over for the try.'[xlviii]

The scrum-half touched down a second time after stand-off Duffort foxed the Australian defence, selling dummies so convincingly that he went almost half the length of the field before handing on. The Australians were reeling and conceded two more tries in the two minutes before the break. Elie Brousse, described as one of the best second rowers of all time, ran forty yards – one of several long bursts he made, swatting off would-be tacklers - to score at the posts. As he did so, Aussie second row Davies clipped the back of Brousse's head with his boot, earning a reprimand from referee Tom McMahon for recklessness. A minute later Raymond Contrastin pounced on a loose ball and took Churchill with him over the line. All Australia had been able to offer in reply was two Noel Pidding penalty goals. Australia 4 France 20 read the scoreboard at half-time.

As the teams turned round, Australia, with possession from the scrums at the rate of two to one, were fully expected to make amends for a disastrous first half. Instead, Contrastin extended France's lead with his second try. Crespo, Merquey and Comes proved far too quick and elusive for the home side, pedestrian by comparison. Crespo completed his hat-trick, Comes also touched down and, despite the wind, Puig-Aubert kicked seven goals. France had three players injured – Genoud, Contrastin and Calixte – but, despite winning the scrums,

Australia did not cross France's line until the 66th minute, when prop Duncan Hall barged over. Second row Brian Davies finished the scoring two minutes from full time, which served only to reduce the margin of defeat. Australia's 35-14 drubbing was their greatest-ever humbling in test football.

The Sydney crowd responded sportingly. As the victorious French sang the Marseillaise and went on a lap of honour carrying the Tattersall Cup, awarded to the winners of Franco-Australian test series, the Aussie fans cheered them almost like their own. After all, the statistics couldn't be more convincing. Australia had suffered a defeat heavier than their previous worst when Great Britain won 27-20 in 1910 in Sydney. France's seven tries had only been equalled twice before – in 1910 and at Swinton in 1948. Puig-Aubert, the focus of attention, had collected individual records: his total of eighteen goals in a series easily beat Dally Messenger's tally of eleven, set 41 years earlier. His 163 points and 77 goals were the highest by an individual player on a tour of Australia – and more was to come. Not only was he praised for his goal-kicking. Tom Goodman, in the *Sydney Sunday Herald*, highlighted 'amazing line kicking, dexterous handling and brilliant tactical play by full-back Puig-Aubert, who was a football magician.'[xlix]

The Australian team were the subject of some scathing comments from their own press. 'The forwards and inside backs tackled like "cream-puffers",' wrote George Crawford.[l] 'Our pip-squeak defence was torn to shreds,' said Jim Mathers.[li]

But the Australian journalists reserved the majority of their copy for praising France.

'The French inflicted the most humiliating Test defeat that Australia has suffered in Rugby League,' wrote the *Sydney Sunday Sun*'s Alan Hulls. 'The score 35-14 reads badly enough, and yet it doesn't truly reflect the overwhelming superiority of the Frenchmen. Stunned by the complete superiority of the bright and spirited visitors, the crowd became strangely silent. Later they were laughing at some of the efforts by the Australians.'[lii]

It might be thought that it was the flashing style and speed of France's backs which accounted for the yawning gap between the two teams. Rather, as ex-test centre Ross McKinnon explained in the *Sydney Sunday Telegraph*, 'The French forwards were the biggest factor in their team's win. They made the Australian forwards look tenth-raters.'[liii] In the same newspaper, France tour manager Antoine Blain indirectly backed that view by nominating Elie Brousse as the key player. 'Second rower Elie Brousse was the French star for the manner in which he was able to penetrate the Australian defence,' he said.

In the *Sydney Sunday Herald*, ex-Leeds centre Frank O'Rourke went further: 'The French plan of campaign was the complete undoing of the Australian side. Realising that the Australian backs would be repeating their standing-up tactics, the Frenchmen obviously decided that the breakthrough must be done by the forwards. So it was that Brousse, Ponsinet, Bartoletti and even Mazon strove to get through the Australian forward line, then to whip the ball to their brilliant backs. The plan succeeded with the most devastating results.'[liv]

Another writer, Jack Reardon, thought that 'France's smashing win ... should sound the death knell of [Australia's] present coaching system... The new world rugby league champions showed up our style of play as painfully orthodox.'[lv]

It was, in short, one of the greatest ever international victories, not just in rugby league but in all of sport, crowning so emphatically and so adventurously a tour which exceeded all expectation. In addition to the Tattersall Cup, France also carried off the Goodwill Trophy, which was awarded to the leading nation at the end of four years' competition, and which therefore consecrated the French as world champions.

By that stage the Tricolores, as they were then known, had played eighteen matches in Australia, winning thirteen, drawing three and losing two, and in the process had already covered the full cost of the whole tour including New Zealand. Up to the point of departure for New Zealand, the tour had grossed £A64,000, of which the French took £A34,088. By contrast, the takings from Great Britain's 1950 tour were £A51,278.[lvi]

It was a formidable record for a team which had arrived

two months earlier in the hope of advancing their rugby league education in the land of champions. They left after giving the Australians a lesson which would be imprinted on the nation's sporting consciousness, one which showed how spectacular rugby league could be when played with rigorous skill, quickness of thought and imagination.

The wider significance of the victory was not lost on one of the older members of the party. Coach Duhau, who, like Samatan, had been present at the birth of French rugby league, reflected: 'The French are at the top of the world after only sixteen years. If only my good friend and old team-mate Jean Galia had lived to see this day.'[lvii]

It was inevitable and appropriate that Duhau should recall Galia, who, on first seeing rugby league played in that exhibition match in Paris on 31 December 1933, had been entranced by the Australian forwards' mobility and passing skills. He called it a game of great beauty. It made a splendid spectacle, he said.[lviii] He knew straight away that this sport was a perfect fit with the French temperament and culture. Now, in 1951, the potential that Galia had identified had been realised and taken to the highest level by his own countrymen. Just as the wildly enthusiastic crowd at the Stade Pershing had rushed on to the pitch and mobbed the Australian players, now the Australian crowds took to the Frenchmen as their own, exuberantly applauding their speed, skill and adventure. Now they were saying, as Galia had said, 'This is what rugby league is about.' It presented a new dynamic. It freed rugby league from convention. Coming after the war years, it was the rugby of optimism.

Chapter 7

•

The French School of Rugby League: 1951

THE TEAM WAS not yet ready to return home in triumph. Three more matches lay in store in Australia, but before that came a short tour of New Zealand, just as Great Britain touring teams undertook. The team would stay less than three weeks in New Zealand and in that time would play seven matches, including one test.

Conditions in Australia had not always been ideal, but in New Zealand the pitches presented their own challenge. At Greymouth, in the opener, the heavy state of the field gave an indication of what was to follow. 'The pitch was a real quagmire,' said Jo Crespo. 'We were unrecognisable by the end of it.'[i] The French beat the West Coast 5-2 before going on to defeat Canterbury 13-7 at Christchurch, where Gaston Comes gave a masterly display at full-back in the absence of Puig-Aubert. A record crowd enthusiastically cheered the French style of play. Similarly at Wellington, an apparently modest crowd of 8,000 established a new record for a rugby league match and saw France win 26-13, using swift handling to outwit their big opponents.

France's first ever test in New Zealand took place in Auckland five days later and was to end in controversy. Once again, a match was billed to decide the world's best national side. New Zealand had beaten Great Britain in both tests of the 1950 tour, following up their victory over the 1946 Lions. As the French discovered, the Kiwis were to prove equally difficult at their Carlaw Park home in 1951. 'Of the many memorable matches staged there, the only test of the 1951 tour stands supreme for sheer drama,' John Coffey observed.[ii]

The French had worries about the availability of Puig-Aubert, who had been suffering from a throat infection and had had to have two teeth extracted in hospital, and Comes, who had an ankle problem, but both were pronounced fit. François Montrucolis came into the side at loose forward for his international debut.

A crowd of 19,229, virtually the same number as saw Great Britain defeated the year before, filled the stadium and saw New Zealand take a 14-7 lead despite losing scrum-half Jimmy Haig with a fractured cheekbone in only the tenth minute. France hooker Martin was sent off midway through the second half. According to certain reports he had thrown mud at the referee after the French had objected to a penalty given against their loose forward for taking the ball out of a scrum; according to others he had backed into the referee accidentally. Martin stood his ground and had to be persuaded to leave by Antoine Blain and the NZRL president. France clawed back the deficit to go ahead 15-14. Cantoni touched down twice, Ponsinet added another try and Puig-Aubert kicked three goals, but the Kiwis, who had defended with greater effectiveness than the Australians, had double misfortune when they lost stand-off George Menzies with a broken jaw. In the very last minute, with France leading by a single point, Contrastin, chasing a loose ball shoulder to shoulder with his Kiwi opposite number Bevan Hough, was penalised by referee Griffin, who had twice previously ruled out French tries. After the full time hooter had sounded, full-back Des White, from close to the touchline, landed his fifth goal for a 16-15 victory.

It was hardly a consolation to the French, who were furious to have had their record tarnished, but the remaining three matches all went their way. Returning to Carlaw Park two days later, the tourists defeated an Auckland side featuring nine internationals, winning 15-10. At Hamilton, South Auckland were beaten 27-7 on a rugby union ground – a detail not lost on the French party – and in the final match of this part of the tour, Taranaki were defeated 23-7 at New Plymouth.

At the end of the New Zealand leg, Kiwi president Redwood wrote appreciatively to his counterpart, Paul Barrière, and spoke of the 'unforgettable' impression made by the tourists.

'Thanks to their victories in Europe, your team was preceded by a flattering reputation. But our players, coaches and fans never expected the exhibition which you have given. It is said here that there is now a French School of Rugby League. This School produces a game of unequalled elegance. All the virtues of your nation are to be found in your team's actions on the field, right down to the smallest gesture…

'You have the good fortune to be the president of a federation which is admirable because it knows how to progress. To move forward is the aim of all sportsmen. But the result, for you, goes beyond all expectation…'

Referring to the feats achieved in Australia, the Kiwi president recalled the enthusiasm of the hundreds of thousands of spectators, whose applause testified to the spectacular quality of French rugby.

'Our players and coaches will remember the lessons given by your team. They were all struck by the flair of your magnificent athletes.'[iii]

The French party returned to Australia for a farewell match which soon multiplied by three. The Australians had asked Antoine Blain for a fourth test, to which the French, coming to the end of a tiring tour, agreed only if it were not recognised as an official international. The two sides agreed and a date was fixed for Melbourne, then virgin rugby league territory. Before that, the tourists, reeling from numerous injuries and the accumulated fatigue of travelling long distances, met a New South Wales XIII in Sydney, losing 29-11.

It was an improvised team also that faced Australia on 18 August, three months after setting out. 'We thought we would get a good hiding,' said Crespo, because we were very tired.'[iv] Loose forward Calixte moved to scrum-half, partnering Maurice Bellan. Hooker Jean Audoubert shifted across the front row to prop. Full-back Maurice André played on the wing, alongside tour captain Robert Caillou, who had not figured in any of the tests. The match was intended as a means of promoting rugby league in Melbourne and indeed, regardless of team changes, the match turned into yet another exhibition of French skill, even in the rain and in front of only 4,460 spectators. Puig-Aubert collected nineteen points from eight goals and a try in the 34-14 victory, André Béraud touched down twice and three more tries came from Maurice André, Crespo and Contrastin. 'We surprised ourselves with the result,' commented Crespo.[v]

Unlike the outward journey, the return was to be made by ship and would take a month. The players boarded the Stratheden at the port of Melbourne, but one final match was to be played on the other side of the country against Western Australia. The team that had been selected flew directly from Adelaide to Perth, where the game turned into a procession, as France thrashed the locals by 70-23.

Before that, as the French party left Sydney, they were given a send-off that foreshadowed their welcome home in France. Thousands lined the streets to cheer the team coach, throwing streamers and confetti and shouting 'Vive la France' or even breaking into a line or two of the Marseillaise.

One striking example of the impression the French made is that the Eastern Suburbs club, nowadays known as Sydney Roosters, who already played in red, white and blue jerseys, are thought to have adopted the cockerel as their emblem in homage to the France legacy.

An official goodbye was read out by Mr Simmons, representing the Australian parliament, before the departure. His words were reproduced in all the Sydney newspapers and were posted on walls all over the city.

'We say goodbye,' the statement began, 'to the most brilliant, spectacular rugby team that we have ever seen. The tour of the French Rugby League has had unprecedented success...

'France is loved more than ever in Australia after their visit. We wish them a safe journey home and hope that they will soon be back among us, so brilliant, so likeable and so sporting.'[vi]

Back in France, Paul Barrière was inundated with congratulations. Bill Fallowfield, on behalf of the Rugby Football League, was one of the first to praise the team's achievement. Recognition also came from the government. The Minister for Sport, André Morice, sent a letter expressing his total satisfaction with 'the conduct and success of our representatives [which] have contributed in the most felicitous manner to the prestige of French sport.'[vii] The Australian Justice Minister and honorary president of the Australian Rugby League, Dr Evatt, had already given his opinion following the first test success. 'You are the best ambassadors France has sent us since the beginning of the century,' he is reported as saying.[viii]

Gaston Roux – he who had tried to broker a truce between league and union four years earlier – joined the chorus of those singing the team's praises. 'I want to congratulate all the *Jeu à XIII* rugby players who have defended our colours so well,' he said. He quoted the French ambassador to Australia, who told the team: 'You are perfect ambassadors. You cannot know how much your presence here serves the cause of France.'[ix]

The stars who had left Marseille in May returned as much bigger stars. George Crawford wrote an article remarking how the French tour had upset the established international hierarchy. They had destroyed Australian illusions of superiority. Alongside, he published a World XIII which included four Frenchmen, though in truth there could have been more.

'The English made us smile when they told us a little Frenchman, a certain Puig-Aubert, was better than Churchill,' he wrote.

'But the English were right and Churchill, for the first time in his career, seemed like the pupil before the master.'

Just three Australians featured in the World XIII; none had played in the recent tests, since they were operating at English clubs.

Crawford explained his selection: 'The two unquestionable centre three-quarters are the Frenchman Comes, for his cannonball-like breaks, and the Englishman Ashcroft. But none of the three-quarters seen during the tour has done better than the little curly-headed Frenchman, Jacques Merquey, who has an exceptional future ahead of him…

'We have seen since the war some excellent second rows but none compares with the one formed by the "terrible twins", Edouard Ponsinet and Elie Brousse.'[x]

Crawford's World team was as follows: Puig-Aubert (France); Brian Bevan (Australia), Gaston Comes (France), Ernest Ashcroft (England), Lionel Cooper (Australia); Pat Devery (Australia), Tommy McCue (England); Ken Gee (England), Joe Egan (England), George Curran (England), Edouard Ponsinet (France), Elie Brousse (France), Ike Owens (England).

More than any other, it was Puig-Aubert who was the focus of press attention. The referee in the third test, Tom McMahon, was quoted as saying that Puig-Aubert was the greatest full-back the world had seen in the past twenty-five years. 'Even with my twenty-one years experience as a referee, I could not anticipate moves Puig-Aubert had in mind. Neither could the Australian players,' he said.[xi]

The Carcassonne full-back and captain of France in Caillou's absence had broken several individual point-scoring records, all previously held by legends of the game. With his total of eighteen goals in the series he had easily eclipsed Dally Messenger's total of eleven, set in 1910. According to Henri Garcia, his two goals in the opening minutes of the third test also put him beyond Messenger's record of eleven successful penalty attempts in a row, an extraordinary achievement.[xii] On the whole tour, including matches played in Australia after the return from

New Zealand, he clocked up no fewer than 236 points, eclipsing Jim Sullivan's 1932 total of 223, thanks to a 20-point haul in the 70-23 victory at Perth in the final match. Both players had taken part in 21 matches.[xiii]

Puig-Aubert himself recalled: 'People recognised me, they stopped me in the street. The newspapers just talked about me. And that's because I benefited from a very favourable situation.

'When we arrived there, the Australian idol was Churchill. They considered him the best in the world. [Soon after we arrived] we went to a match he played in and my team-mates told me, "Hey Pipette, you're going to be up against a tough customer." But I didn't answer. Because – just imagine – on tour I was training, which I didn't do at home, or very little. And I was smoking barely a packet, seeing that I had only been able to bring a few with me. So you might say I was on top form. The best of my career.

'In any case I'd had it up to here with our friend Churchill. Churchill beer, Churchill cigarettes, Churchill shirts. You saw him everywhere you went...

'Like me, Churchill played full-back. And like me, he was the captain. Those were the only two points we had in common... That's why people talked about me so much. Because I outplayed the world's best player. [But] I can assure you that there were plenty of others in the France team as good as me, Brousse and all the others.'[xiv]

As if playing against the world's best was not difficult enough, Puig-Aubert and his team-mates came up against long-held prejudices. Certain ideas needed to be dispelled. He explained that at first the French were not taken seriously. They were seen as 'jokers, gigolos, champagne-drinkers, frog-eaters – the image which a lot of people had, and still have, of the French. All that was missing was the beret. Afterwards, they changed their views.'[xv]

So much so that, at the tour's end, Puig-Aubert, Brousse, Ponsinet and others including tour captain Caillou received huge offers from Sydney clubs to stay in Australia. Brousse, who had been given the nickname of the Tiger of Sydney for the way he clamped his great paws on the shoulders of an opponent to bring him down, was targeted by Manly but, although a single man at the time, was not tempted. Puig-Aubert, who had a wife and daughter, was reported to have been offered a sum quoted as ten million francs to sign for St George.[xvi] 'I would have had to say goodbye to my mates and finish the Australian season,' he said. '...They were offering me a pot of gold.'[xvii] Information reported to have come from a letter written by Puig-Aubert to his wife detailed the offer as consisting of six million francs to sign for just two years; 200,000 francs per month over the two-year period; plus match bonuses and other fees, accommodation, travel to and from France, all of which, it was believed, added up to almost 20 million francs.[xviii] That was the equivalent of £20,000 – an enormous sum at that time. A six million-franc signing-on fee – roughly equal to £6,000 – was similar to what Welshman Lewis Jones would receive from Leeds for a permanent contract when he switched codes the following year. '[In France] I had all I needed,' explained Puig-Aubert. 'And yet [in Australia], without boasting, I would have been a king.'[xix]

A month after setting sail for home on board the British boat Stratheden, after many days of deck tennis, table tennis and nursing bruised bodies, the tourists arrived back in Marseille. The ship docked early in the morning at nearby La Ciotat, where they met up again with their families before an official reception. In Marseille itself, Paul Barrière had taken over two hotels – one, the Hôtel de Noailles, for officials and press, the other, the Hôtel des Deux Mondes, for players and their families.

After the players had embraced their families in a tearful welcome home, they were greeted by a number of the great players of the previous era: Max Rousié, Maurice Bruneteaud, François Noguères, Jean Poch among them. Officials too: Claude Devernois, the Carcassonne chairman Georges Ramond, the Catalan Dr Bonzoms.

At six in the evening the celebrations began, with an American-style tickertape reception. Banners were hung across the façades of buildings: *'Honneur à l'Equipe de France'*, and *'Gloire aux Héros d'Australie'*. The players were taken by motor launch across to the Old Port, where a huge crowd, estimated at a hundred thousand strong, waited for them on the quayside. The main boulevard of the city, La Canebière, was lined ten deep with well-wishers, who clapped, cheered and threw confetti as the team passed by. Each player, plus coaches and manager, was conveyed individually in one of 31 convertible Peugeot 203s, his name prominently displayed across the radiator grille. The Marseille stars, Dop and Merquey, led the way, while Puig-Aubert was placed in the last car. As they waved to the crowd, a shower of little paper cockerels fell from the sky.

That welcome home, lasting four hours on Wednesday evening, 19 September was unlike anything that had gone before. Paul Barrière, the man who inspired the whole project, put it all into perspective in a speech that evening.

'When, on the morning of May 14, our boys flew from Marignane, they carried with them our hopes, our fears and our pride. Pride at having dared to risk this great adventure. Fear of opponents who, on their last visit here, had almost toyed with our team. Hope for a mission, both sporting and peaceful, which, whatever some may think, often does more for the reputation of France than any number of speeches by politicians. There remains an immense satisfaction made all the greater by this unforgettable Marseille reception.'[xx]

The outcome for rugby league in Marseille was predicted to be all positive. Not all the thousands of people who lined the streets of the city that evening were rugby league fans. But many had been won over by the France team's exploits, as the crowd's spontaneous enthusiasm showed.

What also stood out was the closeness between the France players and Federation officials, particularly president Barrière. Among numerous letters written to him from Australia, one from Gaston Calixte, composed just after the third test victory, spoke for all the players.

'We all thought of you before and during the match, and

afterwards we were as happy as little kids in knowing that you would be pleased with your "youngsters",' wrote Calixte to a president barely older than the players.

Calixte spoke highly of the trio who managed the tour: Antoine Blain, who had taken on a 'crushing workload' vital to the tour's success and whose 'gift with words in difficult circumstances created an excellent atmosphere.' It was hats off too to Bob Samatan and Jean Duhau, who 'did not stint in their efforts in the name of rugby league.'

The Villeneuve loose forward added that all the Australian papers had dedicated entire pages to the team's achievements: 'Our success is considered one of *the* events in world sport; they've been going into raptures about the merits and quality of what they call "the French method".

'For sure the France team is playing better than it has ever played. The fact of being together for a long time and our very good physical condition are no doubt the main reasons for that.'[xxi]

While the touring party had been on the other side of the world, Barrière and Devernois had dedicated themselves both to their business interests and the work of the Federation. From the annual congress, which took place at Libourne as the France XIII were carrying all before them in Australia, there emerged a major decision. It concerned the revival of Paris at the highest level, instigated by Maurice Tardy, who had worked tirelessly for that cause. At first delegates decided that Tardy's guarantees were insufficient. The chairmen of Perpignan, Carcassonne and Marseille were especially sceptical but even their reservations, which carried considerable weight, were put aside with the 'spectacular intervention' of Devernois, who combined his duty as Federation vice-president with that of chairman of Lyon XIII, and who personally guaranteed the future of Celtic de Paris in the first division.[xxii]

That took place weeks before the financially successful tour. Before the end-of-tour matches in Melbourne and Perth, the France team had taken approximately £14,100 from its share of the tour profits. That figure exceeded Great Britain's profits from the

1950 tour by over £1,000 even though France's costs were much higher. The outlay for the flight to Australia alone was £9,750.

At the end of the 1950 Lions tour, the English Rugby League distributed £5,500 as bonuses to players.[xxiii] The destination of the French party's tour profits have been the subject of speculation in the long intervening period. Anecdotally it has been suggested that the profits were divided among the participants. After all, the team went off with only the promise of remuneration if the tour takings warranted it and received just £10 a month spending money. On the other hand, it has been thought that the newly-swollen Federation bank account was drawn on to entice rugby union stars to switch codes. It seems likely that, following the British model, the first supposition was true, with players receiving bonuses. Evidence also suggests that the Federation put at least some of the rest towards what might be called capital expenditure.

Jacques Merquey confirmed that the players were given a share of the profits. 'I bought myself a motor-bike,' he said. 'But only a small motor-bike.'[xxiv]

Elie Brousse endorsed the suggestion, saying, 'During the tour Blain gave us a bit of money to buy postcards etc – it was just pocket money. I don't remember how much of the profits we got but it wasn't huge.'[xxv]

But before the party had even returned to France, there was speculation about whether the recently-acquired wealth would be used to fund an attack on rugby union. According to the specialist newspaper *Midi-Olympique,* there was no concerted campaign on the part of the Ligue. Claude Devernois denied any 'offensive',[xxvi] but a list from 'a generally reliable source' was published. On the list figured one-time league players such as centre André Brouat, rated at three million francs, centre Jean Dauger, now nearing the end of his career, but still valued at two million, ex-Carcassonne scrum-half François Labazuy and many others, including members of the France XV, together valued at a putative 27 million francs (roughly £27,000).[xxvii] Barrière and Devernois did not deny that they had covered thousands of kilometres contacting rugby union internationals whom they wanted to bring to clubs such as Bordeaux, Carpentras, Marseille, Avignon and Lyon.

At the start of the 1951-52 season, Devernois agreed that the game would benefit from the success of the Australasian tour but maintained that it was necessary to keep a cool head.

'There has been talk of a general offensive on rugby union players,' he said. 'That is incorrect. We certainly don't intend to pillage rugby union. Why should we spend millions pointlessly? We will simply take on the players we need to complete our various teams.' The top division would stick with fourteen clubs because the main aim was to put out 'good teams capable of playing enjoyable attacking rugby.'[xxviii]

But as *Midi-Olympique* pointed out, despite Devernois' claims not to have launched a raid on rugby union players, a list of players already signed, at the head of which was the Pau trio of middle backs Antoine Jimenez, Jean Hatchondo and André Carrère, represented an impressive tally.[xxix]

The French Rugby Union Federation were worried. As far back as February, French officials had been warned once again by the Home Unions about the unsatisfactory nature of the game in France. British officials were unhappy about the intensity of French competitions, giving rise once again, they believed, to a neglect of 'the spirit of the game', to dubious transfers of players from one club to another, indiscipline and rough play, spectators' threatening behaviour towards referees and the large number of well-known players who had been found positions running cafés.[xxx] The RFU was taking aim at pretty much all of the French game. But what was feared yet again, and on both sides of the Channel, was a return to the situation in 1931, which provided a vacuum for rugby league to prosper.

Now, it was being claimed in the press, war between league and union had been openly declared, with the winner taking all and the loser disappearing altogether. The Ligue, led by 'active, realistic men, has begun its campaign against the antique FFR, which, in the seven years since the "dissident" rugby has

Above: Members of Racing Catalan, formerly XIII Catalan, meet Marshal Philippe Pétain, the Head of State, at Vichy on 6 May 1944. The Catalan team, obliged to play rugby union during the war, were fulfilling an away fixture there. Four months later the German Occupation of France and the Vichy government came to an end.

Fédération des Maquisards
et
Résistants Actifs
DU TARN

DÉPARTEMENT DU TARN

CARTE de TITULAIRE
Année 1945-1946

Nom : BERTHOMIEU
Prénoms : Gabriel
Né le ... Graulhet
Département : Tarn
Domicile actuel : 21 Rue des ...
Carte d'identité N° 1324

Date d'entrée dans la Résistance 6 Juin 1944
le Maquis 6 Juin 1944
Sous le nom de : Le ...

Certifié par le Chef de Groupe,

Date de délivrance de la Carte ...

Le Trésorier,

N° 00725

The Resistance membership card of the future Albi and France second rower Gabriel 'Hugues' Berthomieu, *above*, one of the few survivors of the attack on the German barracks which preceded the liberation of Albi in August 1944

Right: Albi's René Rouanet, who figured in the Resistance attack with Berthomieu, moves in to tackle Marseille winger Casse at the Vélodrome

Above: Toulouse 1944-45 with Jean Galia, French rugby league's great pioneer. Back row: Galia, Chevalier, Moreau, Pérez, Coll, Dax, Morel; Front row: Thiebaut, Sabarthès, Duffau, Teychenné, Duffort, Cougnenc, Vigneau

Left: Lyon-Villeurbanne's pre-war pioneer and captain, Charles Mathon, a *résistant* executed in error in 1944

Above: The Carcassonne team which met Villeneuve in the charity match in Paris in 1945 and which included the two *résistants*, Louis Mathon and Henri Moutou, as well as the Stalag escapee, Félix Bergèse. Back row: Carrasco, Martin, L Carrère, Mazon, Noé, Moutou, Poch, Iriart, Calbète, J Raynaud; Front row: G Llari, Labazuy, Bergèse, Puig-Aubert, Raynaud, Ponsinet

In 1945, Carcassonne's player-coach and mentor, Félix Bergèse, opened the café which bore his name, Chez Félix. The city's famous rugby league gathering-point, *pictured below,* is still run by the family today

Left: The Catalans de France team which beat the Australians 20-5 at Christmas, 1948.
Back row: Bruzy, Vayre, Ulma, Blanc, Négrier, Brousse, Riu, Duhau;
Front row: Trescazes, Maso, Prats, Rouzaud, Comes, Déjean, Casse

Right and inset: The Toulouse Olympique scrum-half Yves Bergougnan, who switched to rugby union with Stade Toulousain in 1944 and was at the centre of a huge scandal in 1947-48 when selected to play for the France XV in the Five Nations tournament

A tumultuous match between XIII Catalan and Carcassonne, in which an altercation between ASC prop Louis Mazon and his counterpart Ambroise Ulma started a mass brawl. Police escort Mazon and Martin Martin off the pitch

Right: Carcassonne v Marseille: the final of the Coupe de France, 1949, at the Stade Vélodrome. Carcassonne front-rower Mazon attacks as Marseille second-rower Brousse covers across; ASC centre Llari has been tackled, scrum-half Guilhem stands behind him and hooker Martin is on the extreme right. Marseille retained the Lord Derby trophy, winning 12-9

Above: The Roanne team backed by Claude Devernois (back row, extreme right) and coached by Bob Samatan (on Devernois' right) became champions in 1947 and again in 1948. As they had done the previous year, Roanne played Wigan at Central Park on 21 May 1949, losing 25-16 in front of 21,000 spectators

Left: The France team which beat Wales 11-0 at Marseille, April 1949. Back row: Duhau, Martin, Bartoletti, Ulma, Ponsinet, Berthomieu, Calixte; Front row: Lespès, Crespo, Puig-Aubert, Déjean, Guilhem, Galaup, Cantoni

Left: Captain Paul Déjean receives the Lord Derby trophy after his XIII Catalan team beat Lyon 12-5 in the 1950 final

Below: The France team which met England at Headingley, 11 November 1950, losing 14-9. Back row: Pérez, Brousse, Ponsinet, Béraud, Mazon, Martin, Duhau; Front row: Contrastin, Duffort, Dop, Puig-Aubert, Galaup, Crespo, Cantoni

Right: In France's match against Other Nationalities at Bordeaux on 10 December 1950, second rower Edouard Ponsinet was concussed by his Australian opposite number, Arthur Clues. Midi-Olympique published this picture of a stricken Ponsinet, who is comforted by Federation president Paul Barrière, while on the left vice-president Claude Devernois stares angrily at the aggressor. *Below*: Ponsinet in action against New Zealand

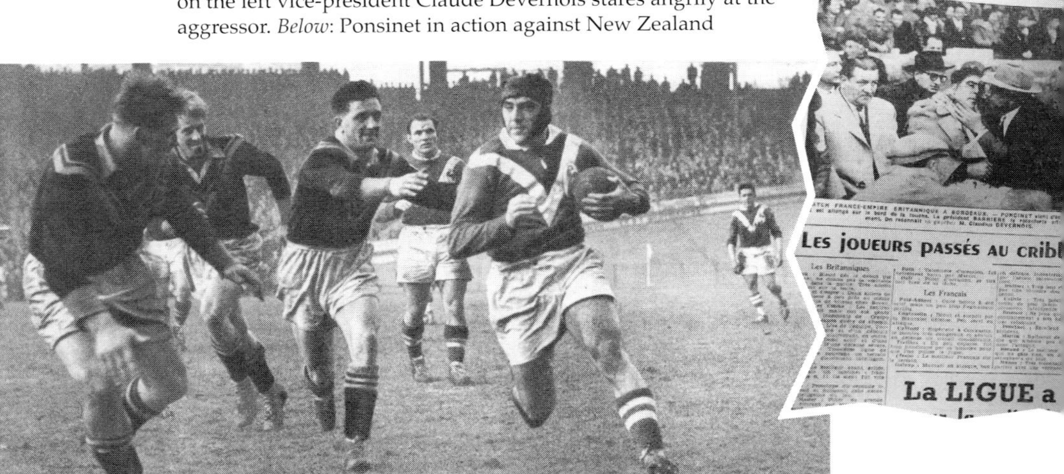

Left: Record points-scorer Puig-Aubert, whose name became synonymous with the France team's dazzling style of play which enthralled Australian crowds on the 1951 tour

Below: From their hotel opposite the SCG, the Lyon trio of Maurice Bellan, René Duffort and Elie Brousse wave to the crowd

Above: The France team which undertook the ground-breaking tour of Australia and New Zealand in 1951. Back row: Audoubert, Lopez, Calixte, Brousse, Delaye, Pérez, Béraud, Ponsinet, Lespès; Middle row: Bartoletti, Duhau (coach), Duffort, Contrastin, Mazon, Cantoni, Blain (manager), Puig-Aubert, André, Genoud, Montrucolis, Rinaldi, Samatan (coach); Front row: Martin, Merquey, Bellan, Caillou (capt), Dop, Crespo, Comes. Missing: Galaup

Classic shots from the thir
at Sydney in 1951: (*Clockw*
Raymond Contrastin is ta
Elie Brousse scores a famo
try; the victorious France
parades the Tattersall Cup
Gaston Comes slices thro

Below: The streets of Marseille throng with supporters as the France team returns home

reappeared, does not seem to have noticed the danger which threatens it,' it was observed. The same writer cited the triumphant tour of Australia and New Zealand, coming after the success in the annual international tournament, as evidence that rugby league was very much alive and well. The possibility of new clubs springing up (Pau and Tarbes among them), the resurgence of Paris, the dominance of league in Bordeaux – though this was something of an overstatement – and Perpignan (where XIII Catalan was taking USAP's best players and actively seeking to hinder the union club) was given as further proof. Meanwhile the FFR was trying to toe the RFU line by diluting the championship, and by employing a more covert transfer régime. Everything was being sacrificed, it was maintained, in order to keep the international matches, the means by which the Federation managed to make ends meet.[xxxi]

Rugby league had now seized the initiative and would maintain the momentum not just with the annual matches against England, Wales and Other Nationalities, but with a forthcoming visit by the Kiwis.

'The antipodean tour has singularly raised the standing of an organisation whose leaders have shown themselves in many ways to be enlightened innovators,' wrote another observer. 'In a word, the Ligue, which, through the tour … has placed itself at the very top level, must maintain that position this season.'[xxxii]

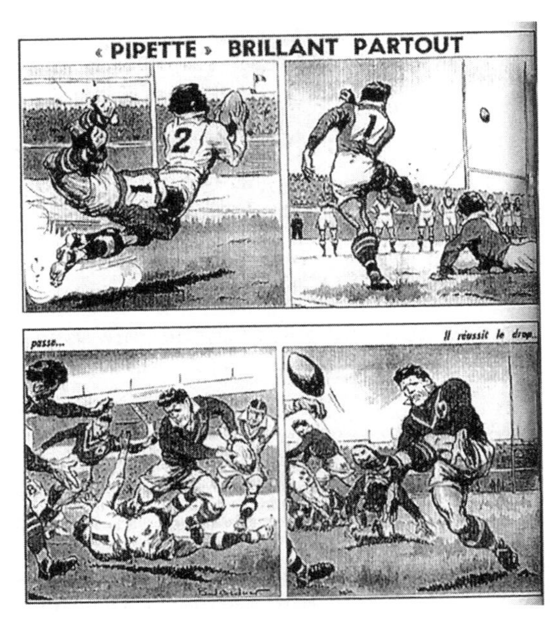

The junior version of *L'Equipe* produced a cartoon strip of the great Puig-Aubert, nicknamed 'Pipette'

Chapter 8

•

Star-studded Teams: 1951-53

AT THE START of the 1951-52 season, treizistes had every reason to be full of hope for the future. The overwhelming success in Australia and the title of unofficial world champions – despite the defeat in New Zealand – had made the sporting media take notice beyond the usual geographical confines.

In a variety of those sports weeklies which abounded in the immediate post-war period, such as *Miroir-Sprint, Miroir des Sports* and *But et Club*, rugby league was featured alongside the major sports of cycling, athletics, boxing, football and rugby union, and sometimes provided the front-cover picture. Once more Puig-Aubert carried the rugby league flag, and with great distinction. Already, at Christmas 1948, the magazine *Sprint* had selected Puig-Aubert as one of its front-page 'wonders' of French sport, alongside, for example, the world middleweight boxing champion, Marcel Cerdan, and, representing rugby union, Yves Bergougnan. In 1951, the respected sports daily *L'Equipe* named Puig-Aubert as France's sportsman of the year – Jacques Merquey was also nominated – and pointed out that in the course of that calendar year, the full-back had scored no fewer than 434 points. Marcel Cerdan, whose father, by coincidence, also came from Perpignan, had been voted number one in the same publication three years earlier. Since it was agreed that no one in rugby league could match Puig-Aubert's celebrity, apart from Max Rousié in the pre-war years, comparison was made between the rugby league player and the champion boxer, darling of the French sporting public. 'Cerdan, like Pipette, is quick on his feet and with his hands,' it was said in *Miroir-Sprint*.[i]

That glorious, unprecedented homecoming at Marseille, which for a day transformed La Canebière into New York's Broadway, had helped erase any lingering indifference in the press. The spotlight was turned on the returning tourists, for whom there was no respite as the new season got under way.

The biggest news on the domestic front was the re-launch of rugby league in the capital with Maurice Tardy's Celtic de Paris, thanks to Claude Devernois, who, as promised, stepped in to give guarantees after the initial bid had failed. Devernois, who retained his interest in Lyon, saw to it that three top players from that club moved to the capital: the two internationals, Duffort and Bellan, and second rower Lasserre. The club also recruited the recently-capped union pair, Roger Arcalis and René Bernard. At the same time, several amateur clubs sprang up in and around Paris, including one at Versailles.

Among other newcomers to the Ligue, Limoux appeared that autumn, though they were not promoted to the national division until a decade later. As had often happened, before the war as well as after, Limoux was one of those clubs which switched from union following a dispute with the FFR, which had refused to rubber-stamp a number of transfers. The former Carcassonne star Félix Bergèse helped to launch the club, but it was Paul Barrière, from his home base at nearby Espéraza, who facilitated the move.[ii] The strengthening of rugby league in his home *département* of Aude became a feature of Barrière's presidency.

The previous season, Villefranche de Rouergue, in the

Aveyron, had also defected to rugby league after a tussle with the governing body, which imposed sanctions that the club officials regarded as unfair. The club was supported and advised in its move by none other than Antoine Blain, who had lived nearby during the war years and had become friends with the chairman.[iii] Like Limoux, Villefranche would not join the top division until a decade later but became another significant addition to the Ligue's roster.

In the national division, Bordeaux, which had provided Contrastin, Lespès and Bartoletti to the squad which had toured Australasia, decided to merge with Libourne and become known as Girondins XIII. The two clubs had finished the previous season in eleventh and twelfth place respectively. That merger, together with the arrival of Paris and the departure of Toulon, who had dropped out after finishing bottom, took the number of clubs to thirteen.

But as rugby league looked forward to the New Zealanders' tour to Europe, the FFR was in a state of anxiety about whether the Five Nations tournament would revert to four, if not in the present 1951-52 season, then in the not too distant future. Some were predicting another showdown once the international season was over.

The rugby journalist and former union international, Marcel de Laborderie, wrote of the difficulties of the relationship between the French and British. His article in *But et Club* described a concept of rugby which seemed a long way off what was happening in rugby league.

'Let us not forget,' de Laborderie began, taking a dispassionate but also conservative line, 'that rugby is an essentially English game…, that the British invented it, perfected it and codified it with the measured pace and prudence which is their nature… Often [French clubs] have disfigured it, and it is because it has moved away from the true face of rugby that Franco-British matches are so valuable and instructive.'

The writer went on to quote an unnamed English international player, who had insisted, 'We guard the true rugby fiercely. We want to keep it in the direct line of our traditions... The universities of Oxford and Cambridge are its sanctuaries and it is [their] students who, imbued with the finest spirit of the game, go forward to spread the good word in our various clubs.'

According to this view, which was undoubtedly prevalent in the mid-twentieth century even though it had not changed since the last quarter of the nineteenth, Franco-British exchanges were useful so that the French could be inspired by examples set across the Channel. De Laborderie observed that the British had in effect 'restricted rugby to an elite, even a caste. The idea that one could make a profit from it, the very thought of professionals plunges them into the depths of despair. They want to believe, or rather, wanted to believe that in France the sacred customs of amateurism were being adhered to, but their confidence has been shaken.'[iv]

Despite the divergence between league and union in almost every aspect of playing and administering rugby, it goes without saying that the concept of the 'spirit of the game' was one recognised by treizistes even if they used less lofty language to describe it. Fairness and respect for the opponent were of course qualities common to both codes.

Definitions were stretched from time to time, though, and most recently by the Australian tour. Some of the games up country, where an element of 'biffo' was seen as part of the game, had more than their share of dirty play, even by the standards of the day. The second test, won by Australia, was described as particularly violent, as had been the match at Swansea two years before.

The French, having risen to the top of world rugby league, were seen by some as fair game. Not that they were necessarily angels themselves. But the match between France and Other Nationalities at Hull on 3 November 1951 was a blemish the game could have done without.

It provided the sequel to the match played at Bordeaux almost a year earlier, which was marked by over-aggressive play, and which resulted in second rower Ponsinet being maimed by

Arthur Clues. If revenge was on the Carcassonne forward's mind, the Australian members of the side had a few things to settle, too.

In a preview which appeared on the morning of the match, Alfred Drewry wrote in *The Yorkshire Post*: 'The ten Australians who will play for Other Nationalities against France in the Rugby League international championship at the Boulevard, Hull, today have a private score to wipe off – by proxy. It was the Frenchmen who humbled Australia's pride in the Tests last summer, and the fact that most of today's Australians were 12,000 miles away from the scene of the outrage scarcely lessened the blow to their national pride.'

Drewry went on: 'It is a long time since the proper attitude towards the ... Frenchmen was one of friendly indulgence. They have been quick to learn the distinction that sometimes exists between spectacular football and winning football. While retaining much of their fantastic skill in handling they have acquired steadiness in defence – and the toughness that goes with it.'

It was a remarkably prescient article, with the *Yorkshire Post's* man concluding that France might suffer from a surfeit of football. 'They will not be like our touring teams if they are all completely fit and fresh.'[v]

In a French report of the match, it was said that the France team did indeed look tired, but the main thrust of the opening paragraphs concerned the apparent vendetta by Ponsinet. '[France's] first mistake, and the most startling, was the violent blow which Ponsinet struck to the face of his opposite number, Clues,' wrote Raoul Raynal. '[It was] a regrettable act which had the double effect of unleashing the opponents' forces and diminishing those of its perpetrator, who seemed overcome by a strange fixation which made him lose all effectiveness and accuracy. And this curious disposition spread to the whole forward pack.'[vi]

In his own report, Drewry called the match an 'astonishing mixture of football and fisticuffs', the latter being provided largely by the French forwards.[vii] After only two minutes' play, the normally self-disciplined Ponsinet targeted Clues, who was carried off and spent the night in hospital with concussion and contusions. The Frenchman was merely penalised by referee Phillips, 'who showed remarkable restraint in the cause of international relations.' The second rower continued the match in a fury. Lionel Cooper, the scorer of three fine tries, was dazed in a Ponsinet tackle before the Leigh forward Burke was knocked unconscious and the Carcassonne man was finally sent off – the first player to be dismissed since France and Other Nationalities joined the championship. In all, France had two players injured; Other Nationalities, who won 17-14, had five. The report ended by adding that France 'would have won through the superiority of half-backs Duffort and Crespo and the centre skill of Comes if they had kept their heads.'

The defeat was a major disappointment for French supporters and created widespread disbelief among the French sporting public in general. The manner of the defeat was also seized upon, according to Jacques Merquey, to reinforce a negative impression of rugby league by pro-union media.[viii]

Three weeks later at Marseille, in front of a record 31,810 crowd, France showed no ill effects, either from the tour or from the so-called 'Battle of the Boulevard' as they regained in spectacular fashion the form they had shown in Australia. England were the victims as France racked up ten tries in a record 42-13 victory. It was England's first defeat on French soil and the heaviest since the European championship had been instituted sixteen years earlier. 'We were run into the ground by a French team which played brilliant football,' an England official was quoted as saying.[ix] Such was the talent available that it mattered little that France had three players who had not been in the Australasian party: the Carcassonne pair of Roger Llari and Roger Guilhem, and, replacing Ponsinet in the second row, Gabriel Berthomieu of Albi. 'It was too easy,' Puig-Aubert was said to have commented, as the mechanical, uninspired play of the English was undone by France's flashes of genius, improvisation and subtlety.[x]

France ended the calendar year of 1951 on a high note by

beating the New Zealanders twice, thus gaining revenge for their one-point defeat in Auckland only four months earlier. The Kiwis had lost all three tests in England, but none by more than six points. Their first match against France, played at the Parc des Princes, was not the kind of classic to entice the largely uninitiated Parisians, but France came back from 3-0 down to take the lead fifteen minutes from the end when the recalled Ponsinet sent Merquey in at the corner to add to Puig-Aubert's 55-metre penalty goal. Contrastin sealed the 8-3 win with a late try. Paul Barrière, was quoted as saying that at half-time he asked his players 'to free themselves from the sort of complex and fear they suffer from whenever they play in front of their Parisian judges, and to play in the French style, audaciously, with conviction, as they do at Marseille, Perpignan or Toulouse.'[xi] The France team, for whom Carcassonne stand-off Gilbert Benausse was making the first of a record-breaking number of appearances, responded with two 'magnificent' tries, which brought 'joy to all the spectators'[xii], including of course Barrière himself.

The second international, at Bordeaux, resulted in a more straightforward 17-7 win for France, though no more than one score separated the teams until the hour. A break by Dop and a jinking run from 35 metres brought France's first try; an interception by Martin the second, soon after half-time. In the last minute of play, with France well on top, Contrastin added a third. Puig-Aubert had not been in best kicking form in the first half but rediscovered his touch with both out-of-hand and place kicks in the second half. Not yet twenty years old, André Carrère, Bordeaux's recent signing from Pau rugby union, made an impressive debut in the centre in the absence of Crespo. 'How much harder rugby league is than union,' said Carrère. 'And how often you touch the ball. I admit I'm tired as I've never been before.'[xiii] Roger Guilhem at loose forward was a model of endeavour and sound judgement. In the centre Jacques Merquey, who remembered nothing of the second half after being knocked out, played a fine game. But more than anything this was another spectacular team performance despite the rainy conditions which made the ball slippery, and despite a New Zealand team which the French regarded as superior to the one which had toured four years earlier. The France team, it was argued, had moved on from simply taking advantage of their opponents' weaknesses and errors and had imposed their own personality and style on the game.

In the championship, Celtic de Paris were winning new friends for rugby league and notched some memorable wins, including one in December over XIII Catalan at Saint-Ouen. The team had sensationally been strengthened by the arrival of arguably the world's best forward, Elie Brousse, who had forged such a reputation in Australia. The 16-12 victory over the Catalans came in a match 'saturated with open play', a deliberate policy designed to attract the Paris sporting public.[xiv] Celtic's captain-coach René Duffort, who went on to guide the national side to success and was thriving as a leader, had instigated a style of play intended to please the crowds, even in defeat, such as the 23-11 reverse at Toulouse in January. It was a far cry from the bulldozing play which had begun to affect the style of one or two other sides. Celtic was not a team disposed to grind out victories, which, however, showed in their final league position of tenth.

Carcassonne remained the team to beat. The Canaries finished the 1951-52 season as leaders, followed by Marseille, Lyon and Villeneuve. They did the Cup and Championship double for the second time. Eighth in the league, XIII Catalan reached the Cup final, played at Marseille, but were well beaten by Carcassonne, for whom Puig-Aubert kicked eight goals, including two drop goals, in their 28-9 victory, their fourth Lord Derby trophy.

In the Championship final at Toulouse's Stade Chapou, watched by 20,000 spectators, Carcassonne beat Marseille, second in the table, by 18-6. As they had done two years earlier, the ASC outplayed their opponents, with rising stars Claude Teisseire at centre and stand-off Gilbert Benausse spearheading their attacks as they opted for uncomplicated, direct play. Benausse touched down twice in the last ten minutes; second row Gacia also scored two tries. It was not a final to compare with the previous season's magnificent fare, but it counted on the ASC's honours board as their fourth triumph in seven appearances.

The international season finished with a 20-12 win over Wales at Bordeaux in April, followed by a 22-12 victory over Great Britain in Paris in May, an unusually late end to the calendar. For the French, it had been highly successful. In eleven matches since the beginning of 1951, they had lost just three: the second test in Brisbane, the Auckland test and the clash with Other Nationalities at Hull.

For the first time, France hosted a meeting of the International Board, which took place at Lyon and of which Paul Barrière acted as co-chairman. Expansion had been on the agenda for a while. In addition to the usual business of arranging international tours and matches, rugby league development in the United States was discussed, and the president of the Italian Federation as well as a Spanish representative were invited to attend. An Italian club, Turin, had already undertaken a short tour in France the previous December. The most important decision, however, for the future of the game was that each nation should put forward its proposals for the inaugural World Cup.

In the close season the thoughts of club chairmen and their committees quickly turned to team-strengthening for the following season. Some recruited from within the elite division, others went scouting in the union ranks, with Paris and Carcassonne believed to be leading the party - 'two names to make the quinzistes tremble', as *Midi-Olympique* put it.[xv] Claude Devernois went off for a break to the Landes region to hunt woodsnipe, as well as a player, it was reported.[xvi]

Union clubs had good reason to fear their ranks being depleted by defections to league. Since the new wave of measures introduced at the behest of the British and the insistence on strict amateurism, no union club was now able to outbid league clubs for players' services. Or so it was thought.[xvii]

The biggest transfer of all concerned the game's biggest star. With the backing of Devernois, who had taken a closer interest in Paris, Puig-Aubert went from Carcassonne to Celtic, thus providing the Parisian side, which had already signed Brousse and Duffort, with three stars of the Australian tour.

It was hard to imagine the ASC without their inimitable full-back, who had been with the club since *la reprise*, even though he had put on a few kilos and was no longer as fit as on the tour. His play had evolved and yet remained essentially the same.

'Pipette's last matches at Domec showed a new facet of his sheer talent. Aubert had comfortably got heavier and, by his own admission, "didn't tire himself too much". But he always guessed where the ball was going to bounce, which he attracted irresistibly like a magnet. His kicking still wrought havoc, as well as his sudden bursts of speed in attack.

'But sometimes when an opponent broke through the Carcassonne defensive line and passed within his reach without his making the slightest effort to catch him, the crowd screamed at him.

'But then, a few minutes later when ASC were in the opposition 22 metres, Pipette moved up to the stand-off position, and, turning on a sixpence, dummied his way through, leaving two or three defenders for dead, and scored under the posts. He kicked the goal and made a mocking gesture to the delirious crowd.'[xviii]

Puig-Aubert had been paid three million francs (roughly £3,000) to play for Paris, but continued to work and train throughout the week in Carcassonne, only going up to the capital for home matches.[xix]

It was an almost impossible task to replace him, but Carcassonne were better able than most to find someone to step into his shoes. The ASC had nurtured their junior teams and produced a string of fine players, first among whom was Gilbert Benausse. Other well-established clubs such as Villeneuve, Albi, Lézignan and XIII Catalan were also producing a stream of young players. Some of the big city clubs – Paris particularly, Marseille, Bordeaux and Toulouse to a lesser degree – did not find it so easy, though Marseille were able to draw on smaller clubs in the area.

When Lyon and Paris Celtic, the two clubs backed by

Devernois, reached the semi-finals of the Cup, there was cause for reflection in some quarters. One writer argued that an expensively assembled team did not make a club.

'If the Catalans of Paris Celtic (there are ten or so of them) were brought together within sight of the Castillet [a Perpignan landmark], under the aegis of the club they secretly think of, not a team in France could depose them... Clubs, I say, not prefabricated teams. For a long time Carcassonne has set the example, Villeneuve fosters its youngsters, as does Albi, and indeed Marseille and Avignon.'[xx]

The writer, the respected Jean Boudey, concluded perhaps more prophetically than he could have known: 'In the future... Monsieur Devernois will see his star teams outstripped by clubs of sub-prefectures [i.e. small towns], inspired by local pride.'

Puig-Aubert's successors had a lot to live up to. Which was true of the game as a whole, given the exploits of the national side, sparkling finals and generally spectacular play which the public had come to expect. It was often said that open, entertaining play was rugby league's raison d'être, the factor which above all distinguished it from rugby union. So when matches fell short of those standards, criticism was not slow in coming. Barely had the 1952-53 season got under way than headlines about 'negative rugby' began to appear.

'The rugby league championship is sinking into negative rugby,' it was claimed in one article. 'The forwards seize on the ball and the backs persist in stereotyped play from which all variety is excluded. Not losing the ball, which was once a virtue, has now become a habit and a flagrant failing.'[xxi]

Apart from the standard of play on the field, Federation officials were constantly preoccupied with development in new areas. While it was said that rugby union had too many clubs to accommodate in a meaningful fixture formula, rugby league had too few, though Barrière and his men were ever aware of the need to extend their network. At the top level, following the Toulon experiment which had lasted just one season, the Ligue was naturally cautious. Pau and Limoges were two projects which could not be covered by appropriate financial guarantees in a climate in which gate receipts appeared to be declining. It was argued that the dominance of Carcassonne, Lyon and Marseille had made the competition too predictable.[xxii] The public was becoming disaffected and choosing its matches. Of the leading trio, only Lyon was making headway on and off the field. Rugby league had not increased its popularity.[xxiii]

One pleasing development was the progress being made by the national junior side, whose most recent performance resulted in a 13-9 victory over England at Leigh. The team included three players from Avignon, three from Albi and two from Carcassonne. Other clubs which supplied team members were Villefranche, Cavaillon, Marseille, XIII Catalan and Lézignan. The only club which surprised by its absence on this occasion was Villeneuve.

An article which appeared in *Midi-Olympique* in October 1952 previewing the international season bore the heading 'A year of transition'. The notion perhaps applied equally to the domestic game.

The first international of the season, against Wales at Leeds, resulted in a below-par team performance which ended in defeat by 22-16 despite some good individual displays, among which was that of Jean Dop. Castleford were reportedly impressed enough to offer the half-back £5,000 to sign for the club.[xxiv]

As a sign of growing media attention, the match was broadcast live from Headingley by French radio. None other than the legendary Max Rousié acted as half-time summariser. The commentator was Roger Couderc, who had been introduced to rugby league by Jacques Merquey. Both came from Souillac, on the river Dordogne. Couderc would go on to become a famous broadcaster but his name, by a curious twist, is forever associated with rugby union. As for the match, it was suggested that the Welsh players, who already had ten or twelve domestic matches under their belts to bring them to match fitness, had the edge over the French, who had only played four or five games by that stage in late October.

There was no such excuse for the 28-10 defeat by Other Nationalities at Marseille a month later. Although half-backs Benausse and Teisseire were relatively inexperienced at this level, and though seven changes had been made, there was plenty of experience throughout the team. France made a quick start through two tries by Merquey and led 10-6 at half-time but conceded 23 points without reply after the interval.

None of this was the ideal warm-up for the three-match series against the Australian tourists, which began five weeks later at the Parc des Princes. As was now the pattern, the Australians arrived from England. There they had lost two tests and won the third at Odsal, a match spoiled by 'mass punch-ups, individual assaults and all manner of clandestine skulduggery'.[xxv]

As in the previous match, against Other Nationalities, France fell away in the second half after Cantoni and Brousse had scored first-half tries to produce a 10-7 lead. Australia had learned some of the lessons of France's 1951 tour and showed some fine passing movements to win by 16-12. But, in the opinion of the Australians themselves, there was one French player who remained unequalled. The Aussies unanimously praised the fine performance of Elie Brousse, who, said Clive Churchill, was the greatest forward in world rugby league and even better than two years previously. 'What speed, what power!' said the Kangaroo captain.[xxvi]

In the second test at Bordeaux, the Aussies slipped back into a forward-dominated style in attack and concentrated on preventing the French from opening the game out. The only try of the game came in the second minute, when, directly from a scrum, Crespo worked a move with loose forward Montrucolis. Benausse in support slipped the ball to centre Carrère, who went over at the corner. Full back André Rives, deputising for Puig-Aubert, converted from the touchline. During the whole of the rest of the match, Crespo made the only clear break. The 23,000 spectators did not get much open football for their money but had the consolation of seeing France level the series with their 5-0 win. 'We understand now,' wrote Jean Boudey, 'why the Tricolores in the Antipodes ... were able to achieve such dazzling success.' Puig-Aubert, watching from the touchline, commented: 'The Australians were wrong to persist with their power rugby. In Australia we had already dominated them in this area.'[xxvii]

Two weeks later at Lyon, France beat the tourists 13-5 to win their second successive series against Australia. It was a more open affair, with plenty of attacking moves to please the 18,000 crowd. Puig-Aubert took the honours with five goals, including two from 50 metres, and stand-off Gilbert Benausse, decisive and quick, scored the sole French try, but the whole team gave an energetic and committed performance.[xxviii]

With various enforced changes to the side, they fared less well in the European championship. With a narrow 15-13 defeat by England in Paris, France had lost all three fixtures. They did, however, make up for the loss by beating Great Britain 28-17 at Lyon six weeks later. In the May heat, France turned on their best attacking style. Puig-Aubert scored thirteen points from five goals and a try; stand-off Jo Crespo and local winger Maurice Voron both touched down twice.

Lyon contested both end-of-season finals. The Championship final, played for the first time at the Stadium de Toulouse, pitched Lyon against league leaders Carcassonne. The ASC, captained by Louis Mazon, scored three tries to two. Loose forward Germain Calbète gave a masterly display, well supported by try-scorer Edouard Ponsinet, in an entertaining, fast-paced final in which Carcassonne retained their title, winning 19-12. The attendance of 22,500 showed an improvement of 6,000 on the previous year's final at Stade Chapou in the same city.

Claude Devernois decided to take his Lyon team away to lick their wounds at Le Boulou, near Perpignan, the city where the Cup final was to be held for the first time. Lyon's opponents were Villeneuve, who were appearing in their first post-war final. Watched by 12,000 spectators in fine weather, the pioneer club came close to upsetting the favourites and, with loose forward Gaston Calixte deputising ably at stand-off, and centre Antoine Jimenez racing 40 metres to touch down, came back strongly in the second half before going down 9-8 despite scoring two tries to one.

At the end of the season, Carcassonne undertook another first. The champion club were invited to make a short tour of the Indian Ocean island of Madagascar, then a French colony. The tour was set up by a police lieutenant stationed there who happened to be a keen ASC fan and was also the brother-in-law of the former Carcassonne player, François Labazuy. Paul Barrière agreed and Carcassonne, reinforced by Puig-Aubert, now with Paris, as well as internationals André Carrère of Bordeaux and Gabriel Genoud of Villeneuve, played exhibition matches there wearing the Tricolores' jerseys.[xxix]

An interesting statistic also emerged from Carcassonne's Championship final against Lyon. Of the twenty-six players on duty that day, sixteen came directly through rugby league clubs' nurseries. Considering that the game was wiped out by the Vichy ban, with the progression of young players to the senior ranks thus completely disrupted, the figure is more impressive than might appear at first sight. As the statistic shows, players who were thought good enough to convert from rugby union were still in demand, and given that the 15-a-side game had many more clubs than league it was not surprising that officials should recruit from that code. But crucially for the future of league, the game was drawing increasingly on its own resources and Carcassonne was one of the clubs leading the way.

Dubbed 'the world's greatest forward', Elie Brousse torments England

Chapter 9

•

Elie Brousse, the Tiger of Sydney

AMONG ALL THE great players in those star-studded teams of the decade immediately after the war, none, with the possible exception of the inimitable Puig-Aubert, stands out more than Elie Brousse. Between 1947 and 1954, the second rower played in eight finals, winning six of them, and was a key figure in some of the most glamorous and extraordinary sides of the day: Roanne, Marseille, Lyon and Paris. A Catalan like many of the great players of the era, Brousse came from the village of Bages, a long way from the town where he first played rugby league professionally.

Brousse still lives in Roanne, where he arrived at the start of the 1945-46 season. It was in that post-industrial town, situated on the Loire some 50 miles north of Lyon, that I met this still physically imposing figure from French rugby league's second great era. A week later the 94-year old was given a standing ovation as the guest of honour at an event to celebrate Roanne rugby league club's eightieth anniversary. With Max Rousié and Jean Dauger, probably the pre-war era's two finest players, Roanne won the last Championship final before the outbreak of conflict in 1939, as well as the Cup in 1938, and restarted afterwards, winning back-to-back championships in 1947 and 1948, beating Carcassonne on both occasions, before Claude Devernois transferred the backbone of the team to Lyon.

Edouard Duseigneur, the international forward of the 1960s, had offered to drive me from Lyon to Brousse's home at Roanne, or rather Le Coteau, on the outskirts. We had lunch at a bistro, Le Sporting Bar, appropriately enough, which had once been the hotel where Brousse and some of his team-mates had lodged. Some seventy years on, there are few people left in Roanne who remember seeing him play, but, judging by those who came over to talk, some of the working people at nearby tables seemed to realise that they were eating their *côte de porc* or *langue de boeuf* in the presence of greatness.

At the time he arrived there, Roanne appeared very different from the Catalan village where he was born and brought up, though both places are recognised for their people's generosity of spirit. Brousse's playing career was exceptional, but his arrival on the banks of the Loire was far from unusual. The Catalan region was, and still is, a plentiful source of rugby talent, where the two codes lived cheek by jowl. From 1940 to 1944, during the ban on rugby league, Brousse played for both USAP, the union club, and Racing Catalan, essentially XIII Catalan forced into playing the other code. At the Liberation in 1944, Brousse played just three rugby league games with the Catalans and remembers each one. 'I played in the first [rugby league] match to be played in France [after the war], against Toulouse Olympique at Toulouse,' he said. Alongside were such great names as Gaston Comes, Paul Déjean and André Bruzy. That was the match, played on 21 October 1944 at the Stadium, which marked the official rebirth of *le rugby à treize*, though other matches had been played in the five weeks since the famous meeting in Toulouse at which the game was relaunched.

'After that, in the championship, against Carcassonne at Perpignan, and Avignon at Avignon' he went on. 'I played just those three matches. At the time you could move easily from league to union after two weeks' wait. So I went back to USAP. It was the former international [of both codes], Jep Desclaux, who suggested it to me. I had played with him during the war in the Languedoc-Roussillon team which won the final of the regional cup competition at Toulouse against Côte Basque-Béarn with the Dauger brothers.'

Desclaux, who had been captain of the France XV before signing for Bordeaux XIII, reverted to union after the war, just like ex-Roanne centre Jean Dauger. Robert Dauger, brother of Jean, remained a rugby league player and played alongside Brousse at Roanne.

'When I was in the [war-time] *chantiers de jeunesse* [youth camps] at Argelès [near Lourdes], we had a team with lads from Agen, Toulouse and so on. We had a really good team; we played against Brive and against the Stade Toulousain reserves. Stade Toulousain wanted me to go and play for them, but it was the Occupation and there were round-ups [by the Gestapo] and so if I had gone there I might have been picked up and sent off to work in Germany.

'At the end of the war, Monsieur Devernois, who wanted to put a great team together like he had before the war, when there were Max Rousié and the Dauger brothers, came personally to Perpignan and signed up Crespo, Riu - five or six Catalans in all. He was staying at the Grand Hôtel. I was just leaving town – I had been asked to have talks with another club. I was at the station and a XIII Catalan official who was a scout said to me, "There's a Monsieur Devernois who wants to see you. He's at the Grand Hôtel. What are you going to do?" I went to see him and afterwards a friend of mine – we played in the same team – said, "I'm glad I've seen you because some officials from the Vichy club want to see you." I said, "It's too late. I've signed to play rugby league."'

Robert Barran, the former Stade Toulousain captain and journalist, described Brousse's departure in his book *Le Rugby des Villages*. 'Being a good son,' he wrote, '[Elie] thought first of his parents, with whom, since his youth, he had sweated on the land

and bought them what in those days was worth the equivalent of a tractor, a mule. Elie's mule, in the Roussillon plain, was more than a bucolic image; it was the mark of a man who, though achieving glory on the rugby field, remained faithful to his origins, aware of the need, for him and his family, to earn one's daily bread.'[i]

Barran, an excellent writer on rugby, portrays a somewhat romantic image of the honoured player who never forgets his humble beginnings. Which, in Elie Brousse's case, is true enough. Except that the detail is wrong. 'Did you actually buy your parents a mule?' I asked him. 'No!' he answered. 'Barran must have confused me with [Raoul] Perez.'

'I never owned so much as a single vinestock and yet I was "the richest proprietor in my village" [according to how a journalist put it at the time]. I was an agricultural worker, that's all. When I was playing at Roanne, I arrived late [for the start of the season] because we were busy with the grape harvest and I was giving my parents a hand.

'My parents had a hectare of vines. If you had a bit of land to grow vines on, it brought in a bit of money because agricultural workers didn't earn a fortune. All the workers, if they could, bought themselves a hectare of vines. It wasn't the dessert wine [for which Bages is well known] that they made, though Muscat and Grenache are made there. It was just ordinary wine they made and sold straight away.'

'When I went to Roanne, I worked in the [Devernois] factory. My wife worked there for 45 years and I for 34. Monsieur Devernois was a well-respected gentleman. He had four factories. When I came in 1945 they were building another. He had at least 600 people working for him. You should have seen it. Two or three of the players who were from Roanne worked at the arsenal, but all the others that he signed worked in the factory.'

Racing Club Roanne started up again in the 1945-46 season, a year later than most of the other top level teams. The Catalan contingent arrived from Perpignan to make Roanne a champion team, coached first by Jean Duhau, then by Bob

Samatan. In the backs were Crespo and Comes; in the forwards Barris, Riu and Brousse, among others. But by 1948, when Roanne were winning their second successive championship, Brousse had already moved on to Marseille, where 'they wanted to put a great team together' and, with a powerful mix of Basques and Catalans, succeeded, because in that same year Marseille won the Cup, and the Championship the year after. But all was not entirely well on the shores of the Mediterranean. 'A lot of promises were not kept.'

'When I was at Marseille,' Brousse continued, 'Roanne had merged with Lyon and the coach was Taillantou, a good player and a good stand-off. 'I remember he found me and said, "Aren't you playing?" I said no and he said "What if Monsieur Devernois took you on at Lyon?" I said, "Listen, I'm not playing and I'm so fed up with all this nonsense that's going on, I'm going to finish." So he said, "I'll talk to the boss." They asked me to go over there and I signed.

'Afterwards, we went to play at Carpentras. It was Christmas Eve. It was terrible weather and Duffort was playing full back because the regular full back was injured. He missed two high kicks from the Carpentras loose forward and at half-time we were trailing 10-0. Towards the end Baldassin scored a try, I scored another and we lost 10-8. We were around sixth in the league table: we would win one, we would lose one. And so Monsieur Devernois, with the Lyon chairman, went to see Samatan. And with Samatan, it was ... well, you had to watch out.'

Lyon reached the final of the Cup, losing to XIII Catalan in that 1949-50 season, and were finalists again the following year, as Brousse made his fourth Lord Derby appearance in a row. They were defeated by Carcassonne, but their finest hour came in the sumptuous Championship final against the Catalans, in which Brousse was the instigator of three of Lyon's five tries in their 15-10 triumph.

Soon after, he was making his name known on the other side of the world. His reputation as one of the world's finest forwards was based on his outstanding performances in the three tests of the 1951 tour of Australia, but not without controversy.

The Brisbane test, the second, was a violent affair 'because the Australians couldn't accept that they had been beaten [in the first].' Brousse was sent off.

'I tackled the centre Hazzard and threw him into touch. He didn't like it, he got up and kicked me on the leg. I defended myself, the referee turned round: "We'll have no trouble from you – off!" In the evening at the disciplinary – three players had just been banned for life; you didn't get off lightly – he said it wasn't true [what I had claimed]. I lifted my trouser leg and there were five stud marks. We left it at that. At the end of the third test, the first person who came to congratulate me was him.'

Noel Hazzard was not the first or the last to be riled by Brousse's particular method of tackling, especially cover tackling.

'I had this way of putting two fingers down the collar of the jersey and pulling like that and throwing [the opponent] into touch,' he said, crooking two fingers and pulling them back. 'In the first few matches, when the Australians saw that – biff! They said to Blain that I was punching, that it was a rabbit chop at the back of the neck. Blain said no, no. They filmed it and saw it wasn't so.'

Or else it was a smother tackle, Brousse circling his great arms around an imaginary figure to demonstrate. Either way, once you'd been tackled by him you no doubt felt it.

The attacking power of the 'Tiger of Sydney' is encapsulated by the famous try he scored in the series-clinching third test. It wasn't just the French backs who dazzled the Australians but the forwards too, as Brousse and fellow-second rower Ponsinet unequivocally showed.

'We were in our own 22 metres and the Australians were on top. We got the ball, Ponsinet and Bartoletti played the ball and I was away. I broke through the forwards, shoved the threequarters out of the way and found myself with nobody in front. I was five metres from the line, maybe less, and the stand-off O'Connell dived and caught the tip of my boot but with my momentum I went over at the post. The second rower Brian Davies was running across and if he'd carried on he'd have smashed his face against the post. He wanted to swerve to the left, he jumped over me but caught me with his boot on the back of my neck. We'd been playing about 20 minutes. I came round at half-time in the dressing room with the doctors around me.'

After turning down the offer to stay in Sydney, Brousse moved to Paris for the 1951-52 season, where a future president of the Federation, the indefatigable Maurice Tardy, with the backing of Claude Devernois, was again trying to assemble a team that would hold its own in the top division.

'They came to see me. Monsieur Devernois wanted to put together a great team and I said yes. I was told that they would get me into the police and I took the exam. I passed the written exam and then the physical tests, and was classed among the top candidates. The director wanted to see me. He said, "You're a professional rugby player." I said, "I'm not a professional. I work in a hosiery factory in Roanne." I unloaded the lorries.

'He said, "You haven't done any military service." I said, "I couldn't. It was the war [the Occupation]." The *chantiers de jeunesse* didn't count. Everything was against me. He said, "If you had gone to Germany, even just for a day, we would have taken you."' The director was referring to the forced labour scheme applied by the Germans. As an agricultural worker, as he had been at the time, Brousse was exempt anyway.

'When I think that my father had lost three brothers in the '14-18 war against Germany, I was disgusted. So I travelled back and forth between Roanne and Paris. There were students and Catalans and Basques – Duffort, Lasserre, Labadie and so on.'

'To sign Puig-Aubert [who went to Paris at the same time] – he had a shop in Carcassonne – Devernois said he should sell his shop and he would set up another in Paris. It didn't come off. He didn't get a shop. It was like me with the police.'

Paris fell apart after two seasons. Their record on the field was acceptable, but the finances did not hold up.

'We didn't get enough money through the gate. When we played at the Parc des Princes, we got good crowds, but when we played at Saint-Ouen, zero.'[ii]

Brousse's playing career straddles that brilliant post-war decade, a time when, he says, you could have selected three or four *équipes de France*, such was the talent available. He didn't say where he had been happiest, but commented, 'Rugby league was at its height. Like me, many players changed clubs.' He has particularly fond memories, though, of that one-off match at Christmas 1948 when a formidable team was put together as the Catalans de France – a homecoming for several of them – and beat the Australian tourists 20-5, the Kangaroos' only defeat in France. It was a precursor to the 1951 tour which confirmed his reputation throughout the rugby league-playing world.

Chapter 10
•
World Première: 1953-54

DESPITE THE CONTINUED rise of rugby league, the annual congress of 1953, held at Avignon, was expected to be an animated one. For one thing, Federation vice-president Claude Devernois, who had supported, both morally and financially, Lyon and Paris, and was thus the object of some envy, was expected to come in for criticism from 'those who had less money than he', as *Midi-Olympique* put it. The same newspaper, in his defence, argued that Devernois was only guilty of the creation of Roanne, both before and after the war, the transfer of Roanne's best to Lyon, once there was no further room for expansion in his home town, and 'massive' assistance to Celtic de Paris. The paper asked whether, if it had not been for Monsieur Devernois, Roanne, Lyon and Paris would have existed. 'It is with officials like M Devernois that towns and cities have had teams of great players winning matches and, what is even better, winning them by playing true rugby league.'[i]

The attacks on Devernois failed to materialise as he and Paul Barrière led the Avignon congress to achieve unanimity on the major questions under discussion. It might have been thought that rugby league was in a healthy position, particularly when compared with what was going on in the other code. Rugby union was heading towards bankruptcy as a result of disastrous financial management, if reports were to be believed.[ii] The 15-a-side game was in further disarray over the new championship structure. The game's masters, the RFU, had long held that the French championship was the ultimate reason for the ills of the game there. The FFR narrowly succeeded in pushing through a reduction in the number of championship matches, which led to the ironic comment that 'the less we play in the championship, the more we become amateurs'.[iii]

Rugby league's concerns centred on improving the game as a spectacle. Despite the reputation the French had earned at international level for a rapid, expansive style of play, the domestic game was considered to be falling short of the ideal.

'The past season has not brought us the joys that we were expecting,' declared Barrière, not mincing his words. 'We wanted an evenly-balanced championship, and it was. But the game itself, except at amateur level, has not improved. On the contrary…

'The game has become monotonous, occasionally brutal. It is less pleasing. Let us give it back its character, romantic and manly at the same time.'[iv]

The finger was being pointed at the play-the-ball rule, which had again been under discussion at International Board level the previous November, and which was proving problematic in England as well, with various solutions being proposed. France, supported by Australia and New Zealand, wanted to scrap the present rule, which stipulated that the dummy half should stand one yard behind the man playing the ball and all other players behind the dummy half. Its detractors said that the rule hampered open play. An Australian newspaper even reported that in France it had made the game 'a shambles.'[v] In France up to 1950, the four-metre rule had been in force: all players had to stand four metres back from the play-the-ball except the dummy half, who retired only two metres. On the 1951 tour of Australia and New Zealand, the five-yard rule applied, though it appears from film of that time that referees did not police the distance rigorously.

Other reforms were proposed: in refereeing, in the administration of the game and in the level below the national division, where the creation of a second division, after much consideration, was judged not to be in the interests of the game at the time.

During the course of the 1952-53 season, the Federation had also moved its headquarters from Bordeaux back to Paris, its original base. Barrière and Devernois believed it was essential that the game should have its head office in the capital, close to the national media, the Ministry and major stadiums, even if Parisians themselves knew little of the game.

All of this indicated a leadership eager to move forward, to question current practices and, above all, not to rest on what had already been achieved. The contrast with the FFR, continually in thrall to the RFU, could not have been more marked.

But there were setbacks. Ironically, Celtic de Paris dropped out before the 1953-54 season got under way, despite finishing the previous season in a respectable seventh place out of thirteen. The difficulties associated with keeping a team together in Paris when several players still lived in their home towns in the provinces, and the problems of attracting a loyal Parisian following proved too much. At the start of the previous season, the former rugby union international hooker René Bernard had complained that the club had reneged on a promise to pay him a fee for signing a new contract, without which he would have difficulty, as a low-paid civil servant, in bringing up a family in Paris. The club disagreed and he was transfer-listed.[vi]

As Paris folded, Puig-Aubert moved from the capital to home territory, signing for XIII Catalan and steering them to a Cup final appearance against Lyon. It was the only occasion on which the Cup final would take place at Cavaillon, but the attendance was a disappointing 8,000 for a match which was full of interest. The Perpignan club led 10-6 at half-time, but two other ex-Parisians, Brousse and Duffort, figured prominently for Lyon, who scored five tries to three in winning 17-15. Appearing in their fourth Cup final in five years, Lyon thus retained the Lord Derby trophy.

If only the Championship final, played a week later at Toulouse and featuring Bordeaux and Marseille, had been as entertaining. *Midi-Olympique* called it the worst final of all time.[vii] André Passamar said it was 'the ugliest final, the biggest failure of a final I have ever witnessed. A dull, grey day and rugby to match. It was a festival of play-the-balls and drives…'[viii] This insipid game was dominated by the forwards and was heading for a 4-4 draw after each side had managed two penalties. The only try, scored by Bordeaux centre André Carrère, came in the final minute.

The *Midi-Olympique* reporter, who pointed out that the English Cup final, between Halifax and Warrington, had ended in a 4-4 draw, was scathing about the present state of rugby league, saying that these low scores were the result of players' fears of giving the ball away.

Echoing a concern that was also common in England, he observed that current play revolved around maximum ball control, and by any means. '[Players] avoid passing to their team-mates, they never kick ahead for fear of giving the ball to the opposition. They content themselves with gaining ground centimetre by centimetre, applying a kind of collision rugby that might be called the "stock-car method"…

'Do you think the public finds satisfaction in these methods? Not at all, I can assure you, and if rugby league does not rediscover its prime qualities, which made it so successful, the stadiums will become increasingly deserted.'[ix]

Antoine Blain also revealed his concerns, arguing that attacking rugby was fundamental to rugby league. The essence of the game, he said, was to win by scoring more points than the opposition. But at the present time, by some aberration, that objective had become perverted so that instead the aim was now not to lose, by preventing the opposition from scoring more points than one's own team.[x]

For their part, Marseille resolved to learn their lesson. A month later, their chairman, Albin Rougier, maintaining that all teams had concentrated too much on forward play, declared that his own club would return to playing open football.[xi] Marseille, as Championship finalists and Cup semi-finalists, continued to figure among the Ligue's most successful clubs. But even they had had difficulty in balancing their books, Rougier declared at the club's annual general meeting. A policy of austerity was indispensable to the club's survival and they would seek to recruit from their own nursery or from neighbouring amateur clubs. That was the only way, argued Rougier, to consolidate and increase rugby league's popularity in France.[xii]

Below the national division, 26 teams were divided into three pools – one of ten teams and two of eight. Pool A, which comprised clubs from the Aquitaine region, mainly along the Atlantic coast, featured Arcachon, Facture, La Réole, Sainte-Foy, Métro, Bayonne, Biarritz, Nay, Pau and Girondins. The Midi-Pyrénées region was represented in Pool B by Pamiers, Lavardac, Tonneins, Miramont, Rodez, Villefranche, Cahors and Albi 'B'. Pool C, with the exception of Limoux and Carcassonne 'B', consisted of teams from Provence: Nîmes, Salon, Orange, Toulon, Estagel and Aix.

The 200 delegates to the 1954 annual congress, held in July at Albi, heard Paul Barrière open the proceedings by declaring, not for the first time, that he was intending to resign owing to the increasing demands of his businesses. 'Power wears a man out,' he said. 'I have been in post for nine years. It is time for someone else to take my place.'[xiii] But there followed some stirring oratory from the lawyer Max Juvenal of Aix-en-Provence, who stated that rugby league was at a turning point. With Barrière at its head, he said, the game had achieved miracles and would continue to do so. Within hours of saying that he was giving it all up, Barrière was persuaded to remain, at least for a few more months. No wonder he found his duties exhausting. The various sub-committees, charged with examining the game's administration and refereeing, worked until four o'clock in the morning. But at the closing session, which took place that same Saturday morning, it was with confidence that the Federation approached the 1954-55 season and, above all, that autumn's inaugural World Cup.

The international matches during the 1953-54 season indicated that, with a full-strength side, France were likely to prove very strong in this first-ever tournament. In the European championship, 20,000 spectators at Marseille saw Contrastin touch down three minutes from the end of the final match, which gave France a 23-22 victory over Wales. The other two matches were also closely contested. Brian Bevan's two tries were largely responsible for France's 15-10 defeat by Other Nationalities at Bordeaux. A last-minute penalty try gave England a 7-5 win in the mud of Odsal, over a France team in which Joseph Krawzyck and Jean Pambrun in the forwards and winger André Savonne made their debuts. France's defence was equal to all that England launched at it - from loose forward to full-back, which could not always be said. That drew the headline: 'Sensation: Puig-Aubert tackles at Bradford', referring to the fact that Pipette, not known for his interest in defending, had reportedly made more tackles in this match than in the previous two seasons.[xiv] It was an unspectacular game which was televised in full, though it was not the first international to be screened. Two years earlier the Great Britain-New Zealand test match had been broadcast live from Swinton.

France continued to be involved in development elsewhere in the rugby league world. After the Italians it was the turn of the Americans to tour France. The American All-Stars had already toured Australia and had achieved some respectable results. Similarly in France, where the team of Californian students led by Mike Dimitro, ended their brief visit with an honourable 31-0 defeat by a full France side at the Parc des Princes.

Three Americans and one Italian were selected alongside British and Australian players in the Rest of the World team which faced the French in Lyon to mark the twentieth anniversary of the birth of rugby league in France. The home side won 19-15 as snow fell, which must surely have reminded the watching Victor Breyer, John Wilson and Harry Sunderland, who all played key roles in the launch of rugby league across the Channel, of the exhibition match in Paris on 31 December, 1933 which gave the French their first taste of 13-a-side rugby.[xv]

The remaining international fixture of the 1953-54 season saw France return to Bradford in April to face Great Britain, who were due to set off on their tour of Australasia. The home side scored three tries to none in winning 17-8, France's points coming from three Puig-Aubert penalties and a drop goal. Despite the clear British victory, France were the more enterprising in attack but for once were let down by poor finishing. They also played with twelve men for the last half-hour after prop Paul Bartoletti left the field with an ankle injury.

The event of 1954 which became a milestone in rugby league history took place in October. The French had stuck their necks out to put on this first World Cup competition, showing commendable persistence in the face of apathy. As early as November 1934, the same year as the game had been implanted in France, the French proposed a world championship involving England, Wales, France, Australia and New Zealand to take place the following year. The semi-finals were pencilled in for Bordeaux and Toulouse, with the final in Paris.[xvi] Again in 1947, soon after the French game had got back on its feet, the same idea was put forward but found no takers. At an International Board meeting in 1953, the tournament was finally approved as France, the hosts, agreed to underwrite the other nations' expenses.

Two decades after the idea was first mooted – but only four years after England made a first appearance in football's World Cup, launched in 1930 – the pioneering rugby championship got under way.

Although Barrière's name is the one most closely associated with the competition, RFL secretary Bill Fallowfield claimed credit for the innovation. 'The possibility of organising a Rugby League World Cup Competition first entered my mind in 1951,' he wrote in the official programme for the 1960 series, 'and

I put the suggestion to the Rugby League Council at their meeting on 3rd January 1952, when it was agreed to place it before the International Board, due to take place nine days later at Lyon.'[xvii] Fallowfield cited opposition to the idea, most notably from the Australians, who believed their clubs would not stand for it, before going on to write: 'One of the few who actively supported my suggestion was Paul Barrière, the young President of the French League... [As] Chairman of the Host Organisation at the time of the Lyon Conference he was automatically Chairman of the International Board during the meetings and he, more than any other, was instrumental in not allowing my suggestions to be turned down out of hand.'[xviii] At a further International Board meeting at Blackpool in November of the same year, '...the French League, after Australia had stated that it was "impossible to arrange the Competition in Australia", agreed to stage the First World Cup Series in France and offered a guarantee of £25,000.'[xix]

Despite the ground-breaking concept, it must be said that the timing could have been better. Great Britain had just returned from a gruelling tour down under, where they surrendered the Ashes to Australia, winners of the test series by 2-1. The Lions went on to beat New Zealand, winning two of the three tests. The final test, in Auckland, was played in mid-August. Just over two months later, the Great Britain players were back in action. Or rather, a handful of them were. Many were either injured or left out or declined selection, so that just three members of the Lions party joined Great Britain's World Cup squad. In the Australian squad, by contrast, all but three had played in the tests against the Lions. The Kiwis presented a squad of which six players had not taken part in the tests against Great Britain, and joined the Australians on the same plane to Europe. The similarities did not end there, as they would later find out.

The Kangaroos and Kiwis were playing out of season; the French were just four matches into theirs; but the British – despite their hastily assembled squad, which travelled to France without a coach, Joe Egan having been left behind after conducting a couple of training sessions – were at least match fit.

France lacked a number of those star players who had faced the Australians and the British in 1953, including the second row pair of Brousse and Ponsinet, and prop Louis Mazon. But still the squad, coached by Jean Duhau and René Duffort, was reckoned to have enough experience of high-level competition.

All the matches were staged in big cities: Paris, Lyon, Toulouse, Marseille, Bordeaux and Nantes, the last-named classed as a development area. It was at the Parc des Princes in the capital that the opening match took place on Saturday, 30 October between the hosts and New Zealand, drawing a crowd of 13,500 spectators who paid almost six million francs. In terms of the quality of play, the opener proved a great success. 'At last a rugby league match worthy of the capital,' ran one headline.[xx]

It was vital for the success of the competition that the French should win in front of their own crowd and that they should do so with style. France's 22-13 victory was indeed carried off with panache. The game was evenly balanced until France pulled ahead in the last twenty minutes when the Kiwis' lack of match fitness began to show. The win was built on the superiority of the forwards, among whom the lively hooker Jean Audoubert and the big second rower Guy Delaye both crashed through to score, adding to tries from Contrastin and Crespo. Puig-Aubert kicked two conversions, two penalties and a drop goal.

The next day at Lyon, Great Britain took on Australia, who had just regained the Ashes and were therefore clear favourites against a completely re-worked British side. But the Aussies were surprised by the remarkable spirit of Dave Valentine's men, who led 12-5 by half-time and went on to dominate the game, winning by an unequivocal 28-13 score.

That British triumph set up a keenly-anticipated clash with the hosts at Toulouse a week later. The crowd of 37,471, which remains a record for a rugby league match in France to this day, did not leave the Stadium de Toulouse disappointed. The gate receipts of 13,675,000 francs (also given as £14,276 sterling) easily established another record.

As the *Daily Mirror's* Joe Humphreys put it: 'In a match

that throbbed out every second there was not a dull moment. Good football in flashes, the rough and tumble of a hectic cup-tie and those oddities with which only the French can spice a match … it was all there.

'In short, as Mr Jim Hilton, the Rugby League Council Chairman, commented: "A great game played in the best traditions of international football."'[xxi]

In the build-up to the game, the press and around 1,500 fans watched a France practice session, during which the squad went through various physical exercises and routines with the exception of Puig-Aubert, whose now portly figure suggested that this was not the first time he had disdained training. Instead he practised his kicking.

'Puig-Aubert placed the ball only three or four yards from the corner flag,' reported Alfred Drewry, 'almost like a soccer winger taking a corner-kick. He leaned on the fence to exchange a few pleasantries with the spectators, turned round and kicked the ball straight between the posts.

'Then he tottered to the half-way line – one felt that he should have been provided with transport – and for half an hour dropped goals from 50 yards' range with the fluent mechanical ease of a conveyor belt operator.'[xxii]

Since Great Britain did not take a coach with them to France – Castleford's Gideon Shaw acted as team manager – they formulated a plan to deal with the French and Puig-Aubert in particular. 'France regards the fabulous Puig-Aubert as a tower of strength,' wrote Drewry. 'Britain believe that he could be a source of weakness.

'Puig-Aubert, for all his chain-smoking and for all his corpulence, is unsurpassed as a sleight-of-foot matchwinner through his dropped goals, but Britain, instead of devising plans to keep the ball away from him, aim to run him off his feet by kicking to his flanks.

'This involves overwork for Puig-Aubert and also for the British pack of harriers but the feeling is that our forwards will not be the first to feel the strain.'[xxiii]

British captain Dave Valentine explained that his team would use similar tactics to those used against the Australian captain and full-back Clive Churchill in that 'all six forwards shall hare after the ball and hunt Aubert from beginning to end.'[xxiv] The expectation was that the French full-back would be forced into returning Jimmy Ledgard's kicks or, if choosing to run, would be stopped by the British forwards. Valentine added that if Britain should beat France, the World Cup would be theirs because they did not expect to lose to New Zealand in the following match. Great Britain would then have won all three matches to claim the trophy. At that stage a final play-off between the top two teams had not been envisaged. Instead a match between the winners and a composite team from the three other nations was planned.

It turned out to be a game full of suspense, with the lead changing hands five times. By the end of a thrilling first half, Britain had put their plans into practice and led by a single point after winger David Rose and stand-off Gordon Brown had touched down and Ledgard had landed a penalty goal. In reply, prop Joseph Krawzyck went under the posts and Puig-Aubert converted after earlier kicking a penalty goal. In the second period, winger Raymond Contrastin finished a fine movement to put France ahead only for Gerry Helme to dummy his way through, Ledgard converting from touch to reclaim the lead. But, with time running out, another magnificent passage of play ended with Contrastin powering his way over to level the scores at 13-all, which brought a roar of approval from the partisan crowd. An even greater roar would have greeted Puig-Aubert's conversion if he had succeeded but the captain had an off-day with his kicking and could not win the match for France. In fact he kicked just two goals from nine attempts and later claimed that he was tired from all the running around he had been made to do.[xxv]

On that same Sunday, Australia beat New Zealand 34-15 – the highest score of the tournament – at Marseille in front of a crowd given as 20,000. The remaining matches, featuring France v Australia and Great Britain v New Zealand, took place the following Thursday.

At Bordeaux, Great Britain soon took a grip on the game and won 26-6 against a New Zealand side which lost all three matches. France had a more difficult task at Nantes against the Australians. But after Puig-Aubert had given the French an early lead with a penalty goal from the touchline, centre Claude Teisseire took advantage of a fumble in the Australian back line, drew full-back Churchill and sent Merquey to score at the posts, Puig-Aubert converting. Merquey, Jimenez and Crespo all combined to put Contrastin over for a 10-0 lead. Australia came back to 10-5 but despite the dominance of their forwards in the second half, it was France who scored again. Puig-Aubert came up into the threequarter line and kicked across field for Cantoni to collect the ball on the bounce and go over for a converted try that gave France victory by 15-5 in front of a 12,000 crowd – a record for a sports event in Nantes.

Only two days later, on Saturday, 13 November, France faced Great Britain to decide who should take the inaugural trophy, which had been provided by Paul Barrière. The Parc des Princes had hosted the France-New Zealand match which had opened the competition two weeks earlier, but almost 20,000 more spectators turned up to the final. Such was the momentum that had built during the competition that the crowd of 30,368 (also given as 33,000), paying £11,395, smashed all previous records for a rugby league match in the capital. As Bill Fallowfield pointed out, 'Fortunately for France there was a play-off ... and the Competition more than paid its way.'[xxvi]

Great Britain put out an unchanged side from the one that had drawn with France in Toulouse. Remarkably the same set of forwards played all four matches. France's pack, in which the Marseille second row of Delaye and Pambrun had adequately filled the gap left by the injured Brousse and Ponsinet, was changed when Delaye suffered a knee injury, Armand Save replacing him. A third loose forward was tried when Gilbert Verdié, normally a second rower, was brought into the role for his international debut.

In the backs, Antoine Jimenez continued at stand-off,

having switched from centre to replace Gilbert Benausse against Australia.

In front of the television cameras, Puig-Aubert claimed the first points with a well-struck 40-metre penalty goal. It was probably the first time British viewers had ever seen a goal-kicker turn his back on the ball before making his run-up. Great Britain winger Rose opened the try-scoring; stand-off Brown also went over, Ledgard converting, and Valentine's team were 8-4 up at half-time, Puig-Aubert having added a second penalty.

France came back in the second half when Merquey made the opening for Cantoni to evade two tacklers and touch down, Puig-Aubert goaling for a single-point lead. But, amid rising tension, they did not hold the advantage for long as scrum-half Helme darted under the posts and Ledgard converted before Brown crossed for his second. On the other French flank the ever dangerous Contrastin inspired another rally as he found a way over the line to renew France's hopes. But Great Britain were equal to the pressure and finished on top to win by 16-12.

The British, showing a formidable team spirit, had grown stronger match by match. Few outside their camp had given Valentine's team any chance of winning the competition, but what was widely considered as being a long way from Britain's best team played with an overwhelming energy and commitment, as well as tactical cleverness. Their unchanged set of forwards had outplayed their counterparts. France's team was also under-strength, at least in the forwards, and, though they made no excuses, they were put off by Britain's defensive tactics, which some regarded as offside. Certainly the one-yard rule at the play-the-ball did France few favours. But the French were dominated in the forwards and their scintillating backs had little room for manoeuvre and not a great deal of possession. Still, the French press praised the attacking style of the both finalists, considered superior to the 'static' play of the Aussies and Kiwis.[xxvii]

What has been called the most ambitious rugby league venture of modern times resulted in a brilliant success at all levels. The expenses of £40,000 (31 million francs) had been easily recouped. The 30,000-plus crowds in Toulouse and Paris established records which still stand. All the matches had proved a fine advertisement for the game, with not a great deal to choose between the standards of all four nations. More than that. 'Rugby league appeared … in a different light,' said one commentator.[xxviii] 'It was a triumph of attacking rugby.'

Chapter 11

•

Confirmation: 1955

IN ANTICIPATION OF the World Cup and the raising of the game's profile, the domestic championship put on its best face and increased from twelve clubs to fourteen. Celtic de Paris reappeared and, in the Basque country, so did Bayonne, led by the 1951 tour captain, Robert Caillou, returning to his home territory.

By mid-season the health of some of those clubs was in doubt. Dr Pierre Mourgues cast a critical eye over the composition of the elite division. He believed that, of the fourteen, Carcassonne, Lyon, Perpignan (XIII Catalan), Avignon, Albi and his own club Villeneuve, to which Cavaillon, Carpentras and Lézignan could also be added, were clubs which, based on solid foundations, had 'magnificently' stood the test of time. But the remaining five – Toulouse, Bordeaux, Marseille, Paris and Bayonne – were having serious difficulties, some financial, some administrative, arising from a lack of officials.[i] He was right about Paris, who were to drop out again only two seasons after rejoining the top division, and Bayonne, who would give up the struggle after four seasons.

Nevertheless Marseille contested the 1955 Cup final, in which they met Avignon, a team which was on the rise. Avignon had signed two outstanding internationals from Marseille - centre Jacques Merquey and prop André Béraud - and to great effect. Béraud had already become a firm favourite in Avignon. The team's captain-coach, he also ran the famous café 'Le Club' in the city centre. He had joined Marseille in 1946 from Biarritz rugby union club and established a reputation as one of France's finest front row forwards. He was one of those players who, as a result of his prowess on the field, was able to raise his social standing, as it was said at the time, becoming a sporting idol in the city and a respected businessman.[ii]

Avignon had reached the final of the Lord Derby competition once before. They were beaten by Carcassonne in the 1947 final, the same year in which, remarkably, they finished bottom of the league table. But that proved to be the year when the Sporting Olympique Avignonnais, who had switched to rugby league in 1944, started to realise its potential. The club owed a good deal to its dynamic secretary, Luc Nitard, whose name is for ever associated with the national Juniors trophy which is played for every year. Nitard was also secretary of the Méditerranée-Provence committee as well as the Franco-Italian committee.

On the first weekend of the 1954-55 season, Avignon faced Paris in yet another example of a team from the capital meeting another from a historically important city. With the World Cup just over a month away, and all that was riding on it, no wonder it was reported that 'Rugby league was in need of this intelligent renewal. Avignon and Paris produced it. [They showed that] it is possible to play a match heavy with consequence and still play attractive rugby. The Parisians and the Avignonnais clearly demonstrated that.'[iii]

By the end of the season, the SOA were still playing open football and beating their Provence rivals for the Lord Derby trophy at Carpentras, watched by 11,600 spectators. Marseille, though reportedly fighting for survival, still counted the likes of full back Maurice André, scrum-half Jean Dop, back rowers Raoul

Perez and Jean Pambrun, prop François Rinaldi and future international hooker Antranick Appelian in their ranks. But it was not for nothing that Avignon also finished top of the league in that year of 1955. Béraud's men played better as a team and moved the ball more quickly despite Marseille's strength in the forwards. Avignon's international winger André Savonne, nicknamed 'the Bison of Vaucluse', showed his finishing power to score three tries in the 18-10 triumph.

In the Championship final, played a week later at Toulouse, Carcassonne, who had finished second to Avignon in the table, met fourth-placed Lyon, as they had done two years earlier. The ASC were appearing in their ninth Championship final since the war, while Lyon were making their third appearance. The 12,000 spectators got good value for their money, even though it turned out to be a low-scoring game. If Carcassonne had once boasted a fearsome reputation, based on their formidable forwards, it was now Lyon who, with the likes of Krawzyck, Audoubert and Vanel as their front row, and Augey and Taterzinski behind, not to mention the wily Duffort at loose forward, dominated up front. But, coached by Félix Bergèse, it was the ASC who offered the most spectacular passages of play, with scrum-half Claude Teisseire and stand-off Gilbert Benausse setting off the attacks. Carcassonne scored two delightful tries as centre Delpoux and winger Husson both brought brilliant attacking moves to a conclusion. In reply Lyon could only muster two Duffort penalties. If Benausse had been on form with his kicking and had converted just one of several opportunities, the ASC would have won. But, five minutes from the end, Krawzyck put winger Voron over the line, despite ASC protests of a forward pass, and Lyon had won their second Championship final. It was an absorbing match, full of high-quality play, which went a long way towards eradicating the memory of the previous season's 'worst ever' final.

The championship had recovered its reputation, which helped soften the blow dealt by the resignation of Federation president Paul Barrière a week before the final. Barrière had let it be known several times before that he intended quitting. No other president could have left such an impressive legacy. Barrière was born at Espéraza in the Aude valley, not far from Quillan, where his uncle Jean Bourrel had sponsored the rise of the local rugby union club, which, with Jean Galia and other Catalans in its team, upset the rugby establishment by becoming champions of France and forming a blueprint for semi-professional rugby of the future. The young Barrière, like many in the region, played some rugby union but did not pursue it after the war, during which he held a position of responsibility in the maquis of Picaussel, where he was involved in assisting Allied parachutists and for which he was awarded the *croix de guerre*.[iv] At the end of the Occupation and aged just 24, he was introduced to rugby league by Marcel Laborde and famously took up the cause for rugby league's reinstatement, being elected officially as president at the Bayonne Congress of 1947. It is hard to overestimate his influence, not just on rugby league in France, but on the international game as well. His vision for rugby league brought about the 1951 tour of Australia and New Zealand and, three years later, the World Cup, though in his lifetime he dismissed the idea that the trophy should bear his name.

Many years later, at a reunion in honour of the 1951 tour captain, Robert Caillou, he declared: 'I was the public face of a fine team. You brought me joys which are rare for a man to be given. It is I who thank you for the page which has been written. In fact we waged and won a war of religion. As a Cathar, that is what pleased me most.'[v]

French rugby league was fortunate in having Barrière's vice-president, Claude Devernois, to continue the battle. The dynamism of both men working in tandem had driven the game forward for the best part of a decade. Devernois had an even longer pedigree than his predecessor, dating back twenty years to the formation of the Roanne club in the pioneer days. His wealth, based on his textile factories in Roanne, allowed him to make important interventions at Lyon and Paris. Devernois took up the role of president immediately on Barrière's resignation and was officially elected at the 1955 Bordeaux Congress.

No sooner had Devernois taken office than the France team was setting off on a second tour of Australia and New Zealand. If the tour of 1951 had been dubbed 'mission impossible', it also looked, four years on, impossible to repeat. Of the 28-man squad, only five – Audoubert, Contrastin, Dop, Merquey (who was named tour captain) and Montrucolis, plus Duffort, now promoted to coach to replace Samatan – had figured among the 1951 party. Two members of the management trio, tour manager Blain and coach Duhau, remained. A whole raft of players were no longer there, either because they were injured or at the end of their career, including Puig-Aubert, Brousse, Ponsinet, Mazon, Martin, Cantoni, Comes, Crespo, Genoud, Bartoletti and Calixte, whose undoubted class and experience would be hard to replace. (Fernand Cantoni replaced his elder brother Vincent, who was injured.)

Between the final of the World Cup the previous November and the Australian tour, the France team played only one international match. Wales provided the opposition at Nantes a few days before the party set off down under. The match served little purpose: the Welshmen had not played for a month and there were withdrawals from both sides. France fielded several players who did not go on tour, with coach Duffort also turning out, but won 24-11.

After leaving by plane in two groups, the France team picked up where they had left off. Their first match in Australia took place at Perth, where they had had such an easy win in the last match of the 1951 tour. It was not quite so simple this time, but Contrastin on the wing and Save at loose forward each scored a hat-trick in the 31-6 win.

Two promotional matches – at Adelaide and Melbourne, where rugby league was not yet played – had been programmed as the French adapted once more to Australian conditions. Both resulted in forty-point wins before they came up against sterner opponents in Canberra and New South Wales, which is where the tour started in earnest. Unlike four years earlier, when, out of the first five matches, they won three, lost one and drew one, the

Frenchmen now found themselves hitting a five-match losing run, starting at Canberra with an 11-3 defeat by Monaro division, and continuing with further losses against a Sydney XIII, Riverina, New South Wales and Southern New South Wales. The year before, Great Britain had fared only slightly better, losing three and drawing one of their first six games.

Not only was France's record depressing but numerous on-field incidents clouded this first phase. At Monaro a brawl quickly spread to spectators, who spilled on to the pitch and police were forced to try to calm the situation. Nor had the heavy pitches been to France's advantage. There was clearly much to be put right following the 25-0 defeat by Sydney on a quagmire.

The interest aroused by France's tour, however, was no less than in 1951. The Sydney Cricket Ground accommodated 67,748 spectators for the opening test – 700 more than for the third test of the previous tour and a couple of hundred more than had seen Great Britain in the last test there the year before.

The Australians had learned their lesson from 1951 and knew what to expect. They were also keen to exact revenge. The ground had suffered as a result of heavy rain over the previous fortnight, which suited the hosts but not the French, who had stepped up their training in preparation for the match. Bordeaux winger André Ducasse and hooker René Moulis of XIII Catalan were called up to make their debut, while 'Hugues' Berthomieu, having returned to rugby league from hunting crocodiles in Africa, was brought into the front row. The experienced Albi forward proved his worth throughout the tour, always willing to take the ball forward through the heart of the Australian defence, proving hard to tackle and shirking nothing in defence. He was to become France's most capped forward.

The one-yard rule in force at the play-the-ball appeared to favour the Australians, as centre or stand-off Antoine Jimenez pointed out in one of a series of articles he cabled back to *Midi-Olympique*.[vi] That view was widely supported in the French camp.

The Australian forwards, 'this block of granite',[vii] took the game to the French, but the tourists defended well and only centre

Harry Wells was able to cross the Tricolores' line in the first half. France produced a fine riposte when Merquey put Ducasse away for a try, goaled by full-back Benausse, but Australia, despite a fine individual try by Berthomieu, maintained the pressure and ground their opponents down to win 20-8.

The party set off on the Queensland leg of the tour, where they would eventually start to find some form. After beating a Brisbane XIII by 21-11, they fell heavily to Toowoomba, losing 35-6. But a 23-17 victory over Queensland was followed by four more wins against sides representing different areas of the state, ending with a 42-26 win over North Queensland at Townsville. After a midweek match against Northern NSW at Casino – lost 18-17 after scoring five tries to two – the Tricolores faced Australia in the second test at Brisbane.

The French had lost in 1951 at the Brisbane Cricket Ground, otherwise known as the Gabba. This time 10,000 more spectators turned up to make a crowd of 45,745, only six hundred fewer than had watched Great Britain perform there the year before. Among several team changes which Blain, Duhau and Duffort made, two of them, positional, proved crucial. Jean Dop, who had played in his usual scrum-half position in the first test, was switched to full-back, with Gilbert Benausse moving forward to stand-off, where he partnered his Carcassonne team-mate Claude Teisseire.

It was a match France had to win, as Berthomieu confirmed. 'We were thinking that back home in France they were expecting a miracle from a team that was not as good as its predecessors. But how to believe it after the drubbing of the first test? And yet we had a faith which moves mountains.'[viii]

The Australians scored an early try and pulled ahead to 15-11 by half-time, France's try coming from centre Roger Rey, with Benausse contributing three penalty goals and Christian Duplé a conversion. After the break, the French came close to scoring on three occasions before Merquey touched down, but it was the Australians who went further ahead to lead 28-16 going into the final twenty minutes. France faced defeat and with it the loss of the brilliant reputation the previous tourists had earned. The French forwards refused to buckle and drove forward to launch a sensational fightback, with loose forward Duplé and front rowers Montrucolis and Audoubert much in evidence. The backs, prompted by Merquey and Benausse, had to risk all. It was at this point that Dop came into his own. On a counter-attack he broke through the Aussie defensive line, drew his opposite number Churchill and sent Rey to the line for his second try, which Benausse converted to reduce the margin to seven points.[ix] It proved to be the turning-point.

Minutes later Dop again took charge and, weaving this way and that, created a gap for Benausse to send Merquey racing past Churchill to touch down, Benausse again landing the goal. The crowd thrilled to watch France's refusal to back down as wave upon wave of attacks threatened to overwhelm the Aussie forwards. Still France were two points adrift, and, despite their heroics, the series equaliser seemed beyond their grasp.

For a third time Dop came up into the attack. For a third time he tormented the Aussie defence. Montrucolis broke, Audoubert backed up and winger Ducasse went through to score, giving France a 29-28 lead with under five minutes left to play. Australia, refusing to give up, as is their style, attacked close to the French line. Winger Watson looked certain to go over and win the match, but his opposite number Voron pulled off a match-saving tackle one yard from the line. Once more the Australians had their chance to pull the match out of the fire when awarded an angled penalty forty yards out. Davies's attempt passed a foot wide of the post. France had won. In a truly remarkable comeback, the Tricolores restored their reputation and silenced their critics. More than that. This match, said Merquey, represented 'the quintessence of rugby league.'[x]

Nevertheless, the French still believed they were suffering from having to play according to the one-yard rule at the play-the-ball, which, it was reported, 'considerably handicapped the France team' and set Antoine Blain on a campaign at International Board level for a return to the three-yard rule.[xi]

Before the decisive third test in Sydney, France played six more matches, winning four and losing two. Some of those games were marked by incidents, as at Ipswich, where they won 19-10 but where obstructions and late tackles were the order of the day. After one such incident, play was held up, causing Blain to go on to the pitch to help restore order.

Came the day of the third test and France's tour record showed 24 matches played, with 14 wins and ten defeats. Again the conditions at the SCG did not benefit the French after rain had left the pitch sodden. Poor weather or not, 62,458 fans turned up to see the decider, meaning that over 175,000 people had watched the three-match series.

It was the home side who once more took an early lead when Davies went over for an unconverted try. But France hit back when scrum-half Duplé, who had switched from loose forward for this match, and Benausse combined to send Contrastin over to level the scores. Benausse could not convert but a Churchill penalty regained the lead for Australia, who were ahead by five points to three. In the second half, the Tricolores played as well as they had done all tour. The only try of the second period came when Merquey made the initial thrust before Rey and Duplé handed on to send Ducasse hurtling through the Australian defence for what proved to be the matchwinner. It was not converted, but Duplé landed a late drop goal to increase the score to 8-5 and despite the Aussies' last desperate efforts that was how it remained.

The French had achieved what had seemed at one point to be beyond their reach. It was not just their speed and skill which the Australian crowds loved and applauded but also their courage and resilience. Those qualities gave them victory in the series against a team which had beaten the Lions 2-1 the year before.

In New Zealand, where they had narrowly and controversially lost the single international match of the 1951 tour, France were scheduled to play two tests. In the lead-up, they won three matches and lost one, at Canterbury. Two weeks after the third test in Sydney, the Tricolores met New Zealand at Carlaw

Park, Auckland and announced a similar team, except that Carcassonne's André Delpoux came in at stand-off in place of the injured Benausse and Jimenez returned at centre. Most recently France and New Zealand had met in the World Cup with the French emerging as convincing winners after an evenly-balanced first hour. So it proved in Auckland, where New Zealand led 6-5 at half-time, France's try coming from Merquey. With Dop counter-attacking from full back, as he had done against Australia, the Tricolores dominated the second period. Second row Berthomieu, probably the outstanding forward of the tour, broke near his own line and sent winger Ducasse sprinting sixty yards to score. Merquey and Ducasse each added another try, prop Vanel[xii] also crossed and Montrucolis took over the goal-kicking duties from Duplé, who had landed a first-half goal, to contribute two points to the 19-9 victory, seen by 21,000 spectators.

A week later the two teams returned to an even muddier Carlaw Park for the second and final test of the tour. Benausse returned to the stand-off position as tour captain Merquey dropped out through injury, Delpoux moving into the centre. The New Zealand selectors kept faith with their side and were rewarded as the hosts ran up a 9-0 lead by the interval from which the tired French could not come back, despite Contrastin's two tries, and New Zealand squared the series with an 11-6 victory.

The Australasian tour had been a second unarguable success. In 1954 Australia had beaten Great Britain 2-1; the Lions then defeated New Zealand 2-1 before beating France in the World Cup final. After France had won the 1955 series in Australia and drawn in New Zealand, they had regained at least equal status with the British.

In financial terms, though, the tour produced mixed results. At the end of the Australian leg, which provided by far the biggest gates, tour manager Antoine Blain predicted a record tour profit of around £22,000, which would have been greater than the Lions had achieved the previous year.[xiii] France's expenses, however, were higher as air travel, which was used more than on the previous tour, was alone believed to have cost around

£25,000.[xiv] It was announced that, at the end of the full tour, profits were expected to be around 30 million francs, based on the fact that the two Sydney tests had receipts of 22 million francs each and Brisbane 14 million.[xv] In fact the figure of 30 million francs actually represented the amount of receipts, not profit, as president-elect Devernois clarified: 'For the tour to Australia we took risks and I personally took on the largest share. Fortune was favourable to us. But when the final accounts are drawn up … I am sure that they will show a small deficit.' That came as a shock to those clubs which had expected a providential hand-out to help them over financial difficulties. Devernois added: 'But the moral success, and this is important, will compensate for the financial loss.'[xvi] At this moment of triumph, though, that was not quite what club officials wanted to hear.

Tour captain in 1955, centre Jacques Merquey was a prolific try-scorer

Chapter 12

•

Jacques Merquey: Order and Disorder

AN UNDISPUTED STAR of the fifties, Jacky Merquey burst on to the international scene in rugby union's Five Nations in 1950, playing in all four matches. Merquey was studying pharmacology at Marseille and playing at the same time at Toulon, which he had joined from his native Souillac. He was quickly signed to play rugby league by Marseille XIII, who offered him the opportunity to play at the top level as well as supplementing his student's allowance. 'To think that, only a year before, I was still in the sixth form,' he recalled.

This quick-witted centre, small of stature, was a key figure on the Australasian tours of 1951, 1955 – when he was made captain – and the first three World Cups, in 1954, 1957 and 1960. From Marseille, where he was a Championship finalist in 1952, he moved on to Avignon, where he appeared in three Cup finals, winning two, and a Championship final. He was later signed by Villeneuve, with whom he won the Championship in 1959 and 1964.

Some sixty years on, there were half a dozen of us around

the table at the Merquey family home at Souillac, situated on the river Dordogne in the Lot, to which he returns every summer. Another guest was his former Villeneuve and France team-mate Antoine Jimenez, a tourist in 1955 and again in 1960, when he captained the team, and a World Cup player in 1954 and 1957. The pair played alongside each other in Villeneuve's 1959 Championship-winning team, and played on opposite sides when Villeneuve beat Avignon in the Lord Derby final the year before.

As one of those exciting French backs who both thrilled the Australian crowds and frustrated their players in 1951 and again in 1955, Merquey, who still thinks deeply about the game, has a theory with which few would disagree.

'When you defend you need a very organised system,' he explained. 'You must have order. But when you attack, you have to create disorder in the order of the opponent. But how do you do that? You have to have someone who penetrates and creates something out of the ordinary in the opposition defence and everyone must be quick to support this disorder which has been created so as to get to the goal-line.'[i]

As one of the two coaches on the 1951 tour, Bob Samatan is often credited as the architect of the French style of play. But Merquey disagreed, saying, 'I think he was a good coach, a pragmatic coach who worked with the players he had and effectively constructed a team which gave the maximum in terms of the qualities they had.

'[But] it was the players who organised this French style of play. Samatan was by reputation a pioneer of a well-organised style of play. If we won in '51 it was not because of that, it was thanks to guys like Dop, like Puig-Aubert, who created something in the opposition camp. I come back to the matter of order and disorder. They created the disorder which others were able to exploit. I think you need a coach who is very good at organising the defence and who can reposition and always be effective and alive [to what is happening]. But the attack depends on the players you have.

'Where we won in Australia was exactly because of this

variation, attacking from all directions, with passes of fifteen or twenty metres; Dop and Puig-Aubert counter-attacking; Dop at the scrum base, going left, going right. The Australians and even we didn't know where he was going but you had to follow him, and when you did, it was always beneficial.'

Jimenez, who like Merquey, was capable of playing either centre or stand-off, became France's first national technical director in 1968. He interjected: 'I didn't go on the '51 tour but I can say that, whatever the team, it is up to the coach to decide on the style of play according to the qualities of the players he has. That is the first article of coaching. If you have players who aren't up to it, even with the best coach in the world, the team won't go very far.'

'The '51 tour confirmed that there was a French style of play,' he added.

'You're right,' said our host, 'but this French style came about despite everything being against it. It was not the coaches who had us play like that. It happened, as far as I'm concerned, because there was Dop, who I admire a lot. Around the scrum he would set off in any direction, do anything...'

'No one could do what Dop did,' said Jimenez.

'There were people like Teisseire, who was capable [of playing like that], and Fabre, of Albi, but you have to have the nerve. I think it's an enormously important quality to be able to create like that. You have to have that spark. For me, Dop in '51 and '55 was a catalyst.'

I mentioned that I had read that, before the last two test matches, coaches and players watched the film of the previous test in order to analyse performances.

The idea seemed to surprise Merquey. 'In '51?' he queried. 'We were never told how we should play. Never. Up front? The forwards played like forwards should.

'In the third test, Dop didn't play. Crespo was at scrum-half, Duffort at stand-off. But we had the ascendancy. We had to play serious, businesslike rugby.'

In 1955, with Merquey as captain, France did it again,

though with a team which was not quite as brilliant as its predecessor.

'That's true,' said Merquey. 'There weren't the big stars. There was no Brousse, no Puig-Aubert. We had to make do with the players we had; we played differently.'

'We had to do without Puig-Aubert,' added Jimenez, who played stand-off in the first test, 'and that's what we did.'

'Some matches were very difficult because we played in mud. It rained non-stop. We trained in the mud. We were in a hotel with limited facilities; there was no heating and we couldn't get our rugby kit dry. When we went to Queensland, in the warm, it was great and we recovered.'

In 1956-57, however, the Australians went to France and won all three tests, suggesting that they had learned from their experience at the hands of the French.

'I had a conversation with the Australian who played opposite me,' Merquey continued. 'When we talked about the second test [Brisbane, 1955], they said they should never have lost. They learned their lesson. Which was that when we attacked in every direction, they were all lost. The defence lost the thread. That's how we were able to score three tries a quarter of an hour from the end. That opened the door to the third test. We buckled down and won it.'

The 1951 tour in particular was a financial success, though it remains unclear exactly how the profits were used. Neither Merquey nor Jimenez was able to shed any light.

'We never talked about money,' said Merquey. 'We didn't know if it was a financial success or for whom. For the Federation, I hope. The '51 tour was the first time that a French team had gone on tour abroad. They [the Federation] didn't know [what it would be like] where they were going. They had tapped up the clubs for financial guarantees in case it didn't work out and they told us straight away once we'd arrived that if it didn't work out we'd be going home on a cargo boat!'

Despite the flamboyant play which gave France victory in those first two series in Australia and won many fans, it was perceived at home that, in between the tours, play had become dull, hard though that is to believe. Paul Barrière had raised his concern in 1953 and lobbied at International Board level for a change in the play-the-ball rule which forced the defending side to retreat only one yard.

'It's hard for players to say whether the play is attractive or not. We don't question it, we just play to the rules,' said Jimenez.

'What poisoned play at the time,' said Merquey, 'was not the distance of one metre or whatever, it was the fact of being able to intervene at the play-the-ball, in other words to kick at the ball [while the opponent is playing it]. Fifty years on, it is forbidden and it has totally changed the psychology of the game. It was a source of confrontation and anger. I'm sure that if we had been able to play the ball in an unobstructed way, and to get the ball away backwards, the game would have been much clearer and quicker.

'In fact, if there had not been the problem of kicking at the play-the-ball, we would have had better tours. I think that the fact of being able to challenge the [tackled] player at the play-the-ball very much upset the France team and the French spirit. We became enervated and lost the sense of the game. If we had known we could play the ball [without interference], we would have been more effective.'

In the year before that second tour, France had had to get over the disappointment of narrowly losing to Great Britain in the World Cup final play-off. It was a tournament they could easily have won.

'We had played New Zealand at the Parc des Princes,' said Merquey. 'We played well and won. We played Great Britain at Toulouse, a draw, and we played very well against Australia at Nantes, where we won with difficulty in a very hard game, but it cost us dear because we lost our second row, Pambrun and Delaye, who had done well to replace Brousse and Ponsinet. That was a shame because we had found a good second row who had played well against the Australians, who were very strong up front. It was a match with a lot of commitment on both sides and we won.'

In the final, Great Britain were said to have deliberately kicked towards Puig-Aubert, who they believed would tire, a tactic which seemed to have paid off.

Jimenez countered, 'It has to be said that Puig-Aubert in '54 was not the Puig-Aubert of '51, but he was still the best in his position.'

'I don't think that's why we lost,' said Merquey. 'We lost it up front. We had a weakened pack. The reserves who came in were not as good as the players we had at the start.'

Some have seen the outcome of the final as one of rugby's great 'if only' situations. 'It needed victory for [rugby league] to be able to widen its audience and quickly build the solid foundations which time has given to rugby union,' wrote Jean-Pierre Bodis.[ii] It didn't happen, but France were already unofficial world champions in 1951, albeit crowned on the other side of the world. Rugby league's eventual failure to increase the momentum which had built up in that first post-war decade derived from other factors. Merquey is not one of those who believe that the World Cup final defeat changed the course of French rugby league history.

'I think that the Federation lacked important structures, national representation, people who carried weight, people of quality, of which there were some, but not enough. It depended on many things, not always to do with what happened on the field.'

Merquey had previously mentioned rugby league's failure to grasp the importance of television as a means of popularising the game among a wider public. He himself had introduced the presenter Roger Couderc to the Federation. A native of Souillac, like Merquey, Couderc did indeed broadcast radio commentary of rugby league matches before going on to become synonymous with televised rugby union, a role he could well have covered for rugby league.

The '51 tour gave rise to what Merquey calls a 'euphoric

period'. He recalled the 'parade through the streets of Marseille, like in New York, and the extraordinary reception the team had, the great enthusiasm for rugby league.'

But that euphoria was short-lived. Not enough was made of it. Imagine if it had been the national rugby union team that had pulled off this remarkable exploit. There was also an unfortunate follow-up.

'We went to play against Other Nationalities at Hull. It was an awful match, full of incidents.'

The worst was Ponsinet's revenge on Clues, who was knocked out in retribution for the damage he had caused to his opposite number at Bordeaux eleven months earlier. It was the first match France played after their homecoming. 'It took the shine off the tour,' said Merquey. 'The anti-treiziste media seized on incidents like that.'

Despite what France had shown in Australia, the game on the domestic scene could at times appear negative. In the era of unlimited tackles, it was a problem recognised in Britain too. But in France especially, the tactics whereby one set of forwards kept the ball to themselves, thus producing 'zero spectacle', went down badly. 'It harmed the image of rugby league,' said Merquey.

His first club, Marseille, a glamour club, attracted plenty of attention. Like others such as Paris or Toulouse, it also attracted its critics, who believed that the club did little, or at least not enough, to encourage junior rugby and produce its own players. Marseille tended to sign big-name players instead.

'In Marseille, rugby grew up alongside the OM football club, a team of stars. So the directors of the rugby league club felt obliged to go in the same direction, in other words, to bring in players in order to create a climate of rugby, which did not exist there at the time. They were obliged to sign stars such as Brousse, Béraud, Dop, Delaye later. There were many Basques there too, such as Hatchondo. But the club had no infrastructure like for example at Avignon or Villeneuve [Merquey's other clubs]. There was no social life there.

'There was absolutely no comparison between Marseille

on the one hand and Avignon and Villeneuve on the other. Marseille was formed, in a way, artificially, although Monsieur Rougier and Monsieur Ricard were very devoted to it. But they were surrounded by incompetents. Everyone was very good to me and then I got a cartilage injury. The medical department of the club said that I was not injured. Now at the time I was working at the hospital and living there. I was operated on and after that I thought I never wanted to play for Marseille again.'

In 1953 Merquey moved to Avignon, teaming up with André Béraud. Life took a turn for the better, with back-to-back Lord Derby trophies. Not only that.

'Avignon was a very old club [founded in 1916, the SOA switched to rugby league after the Second World War]. It was very much representative of the city. The rugby there was almost exclusively treiziste. Everything was perfectly in order and I spent a few years there. Then the Algerian war broke out and I went into the Army team as captain. After that I went to Villeneuve, where we had a pharmacy which my wife ran on her own. It was very good at Villeneuve, though quite different from Avignon. The people of Provence and the people of the south-west are quite different. In the south-west they are more quarrelsome. Villeneuve had a fine team and were champions in '59. There were junior internationals there and the [first] team was an extraordinary mixture of players developed by the club and a few outsiders. There was the extraordinary vice-chairman, Dr Mourgues, as well, a man of letters and many other things besides.

'The main difference between Marseille and these two clubs was development. Avignon and Villeneuve produced young players. And then you needed personalities who were out of the ordinary. That's why rugby league succeeded in places like Perpignan, Carcassonne, Avignon, Albi and Villeneuve.'

Chapter 13

•

New Tests: 1955-60

FOR THE SECOND time the France rugby league team returned in triumph from a tour down under. It was another remarkable achievement. But not like the first. The reception given to the team as they landed at Le Bourget airport on the outskirts of Paris bore no comparison, either, to the euphoria of Marseille four years earlier. It lacked the sparkle which Paul Barrière, with his sense of the spectacular – he later transformed the Carcassonne music festival into a large-scale international event – would almost certainly have brought to it.

But there was more to it than Barrière's absence. By their successes on tour, France had regained the right to be regarded as the best team in the world, even if the World Cup of nine months earlier had changed the perception of the French public. By any reckoning, France had recovered its international standing. It certainly did not appear that rugby league in France was at a turning-point. Yet the five or six years following the 1954 World Cup saw the French game encounter difficulties it had never before faced in peacetime.

The rugby historian Jean-Pierre Bodis suggested that France needed to win the final in order to spread the game and allow it to deepen its roots.[i] Bodis also suggested that the quality of play had declined – a matter which the Federation had worried over – giving that as a second reason why 'the amateur [sic] Federation [i.e. rugby union], after biding its time in the face of the competition, was able to bestir itself and return to its lofty disdain for the new code.'

Bodis wrote that rugby league 'was deluding itself' and stated, accurately enough, that treizistes, in spite of all efforts, did not have an international competition that was as ingrained in the public's consciousness as rugby union's Five Nations. The historian added that rugby league's player base was too narrow, which is also true. He went on to give an example: that even in Villeneuve-sur-Lot, the town known as the 'academy' of rugby league and the 'point of entry' of the game in France, schoolboys were 'first and foremost urged to play rugby union.'[ii] But Bodis did not say why that should be so.

The reason lies, almost inevitably it seems, in a legacy of the Vichy era, when Jean Borotra, followed by Jep Pascot as overlord of French sport, made sure that the union code was played in French schools. Rugby league has never been able to compete with that special advantage. It was not until 2012 that the Federation at long last put an agreement in place with the Ministers of Education and Sport, theoretically allowing rugby league to be played in schools. In 2015 it was agreed in principle that the game could form part of the curriculum of trainee physical education teachers.

Furthermore, there is anecdotal evidence from Bodis himself that Villeneuve had been targeted by the FFR. Robert Fassolette states that Bodis told him that FFR president Albert Ferrasse, who was also chairman of nearby Agen RU, asked intermediaries within the Education ministry to nominate quinzistes to schools in treiziste territory, such as Villeneuve, in order to render it 'barren'.[iii]

As Fassolette also argues: 'It is interesting to note that the five team sports in which France has had consistently world-class results are association football, basketball, handball, rugby union football and volleyball. These five sports were officially included in the PE curriculum of the Vichy regime on 1 June 1941 ... and the list has never been modified since then. In other team sports, such as hockey or water polo, France has had no prominent results. Had rugby league football been included in the list, or even added after the war ... the sport would still be a major source of pride for the French nation.'[iv]

The Vichy period, when French sport was nurtured in institutions to a greater extent than it had ever been, laid the foundations for future development at all levels. In schools and universities, rugby union, basketball and volleyball all increased participation almost three times over.[v]

Fassolette examines the case of handball, almost unknown in France before the war, except in Alsace, where there were but eight clubs. Across the Rhine, however, it was a major sport. The German national team were the world champions. It was not long before Vichy obligingly added the sport to the PE curriculum. Fassolette maintains: 'It would appear to be the case that, without its inclusion on the school curriculum, French handball would never have reached the upper echelons of world rankings where it figures permanently nowadays, despite almost no television coverage at all.' He puts forward a clinching argument: 'It is perhaps not stretching the imagination too far to envisage that rugby league, given the potential shown by the sport in France before the war ... could have been at least as successful as handball and France would still be a first-class league-playing nation.'[vi]

Bodis referred to the decline in the quality of play of rugby league, with the abuse of the 'monotonous' play-the-ball as the major factor. It is evident that the Ligue was equally concerned that the game sometimes failed to live up to the spectacle with which it had been associated before the war and immediately after. The trenchant Dr Mourgues went so far as to suggest that the French had lost the World Cup final because of the 'disastrous' way club teams played, allowing forward domination to hold sway over open play. 'This sterile, repugnant combat played out by forwards more concerned with demolishing than constructing has produced the impression of robots …' he claimed.[vii] Few would have agreed, however, with that explanation for France's defeat in the World Cup final, citing instead France's lack of forward domination, caused by late changes to the pack.

Barely had the 1955 tourists set off for Australia than Mourgues was claiming: 'The squad … is unarguably weaker than the previous one… It is weaker because for several years our players have played a more and more negative style of rugby.' The Villeneuve official and member of the Federation management committee cited the 1954 Championship final as the height of mediocrity, though the following season's final was, he said, 'worthy of the cause' and a sign of the game's recovery. Club officials, he maintained, were responsible for the 'degeneration' of rugby league, because they were obsessed with results, no matter how they were obtained. The fact that the France squad brought off another astounding success in Australia made Mourgues' claims seem extravagantly pessimistic, yet the concern was a real one.[viii]

In Britain too there was much discussion throughout the 1950s about how the play-the-ball rule could lend itself to negative tactics. RFL secretary Bill Fallowfield even held it responsible for the falling-off of attendances during the decade.[ix] Before the four-tackle rule was eventually introduced in 1966, followed by the six-tackle version, Fallowfield had proposed reverting to rugby union's method of playing the ball. It was the French Federation secretary, Antoine Blain, who dismissed the idea, saying that 'to adopt the rugby union method would be to step back fifty years.'[x] It is hard to imagine, in any case, that rugby union, with its rucks, mauls and endless kicking, could offer anything more attractive to spectators.

The decade following the end of the war had belonged to rugby league, whose international achievements left the other code trailing in its wake. Rugby union had suffered one crisis after

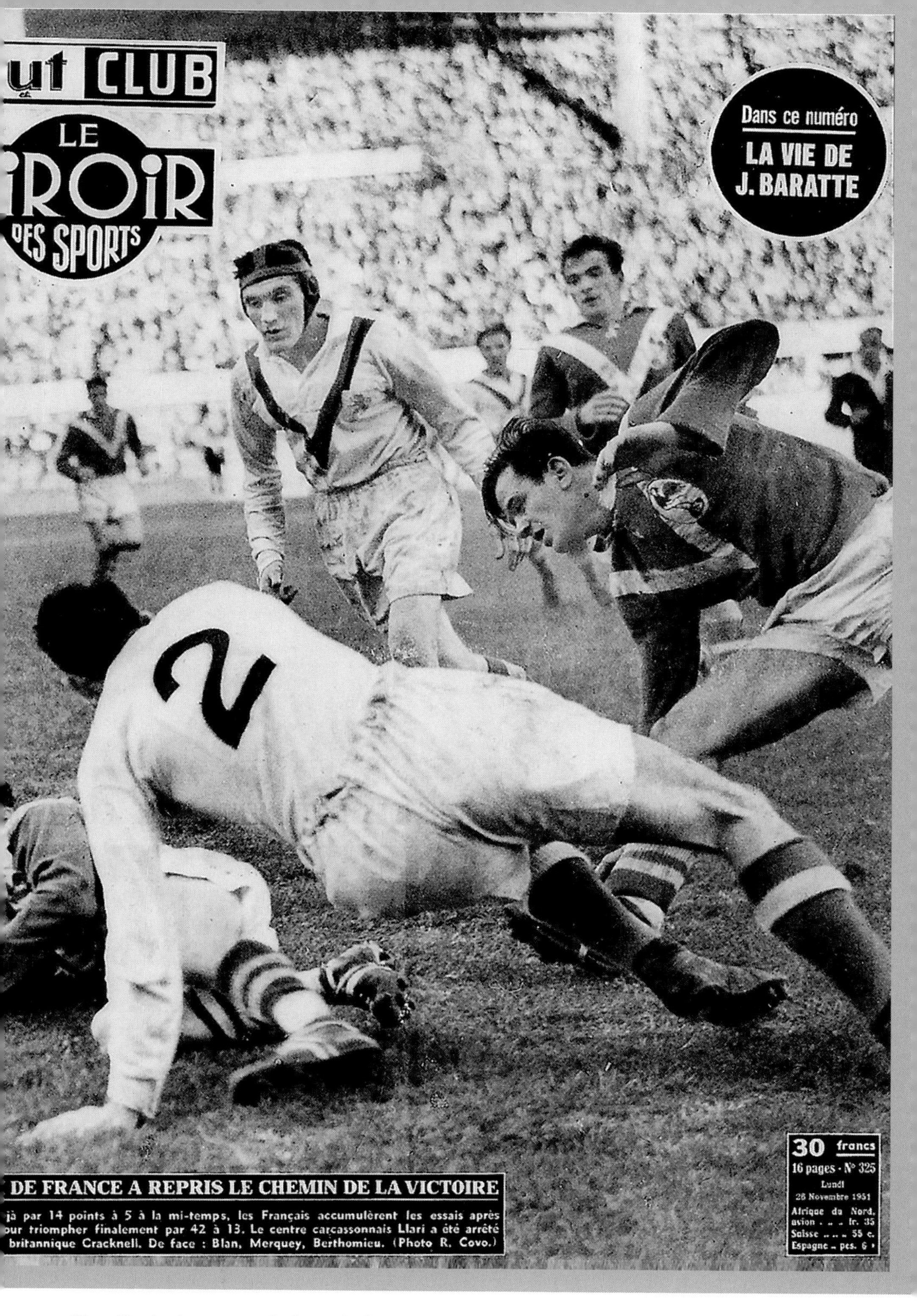
ut CLUB

LE
IROIR
DES SPORTS

Dans ce numéro
LA VIE DE
J. BARATTE

30 francs
16 pages · N° 325
Lundi
26 Novembre 1951
Afrique du Nord, avion . .. .. fr. 35
Suisse .. .. .. 55 c.
Espagne .. pes. 6 »

DE FRANCE A REPRIS LE CHEMIN DE LA VICTOIRE

jà par 14 points à 5 à la mi-temps, les Français accumulèrent les essais après
our triompher finalement par 42 à 13. Le centre carcassonnais Llari a été arrêté
britannique Cracknell. De face : Blan, Merquey, Berthomieu. (Photo R. Covo.)

Above: Rugby league regularly made the cover of sports weeklies. Their first match since returning from the 1951 tour was won 42-13 against England at Marseille and merited full coverage. In this shot, centre Roger Llari is stopped by England winger Dick Cracknell with Billy Blan and France's Jacky Merquey and Gabriel Berthomieu in attendance

Right: Centre Jacky Merquey, one of the undisputed stars of the fifties and captain of the 1955 tour, gives a reverse pass to winger Contrastin in the match against New Zealand at the Parc des Princes in December 1951

Below: France winger Vincent Cantoni, a double try-scorer in the rout of England at Marseille in November 1951

Below: The skilful and athletic international loose forward Gaston Calixte, in action for Villeneuve against Celtic de Paris in November 1951

Below left: The Lyon club, backed by Claude Devernois, guided by the '51 tour coach Bob Samatan, achieved success after Roanne's leading players were transferred there. In the early fifties, stacked with stars, the club won two Championships and two Lord Derby trophies. The 1951 team: Back row: Villagra (director), Baldassin, Vanel, Riu, Brousse, Lasserre, Montrucolis, Audoubert, Samatan (coach); middle row: Delahaie, P Sabeyrac, L Sabeyrac, Devernois (chairman), Voron, Taillantou, Rey, Lecuyer; front row: Rascol, Crespo, Duffort, Lhoste, Bellan

Above: Half-time between Albi and Libourne at Albi's Stade Lagrèze, 1952. The home team includes Verdié, in the middle, looking to camera, Balent, next to him on the right, Viguier, Heuillet and Cesse. Coach Barbazanges, in scarf and overcoat, is on the left of the picture

Left: Winger Maurice Voron, who scored two tries on home territory in Lyon as France beat Great Britain 28-17 in May 1953

Right: Cup-winners Lyon, who defeated XIII Catalan 17-15 in May 1954 at Cavaillon. At the front: Crespo, Lucia, Brousse, Augey, Duffort (capt); standing behind: Audoubert, Bastianelli

Left: After winning the Cup twice and the Championship once in the late forties, Marseille carried on in the early fifties by contesting the Championship final three times and Cup final once. They went on to win the Lord Derby trophy in 1957. The leading figures were scrum-half Dop (front, fourth from left), full back André and forwards Appelian, Rinaldi, Delaye and Pambrun

Left: Former *résistant* Paul Barrière, Federation president from 1947 to 1955, formed a dynamic partnership with vice-president Claude Devernois at the head of the governing body and was responsible for major innovations including the first tour to Australia and World Cup

Below: The teams of France and Great Britain at the playing of the national anthems before the inaugural World Cup final play-off at the Parc des Princes, Paris on 13 November 1954. The World Cup trophy, presented by French Federation president Paul Barrière, is on prominent display and was to be won by Great Britain, who triumphed by 16-12

Left: Scrum-half Jean Dop, one of the stars of the 1955 tour with his clever, unpredictable play, gets the ball away under pressure from the Australian defence

Above: The France team which defeated Great Britain 17-5 at the Parc des Princes in December 1955. Back row: Rinaldi, Appelian, Tarozzi, Save, Berthomieu, Duplé; Front row: Ducasse, Merquey (capt), Ambert, Dop, Eïto, Delpoux, Alberti

Right: Loose forward Christian Duplé, of Bordeaux, faces up to Great Britain winger Mick Sullivan in the December 1955 match against Great Britain. Merquey and Berthomieu are in support

Right: Captain of the 1960 tour, centre Antoine Jimenez, seen here in action in the 24-7 victory over New Zealand at Toulouse in 1956, linked up with Merquey at Villeneuve. He went on to become French rugby league's first National Technical Director in 1968

Left: The headquarters of the French Rugby League Federation (Fédération Française de Jeu à XIII) in Rue Marbeuf in Paris – the governing body's first postwar site in the capital

Below: Playing at Grenoble for the first time, the France team was defeated by Great Britain 23-9 in March 1958, watched by a 17,000 crowd. Back row: Appelian, Andrinople, Lacans, Tonus, Verdié, A Lacaze; Front row: Contrastin, A Carrère, Benausse, J Rouqueirol, Duplé, Jimenez, A Savonne

Left: International forward Edouard Duseigneur on the attack for the Bataillon de Joinville against his home club, Lyon, October 1960

Below: In a heated match against Great Britain at Toulouse in March 1960, France came back to win 20-18. Back row: Casas, Quaglio, Majorel, Barthe, Bescos, A Lacaze; Front row: Gruppi, Jimenez (capt), Fages, P Lacaze, Mantoulan, G Benausse, R Benausse

Below: Albi's international forward Marcel Bescos leaves the field with a dislocated shoulder in the 1962 Championship final against Villeneuve. He soon returned to help his team, *right*, win the Max Rousié shield 14-7

Left: Albi and France front-rower Honoré Conti, a coal miner, makes a presentation to the President of the French Republic, Charles de Gaulle, on his visit to the mining town of Carmaux, where Conti worked

Below: In the 1969 Championship final, won by XIII Catalan, St Gaudens winger Serge Marsolan seeks to evade Catalan centre Claude Mantoulan

Left: The France and Lézignan attacking trio of full-back André Carrère, scrum-half Claude Teisseire and stand-off Gilbert Benausse

Above: Georges Aillères, captain Toulouse and France's 1968 Wor Cup team and a cornerstone of t French pack throughout the 196

another, culminating in the famous mutiny in 1952 of the 465 clubs who refused to accept the hierarchy's view, prompted by the British, that their championship should be abandoned because it fostered all that the RFU disapproved of, chief among which was suspected professionalism. It resulted in the resignation of the president, Alfred Eluère, whose successor, vice-president René Crabos, enjoyed particularly good relations with the upper echelons of the British game and managed to talk them round. It can hardly be stressed enough how important this negotiation was for the French Rugby Union Federation, who had an all too clear memory of how they had been cut off by the British in 1931, leaving the way open for rugby league to become a popular success. The Five Nations tournament was of vital importance: it was the focus of the season. Spectators turned up in Paris in far bigger numbers than for any domestic match and what they paid kept the Federation financially afloat. Media interest was always intense, which until the mid-fifties meant the press and radio. Soon television was to make an impact. The first rugby union match was televised in 1954, the same year that the Rugby League World Cup was broadcast. But it was on rugby union that television would have an increasingly positive effect.

The France XV had slowly begun to accumulate some success. The French won for the first time at Twickenham in 1951, twelve years after the France XIII beat England at St Helens. The national side shared Five Nations honours in 1954, when they finished top alongside England and Wales, and in 1955, when they were equal first with Wales. Compared with their league counterparts' achievements, the union team's success hardly amounted to much at all but it had a legitimacy conferred on it by the overwhelmingly important institution of the tournament, which was widely reported on. In the February before the France XIII beat New Zealand and Australia but lost the final play-off of the first World Cup, the France XV beat the All Blacks for the first time, winning 3-0 in front of 25,000 spectators in Paris, which was enough for the readers of *L'Equipe* to vote them France's team of the year. Where the France XV went, the France XIII had trodden that path before. Puig-Aubert's men had beaten New Zealand in Paris – and again in Bordeaux – three years earlier, except that the All Blacks had an aura that for many people eclipsed the Kiwis.

After returning, in the summer of 1955, from their second successful tour of Australasia, France played two matches before again facing New Zealand, with whom they had just drawn the two-match series in Auckland. Other Nationalities had already beaten England and went on to defeat France under floodlights at Leigh in October, winning 32-19. Wigan's Billy Boston scored two of the 'home' side's eight tries, though France's stand-off Gilbert Benausse was the outstanding player on the field with a solo try and five goals.

Two months later at the Parc des Princes, a year on from the World Cup final there, France got their revenge, of sorts, by beating Great Britain 17-5 in front of 12,894 paying spectators, though estimates suggested a total crowd of 18,000. The Tricolores, despite having just four seasoned internationals in their line-up – Dop, playing at full-back, centre Merquey, second row Berthomieu and prop Rinaldi – seized every opportunity to show their worth, outplaying a strong Great Britain side led by St Helens prop Alan Prescott. Well served in the scrums by debutant hooker Antranick Appelian, France ran in three tries through winger André Ducasse, who touched down twice from moves initiated by loose forward Christian Duplé, in outstanding form, and Villeneuve prop Ernest Tarozzi, whose club team-mate, scrum-half Pascal Eïto, kicked four goals. 'France played at express speed,' reported Allan Cave in the *Daily Herald*. 'Britain were barges by comparison – slow and cumbersome, and so orthodox against a team with a trapdoor defence... The second half was one of protracted wonderment for the crowd. Just as [the French] never missed their man in the tackle they never failed to find their man with trigger-snappy passes... Even the expressionless mademoiselle, smoking a Churchillian-size cigar on our right, lost herself in the excitement at one ten-piece movement which split the British defences.'[xi]

In January 1956, in the first match of a series expanded for the first time to three, the Kiwis met France at Toulouse. Watched by 12,250 spectators, France scored six tries to one in their 24-7 victory, stand-off Benausse touching down either side of half-time as the French got the better of the forward-dominated New Zealand style. At Lyon in the second encounter, seen by a crowd of 7,864, the embattled Kiwis, nearing the end of a long tour, found the strength to level the series by winning 31-22 against a French team deprived both of Dop, who had arrived late and been left out, and the injured Puig-Aubert. But a week later in Paris, witnessed by a crowd of 14,752, the tourists were unable to put up much resistance as France raced to a 24-3 victory and a series triumph.

The 1955-56 international season was more than satisfactory, even with a changing team. Writing about the New Zealand tour, the radio reporter Roger Couderc, later to become indelibly associated with televised rugby union, reported that, compared to the French, the Kiwis seemed ten years behind in their style of play. Couderc appreciated rugby league but was essentially a union man, though that did not prevent him from saying candidly, 'On the threshold of the Five Nations tournament, I wish with all my heart that our national XV can triumph with as much panache as the XIII has shown.'[xii] Once more, rugby league was setting the example for union to follow. Except in terms of its following. When the France XV was in with a shout of winning the Five Nations in 1955, 'an incredible enthusiasm' took hold of the French public, with the result that a crowd estimated at 62,000 packed the Colombes stadium in Paris for the match against Wales. France lost, but the potential of this annual tournament was amply demonstrated.

The New Zealanders, on their return home, were full of praise for the French. Their tour manager was reported as saying that the French players were 'extremely good,' and that France was probably capable of putting out three teams capable of beating any other international side.[xiii] The writer who reported these comments, the experienced rugby league journalist Jean Boudey, took the New Zealander at his word and drew up three hypothetical teams, all of them of a respectable international standard. Boudey concluded by adding: 'French rugby league is certain not to experience too many disappointments in the years to come.' Though his team selections were sound enough, Boudey's predictions would prove to be a little wide of the mark.

In the spring France suffered an 18-10 defeat under floodlights at Odsal, where a Great Britain side containing five newcomers overcame a below-par French side. But a month later at Lyon the French, guided by stand-off Benausse, were back to form, beating England 23-9. It was Puig-Aubert's forty-sixth and final match in the Tricolore jersey. Only Benausse would earn more caps for France. Puig-Aubert was easily the biggest star in post-war French rugby league. His remarkable feats of goal-kicking or unpredictable attacking play, achieved with a maximum of nonchalance and minimum of training, provided journalists with an exceptional fund of material. Even *Paris-Match* paid tribute to this 'stadium god' who was hardly the model athlete but who 'made anything possible'.[xiv]

As a prelude to the Kangaroos' tour in the autumn of 1956, a Rugby League XIII played France at Marseille on 21 October. A late interception try by scrum-half Jeff Stevenson gave the visiting team an 18-17 win but the match was a bad-tempered affair, which one pressman excitedly called the 'Marseilles Massacre'. Two players were sent off, there was a touchline brawl between two others and several players were injured. The referee was roundly criticised after awarding 22 penalties to France and only nine to the British and generally for failing to take control of the game.

The Australians arrived eager as ever to make up for three consecutive series defeats at the hands of the French, in Australia in 1951 and 1955, and in France in 1952-53. As in 1952, the first test was played at the Parc des Princes, where the crowd of 10,789 was 4,000 fewer than had watched New Zealand ten months earlier. France second rower Augustin Parent touched down in the first minute, but they sorely missed the goal-kicking ability of Puig-Aubert as his replacement, Bordeaux's André Audy, landed only one goal out of six. Aussie scrum-half Keith Holman, with two tries, was the architect of his side's 15-8 victory. Merquey scored France's other try.

The Kangaroos then left France for England, returning in late December, after losing the series against Great Britain 2-1. They found winning form again at Bordeaux, where they edged out France by 10-6, watched by 11,379 spectators – less than half the number who had seen the corresponding international four years earlier. The French became locked into a forward battle they could not win and failed to open up in the backs to counter the Australian tactic, despite Duplé's efforts at loose forward. In another close contest, the Kangaroos made a clean sweep of it, winning the third test at Lyon 25-21 and the series 3-0. They had gone through the French leg of their European tour without losing a game. The French Army, made up of leading young players on national service, drew 11-all with the Aussies at Limoges. Albi, the 1956 champions, almost pulled off a sensational win but went down 25-20 and the Catalans de France also gave the Aussies a hard time before being beaten 20-14.

France also struggled in matches against Great Britain. In November 1951, the French had racked up the highest score in matches against Great Britain or England, when they triumphed 42-13 in Marseille. In January 1957 at Headingley, where a crowd of 19,000 was present, the British team made amends. Though they led only 19-12 early in the second half, Alan Prescott's men scored three tries in a five-minute blitz and ran up a 45-12 scoreline. But the game was far from one-sided. As well as appreciating the artistry of Leeds centre Lewis Jones, an inspiring try by the captain and the all-round abilities of forwards Derek Turner, Geoff Gunney and Sid Little, the Headingley crowd also admired 'the magnificent duel between [wingers] Billy Boston and André Savonne', 'the Frenchmen's delightfully fast and adventurous passing', as well as 'the artfulness of Teissiere at half-back, the deft skill of Merquey in the centre and the rampaging runs of Parent and Pambrun in the pack'.[xv] That match also entered the record books as the first official test match – rather than simply an international match – between the two countries.[xvi] It is not clear how it came about that the French, who had proved their international worth long ago, should only be granted test status, alongside Australia and New Zealand, at such a late stage in their history.

Thanks to a controversial penalty, converted by Benausse, the French managed a 19-all draw two months later in Toulouse, Merquey touching down twice. But in the last international before both teams headed for Australia and the 1957 World Cup, Great Britain won 29-14 at St Helens.

It was at Sydney Cricket Ground, scene of the Tricolores' greatest triumphs, that France next met Great Britain as the second World Cup got under way. The Australians, doubtful of the value of the competition before it first took place in France, were now enthusiastic hosts, looking forward to celebrating the fiftieth anniversary of the founding of the game in their country.

Great Britain, who had comfortably won the Ashes six months earlier and now presented much the same team, were favourites to win the competition, whereas France was still in the process of rebuilding the national side. A crowd of 50,007 fans watched as the British made a strong start to the tournament, winger Mick Sullivan scoring two of their five tries in their 23-5 opening win. France's only reply came from a try by their captain, Merquey, and a Benausse conversion.

Only two days later in Brisbane, France faced New Zealand in front of a 22,142 crowd. In a tight contest, Villeneuve centre Jean Foussat, in only his second outing in the Tricolore jersey, accounted for both of France's tries; Benausse's four goals made the difference between the two sides in France's 14-10 victory.

The following Saturday, a week after the start of the competition, France were back in action when they returned to the SCG to take on the host country. France's fine record in Australia made the 35,158 spectators keen to see how the current side would fare against their own boys, who had already beaten New Zealand 25-5 and swept aside Great Britain's challenge by 31-6. France showed up better, but Australia, boosted by Brian Carlson's seven goals, were successful by 26-9 to win the tournament undefeated. Benausse scored all France's points with a try and three goals. Like

Great Britain and New Zealand, France had one victory to their name, which, taking into account other international matches played over the past couple of years, once more showed the closeness in standard of the four nations.

Except that France were making a habit of losing against Great Britain, who opened the 1957-58 international season with a 25-14 victory at Toulouse, though the scores would have been much closer if the French had had a reliable kicker. Whereas Oldham full-back Bernard Ganley landed five goals to go with Britain's five tries, his opposite number André Rives managed only one. In the return match at Wigan, Ganley once more played a significant role, converting ten goals from eleven attempts in the inflated 44-15 scoreline. Wigan stand-off Dave Bolton scored a hat-trick, while the performance of Derek Turner led journalist Harry Sunderland to predict that the Oldham loose forward could finish as one of the all-time greats. Once again Billy Boston was involved in an absorbing duel on the wing, this time with Raymond Contrastin, who, like his opposite number, was a powerhouse in both attack and defence. Antoine Jimenez, moved from centre to stand-off, also gave an outstanding performance in a beaten side.

Grenoble hosted a rugby league match for the first time, producing a capacity attendance of 17,000, when the two nations met in March 1958. Despite referee Jep Maso's profligacy with penalties awarded to France (two dozen to the home side but just two to Great Britain), a Jeff Stevenson-inspired British team came from behind to win 23-9. At Leeds, against a Rugby League XIII which featured two of the game's greatest-ever wingers, Brian Bevan, who scored one try, and Tom van Vollenhoven, who scored two, France again lost an early lead to go down 19-8, their tries coming from Contrastin and Jimenez.

In the 15-a-side code, the French national team had made slow progress in the decade since the end of the war, but following the victory over the All Blacks there came another sign of re-awakening. Seven years after France's rugby league team had made their pioneering, brilliant tour of Australia, the national rugby union side undertook a daunting tour of South Africa, where the Springboks had not lost a series that century. The memory of the South Africans' crushing 25-3 victory in Paris in 1952 was also fresh in French minds. Two international matches took place, the first at Cape Town, where France's drop goal cancelled out South Africa's earlier try for a 3-3 draw. In the second, at Johannesburg, a penalty goal and two drop goals gave France an astonishing 9-5 victory and with it a series win. The wider significance was enormous, though the style of the triumph – two grinding victories without scoring a single try[xvii] – had nothing to compare with the treizistes' try-fests of 1951 and 1955.

The quinzistes' South African venture also courted controversy. Just as rough play had been a feature of the rugby league tours, so the union tour had been peppered with brutality. Though it was never admitted by the governing bodies, the International Board had reportedly sent a telegram to the French party before the second test, threatening another breaking-off of international relations if any incidents took place in the match. Once it was over, the British, acting in their capacity as head of the International Board, denied sending such a threat, just as the French denied having received it.[xviii] Three months later, on Armistice Day, now that the importance of the feat had sunk in and the increased value of France to the Five Nations had become apparent, the British declared a hope that the French 'would remain our great friends'.[xix]

The France XV's triumph over the Springboks created a media sensation. More was to follow a few months later. The 1959 Five Nations ended with France winning the tournament for the first time. In 1960 and 1961 the French were undefeated. This international success, widely reported, heralded a pivotal period in the progression of rugby union in France. Even with the innovation of the World Cup, the competitions which rugby league had to offer were, by contrast, irregular and thus less meaningful as far as the general public were concerned. The annual European championship, involving England, Wales, France and Other Nationalities, turned into a desultory affair which never managed to find a fixed place in the calendar. When

France played Wales at Toulouse in March 1959, it was the first time the two nations had met for four years. Over the course of the next decade, they would only face each other once.

It has often been argued that rugby league in France was slow to see the advantage of television and allowed rugby union to steal a march in terms of popularisation through that medium. If the French Rugby League Federation was insufficiently far-sighted, it was hardly different from any other governing body of a team sport. The French Football Federation, for example, was initially hostile to television's overtures.

'The conflict which has broken out this week between French television and the French Football Federation is simply the outcome of a long-standing mutual incomprehension,' ran an editorial in a December 1955 issue of *Miroir-Sprint*. 'And with this result – the FFF now refuses to allow football matches to be televised, and for their part TV has decided not to give the results of championship matches.' The editorial went on to say that television could work as a very useful propaganda tool for sport, as increasing numbers of viewers became used to watching sporting events in their own homes. 'It is worthwhile noting,' the article continued, 'that millions of viewers were able to see the football World Cup in 1954, and that hundreds of thousands of French people sit down every Sunday to watch a boxing match or cycling race which were previously reserved for a few thousand privileged Parisians. Not to mention the latest France-Great Britain rugby league match, played in front of however many hundreds of thousands of sports-lovers (or non-sports-lovers) in France and abroad. What publicity for this sport!'[xx]

However spectacular and well-suited to television, annual matches against Great Britain could not compare, in the eyes of the viewing public, with the annual Five Nations tournament, when each country played four matches beginning in January and ending in April or March. France's home matches were played in Paris, which emphasised rugby union's development from what had previously been seen as a regional sport to a national one.

The Five Nations began to be televised regularly from 1957

and found an unlikely audience in the presidential palace. General Charles de Gaulle, embodiment of the Liberation in 1944, head of the provisional government until his resignation in 1946, returned to the forefront of the political scene in 1958 when he was appointed Prime Minister against the background of the Algerian crisis. He became President of the Fifth Republic later that year. De Gaulle was an unlikely rugby union fan. Born in Lille and brought up in Paris, at the opposite end of the country from the heartlands, he nevertheless became attracted to the sport once the national side began to achieve success. It fitted with his vision of national unity and of giving back to France the grandeur it had historically enjoyed. On Saturday afternoons during the Five Nations season, de Gaulle could not be shifted from his armchair in front of the television screen. 'The press gladly reported that General de Gaulle was an ardent supporter of the France national team and that he never made appointments on Saturday afternoons when a Five Nations match was on. To a question on the subject, he replied, "I like it when France win".'[xxi] With that kind of endorsement from the very top, rugby union's momentum grew. As Augustin and Garrigou point out, rugby union developed from a regional sport – in terms of where it was actually played - into 'a national totem'.[xxii] It was hardly surprising that rugby union in France was becoming increasingly associated with the establishment. If a reminder was needed that it had been so since time immemorial in Britain, the France-England match of 1956 saw Denis Thatcher, husband of the future Prime Minister, doing duty as a touch judge.[xxiii]

The Eurovision network, which had broadcast the rugby league World Cup in 1954, ensured that Five Nations matches away from home could be beamed back to France. A key element in all of this was the commentator Roger Couderc, who had been introduced to rugby league by Jacky Merquey. It was not a case of abandoning rugby league, more a matter of returning to the rugby he was familiar with, following a trend which saw union reclaim the limelight. Rugby union fans and even those who had previous little interest in the sport easily related to Couderc's commentaries.

Unlike most of his contemporaries who tended to talk down to the audience, he spoke like a fan. With his local accent, with his obvious enthusiasm, he was unashamedly partisan, urging on the France team with what became his catchphrase: '*Allez les petits*' ('Come on lads'). His own technical deficiencies – 'I don't think I'll ever understand the offside law', he once said – simply made a deeper connection with his audience. Of course, if Couderc had been commentating on a team which lost most of its matches, his presence in the commentary box would have made little difference. But the France XV had accounted for the All Blacks in 1954, the South Africans in 1958 and had won the Five Nations outright for the first time in 1959. And this at a time when soccer was going into a period of decline after the 1958 World Cup.

Not that the national rugby league team was doing badly. In the 1958-59 international season, the Tricolores won three of their four matches.

Against a Rugby League XIII at St Helens, France were so dominant that it was reported that they 'found themselves so much on top that when Voron scored their sixth and last try in the gathering gloom he strolled contemptuously over the home line, no defender apparently having the urge to lay a hand on him.'[xxiv] Remarkably this 26-8 victory was France's first in twelve encounters on English soil since Wembley 1949. They followed up with a 25-8 win over Wales at Toulouse in March 1959 before travelling to Leeds to face Great Britain two weeks later. On the Headingley pitch, the French were brought down to earth as they suffered their heaviest defeat ever, losing 50-15 in front of 21,948 spectators. A strong British side, which had won the Ashes by a thumping 40-17 in Sydney the previous July, was captained by Eric Ashton and inspired by a sensational performance from 19-year old scrum half Alex Murphy, who ran the French ragged to score four tries, even overshadowing winger Mick Sullivan, who scored three.

But France always seemed to have the capacity to bounce back. They did so in April, playing for the second time at Grenoble, this time watched by a crowd of 10,000 – 7,000 fewer than the year before. Leading 19-0 at half-time, and well directed by the returning Gilbert Benausse at stand-off, France won 24-15.

The discussions which took place at the annual Congress of 1955, held at Bordeaux, show officials' continuing concern to improve the game as a spectacle and to increase crowds. It was noted that fifty per cent fewer penalties had been given by referees in the 1954-55 season, which, it was supposed, had led to a better quality of play and fitted with the Ligue's ambitions for the game's recovery. Attendances and gates had improved. XIII Catalan, though seventh in the table, had seen a total increase over the season of 6,000, Avignon's attendances had improved by 11,000. Lézignan had doubled its total, Cavaillon had seen an increase of 6,000, Carcassonne 13,000 and Albi 10,000. On the debit side, Carpentras and Villeneuve had seen a slight decline of under a thousand; Lyon by 3,000. More worryingly, Toulouse and Marseille had lost 8,000; Bordeaux more than 10,000. Figures for Paris and Bayonne – unlikely to have given comfort – were not made available. If the overall figure for the championship had increased by the relatively modest number of 25,000, officials could be satisfied that the flow away from the game that had been registered since 1950-51 had been stemmed. The fact remained, however, that compared to that season, the Ligue was attracting 60,000 fewer people through the gates. The conclusion that was reached was: 'The 1953-54 season, which ended with the awful Marseille-Bordeaux final, remains the darkest [in recent years] and we cannot say that we have completely emerged from the tunnel.'[xxv]

An innovation which also emerged from that same season concerned the running of the elite clubs. It had begun at Lézignan – though short-lived – and was picked up at Marseille, who had found themselves short of officials willing to take responsibility for how the clubs were managed. At Marseille a kind of workers' cooperative replaced the board of directors, who had thrown in the towel following a financial crisis. Six players, led by Jean Dop, made huge cuts in the budget, throwing out contracts and even match bonuses, replacing formal arrangements – at least temporarily – with the promise of a share of receipts.[xxvi] It proved not to be the way forward but, as much as anything, this development revealed the problems which faced the game: declining crowds – despite the improvement seen in 1954-55 - and a lack of individuals willing to take charge of clubs.

In the second half of the decade the more solid structures in place at clubs outside the big cities was reflected in success in the Championship and to some extent in the Cup. Similar evidence was provided by rugby union. The fifties began with titles for Castres and the little mining town of Carmaux, both of them situated in the Tarn, before Lourdes, another small town famed only for its pilgrimage site, exerted a stranglehold on the competition, winning six out of eight final appearances, giving rise to the well-used phrase, 'the second miracle of Lourdes'. The tradition of small-town clubs, with all their local fervour, outperforming bigger rivals, had first found expression in the famous 1929 final between two clubs from the Aude département, Lézignan, a decade before converting to league, and Jean Galia's Quillan.

The FCL continued the tradition in rugby league. 'Alongside Avignon, Marseille, Lyon, Bordeaux, Toulouse, etc., we might ask what the small town of 7,000 inhabitants that is Lézignan is doing here,' queried *Midi-Olympique*, before answering, 'Quite simply, Lézignan is a capital of rugby.'[xxvii] Though the decade after the war had seen lean times for the FCL, they were renowned for their junior teams. Those efforts bore fruit as the senior team won the Championship for the first time in 1961, the year after they lifted the Cup. Their immediate predecessors as champions were Roanne, Villeneuve, Albi (twice) and XIII Catalan. Of the big city clubs, Lyon won their last title in 1955. Toulouse managed to break the pattern in 1965.

Carcassonne were no longer at the peak of glory, but were good enough to reach the Championship final in 1955, 1956 and 1958, under the tutelage of Félix Bergèse. Suffering a three million franc deficit at the start of the 1955-56 season, the club had been forced to sell the Benausse brothers, Gilbert and René, who left for

Toulouse and eventually moved on to Lézignan, where they joined forces again with player-coach Edouard Ponsinet, credited with kick-starting the FCL's revival, and half-back Claude Teissiere. These were major acquisitions for Lézignan and serious losses for Carcassonne. Of Gilbert Benausse it was said that many considered him the best stand-off in either code of rugby, perhaps in the world.[xxviii]

Albi were also on the rise, inspired by the highly experienced forwards, 'Hugues' Berthomieu and Marcel Blanc, winning the championship in 1956 and 1958 at Carcassonne's expense. In 1957 XIII Catalan came back into prominence and with a courageous, match-winning performance from José Guasch, playing at hooker, beat Avignon to the title. Villeneuve, now with Merquey alongside Jimenez at centre, got the better of Benausse's Lézignan to take the 1959 Championship title in a final described by André Passamar as a masterpiece of attacking play.[xxix] These were the clubs, those which reached the final in the second half of the decade, which would endure and prove to be the major supports on which French rugby league would be built in the future.

Chapter 14

•

Big City Limits: 1960-69

MID-SIZED *PREFECTURES* LIKE Albi, Avignon, Carcassonne and Perpignan, or smaller towns such as Lézignan and Villeneuve was where rugby league fitted best and longest. So much had become clear over the previous decade. In the mid-fifties to early sixties, Albi was the most successful club. When, in 1944, rugby league became once more a legitimate pursuit, it was natural that the Racing Club Albigeois, still with Dr Simon Bonpunt as chairman, should be among the first to restart, just as, ten years before that, the capital of the Tarn had responded to Jean Galia's initiative.

It remains one of French rugby league's most lasting sites. Six decades on from his debut in that most successful team, and even when the city boasted a professional rugby union club with a budget swollen to ten times that of the rugby league club, the former international prop forward Honoré Conti could still say without fear of contradiction, '*Albi est treiziste*.'[i]

Every other year, between 1956 and 1962, Albi appeared in the Championship final, winning three of them. The chairmanship of the club had been taken over by René Mauriès, described as the archetypal self-made man. Mauriès had started his working life as a car mechanic before owning a car dealership as well as selling agricultural machinery, even second-hand aeroplanes, with 500 employees working for him.[ii] Under his leadership a winning rugby league team was put together, comprising half a dozen players brought in from outside and others chosen from an outstanding crop of juniors. Signings from rugby union included full back André Rives, second rowers Gilbert Verdié and Serge Tonus, and props Marcel Bescos and Jean-Marie Bez, all future internationals. Rives arrived from St Girons in the Ariège, Verdié from Decazeville via Brive, Tonus and Bescos from Tarbes, and Bez from Carmaux. Among those who had come through Albi's junior section were three more future internationals in Conti, scrum-half or centre Bernard Fabre and scrum-half or loose forward Georges Fages.

Bez had played for Carmaux, a small coal-mining town fifteen miles north of Albi, in the 1951 Championship final when they sensationally took the title against a Tarbes side featuring the future Albi forward Tonus, though one observer called it a game of 'deplorable mediocrity'.[iii] Bez claimed that he played his first game for Albi without anyone having explained the rules to him, which was particularly unfortunate because at the first scrum, against Carcassonne, he came face to face with the feared Henri Vaslin.[iv] But the prop forward settled quickly, was twice selected to play for France against Great Britain and remained in Albi for the rest of his life. At the time he was playing in the rugby union final, the French rugby league team, he admitted, could not have been better or the game more spectacular. No wonder the same observer who deplored the 1951 rugby union final claimed, 'Rugby league had no difficulty in taking pride of place.'[v]

Before he arrived at Albi, Gilbert Verdié had no playing experience of rugby league either. But in the second row alongside the experienced Berthomieu he learned quickly. 'I owe my whole career to him,' he would later say.[vi] He was immediately taken with the game. 'When I saw the forwards play like threequarters,

I was filled with enthusiasm. I said to myself, "What a great game this is!" I never had so much pleasure playing rugby union as I did rugby league.'[vii] Soon international recognition came his way. His debut could not have happened in more demanding circumstances. Because of injuries sustained by other back row forwards two days earlier against Australia, Verdié was selected at loose forward, a position in which he had rarely played, in the France team to face Great Britain in the World Cup final, and, not having played for three weeks, found his fitness brought into question. 'In all honesty I didn't play well that day. We had a good threequarter line but we couldn't develop our game. The fans kept shouting for us to open up, but the English [sic] defence was always offside, and I say that without malice. If we had won, it would have done French rugby league a lot of good, but fate didn't favour us that day.' Verdié went on to play for France four more times and for Albi another dozen years, becoming a personality in the town he never had any desire to leave.

Rugby league was an essential part in the lives of many of his fellow-citizens. Indirectly the game also became part of the cultural life of the city. A group of artists, writers, teachers and poets figured prominently on the cultural scene; many had a common interest in rugby league. Among them were André Passamar of *La Dépêche* newspaper, later of *L'Equipe*, the doyen of rugby league writers who became known as *'le Pape'* ('Pope'); Jean Roques, teacher of classics at the prestigious Lycée Lapérouse, author of numerous books on Albi as well as the annual *Calendrier-revue* of RC Albi; and the painter Francisco Bajén, an Anarchist refugee from the Spanish Civil War who included paintings of rugby league among his oeuvre and who claimed that the game helped his integration into French society. The group met at the Café de Paris in the middle of town which, with a mural painted by Bajén, served as the club headquarters, as did the Café de la Poste at other times. They called themselves *Les Bizarres* and amused themselves by, among other things, mocking the bourgeois quinzistes at the café across the road.

If the game had already been woven into the fabric of Albi

life almost from the start, and certainly after the Championship-winning year of 1938, it became even more a focus of interest after the team won the 1956 Championship, and again after the victories of 1958 and 1962, when everyone wanted to become associated with the club's success.

Honoré Conti, a coal miner who worked at Carmaux and turned down selection for the 1960 tour of Australia owing to work-related exams, recalled that players were so highly thought of that sometimes when they went into a shop the shopkeeper refused to accept payment. 'We were spoiled,' he said. There were two or three school teams which played ad hoc matches among themselves (though of course rugby league was never on the curriculum); and the club itself had enough youngsters for three teams. 'From the surrounding countryside they came to watch Albi play,' he said. 'From as far as Castres and Carmaux they came. Rugby union did whatever it could for rugby league not to be successful, but in Albi the quinzistes picked up the crumbs. They might have a hundred people at their *championnat de campagne* [country competition]. At rugby league matches there would be five or six thousand.'[viii]

Alongside 'Hugues' Berthomieu in the second row of the team which won the 1956 Championship final was another former *résistant*, Sergio (Serge) Tonus. Many players of Spanish immigrant stock, whose families fled fascism in the 1930s, have made a significant contribution to rugby league. Far fewer are those who arrived from Italy, as the Tonus family did when leaving their village in the Veneto during Mussolini's rise to power. At the very same time as Berthomieu was helping to liberate Albi from German occupation, Serge Tonus, aged just seventeen, took part in the liberation of L'Isle-Jourdain in the Gers, where his family had settled. Determined to avenge the killing of his best friend's parents, Tonus joined the local resistance unit, was armed with a Sten gun and took part in the combat on the bridge over the river Vienne before joining Liberation forces elsewhere in the region.

In the first of the two finals against Carcassonne – both watched by a crowd of 16,000 – the leadership and experience of back-row forwards Berthomieu and the Catalan Marcel Blanc counted for a good deal. Homegrown winger Jean Couveignes stole the show with two tries, centre Pierre Lataste adding another, with the excellent André Rives kicking two goals. It was the logical conclusion to the season, during which Albi had been league leaders, as they were to become two years later. In 1958, in less favourable conditions, three penalties and a drop goal from full-back Rives were sufficient for victory for the team now coached by Blanc. Two years after, in the 31-24 defeat by Roanne – a 'splendid' game, reported Passamar[ix] – full-back Claude Deffez contributed a try and six goals, while stand-off Bernard Fabre, second row Pierre Laurent and centre José Vergniory each scored a try. In the 1962 victory over Villeneuve, in which prop Marcel Bescos dislocated a shoulder but returned to the field, full-back Jean-Louis Bonnet and Fabre, now at scrum half, were outstanding. Bonnet scored two tries, Deffez landed three goals and stand-off Jean Villeneuve a drop goal.

Albi's Junior team, under the guidance of the highly respected educator Basile Lagasse, won the national title several times. To be able to call up local players of that quality was naturally of great value to the senior team. The club's finances were in a healthy state, so that 'the Federation can say that Albi XIII may be cited as an example in every respect.'[x]

It was no surprise that a double-page feature by Robert Barran in *Miroir-Sprint* should bear the title 'Albi: Rugby League Stronghold'. Barran, who had played rugby league as a student with Albi before the war and later became captain of Stade Toulousain, began: 'From its religious history, Albi maintains its reputation as a nonconformist city. The [Albigensian] crusade … at the start of the thirteenth century remains a bloody memory. In terms of sport, and rugby in particular, Albi was also one of those towns which, some twenty-five years ago, rose up against the rugby union orthodoxy.' The difference between Albi's first championship in 1938 and its third, twenty years on, Barran wrote, was that the 1958 team was mainly composed of players who had come through the club's junior ranks. Giving the lie to a persistent misunderstanding that top rugby league players were full-time professionals, Barran went on: 'The Albi rugby league team is made up of working men, often in the hardest jobs. The ovation on the famous Place du Vigan which greeted their return after the final revealed the support of an enthusiastic population.'

Barran, a wise and experienced observer of both codes, concluded, however, on a less optimistic note. 'Rugby league absolutely needs to regenerate itself. But has the alarm been sounded too late? ... From conversations we have had with prestigious former players like Max Rousié and Vincent Cantoni, as well as with Berthomieu, with officials ... like Messrs Tardy, Mauriès and Devernois, there emerges an obvious willingness to put the game right in terms of modification of the rules, improvement in the attitude of players, restoring the standing of referees and respect for the rules.'[xi]

At international level, those last two points were regularly called into question. There had already been several examples of what appeared, to British eyes at least, weak or one-sided refereeing before France met Great Britain at Toulouse on 6 March 1960. The British had scored three fine tries to establish an 11-0 lead when an incident occurred involving, as it happened, two Albi players. According to Harold Mather of the *Manchester Guardian*, 'Fages, heavily but fairly tackled by Turner, kicked the British loose forward under the chin. Not surprisingly in the heat of the moment, further retaliation was made ... Bescos, prominently, and several others on both sides joined in.'[xii] Referee Martung sent Turner off but the loose forward stood his ground, waiting for Fages to accompany him off the field. RFL secretary Bill Fallowfield was obliged to intervene and after several minutes Turner went off and play resumed with Britain leading by just 18-17. They had already lost stand-off Claude Mantoulan with a shoulder injury, but the French went on to show the best of their abilities by scoring the winning try through Aldo Quaglio with a dazzling combination using eleven pairs of hands.

A different version of events was given in the French press. Jean Marquet in *L'Equipe*, describing France's comeback, wrote:

'The [French] forwards fought with admirable bravery, which so surprised the opposition that they lost their legendary (and debatable) self-control. Enervated, irritated, it was loose forward Turner who was responsible for the deplorable deed and for whom the only sanction could be dismissal. He deliberately kicked ... Fages, who was on his own with the ball on the ground. He kicked him until Quaglio stepped in to save his team-mate. I do not know what the reaction of Great Britain will be – none probably – but it is quite certain that Turner should never wear his country's jersey again.'[xiii]

Bill Fallowfield was also quoted as saying, 'The referee was perfectly correct in sanctioning Turner's kick, but the English players thought that a French player had also been sent off. They didn't understand what the referee was saying and the loose forward refused to leave his team-mates for that reason.' Language problems were obviously an issue, even if not for Fallowfield, who spoke French. But the matter went deeper.

The two newspaper accounts differ wildly. Mather began his report by writing: 'International rugby league matches in France rarely produce good football. Indeed they often degenerate into a shambles, usually because of bad and of weak refereeing. One therefore is well prepared in advance for any eventuality. But, even so, today's game was the worst your correspondent has ever seen there.' Marquet, on the other hand, focused his report, in this 'sensational' match, on the French fightback which allowed them to wipe out Britain's commanding eleven-point lead, even with Mantoulan sidelined before half-time. 'There was a big difference between the pleasant match at Grenoble's municipal stadium in April 1959 and the bitter, intense, moving, finely-balanced struggle involving thirteen French players determined to win, yesterday at the Stadium de Toulouse in front of a crowd by turns disappointed, cruel, enthusiastic, worried and delirious.' It was clearly a matter of perception, as may often be true of different versions of the same event, though it can also be said that the *Manchester Guardian*'s account, with the heading 'French Score Decisive Try After Period of Fisticuffs' and sub-heading 'Turner sent off amid wild confusion', can have done little to improve the public perception of Franco-British rugby league relations.

Disciplinary problems also marred the first test of the Kangaroos' 1959-60 tour, played in Paris and won 20-19 by Australia. The Kangaroos led throughout. In his first international, Aldo Quaglio, supporting Jacky Merquey and Maurice Voron, scored the only French try, but eight goals from another debutant, full-back Pierre Lacaze, including two drop goals, kept France in contention. The tourists almost walked off the field ten minutes from the end, already exasperated at referee Jameau's awarding of 24 penalties against them. When the referee penalised the Kangaroos again, centre Harry Wells grabbed him by the jersey and was then ordered off. Wells refused to go but captain Keith Barnes persuaded him to apologise. Fallowfield, secretary of the International Board as well as of the RFL, said that French referees' interpretation of the rules would be discussed at the Board's meeting three weeks later.

After that first test the Kangaroos flew back to England, where the tour had started, returning to France a week before Christmas, first to defeat the French Army team at Nantes and then to win the second test 17-2 at Bordeaux, watched by a crowd of 8,848. The third test was due to be played at Lyon, the Aussies' last match before returning home. But the pitch was frozen and for the first time ever it looked as though a test match would have to be cancelled. It was switched to Roanne the following Wednesday afternoon, when there would have been very few spectators had it not been for the intervention of Claude Devernois, who persuaded fellow directors of the town's factories to allow their employees time off to attend the match. In the end, a crowd estimated at 5,000 watched as France held Australia at 8-all until injuries took their toll and a team reduced to ten men lost 16-8. Unlike on the previous tour, however, the Kangaroos did not go through the French leg unbeaten. Albi defeated an Australian side containing ten test players by 19-10 on Christmas Day, winger Célestin Aymé achieving an historic hat-trick on the swamp-like pitch, which required the fire brigade to pump water from it before play. A combined Carcassonne-Lézignan team scored seven tries in their 32-9 triumph in what was the Aussies' third match in four days.

For France, the decade had got off to a poor start. The defeat in the third test had resulted in a 3-0 series victory for the Australians, as in 1956-7. Not only that, but on home soil the French had only managed to score two tries in the three matches, which was not what the public expected to see.

They fared better against Great Britain, following up their win in the controversial match at Toulouse with a 17-17 draw at St Helens three weeks later. A magnificent try by centre Jean Vergès, Montpellier's first international, three minutes from the end, earned the draw after France again pulled back a double-figure deficit. That match was France's last before they embarked on their third tour of Australia and New Zealand.

The composition of a touring party generally reflects the dominant clubs. In 1951, half the squad came from Marseille or Lyon, with Carcassonne being represented by four players and Bordeaux three. In the 1955 squad, Lyon, champions that year as in 1951, and Carcassonne both provided five players, Bordeaux four and Marseille three. By 1960, though, Bordeaux were not represented at all, and Marseille and Lyon each provided only one player. Villeneuve were represented by five players, as was champion club Roanne, who had reappeared in the top division in 1957, while Albi, beaten by Roanne in the final, contributed four.

The Ligue had achieved some stability in the decade since the rebirth of the game at the war's end. The same fourteen clubs contested the 1955-56 championship as the year before, and again in 1956-57, but with one significant difference. In 1956, Paris had finished the season with only Bayonne below them. Both clubs had rejoined the national division two seasons before. With Paris at one end of the rugby league-playing country and Bayonne at the other, neither club was able to attract away fans and had little local support to count on either. Nautique de Bayonne XIII, with 1951 tour captain Robert Caillou a leading figure, was responsible for raising the treiziste flag amid a host of rugby union clubs at the western end of the Pyrenees. A Bayonne official, Félix Abéradère, reflected, in a phrase much-repeated by treizistes since then, and possibly before, 'Rugby league does not have the audience which the quality of its athletes deserves.'[xiv] Although Bayonne officials could applaud the efforts of clubs such as Avignon, who saw many a lean year before its investment in its own junior teams paid off, it proved more difficult for a club deep in Basque country to emulate the pattern set in Provence. Bayonne had developed some notable players, such as the international forward Robert Eramouspé, but travel costs were prohibitive and the club was forced to concentrate its limited resources on the first team and its fortnightly forays from Bayonne to Carpentras, Marseille, Lyon, Avignon, Cavaillon or Paris. Abéradère gave an example: 'When we travelled to Lyon, the team set off at six o'clock on Saturday evening… Our players took their evening meal with them. They arrived at Lyon at nine o'clock on Sunday morning, setting off back again at nine in the evening to end their journey at eleven o'clock on Monday morning. Do you think that, in these conditions, you can put out a full team with a winning mentality? And then you have it all to do again a week later. When you use up fifty to a hundred thousand francs per trip, you can't even think about "building" [a club].'[xv] Consequently Bayonne made a loss season after season but were propped up by the Federation, who asked in exchange that the club guarantee minimum receipts of 100,000 francs per match. Eventually other clubs refused to support Bayonne and the Federation withdrew its aid.[xvi]

Nautique de Bayonne XIII soldiered on for another three seasons, which was three seasons longer than Celtic de Paris, who faced similar, though not identical problems. Bayonne benefited from first-class amenities in a land where 'eight-year olds could sell a dummy before they knew their nine times table'[xvii], even if most of the rugby was played with fifteen players. Paris XIII tended to shift from one stadium to another and both supporters and players came mainly from the provinces. But the Federation considered Paris too important to let slip from their grasp. Celtic, beset with financial problems, was finished, but rugby league in the capital was not. The Federation's secretary, Antoine Blain, negotiated an agreement with the Army to put together a rugby league team made up of top-level players on national service. The team could be run at little expense to the Federation, since the Army would provide training facilities, transport costs and a stadium, though existing clubs would be deprived of players who might otherwise be expected still to play for them while on weekend leave. The Army team entered the national division at the start of the 1956-57 season and finished the campaign in seventh place out of fourteen clubs.

In the close season of 1955, after finishing thirteenth out of fourteen, Toulouse continued to give concern. 'At Toulouse there is nothing. Or almost,' it was reported. 'An incomplete team, phantom officials and especially a deep disaffection on the part of supporters, who have so often been disappointed.'[xviii] But the Ligue regarded this club, set up in 1937 by Galia himself, as a vital component of its top division. The Villeneuve pair, vice-chairman Dr Mourgues and secretary Jean Barrès, were invited to act as mentors. They would build a team, put a group of officials together, in short re-establish the club. To this end, the Ligue would find 'not negligible' means to help get the club back on its feet.[xix]

Lyon, another important big city, also found itself in a problematic phase. Cup-winners in 1953 and 1954, champions in 1951 and 1955, Lyon stalled in the 1955-56 season, when the team finished tenth in the league table. That was the season when Claude Devernois stepped back from the club in order to concentrate on his duties as Federation president. Six years earlier, Devernois had launched the club as a major challenger for titles when he transferred the best players from Roanne. His departure precipitated a crisis. First there was a lack of officials capable of leading the club forward and second it was hard to find players able to replace the likes of Elie Brousse and Jo Crespo who were coming towards the end of their careers. An unfortunate coincidence was that the club's international forwards, Jean

Audoubert, Joseph Krawzyck and Joseph Vanel sustained long-term injuries. Fortunately Lyon had an exceptional crop of juniors, who won the national championship in 1956 by beating Avignon in the final at Toulouse. For the club as a whole, the 1955-56 season was labelled 'transitional'. At the end of the campaign, it was forecast, 'Lyon XIII will need [new] players but even more it will need officials to help current chairman M. Briand.'[xx]

Despite having structures in place which produced the next crop of young players, Lyon never managed to rise above that tenth place in the table. As one of their outstanding junior players, international forward Edouard Duseigneur experienced at first hand Lyon's problems between the mid-fifties and early sixties.

Duseigneur came up through Lyon's junior system and never played rugby union. He estimated that around four hundred youngsters played at *minimes, cadets* and *juniors* level there. He made his senior debut at the age of seventeen in 1956, the season when several junior players were thrust into the senior ranks. Like other top young players throughout the land he later joined the Army team based in Paris, otherwise known as the Bataillon de Joinville, which had replaced Celtic de Paris in the national division with a home ground at La Cipale and a training ground at Vincennes. That, of course, was another drain on the playing resources of clubs like Lyon, which were already stretched. But Duseigneur gave another reason for Lyon's decline. 'There was a lack of officials to run the club,' he said. 'By 1959-60 young players were leaving for rugby union.' One of those converts to rugby union, he added, was Michel Greffe, who won five international caps in the France XV. The Lyon back-rower was offered 50,000 francs (in a suitcase full of banknotes) by Lézignan, plus a job in the wine-making industry, but turned down the offer to join Grenoble rugby union club.[xxi]

Six years after becoming champions, Lyon dropped out of the national division in 1961. They folded in 1966. The club was subsequently relaunched twice. In a reversal of fate, Lyon's demise coincided with the revival of Roanne. Duseigneur was among those recruited by Devernois' home club, which had also enlisted René Duffort as coach. International winger Maurice Voron, another homegrown Lyon product, joined the club alongside other substantial signings, a number of them from rugby union. Recognised by many as the world's best forward, Jean Barthe, the captain of the famous Lourdes FC who had also led the France XV and figured prominently on the 1958 tour of South Africa, arrived at Roanne, as did another forward from the France rugby union team, Aldo Quaglio, who had played for Mazamet against Barthe in the 1958 Championship final. Claude Mantoulan, stand-off or centre, was signed from Pau after being capped once for France. In the second row came the Basque, Robert Eramouspé, and Serge Estiau, originally from Nantes. All were to make an impact at RC Roanne, which once more bore the imprint of Claude Devernois, and in the national team.

After winning the 1960 Championship final against Albi, in which stand-off Mantoulan kicked seven goals and a drop goal, Roanne reappeared the following year to face Lézignan. Former Carcassonne half-backs Gilbert Benausse and Claude Teisseire dictated play for Lézignan, who scored the only try of an intense match when a pass from Benausse put André Carrère into a gap. The full-back broke away and kicked infield for second row Antoine Lécéa to touch down under the posts for a try that went down in FCL history. Roanne were defeated 7-4 but went on to win the Cup the year after. Mantoulan was in fine form at centre, creating two tries for his winger Jacques Fernandez, scoring another himself and kicking two goals in Roanne's 16-10 victory over Toulouse. It was Roanne's last final. Just two years later, in 1964, the club found itself in financial difficulties and was disbanded by its chairman, Devernois' son-in-law, Jacques Gotheron, who had presided over its three years of success. The Racing Club de Roanne was relaunched at a lower level in 1967.[xxii]

Lézignan proved more durable and would appear in finals in every decade up to the present day, with the exception of the eighties. In 1963, coached again by the former Villeneuve international loose forward Gaston Calixte, the FCL won the

Championship for a second time, this time against St Gaudens, who were defeated 20-13 in their first final.

Among the new wave of clubs, which included Limoux, Villefranche de Rouergue and Montpellier, St Gaudens became the first to reach the Championship final. The club from the foothills of the Pyrenees achieved the feat no fewer than eight times between 1963 and 1974. There had been a St Gaudens rugby league club, successfully operating at amateur level before the war, but it did not restart. It was not until 1958 that the game was resurrected at senior level when the Racing Club Saint-Gaudinois came into being, with the Soubie family its progenitors. The Soubies originated at Duras, not far from Villeneuve-sur-Lot, where they learned their rugby league. As livestock traders, they made regular business trips to the markets in and around St Gaudens and finally decided to set up there. Not long after, they played a major part in founding the rugby league club, which benefited from their financial backing at a time when grants from the local or regional council amounted to very little. A star-studded exhibition match was put on in the May before the club's first season. Gilbert Benausse, Puig-Aubert and Vincent Cantoni all took part. But it wasn't so simple. The behaviour of local quinzistes suggested that the ghost of Vichy still haunted St Gaudens, as it did many other places. The publicity material which the fledgling club produced was energetically hunted down and destroyed, and even on the day of the match a sign was put up in front of the stadium, directing the crowd to a training pitch.[xxiii]

But the treizistes were not to be put off. Fernand Soubie drove the club forward after first playing as a back-row forward and then took over from his father Jean as chairman, with his brother Robert doing much to assist the development of the game in the surrounding villages. St Gaudens had no compunction about making some judicious signings from rugby union as well as recruiting established rugby league players. The forwards Roger Biffi and René Zaccariotto were among the first, both arriving from Lannemezan, and winger Serge Marsolan from

Auch. Others followed, including forward Henri Marracq from Pau. Test stars Claude Mantoulan and Jean Barthe were signed from Roanne, veteran André Rives returned closer to home from Albi, which also saw the departure of Michel Molinier. Fernand Soubie went on to be closely identified with the club for half a century, as well as taking on roles at the Federation, including that of France team manager.

Both Villefranche de Rouergue and Limoux rugby league clubs were formed in protest against the rugby union authorities. Villefranche, in the *département* of Aveyron, was founded in 1950 when the FFR, through its regional committee, suspended the Stade Villefranchois XV ground following an altercation involving players, spectators and the referee, who was jostled. The club members thought they had been been hard done by but were banned from playing even friendly matches from the January of that year, when the incident took place, to the end of the season. The following month the club switched to rugby league by an almost unanimous decision. Ligue secretary Antoine Blain, who had spent part of the war in a nearby village, assisted the club in its move to league.[xxiv]

The year after Villefranche changed codes, Limoux also made the decision to switch. The FFR had refused to allow certain player transfers, the club directors rebelled and, following an extraordinary general meeting, became a rugby league club. Carcassonne's Félix Bergèse, at the request of Paul Barrière, who lived not far away at Espéraza, led the early training sessions with players who had mainly come from union. Within a couple of months Bergèse was called upon to help Toulouse out and handed over to player-coach René Peytavi. The club was promoted to the national division in 1962 and was granted a substantial loan in order to recruit players good enough to play at that level.[xxv]

Montpellier, created in 1953 in a city where football dominated, made their first showing at the top level in the 1957-58 season, when two pools of eight clubs contested the first phase of the championship. *Les Diables rouges* were good enough to qualify for the second phase, in which they finished the season ninth out of ten. Montpellier's rise was master-minded by Jean Dop, who had joined the red and blues from Marseille and introduced an attractive, open style of play. As might be expected, his philosophy was based on the notion that attack is the best form of defence.[xxvi]

Montpellier were joined the following season by Nîmes, who had earned promotion from the second division and ended fifteenth out of sixteen, just above Bayonne, who dropped out. Although they were not present at top level in 1959-60, Nîmes reappeared in 1960-61, when the first phase of the season comprised five pools of four and included other second division clubs. In Pool 1, for example, Nîmes played against Roanne and two clubs from non-traditional areas, Mulhouse, on the Swiss border, and St Etienne, better known for its football club. Limoux, St Gaudens and Villefranche de Rouergue all appeared for the first time at this level. Joining them were Salon, Pamiers, Miramont and Tonneins. Among the new clubs, Montpellier fared best, finishing the second phase – when the number of clubs was reduced to thirteen – in fourth place. After the pool format had been dropped, St Gaudens finished the 1962-63 season in fourth place and did even better in 1963-64, when they led the league – a remarkable achievement – ahead of a revitalised Toulouse, with Limoux in eighth place and Villefranche just behind.

Although the Championship final is a better indicator of which clubs dominated a given season, the Cup can also throw up interesting pointers. The 1956 Cup final proved to be Bordeaux's swansong. After winning the Championship two years before, they could not prevent Avignon from taking the Lord Derby trophy by 25-15 despite having internationals of the calibre of Raymond Contrastin, André Ducasse, Jean Hatchondo, André Audy, Christian Duplé and Armand Save in their side. Avignon contested four Cup finals in five years between 1955 and 1959, winning twice, with Jacky Merquey and André Béraud important influences in the first three. Marseille, no longer the team of stars of the late forties, but with Jean Duhau back in charge, were still good enough to win the Lord Derby trophy in 1957, beating champions XIII Catalan 11-0, and took the trophy again in 1965 and 1971. Villeneuve lifted the Cup in 1958 at the expense of Avignon; it was a prelude to their sensational performance in the Championship final of the following season. Avignon lost again in 1959, this time to the Catalans, who won 7-0.

In 1960 Carcassonne had seen seven lean years – the longest period in their history up to that point without winning a trophy, although they had been runners-up in the Championship finals of 1955, 1956 and 1958. Now they met local rivals Lézignan in the Cup final at Perpignan, watched by a 16,000 crowd. Five former ASC players were included in the Lézignan side and three of them – Claude Teisseire and brothers Gilbert and René Benausse combined to create the try which broke the deadlock and, by 7-4, take the trophy back to the Stade du Moulin. The final of the following season, contested by the same two teams, was even closer. At full time, the score was still locked at 2-all, resulting in a period of extra time. In the 106th minute of play, young Carcassonne winger Laurent Roldos touched down to give the ASC revenge and their first trophy in eight years.

The revival of Toulouse was also signalled by three consecutive Cup final appearances between 1962 and 1964. They lost all three, to Roanne, Carcassonne and Villeneuve. There was double disappointment for Toulouse in 1964, when they also went down to Villeneuve in the Championship final, losing 4-3 despite scoring the only try of the match through winger Jean Etcheberry. When the same teams met again in 1965, Toulouse coach Vincent Cantoni, the former international winger, made sure his troops were well prepared. With Georges Aillères, all power and craft at loose forward, and the inimitable Pierre Lacaze at full-back, profiting from the gaps carved out by '*le Cube*', Toulouse piled on the pressure in the blistering heat to score nine tries and rack up the highest total of points in a final when they won 47-15. The elusive '*Papillon*' Lacaze, with his refined skills, accounted for 26 of those points – another record – from two tries, nine goals and a drop goal. It was Toulouse's first Championship title.

Over a period of five years, Toulouse had managed to get

back on track, with Cantoni playing an important part, as did a previous coach, Jean-Marie Vignals, who had formerly coached Albi. The club's chairman during this period, Pierre Yassonowski, made a number of key signings, including Lacaze, who had played alongside Barthe and Quaglio on the France XV's 1958 tour of South Africa; international loose forward André Lacaze (no relation); as well as future France captain Aillères, a former rugby union junior international from nearby Rieumes.

That 1965 Championship final set a trend for high scores, as Carcassonne, still mentored by Félix Bergèse, came very close to emulating Toulouse's feat in 1966 and 1967, each time at the expense of St Gaudens. At the start of the season, Carcassonne had signed Jean Barthe, now a 33-year old veteran who had previously been a major force at Roanne and St Gaudens. But in the 1966 victory, it was the half-back pair of Jean Colombiès, a local product in at stand-off for Gérard Chalet, and François Gril who led the onslaught. Colombiès scored 19 points from a try, seven goals and a drop goal, and Gril three tries in the 45-20 triumph. The following season of 1966-67 turned out to be Carcassonne's best in more than a decade. In front of a crowd of 16,250 at Gilbert Brutus stadium, the ASC faced local favourites XIII Catalan and came away with the Lord Derby trophy by 10-4. In the Championship final two weeks later they again undid St Gaudens by a score only slightly lower than the previous year. Another nine-try haul, with scrum-half René Castel, loose forward Pierre Escourrou and Colombiès each touching down twice, Colombiès kicking six goals, was a feature of a 39-15 victory. Carcassonne backed up the following year, retaining the Lord Derby trophy by beating Toulouse 9-2 with Escourrou scoring the only try of the match.

The other top-flight clubs in the Aude *département*, Lézignan and Limoux, were snapping at Carcassonne's heels. In 1966 Lézignan won the Cup for the second time in their history when they beat Villeneuve 22-7. The FCL were again successful in 1970, when, with ex-Toulouse full-back Lacaze kicking four goals and Richard Alonso scoring two tries, they defeated the same opponents by 14-8 in an exceptional final. In their enthusiasm, the Lézignan supporters paraded a horse painted in the club colours of green and white around the ground.

Limoux had their finest hour in May 1968, a time of protest, unrest and upheaval throughout France. Facing favourites Carcassonne, who were appearing in their third Championship final in a row, the Sporting Club Limouxin proved the equal of their elders. It was 2-2 at half-time, then 6-6 until Barthe put winger Michel Blanc over to make the score 9-6. Five minutes from the end of a thrilling match, loose forward Jean-Christophe Vergeynst played the ball to himself and put the ball over the line for a try hotly disputed by Carcassonne. In extra time, ASC captain Henri Castel thought he had scored the match-winner, but two subsequent penalties from Guy Andrieu gave Limoux their first title by 13-12.

The season 1968-69 belonged to the Catalans. On home territory in the Cup final they beat Villeneuve 15-8, winger Jean-Claude Michan touching down twice. A fortnight later, at Toulouse, they got the better of St Gaudens, who were appearing in their fourth Championship final but were no more successful than in the previous three. As Limoux had done the year before, XIII Catalan won by a solitary point despite scoring two tries, through Jean Capdouze and André Clerc, to their opponents' three, scored by Michel Molinier, who touched down twice, and Serge Marsolan.

By the beginning of the seventies, Bordeaux and Lyon were no longer present among the Ligue's top clubs. Their places had been taken by St Gaudens and Limoux, who were more than useful assets, although, as small towns, they did not carry the same strategic weight as the two big city clubs. But what the creation of St Gaudens showed, as late as 1958, was that rugby league still had a vibrant future despite what its critics might believe. That view was reinforced later by the appearance of three more clubs – St Estève, Pia and Le Pontet, who also contributed to the strength of the championship.

The France team which toured Australia and New Zealand, 1960

Chapter 15

•

The Tricolores Regain Respect: 1960-68

LIKE THE FIRST two tours, France's third trip to Australia and New Zealand held no great expectations, despite the successes of 1951 and 1955. Only two members of the 1960 party, Gilbert Benausse and the captain, Antoine Jimenez, had previously toured down under, though the management trio of Antoine Blain, Jean Duhau and René Duffort had figured twice before.

France started this third venture brightly enough, winning the first four games, but then lost five of the next six, the last of which was a 25-7 defeat by New South Wales in Sydney, a week before the first test was due to be played there. But in their first encounter with Australia, who had won all three tests in France only months before, the Tricolores once again defied predictions.

Those who came expecting adventurous passing from the French backs saw instead a tough defensive effort, especially from the forwards. Neither side scored a try. In the final minute, Australia led by four Keith Barnes penalties to three from Pierre Lacaze. With thirty seconds left, France were awarded a penalty.

Full-back Lacaze, in his fifth test, showed the required coolness to send the ball between the posts for an 8-all draw.

By contrast, the second test, played at Brisbane, was a disaster for the tourists. Though lacking Benausse in the centre and prop Aldo Quaglio, the France team was not significantly weaker than the one which drew in Sydney. But their woes began when scrum-half Bernard Fabre sustained a knee injury in the opening minutes, loose forward Georges Fages suffered a similar handicap shortly afterwards and centre Jean Foussat left the field early in the second half with a dislocated shoulder, leaving the Tricolores with ten fit men. For the second time in their history, they conceded fifty points as the Aussies ran riot, winning 56-6, France's heaviest defeat. It was also the Australians' second-highest total, only exceeded by the 63-13 victory over England in the Paris exhibition match of 1933.

On their return to Sydney for the third test, two weeks later, France were literally a different team. The party had been much reduced by injury, resulting in nine changes (four of them positional) from the XIII which lost so comprehensively at Brisbane. The Australian public was not impressed. Whereas 50,000 attended the first test, fewer than 30,000 turned up for the third. But what those 30,000 witnessed was a spectacular turnaround.

'It seemed unthinkable,' wrote Henri Garcia in *L'Equipe*, 'that this bruised and bloodied team could last out.'[i] But they did, with Jean Barthe, Marcel Bescos, Aldo Quaglio and Angelo Boldini rocking their big Australian counterparts back on their heels throughout the first half. Claude Mantoulan opened the scoring with a penalty and though winger André Marty had more than one chance to cross the Australian line, the first try did not come until late in the second period after Barthe appeared from nowhere to halt a break by Reg Gasnier, who, of all people, lost the ball. It was snapped up by winger Jacques Dubon, who raced over for a try – France's sole try in the series – converted by Mantoulan for a 7-0 lead. In a furious final quarter, the Australians threw everything at their opponents, but in vain until the tourists found themselves a man down. Fabre was dismissed – unjustly, according to at least one report – for having kicked winger Ken Irvine, who had been concussed in a double tackle by Marty and the excellent full-back Louis Poletti, replacing the out-of-form Lacaze.[ii] Aussie centre Harry Wells took advantage, creating the break which led to a try for Bob Bugden, converted by Barnes to bring the score to 7-5. Three hectic minutes remained for France to maintain their slender lead as the Aussies drove forward. With Barthe still leading from the front, the Tricolores stopped the green and golds from scoring again and thus halved the series. On the morning of the match, tour manager Antoine Blain had assembled his troops in the rain in front of the monument to the French explorer Lapérouse, where they gave a full-throated rendition of *La Marseillaise*. That spirit carried them through the match, and the Tricolores maintained their proud record of never having lost a test series in Australia.

The Tricolores had now twice called up all their national fervour to maintain the spirit of 1951. New Zealand awaited at the end of an already arduous tour of Australia, in which twelve matches had been won, eight lost and two drawn. The New Zealand leg produced bigger receipts than before, but, as in 1951 and 1955, the Kiwis proved hard to beat. The two tests, both played at Auckland on the traditional Carlaw Park mudheap, provided almost identical scores. In the first, the Kiwis won 9-2 after Bescos, the 'undisputed hero of the Australian tour'[iii], had been sent off in the first half for jostling referee Belsham – accidentally, claimed the French, who threatened to pull out of the tour if the same referee was appointed for the second test. But he was, and a tired French side, though 3-0 up at half-time thanks to a try by winger Foussat, lost 9-3. Of the nine matches played in New Zealand, six were won and three, including the two tests, were lost.

Despite the heroics against Australia, the French therefore went into the 1960 World Cup, hosted by Great Britain, on a losing note. In their opening match, in which they faced the Australians at Wigan in front of 20,278 spectators, France came desperately close to making a winning start. With Jacky Merquey returning to the side at stand-off, it was difficult to separate the two teams in what Henri Garcia called 'a sublime match'.[iv] With 17 minutes remaining, Australia led 13-12. The game was there for the taking as France pressed the opposition line again and again, but no fewer than four desperate drop goal attempts were fluffed, and the Aussies claimed their one-point victory.

The following week at Swinton, watched by 22,923 spectators, France took on favourites Great Britain. After the hosts had established a 13-7 half-time lead, France unwisely tried to out-muscle the formidable British pack of Jack Wilkinson, Joby Shaw, Brian McTigue, Brian Shaw, Vince Karalius and Johnny Whiteley. The French captain, Barthe, and Karalius were sent off for fighting as Britain ran away with the match, winning 33-7. The match also showed up differences in method of the two countries. 'Great Britain play as a team, cohesively,' wrote Jean Boudey, 'without making errors and limiting the risks. We follow our inspiration, with a certain dilettantism, without clear method, and by a lack of finishing we let pass major opportunities of which our opponents would have known how to take advantage.'[v]

Britain went on to beat Australia 10-3 in a bad-tempered decider at Odsal – a match widely condemned for its brutality and dour play in the mud – and won the competition for the second time. France, on the same afternoon, in front of a crowd of just 2,876 at Wigan, met New Zealand for the wooden spoon. The French, with four players injured during the course of the match and Eramouspé sent off, lost 9-0 and thus ended the tournament without a win to their name.

Although they had met only two months earlier, France and Great Britain honoured the usual home and away fixtures, which were by now the only regular international competition either nation could guarantee, apart from tours and World Cups. France lost both matches, the first by 21-10 at Bordeaux, the second by 27-8 at St Helens. After the first, one observer wrote, reflecting on the attendance of 5,320 paying spectators: 'Rugby League football in France seems to be short at the turnstiles, as

Rugby League is in England... [The attendance at Sunday's match] must stand as the lowest since the Test series between Great Britain and France was launched in 1955, and compares poorly with such figures as 18,000 (Toulouse, 1957) and 18,000 (Grenoble, 1958). What is more, it looks desperately thin alongside the 23,250 at St Helens in 1957 and the 22,000 at Headingley in 1958.'[vi] Or, he might have added, the 23,419 recorded at the same Bordeaux stadium for the France-Australia match in 1953.

The writer went on to point out that the choice of venue, 'the magnificent Stade Municipal at Bordeaux' accounted as much as anything for the attendance (an estimated figure, including free pass-holders, was given as 10,000). He referred to the fact that Bordeaux was 'a city in which there has not been a Rugby League club, I am told, for the best part of two years.' This international match, he claimed, was 'a venture to see what the prospects were of Rugby League revival in the city which once was the French home of the game.' Indeed the French Federation headquarters were situated in Bordeaux both before the war and after, until the early fifties. But midway through the 1959-60 season, the Bordeaux club collapsed and did not complete its fixtures. The staging of international matches in the city did little to revive interest. In 1961 France met New Zealand there, drawing 6-6 in front of 2,375 spectators; a figure improved on for the match against Australia in 1963 (4,261), before a pitiful crowd of 1,581 for the World Championship match against England in 1975 told its own story.[vii] Bordeaux did, though, reappear in the championship for the 1963-64 season, finishing thirteenth out of sixteen.

That 6-all draw hinted at the growing superiority of New Zealand over France in the early sixties. The Kiwis had beaten France 9-0 in the last match of the World Cup, though the French reversed the result five days later in Paris, when it was too late. In a game of no great significance, the homeward-bound Kiwis lost 22-11 before returning to France a year later to play three tests. After the drawn match at Bordeaux, the Kiwi pack out-muscled the French in the second test at Perpignan to gain a decisive victory by 23-2, watched by a crowd of 9,000. In the third test, a remodelled French side could do no better than in the first. A 5-all draw was played out at Stade de Paris, on the northern outskirts of the capital at St Ouen, where only 3,300 spectators turned up. With two tests drawn and the other won by the visitors, the New Zealanders triumphed in a series in France for the first time.

With a modest record since the Australian leg of the tour down under fifteen months earlier, the France team, now relegated to fourth place in the international order, appeared to be in decline. So did the France rugby union team, who, despite their Five Nations success, lost all three tests on their 1961 tour of New Zealand, with their heaviest-ever post-war defeat coming in the third, by 32-3. Henri Garcia called the tour 'a fiasco' and said that the France XV had 'lost its soul'.[viii]

For France's national rugby league team, however, the calendar year of 1962 began with a notable success and continued in that vein through 1963. At Wigan on 17 February 1962, the French recorded their first victory over Great Britain on British soil. Almost exactly 23 years earlier, it was the national team known as England that France had beaten at St Helens to claim their first cross-Channel victory; similarly at Wembley in 1949, it was England who were defeated, not Great Britain. But at half-time at Wigan on this February afternoon in 1962, with 17,277 in attendance, Great Britain appeared to be heading towards another victory. They had scored three tries through Huddart, Ashton and Sullivan to lead 13-2. But in full-back André Carrère France had a match-winner. A devastating defender, he twice produced tackles to stop certain tries by Bolton and Boston before launching magnificent counter-attacking runs which provided the impetus for France to launch an assault on the British line. With loose forward Barthe prompting, Mantoulan, Benausse twice and Dubon all touched down in a blistering spell of scoring and, with Benausse contributing four goals, France won by 20-15.

France backed up by winning the return fixture at Perpignan, at the newly-opened Gilbert Brutus stadium, where they established a match-winning first-half lead of 21-5 before triumphing 23-13. Carrère and Barthe once again were the catalysts, with Carcassonne scrum-half Louis Vergé scoring two tries, the first of which gave the French team belief that they could overcome their rivals for the second time in three weeks, as well as wiping out the memory of the previous year's defeat against New Zealand in this same city.

Though beaten by the team called England – which included several newcomers but also the likes of Ashton, Fox, Sullivan, Huddart and Turner – at Leeds in November 1962, France went on to register another victory over Great Britain the following month on their return to Perpignan. Jean Barthe inspired his side to a 17-12 victory as Great Britain narrowed the margin by ten points in the last ten minutes. The French made short work of a Welsh XIII, full-back Carrère contributing two tries to the 23-3 win in Toulouse, but they were unable to repeat their feat of fourteen months earlier at Central Park. Great Britain ended a sequence of three successive defeats against France, winning by the handsome score of 42-4, of which centre Neil Fox claimed half the British total with nine goals and a try. It was an undistinguished performance from the French, who had made eight changes from the side which had beaten Wales.

The Australians embarked on their fifth post-war tour of France in December 1963 with the record of having won three of the previous four series there. The Kangaroos had just regained the Ashes, after beating Great Britain 2-1, including the record 50-12 victory at Swinton. Against one of the greatest-ever Australian touring teams, France fared no worse, even slightly better than the British, winning the first test at Bordeaux 8-5 before losing the second 21-9 at Toulouse and the third 16-8 at the Parc des Princes. Sadly the three-match series was watched by a total of just 17,000 paying spectators. Laurent Roldos, the Carcassonne winger who was making only his second appearance in the Tricolore jersey when he appeared in the first test at Bordeaux, reflected on the 'exceptional' physical abilities of the Australians. Roldos singled out the sprinters on the wing, Ken Irvine and Mick Cleary; Reg Gasnier, 'perhaps the greatest centre of all time'; and Graeme

Langlands and Ken Thornett, who 'surged through the wide open spaces left by the French defence, as in the second test at Toulouse. The speed of the Australian sprinters left the French three-quarters, of whom I was one, powerless.' In an analysis which said a great deal about the changes which had come about since the French tour of 1951, or even 1955, Roldos commented: 'Australian rugby league, French rugby league – two completely different worlds: in their conception of play, in the attitude of the players, in the preparation of the players, and in the interest shown in them. Australian rugby league is at the present time the best in the world and for this reason I believe that the French should take their inspiration [from there] at least in certain areas and especially in physical preparation, rigour of application and attitude.'[ix]

That was, and is, undoubtedly true. But sometimes a team puts in a performance which defies all pre-match expectation. Apart from the first test, the Australians had won all their tour matches in France when they met the Catalans on New Year's Day at Gilbert Brutus stadium. Unlike the pure Catalans de France team of 1948, which brought in émigrés like Elie Brousse, the 1964 version was pretty much the XIII Catalan club side, coached by their regular mentor, René Duffort, and including outsiders such as Claude Mantoulan, originally from Pau, and Edouard Duseigneur, from Lyon, not to mention prop Francis Mas, signed from Béziers. With the likes of Hervé Larrue, Henri Chamorin and especially stand-off Yves Castany closing the opposition out, the Kangaroos were allowed little room in which Gasnier, Raper, Langlands, Irvine and co. could manoeuvre. Playing like men inspired, the Catalans took a 12-3 lead. But the Aussies gradually clawed back the margin to come within a point of their hosts. Finally centre André Bourreil, with a solo try, gave the Catalans a second historic victory, winning 15-11, the Kangaroos' only defeat in France apart from the first test.

Six members of that Catalan side were selected to tour Australia and New Zealand later that year. But first there was the small matter of the annual home and away fixtures against Great Britain. In early March, when snow covered not only Mont

Canigou but also the Gilbert Brutus pitch until it was cleared shortly before kick-off, the British, who included five debutants, beat France 11-5, watched by a 6,000 crowd. In the return match at Leigh, the British victory was much more emphatic. France's 39-0 hammering – a record margin of defeat in England – was no preparation for what was to come.

In a preview of the Australasian tour, André Passamar wrote: 'The France rugby league team is setting off on a new adventure, one heavy with consequence for the future of the entire movement. They will have to prove the vitality and quality of the French style, and to register performances which, 20,000 km away, will affect opinion. They will have to attract the Antipodean public so as to ensure the profitability of the operation, which, if successful, may allow the rickety edifice to be shored up and endorse new ambitions…

'French rugby league – and this is the problem it suffers from above all – is not as rich in players as in the past. The handicap of the present lies essentially in the absence of key elements like Jean Barthe, Marcel Bescos, Aldo Quaglio, Gilbert Benausse, Jean Foussat, Antoine Jimenez and Jo Guiraud, who, in 1960, served with panache a team which returned with a commendable record.

'It will be hard, very hard to oppose nations which have an immense pool of players.'[x]

The tour was managed by Jean Barrès of Villeneuve, a future Federation secretary, with the now ailing Antoine Blain as co-manager. René Duffort was still there as coach, in tandem with Carcassonne's Félix Bergèse. Bernard Fabre of Albi captained the team. There were few established internationals in the squad, with Claude Mantoulan, André Carrère, Georges Fages and Robert Eramouspé the most experienced.

Passamar was correct. By common consent, the tour was a catastrophe. In Australia, only nine matches were won for sixteen lost. The Australians took all three tests, by 20-6, 27-2 and 35-9. Ditto in New Zealand, where the hosts won by 24-16, 18-8 and 10-2.

Edouard Duseigneur, who played in 22 of the 26 matches in Australia, commented: 'We had no preparation for the tour. We were amateurs compared to the Australians. That's where I saw the difference. Only when we got to Australia did we have a professional régime, with regular training sessions and two matches a week.'

Failure on the field meant disaster at the bank. In 1960, the attendances for the first and third tests at Sydney Cricket Ground were close to 50,000 and 30,000, with 32,000 for the second test at Brisbane. Not quite up to the levels of 1951 or 1955, but still very satisfactory. In 1964, the first and third tests drew only 20,000 and 16,000 to the SCG, and 20,000 to Brisbane. Sensing further financial quandaries, the Australian Rugby League withdrew from the World Cup which had been scheduled for 1965, effectively putting the whole concept of a world series on hold.

With ten international defeats in a row, France was clearly having trouble bridging the gap between themselves and the other three nations. Remarkably, though, the Tricolores sprang back with an 18-8 victory over Great Britain at Perpignan four months after returning from down under. 'Far from being the poor team their results on tour had suggested,' wrote one observer, 'France played well and deservedly beat Great Britain…

'For this happy state of affairs – and the victory surely should do the game in France much good – the French were greatly indebted to Bescos. Indeed, on his return to international football after an absence of two years, Bescos was not only a splendid captain in marshalling his forces, but also a source of inspiration to his colleagues.'[xi]

Catalan winger Guy Bruzy marked his debut with two well-taken tries, Villeneuve stand-off Etienne Courtine landed two drop goals and Toulouse full-back Pierre Lacaze kicked four goals in all. It proved a heartening send-off for Claude Devernois, who had stepped down the day before, following almost a decade as president of the Federation. Now aged 65, the man who had done so much to maintain the profile of rugby league since succeeding Paul Barrière in 1955 would now concentrate on his flourishing

Devernois fashion label. He was followed by the former XIII Catalan chairman, the well-respected Dr Raphael Joué, who was to remain at the head of the Federation for the next three years.

Dr Joué was co-opted and approved by the Council within hours of the France team's victory in Perpignan. The return fixture at Swinton, six weeks later, in January 1965, sparked the kind of incident which would make the new man realise, as he had surely done already, that controversy was never far from the treizistes' door.

On the hour mark, Neil Fox's fourth penalty goal gave Britain a one-point lead after France had gained the upper hand with a brilliant try by winger Bruzy and two Pierre Lacaze goals. From a scrum, referee DTH Davies gave the home side a penalty, which France captain Marcel Bescos, displeased at the number of times his team had been sanctioned, contested and refused to retreat ten yards. Referee Davies, not a man to brook dissent, sent Bescos off, causing wholesale confusion for the next few minutes, both in the ground and in front of television sets. Bescos stayed put, officials came on to the field and, seeing deadlock, the referee himself made as if to leave the field, followed by most of the French team. Finally order was restored, but the French, now down to twelve men, appeared to take little interest in the rest of the game, during which winger Berwyn Jones scored Britain's only try and Fox extended the lead, producing a 17-7 score. The French had earned praise for their handling, 'delicate like rare perfume', but opprobrium for their 'excitable' temperament.[xii] Another reporter wrote: 'Their backs, handling the greasy ball with impressive ease and running and backing up well in the clinging mud, frequently earned ovations from the home supporters for their bright attacking play in the early stages.' The same writer added: 'The French showed, in their flashes of good football, that they have improved immensely since their Australian tour form which prompted the postponement of the World Cup competition. If France continue along present lines and concentrate on their fine football with less of the footbrawl [sic] they should be quite a force in the next world series.'[xiii]

Despite the outcome of that match, it marked a turning-point. Up to the Perpignan test in December 1964, which had ended a ten-match losing streak, France had needed to regain credibility, and they did. After the Swinton clash, they lost just one out of the next ten.

The Kiwis' 1965 tour of France gave the opportunity for the Tricolores, coached by Jep Lacoste and Vincent Cantoni, to restore their self-confidence, and they took it. In the forwards, the formidable back three of Georges Aillères, Henri Marracq and Jean-Pierre Clar led the way. Unimaginative New Zealand suffered a 3-0 whitewash, after losing two and drawing one test in Great Britain. France's 14-3 victory at Marseille was followed by a 6-2 win at Perpignan and by 28-5 at the Stade des Minimes in Toulouse. In all matches between the two countries, those three consecutive successes brought France level with the Kiwis with eleven wins each.

The two tests against Great Britain, in January and February 1966, were both won by France. At Perpignan, Pierre Lacaze kicked three penalties in the last ten minutes for an 18-13 victory, and at Wigan the French opted for an unspectacular and untypical kicking game, which paid off with an 8-4 win in a match sans tries.

One year later, the honours were shared, Great Britain winning 16-13 at Carcassonne, thanks to a last-gasp try from Clive Sullivan on his debut, and France triumphing by 23-13 at Wigan, before both nations faced Australia in the autumn.

The Kangaroos arrived in France after winning the Ashes for the third time in a row, but could only manage a 7-all draw in the opening test at Marseille. Loose forward Georges Bonnet, following up from a break by Aillères, went over for the equalising try converted by Lacaze. On Christmas Eve at Carcassonne, which hosted a test match for only the second time and attracted just 4,500 spectators, France reverted to the kicking game which had won them the match at Wigan ten months earlier. This time it was debutant stand-off Jean Capdouze, signed by XIII Catalan from Pau, who accounted for all France's points with four penalties and a drop goal for a 10-3 win. The outcome of the series depended on the third test at Toulouse in the new year of 1968. In front of a similar-sized crowd to the one at Domec, the Aussies unleashed attack upon attack but could not shake off the Tricolores, for whom local winger Pierre Surre had scored a try laid on by debutant centre Michel Molinier. With the score at 13-11 to Australia, Villeneuve winger Daniel Pellerin burst through to score the match-winner and, with a 16-13 victory, France had once more defied the odds to win the series.

Although in the next couple of months Great Britain beat France, first at the Parc des Princes, then at Odsal, the French had now regained the respect which they had practically lost in 1964. There was no longer any question, as there had been before the aborted 1965 World Cup, about their worthiness to compete alongside the other three nations in the 1968 version. With their impressive series win over the Kangaroos, the French had convinced the leading doubters in the best way possible.

Staged by the Australians, as in 1957, but this time with two matches played in New Zealand, the competition was scheduled to climax with a play-off final between the top two teams. In the opener Australia beat Great Britain 25-10 in Sydney, before France met New Zealand at Carlaw Park, Auckland. Stand-off Capdouze was the star, scoring the only try of the match from a break by Molinier, and kicking five goals in France's 15-10 win. Roger Garrigues added a drop goal, whereas New Zealand were restricted to five penalty goals by Ernie Wiggs. The French stayed in Auckland to face Great Britain on a Carlaw Park pitch that was by now even heavier. They again scored the only try of the match, this time through winger Jean-René Ledru of Marseille, which, with a 7-2 score, proved enough to send them into the final. But first they had to complete the group stage by facing Australia, who had already despatched New Zealand 31-12. It was the final before the final, and Australia made clear their intentions in front of 32,662 fans in Brisbane. They hammered France 37-4. Just two days later in Sydney the same two teams clashed for the right to be called world champions. Watched by a crowd of 54,290 at the

SCG, the French defended bravely but could not match the quality and physical presence of their opponents, who were blessed with no fewer than five of Australia's 'Team of the Century', named in 2008. France lost 20-2, but, as finalists in a world series for the second time, they had done as much as anyone would have dared to expect only four years earlier.

Team captain Georges Aillères even went so far as to say: 'I think we could have done better. We had a big set of forwards but we were overawed by the Australians.'[xiv]

Coached by Jep Lacoste, the France team had, in the circumstances, produced a noteworthy performance. Unfortunately it failed to get the media attention it deserved, though the team was accompanied by journalists Jean Boudey and André Passamar and radio reporter Alex Angel.

The Tricolores' achievement was submerged by the events of May '68, which shook France to the core. Starting in Paris as the protests of students objecting to what they saw as the repressive attitude of the authorities, with de Gaulle as the symbol of an old order that was becoming increasingly out of touch, the revolt was taken up in solidarity by workers throughout the country who had their own grievances to express. Demonstrations and strikes spread, so that by mid-May factories, mines, airports and railway stations were all forced to close, paralysing the country.[xv] As the historian Rod Kedward observed, 'No one missed the fact that this was the biggest general strike in French history.'[xvi]

When the France team returned home in mid-June, as order was being restored but signs of upheaval still apparent, what they had accomplished seemed to count for little. And yet it was an achievement to have improved so obviously since their previous appearance down under. The lack of preparation in 1964, so lamented by Edouard Duseigneur among others, had been noted. The squad had undertaken two training camps of a week's duration at Font Romeu in the Pyrenees and a further two weeks of preparation at the regional centre for sporting excellence in Toulouse.

Avignon winger André Ferren, who played in two of the

Tricolores' four matches, recalled the experience. 'We left on the last plane out,' he said, 'from Toulouse to Paris, then to Kuala Lumpur, then Sydney. In New Zealand and Australia we had no communication with France and didn't know what was happening there, apart from what we saw in the papers. We saw the headlines 'Civil War in France'. We were completely cut off, like Gauls lost on the other side of the world.

'Jep Lacoste used the situation to motivate us, saying that it was our duty to represent our country with dignity. He actually moved us to tears. He was a fine actor and a very good psychologist. He knew our strengths and weaknesses and we played accordingly. There was a huge amount of cohesion in the group. France had never won in New Zealand before [except in 1955], and then we won against England [sic]. There were no cliques within the group of 18 players. There was a great spirit which gave us confidence and Jep Lacoste was the glue that bound us together. He was well supported by Georges Aillères, the captain, and Henri Marracq, the vice-captain. Our performance ought to have relaunched [French rugby league]. Instead we returned to France in total anonymity.'[xvii]

France team, 1978

Chapter 16

•

Emerging from the Tunnel: 1970-79

IN MAY 1970, Racing Club St Gaudinois, created just twelve years earlier, were contesting their fifth Championship final. They were facing XIII Catalan, the same team they had met the year before, when the Perpignan club had won narrowly, 12-11. A year on, a record crowd of 24,300 paying spectators – at least twice the usual attendance – filled the Toulouse Stadium, many of them sensing that St Gaudens' time had come. They were not disappointed.

It was a magnificent spectacle, a match brimming with commitment and speed of action, which, as André Passamar pointed out in *L'Equipe*, merited all the superlatives; and it was St Gaudens in particular who deserved the accolades. 'Under the impetus of [loose forward] René Zaccariotto, imperious of vision, and of [second row] Roger Biffi, who has joined in reputation the most illustrious rugby league forwards ... the St Gaudens pack scattered the Roussillon forwards, thus creating the ideal conditions for a prodigious collective exhibition in which [centre] Molinier and especially the quick little [winger] Marsolan, dazzlingly fast off the mark, were to play a decisive role.'[i] After building a 12-3 half-time lead which clearly showed the intentions of coach Jep Lacoste's men, St Gaudens got away from the Catalans in the second half with their sweeping movements and greater penetration. In the 32-10 triumph, Biffi scored two tries, one of them over eighty metres; Marracq, Marsolan, Molinier and Raufast also touched down and Pujol kicked seven goals. Against this onslaught, all the Catalans could muster was a try apiece from Michan and Capdouze, who kicked two goals.

With such quality of play, watched by such an unusually large audience, French rugby league appeared in rude health. No wonder Federation secretary Jean Barrès felt able to report, at the annual Congress: 'We are capable, and we have proved it, of attracting the crowds… What organisation, comparable to ours in terms of manpower, can pride itself on attracting 25,000 people for a final?'[ii]

What was not said was that most of the stars singled out for praise had come from rugby union. St Gaudens chairman Fernand Soubie, who was indelibly associated with the club, could rightly point to his Juniors, also champions that year, or that 200 youngsters were playing rugby league at his club. Some, though not all, clubs could boast of similar numbers in the lower age-groups. But rugby union had a much wider spread, an obvious consequence of which was the production of more top-level players.

Not that the traffic was all one way, in spite of rugby union's own strict rules on amateurism. As Louis Bonnery has pointed out, 'Contrary to received ideas, rugby union had always endeavoured to recruit young players from rugby league. The junior internationals Jo Maso, Greffe, Carreras, Pujol, Médus were among those who, as soon as they had been selected for France Juniors at rugby league, went off to swell the ranks of rugby union.'[iii]

One of the first actions of the newly-elected Federation president, René Mauriès, was to complain to rugby union's International Board about the poaching of rugby league players by union clubs. That resulted in a bilateral agreement, if such a word can be used, similar to the one enacted by Gaston Roux in

1947, which had long since been forgotten, as Roux himself had predicted at the time.

In 1972 under the aegis of the Ministry of Youth and Sport, René Mauriès signed a ceasefire with his counterpart, the truculent Albert Ferrasse, in order to curb the taking of one federation's players by the other. This agreement – a kind of non-aggression pact – was known as the protocol and was unique to France. It may have sounded reasonable, if not amicable, but privately and often not so privately, Ferrasse was fuming that Mauriès, who initially had had no response from the FFR regarding his complaints, should go above his head to complain to the International Board, whose stance on amateurism was part of its raison d'être.

Essentially the terms of the protocol were that any player under the age of 21, provided that he was not an international and had not received payment for playing, was free to transfer to the other code. Players over 21 operating in the top two divisions in rugby league and the top three divisions in union were not allowed to switch codes.

A consequence of the protocol was that the French Rugby League, more than ever, paid attention to the development of players. The circumstances which brought about that glorious period of the 1950s, when rugby league was blessed with dozens of high-quality players, a number of whom had arrived from rugby union, no longer pertained. Some well-established clubs did still run successful *écoles de rugby*, each with dozens, even hundreds, of youngsters playing rugby league regularly. But, as was expressed by Paul Tancrède, the Federation official responsible for the junior section, 'leaving aside the traditional *écoles de rugby*, established in the traditional centres, there was no national policy on [development]. There was no thought given to producing the next generation of players. We counted on being able to use wealthy patrons indefinitely to draw from the ranks of the sister organisation.'[iv]

In order to increase the numbers of participants, Mauriès knew that it was vital to make rugby league an attractive sport to watch and play. The international game had a crucial role and its pinnacle was the World Cup.

The commitment of the four nations towards the competition, collectively as well as individually, changed significantly. The 1960 world series was the third such tournament, but France's perceived fragility accounted for an eight-year gap until the fourth. There was no logical pattern to be detected when the 1968 competition was replicated only two years later.

The 1970 version, held in England, was won by Australia, who beat Great Britain, hitherto undefeated, in the final. The group stage had been very even, with only one big score, when Australia thrashed New Zealand 47-11. Each nation other than the hosts recorded one victory, with Australia going through to the final ahead of France on points-scoring difference, thanks to their haul against the Kiwis. The French paid the price for losing by a single point to New Zealand, by 16-15 at Hull, where winger Serge Marsolan scored a try which went down in World Cup history, a length-of-the-field solo effort which started from behind his own line. The St Gaudens winger touched down twice in that match and scored two more in the 17-15 win over Australia at Odsal, with a 40-yard drop goal from Capdouze earning the victory. In between, though, the French were defeated by Great Britain 6-0 at Castleford in a try-less, penalty-ridden match. Matches between Frenchmen and British had often been criticised in the past for bad-tempered rivalry. Not so this time, but the final between Great Britain and Australia simply proved that brawls featured at least as often when these two nations met. Towards the end two players were sent off before a mass punch-up took place, all broadcast on television.

That was not the kind of spectacle René Mauriès had in mind when putting France forward as the hosts of the next edition, held in 1972. In the intervening two years, the France XIII had won just two and drawn one test out of the nine played, including a series defeat by New Zealand in the autumn of 1971. It's worth noting, however, that Great Britain, playing on home soil, had also lost the test series to the Kiwis. But Mauriès was banking on all four countries to provide the kind of entertainment and drama which would show rugby league in its best light. Matches were staged for propaganda purposes at Pau, Grenoble and Lyon, three cities where it was hoped that the game could be resurrected.

To stage the competition in France, and thus promote the sport there, was, said Mauriès, 'an absolute necessity.'[v] The president pointed out that the World Cup, 'born of a French initiative', had not been held in France since 1954. In line with the Federation's policy of expansion, both in terms of increasing the number of players and the places where the game was played, Mauriès wanted to show that French rugby league had ambition. The World Cup, he claimed, 'will confirm in the most concrete manner the dynamic and constructive intentions of the Federation.'[vi] There was, he maintained, another reason for putting on the competition in France, which was that 'for a long time, too long, our foreign partners have imagined that sclerosis had taken hold of FFJXIII [Fédération Française de Jeu à XIII].' The World Cup was a means of persuading the other three countries of France's good faith and effectiveness. Failure was out of the question. 'Assuming our responsibilities, we ask only one thing: that the public understands and appreciates our effort and supports us. We need it. Our future depends on it.'[vii]

In order to allay fears expressed by the other three nations regarding the viability of the project, the Federation, with the backing of the Ministry of Sport, gave guarantees to ensure that it went ahead.

In the event, the public did generally support the initiative, to the extent that the aggregate attendance for the group matches was slightly better than in England two years earlier. The tournament was a financial success. The competition made a rousing start with France's 20-9 victory over New Zealand at Marseille, even if some of the crowd of 20,748 had come to the Vélodrome to watch the Olympique de Marseille football match which followed. However, France's success ended there and, as in 1970, Great Britain faced Australia – who, like the French, had won just one game - in the final, which ended in a 10-all draw. It was a magnificent contest, fit to grace any final, but one which went largely unappreciated. Without the host nation, and played in Lyon, where rugby league had been struggling to re-establish itself, the attendance of 4,231 was much less than the competition deserved. Great Britain had the consolation, not only of Clive Sullivan's 80-yard try, but of claiming the trophy on the basis of winning all three of their group matches.

France was entering a dismal period on the international field, losing twice at home to Australia in 1973, twice to Great Britain in 1974, as well as to Wales and England in a resurrected European championship in 1975. The French were to play ten international matches in the calendar year of 1975, ironically when they fielded one of their weakest squads. The World Cup had been replaced by an ultimately unsatisfactory World Championship, with the five teams – Great Britain was split into England and Wales – facing one another home and away. France began the competition by beating Wales 14-7 at Toulouse – their first win since beating New Zealand in the World Cup of 1972. Apart from a 12-all draw with New Zealand at Marseille, they lost all their remaining matches, including a particularly poor performance in a 48-2 loss to England at Bordeaux, watched by a meagre crowd of 1,581 in a former stronghold of the sport. Australia won the competition, which was a financial failure, and France finished bottom of the table.

After cramming so many matches into a single year, and all to little effect, the International Board left 1976 blank, in preparation for the next World series the following year. It was to be the fifth such contest in nine years. Before the 1977 competition in Australia and New Zealand, France took both Wales and England by surprise to win the Jean Galia Challenge. Captained by Saint-Estève stand-off José Calle, the French beat Wales 13-2 at Toulouse before defeating England 28-15 at Carcassonne. That match saw the flowering of an exceptional talent in centre Jean-Marc Bourret, who, in only his second international, scored two tries and kicked five goals.

As part of their preparations for the 1977 World Series,

France met Papua-New Guinea for the first time. Thrown off their guard by conditions at Port Moresby, the bewildered French were beaten 37-6. They went on to open their campaign at Auckland, where they played Great Britain and slipped to a 23-4 defeat. At Sydney Cricket Ground, France tried in vain to summon the spirit of Puig-Aubert and Elie Brousse, going down 21-9 in a dull game. Returning to Auckland, they matched the Kiwis' four tries, but the home side's four penalty goals swung the game as the French lost 28-20 and ended the tournament without a win to their name.

Outclassed by the Australians at Perpignan and Toulouse on the 1973 Kangaroo tour, the French had no great expectations when the Kangaroos returned in 1978. Bob Fulton's men, with star players in almost every position, from full-back Graham Eadie to loose forward Ray Price, had just beaten Great Britain 2-1, winning the third test at Headingley with ease.

President Mauriès decided that the time was right to make changes. With Louis Bonnery, who had taken over from Antoine Jimenez as national technical director in June of that year, and team director Henri Planel, Mauriès appointed ex-test scrum half Roger Garrigues to coach the France team, aided by Bonnery. 'They are not magicians,' stated an editorial in *Treize-Magazine*.[viii] 'What we would wish for is that they continue the work of their predecessors. In their own way, certainly, but with the firm intention of utilising to the full the abilities of the new wave, which, as we approach the eighties, will hopefully restore the national team's vigour and dynamism.'

Despite those promising young players, it was still a tall order. France had not beaten Australia since the 1970 World Cup, when they won 17-15 at Bradford, and had not won a test series against the Kangaroos since the 1967-68 season. But in this 1978 series, France stepped out without inhibitions at Carcassonne in the first of the two tests. Led by an inspirational captain and loose forward, Lézignan's Michel Maïque, France held Australia to 8-4 at the end of a first half in which José Moya's two penalties had kept them in touch as their opponents twice crossed their line in the shape of Mick Cronin and Graham Eadie. After the break,

France's huge commitment in defence never wavered. Not only that, they scored the only try of the second period when centre Michel Naudo fastened on to a high kick and touched down. Moya added three more penalties and France were triumphant by 13-10. 'France achieves the impossible' ran the heading to André Passamar's match report in *L'Equipe*.

Two weeks later at Toulouse, the Australians were not expected to make the same mistake twice. After Moya and Cronin had exchanged penalties, Australia were first to the try-line when Steve Rogers went over, but France hit back immediately through Naudo. Both tries were converted and the sides were level at 7-7 as they went in at half-time. The second period was as full of suspense as the first. Moya landed another penalty, giving a short-held lead as moments later Kerry Boustead dived over for an unconverted try. On the hour, stand-off Eric Waligunda dropped a goal – now worth one point - to bring the sides level again. The match was heading for a draw when substitute Jean-Marc Bourret stepped up and landed a 77th minute drop goal which won it for France by a single point and wrapped up the series with a second sensational victory.

'The Kangaroo machine was extraordinary,' recalled Maïque, 'but like all machines it could be derailed. It was just a question of finding players capable of putting their bodies on the line. And the front five of Malacamp, Hermet, Castanon, Zalduendo and Daniel showed extraordinary bravery and selflessness.' Behind the forwards, 'Waligunda, Borreil, Bourret and Naudo were all quick and capable of making the difference...'[ix] The Villefranche de Rouergue pair, full back Francis Tranier, showing assurance under the high ball, and centre Christian Laumond also played their part. It was Laumond, supporting Carlos Zalduendo's crucial midfield break from Waligunda's pass, who handed the ball round the back of an opponent to try-scorer Naudo.

'The team was highly motivated,' said Zalduendo. 'Personally, I had never played second row, which requires different qualities from prop, where I had always played, so it was a big gamble. But like everyone else I was so keen to play. I'd prepared all summer, before the training camps. We studied the Australian game closely. We used an in-line defence, which was new then but is standard now. The Australians had developed that, but we didn't try to play like them – we played *à la française*. We had some quality players and a good captain in Maïque. We stuck to our task and surprised them.'[x]

In between the tests, and for good measure, France Espoirs had beaten an Australian team very similar to the test side. At Albi, the Under-24s took full advantage of a massive penalty count in their favour to defeat the Aussies. The goal-kicking full-back Alain Touchagues of XIII Catalan landed ten goals to score all the Espoirs' points in the 20-5 victory.

These victories, claimed a *Treize-Magazine* editorial, gave unambiguous proof that French rugby league was 'ready to come out of the long tunnel in which it had become lost.'[xi] If only subsequent internationals had proved that statement correct. France ended the decade by beating international newcomers Papua-New Guinea twice at home but never beat Australia again.

At club level, the Championship was won by seven different clubs between 1970 and 1979. St Gaudens, Carcassonne and Toulouse each won the trophy twice; St Estève, Albi, Lézignan and XIII Catalan once. No attendance came close to bettering the 24,300 of the 1970 final.

The crowd at the 1977 final, contested by Albi and Carcassonne, was the second biggest of the decade. The venue was switched from Toulouse, where the pitch was made unplayable by the rain, to the home of one of the finalists. On the only occasion between 1951 and 1993, Toulouse did not host the final. It was held instead at the Stadium d'Albi, home town of the Federation president. The match attracted 18,325 fans, who saw the locals take their fifth title as they beat ASC 19-10.

Five years earlier, Carcassonne had played their part in a final described by André Passamar as 'sumptuous'.[xii] Their opponents, St Gaudens, were appearing in their fourth final in a row. Despite two tries from winger Serge Marsolan, St Gaudens went down 21-9 in a match much closer than the score suggests, an 80-metre try from 19-year old ASC centre Bernard Guilhem proving to be the turning-point.

Championship final attendances during the seventies only twice dipped below five figures, when exceptionally small crowds of under 6,000 turned up in 1974 for St Gaudens-Villeneuve and, on a rainy day in 1975, for Toulouse-St Estève. Yet Toulouse's previous appearance in 1973, their clash with Marseille, who were figuring in a Championship final for the last time, produced an attendance of close to 14,000, the same figure as witnessed the Carcassonne-Lézignan encounter in 1976.

Though Cup finals tended to attract fewer spectators than Championship finals, a 10,000 crowd was not rare, as when Carcassonne met St Gaudens at Albert Domec in 1973, or when Carcassonne and XIII Catalan clashed in 1977. When the Catalans reappeared in the following year's final, their third in a row, almost 16,000 fans passed through the turnstiles at Narbonne to see them beat Lézignan 18-7 and claim the Lord Derby trophy for the seventh time.

The upper levels of the domestic championship gave the impression that rugby league was thriving, particularly when, in the 1972-73 season, no fewer than twenty-three teams were divided into two pools for the first phase of the season. This formula, which effectively threw together the first and second divisions during the opening part of the season, had been tried before and was now set to continue for ten seasons. Thus in the autumn of 1972, newcomers Pau and Grenoble, a second team from Toulouse (TOAC, based on workers in the aerospace industry) and a third from the west of the city, Auterive, competed alongside a second Carcassonne team, St Jacques, and a resurrected team from the Bordeaux area, Facture. Villeurbanne's presence signified a return to the top level of the Lyon area, as well as Roanne, reappearing after an absence of almost a decade. All the usual contenders were present, including Marseille and Montpellier. Pamiers joined them the following season, as did Pia. In addition to Avignon, Carpentras and Cavaillon, two more clubs from the south-east, Entraigues and Salon de Provence, joined later. Three teams from the Paris region, Charenton, Châtillon and St Maur, featured at various stages, as Tonneins, La Réole (both situated to the west of Villeneuve) and Cahors (east of Villeneuve) were to do later. Some of these clubs, however, did not last long and disappeared from the upper echelon once a single pool of fourteen clubs was reintroduced in the early eighties.

The two which made the biggest impact both came from the Perpignan area. It could be argued that the arrival of St Estève and Pia did not represent growth, merely a splitting-up of what was already there. But divisions and fusions had characterised Catalan rugby of both codes well before the launch of rugby league in 1934 and continued to do so. Player movement between the codes was also probably more prevalent here than in any other area.

St Estève, a suburb of Perpignan which numbered around 1,500 souls, had had a rugby league club, founded in 1951, which had later switched to union. Rugby league quickly found a new expression when AS St Estève XIII was founded in 1965 with a number of XIII Catalan players in its ranks, and soon made its mark.[xiii] Admitted to the top division in 1967, the club finished second in the 1970-71 league table, four places above the senior Perpignan combination, and, steered by stand-off José Calle, captain of France's World Cup team four years later, went on to win the Championship final 13-4 against St Gaudens. In the following year of 1972 they beat Villeneuve 12-5 to take the Lord Derby trophy at the Gilbert Brutus stadium, a homecoming for the likes of Jo Bonnet and the other former XIII Catalan players.

Three years after St Estève, Pia got their hands on the Cup, their first-ever trophy, when they beat Marseille 9-4, also at Perpignan. Like St Gaudens and the Soubie family, the name of Ambert is forever associated with Pia, the village on the outskirts of Perpignan with a population at the time of just over 2,000. Marc and Philippe Ambert both played in the 1975 final. Their father, Daniel, was the founding chairman of the club in the early sixties. Like St Estève, Pia was regarded as a feeder club for XIII Catalan before joining the upper level of the competition in 1973. Twenty-five clubs, divided into three pools, competed in the top flight in that season.

Through the seventies, despite the vicissitudes of the national side, rugby league in France was making encouraging progress. In 1971 André Passamar made comments which could have applied to the whole decade. 'The movement is becoming reinvigorated,' he wrote. 'The number of players doubles, then triples… The French Rugby League Federation, yesterday convalescing, is now more than in good health. But we should be wary of stating that the movement's condition is a glowing one. For 37 years it has always had to find a way past the same opposition and overcome the same prejudices. It is nonetheless official that it is extending its audience. The reform of the rules and the introduction … of the four-tackle rule [the six-tackle rule was introduced in 1972], have got rid of dismal one-man rugby. They have given back to the game its original vigour and variety.'[xiv]

The insidious influences which, as Passamar states, rugby league had constantly to battle against, should not be underestimated. Those 'same prejudices' did not always emerge from the dark shadows of their natural habitat, but glimpses could be had, as the Avignon winger and, later, Marseille player-coach André Ferren could testify. What he experienced in the 1960s was exactly the same as players in the 1930s who suffered from the cartel set up by rugby union in concert with other federations with the specific purpose of cutting off rugby league players from taking part in other sports.

'Before playing rugby league, I took part in athletics,' said the former 400 metres hurdler who had come third in the France junior championships. 'But when I played rugby league as a junior in 1962, I was banned from athletics for having played as a "professional". So was Jean-Marie Bonal of Carcassonne, a former rugby union international, who was banned [a decade later]. I was stunned. Sport is supposed to be synonymous with freedom.'[xv]

Chapter 17

•

Turbulent Times: 1980-89

THE LIGHT AT the end of the long tunnel, which *Treize-Magazine* appeared to detect in December 1978, was all but snuffed out by two damaging events at the start of the next decade.

The international season of 1980-81 had begun well enough with a narrow 6-5 victory over the touring Kiwis at Perpignan on 23 November. France's points came from two tries scored by centre Jean-Marc Bourret within the first ten minutes. Two weeks later at Toulouse, watched by fewer than 2,000 paying spectators, New Zealand got their revenge, winning 11-3. Again France's points came from a try by Bourret, though he admitted he had not been at his best.[i] An outstanding talent who had joined Pia from XIII Catalan, Bourret was not fully fit for the test, but might also have had other things on his mind. Four days after the second test, it was announced that he had sensationally signed to play rugby union with the Perpignan club, USAP. The news caused uproar. Some XIII Catalan supporters had not forgiven him for going off to Pia. Signing for *la maison d'en face*[ii] was inexcusable.

One of Bourret's former team-mates called him 'a

mercenary'.[iii] Most refused to judge him, but found it hard to understand why he would want to leave in mid-season. Louis Bonnery, the national technical director and co-coach of the France team, said that the Pia star had 'deserted his club and his Federation.'[iv]

Bourret's departure appeared all the more shocking because a couple of months earlier, on 25 September, the two Federation presidents, René Mauriès and Albert Ferrasse, had agreed to maintain the essential points of the protocol. The two men had met at Cordes, the medieval hilltop village north of Albi, known for its steep cobbled streets and picturesque views. There was nothing quaint, however, about *les accords de Cordes,* which continued to restrict the movement of players between the two codes. It's hard to imagine the meeting as especially cordial. By mid-November there was outright hostility. 'If treizistes want war, they can have it,' thundered Ferrasse from distant South Africa, where the France XV had been helping the Springboks emerge from international quarantine and losing 37-15. The quinziste president accused his treiziste counterpart of flouting his commitment to the protocol agreement and threatened to give free rein to union clubs to sign whoever they wanted from rugby league if Mauriès did not make his own clubs toe the line.[v]

Ferrasse was alluding principally to the junior international full-back Serge Costals, who had been signed by St Estève from USAP. But Ferrasse did not reveal the intransigence within his own federation which led to Costals turning to rugby league, a sport he had never played before. Costals wanted to leave USAP and join Thuir rugby union club, a move which his chairman strongly opposed. The FFR backed USAP and handed Costals what was known as a *licence rouge,* meaning that he would not be able to play for another club for two years.[vi] Which is where St Estève, who at the same time lost winger Gilbert Dutren to the same club, stepped in.

Nevertheless, rugby league once again became the focus of Ferrasse's ire. 'We will begin hostilities on December 7, immediately after my re-election, if, in the meantime, the treizistes

Below: Centre Michel Molinier, who, with winger Serge Marsolan, formed a prolific partnership for St Gaudens and France in the late sixties and early seventies

Left: Loose forward Jean-Pierre Clar, selector Puig-Aubert and technical director Jean Cabrol at half-time in a test match at Toulouse

Left: France World Cup squad, Sydney, 1968. The French reached the final but lost to Australia. Back row: Garrigues, Serrano, Clar, De Nadaï, Mazard, Ferren, Alesina, Sabatié; Middle row: Pellerin, J Gruppi, Molinier, Cros, Capdouze, Lecompte, Frattini, Bégou, Ledru; Front row: Estirac (physio), Marracq (vice-capt), Soubie (co-manager), Guiraud (co-manager), Forges (co-manager), Aillères (capt), Lacoste (coach)

Above: The France team which followed up their success in the first test against the 1978 Kangaroos by winning the second at Toulouse by 11-10. Back row: Maïque, Hermet, Zalduendo, Castanon, Malacamp, Daniel, Dr Prévot; Front row: Garrigues (coach), Moya, Naudo, Waligunda, Tranier, Castel, Laumond, Borreil. Missing: subs Bourret, Roosebrouck

Left: France second rower and man of the match Carlos Zalduendo, future Toulouse chairman and president of the Federation, is tackled in the second test against Australia at Toulouse

Right: Loose forward Michel Maïque, captain of the 1978 France team and Lézignan's Championship-winning side of the same year

Left: France and Pia centre Jean-Marc Bourret, here playing for XIII Catalan against Lézignan, created a storm of protest when he signed for the Perpignan rugby union club in December 1980

Left: Villeneuve loose forward Joël Roosebrouck, France's captain on the 1981 tour of Australia

Right: Australian forward Tas Baitieri, player-coach of Paris-Châtillon before becoming France coach in 1985 at the age of 28. He was later seconded by the ARL to act as international envoy to France and was much involved in the creation and administration of Paris Saint-Germain

Right: St Gaudens and France stand-off Gilles Dumas, who went on to coach his home town club as well as Toulouse and France, tackles Great Britain's Shaun Edwards in a 26-10 defeat in January 1989

Inset: Dumas' half-back partner, Avignon and France scrum-half Patrick Entat, who signed for Hull in 1990

Above: The France team which upset Great Britain at Headingley on 7 April 1990, winning 25-18 and the two-match series. Back row: Verdaguer, Jorda, Marquet, Divet, Cabestany, Moliner, Fraisse, Rabot, Buttignol, Valéro, Tisseyre, Grèze, Bonnery; Front: Sokolow, Delaunay, Entat, Dumas, Ratier, Biénès, Pons, Lopez, Frison

Left: The joy of France coach Jacques Jorda as he sees his team beat Great Britain at Headingley

Right: Jacques Fouroux, who had launched his France Rugby League summer tournament before establishing the Paris Saint-Germain team in Super League, meets Bernard Guasch, former XIII Catalan player and instigator of Union Treiziste Catalane, which became the Catalan Dragons in Super League

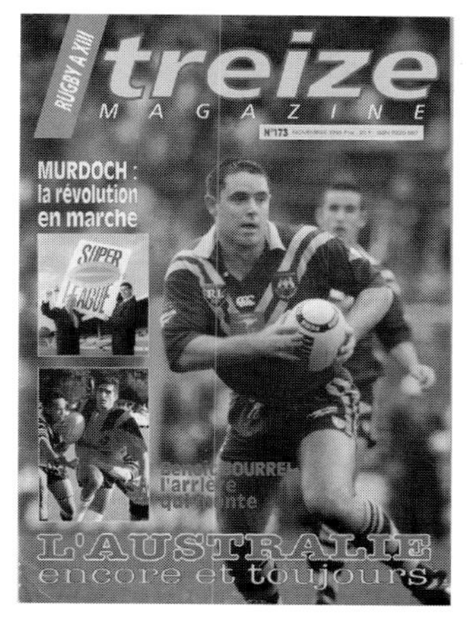

Left: Treize magazine gets excited by the potential of a new landscape for international rugby league

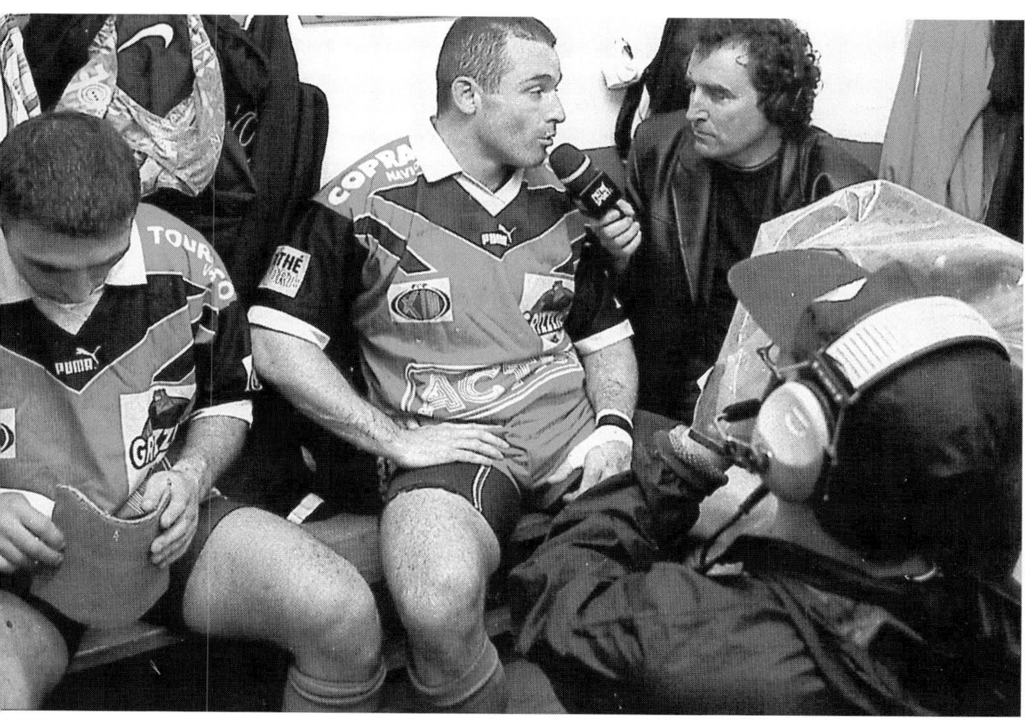

Above: Former international half-back Hervé Guiraud, ex-chairman of Limoux and secretary of the Federation, speaks to players in the Limoux changing room in his other role as pitchside interviewer for Pathé Sport

Right: Paris Saint-Germain centre and captain Pierre Chamorin in action against Workington in the club's first Super League season at the Charléty Stadium

Below: A jubilant 1996 cover of *Treize* magazine

Above: The first Paris Saint-Germain team which defeated Sheffield Eagles in Super League's opening match on 29 March 1996 in the French capital. Back row: Pech, Sands, Chamorin (capt), Cabestany, Kacala, Adams, Torreilles; Front: Brown, Banquet, Entat, Piskunov, Lucchese, Cervello

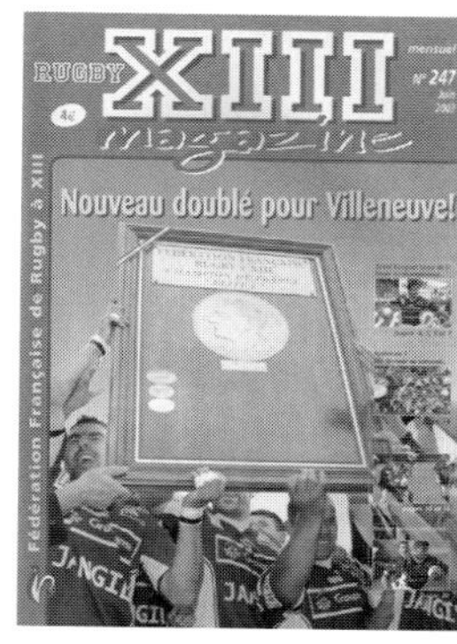

Left: Full-back Fred Banquet in the 2003 Championship final, in which Villeneuve beat St Gaudens 31-18 at Narbonne. Banquet also represented his home town club of Carcassonne, Paris Saint-Germain and three English clubs

Above: The Catalan Dragons, Challenge Cup finalists in 2007, their second year in Super League. Back row: Howe (conditioner), Croker, Casty, Ferriol, Fellous, Fakir, Raguin, Griffi, Touxagas, Chan, Munoz (director of rugby); Middle row: Pignol (physio), A Bentley, Berthezène, Khattabi, Duport, Mounis, Mogg, K Bentley, L Teixido, Gossard, Roques (director); Front row: McFadden (asst coach), Wilson, Greenshields, Pelo, Guisset, Potter (coach), Stacey Jones (*pictured left*), McGuire, Bosc, Murphy, Frayssinous (asst coach)

Left and below: Benjamin Garcia scores a try against Warrington as the Catalan Dragons make history in becoming the first French winners of the Challenge Cup, at Wembley on 25 August 2018

Below: Toulouse Olympique competed in the British Championship in 2017 and 2018, taking part in the Middle 8 Qualifiers in 2018. Back row: A Bentley, Maurel, Mika, Rapira, Puech, Marion, Hepi, Bouzinac; Middle row: Polesel (physio), Innes (conditioner), White (welfare), Barthau, Marguerite, Ader, Canet, Sangaré, Marcon, Pettybourne, Toustou (asst coach), Ferrié (medical), Devey (medical); Front row: Kriouache, Robin, Planas (capt), Sarrazain (chairman), Houlès (coach), Garcia (general manager), Ford, Curran, Kheirallah. Missing: Boyer. (*Dominique Viet*)

do not return to legality,' declared the FFR president.[vii] Ferrasse was duly re-elected on Saturday, 6 December and was as good as his word. The France XIII's biggest star was snared by the quinzistes the following Wednesday afternoon.[viii] Ferrasse strained credibility by insisting that he was unaware of what sport Bourret had been playing in recent years, maintaining that he was now simply returning to the club he had once played with as a teenager.

'I'd been contacted before the tests against the Kiwis,' said Bourret. 'It was during the summer, in June or July, but they [USAP] didn't have the consent of the Federation [XV]. They were waiting for the green light.

'I'd played rugby union up to the age of thirteen or fourteen. Then Michel Naudo went from USAP to XIII Catalan *école de rugby* and I went with him.'[ix]

Though the signing-on fee was never divulged, it was assumed that it was substantial. But Bourret denied that supposition. 'It was not huge at all,' he laughed. 'In the France [rugby league] team we were not really professionals, unlike the English, Australians or Kiwis. When I went to Pia, they made an effort to pay me more or less what I was getting at XIII Catalan, around 500 francs [£50] a month. At USAP I got a bit more than in rugby league, but in my working life it was a big help. When I set up as an insurance agent, I was put in touch with companies through the club. That's how it works, and it secured my future.

'The big problem in rugby league was that it was always the same teams you played against in the final stages. For four or five seasons it became a bit monotonous. That was my main reason for leaving. I have always worked on the principle of being true to myself.'[x]

Bourret thus made the move, short in distance but long in consequence, to the Aimé Giral stadium. His transfer created fury among treizistes, who were, he says, 'at least as numerous as quinzistes' in Perpignan. Once more the town was divided, just as in French rugby league's earliest days.

'For my first match at Avignon, the team bus was escorted by two police motorbikes all along the motorway. They thought people might try and stop me playing. There were death threats and I had to move out to my parents-in-law [former XIII Catalan scrum-half Irénée Carrère and his wife].'

The star threequarter was also given the added protection of a minder in the imposing shape of USAP's international forward Jean-François Imbernon, who lived in the same village of Néfiach. They travelled to Aimé-Giral together in a rather cramped police Renault 4L.

Bourret's transfer came to the attention of the Rugby Football League. Taking action reminiscent of their condemnation of the Bergougnan affair more than three decades earlier, the RFL publicised the fact that the Pia centre had been paid to represent the France rugby league team. Just as his predecessor, Bill Fallowfield, had done in 1947, RFL secretary-general David Oxley took up the case with the RFU, writing to his opposite number to say that Bourret had played rugby league professionally for club and country and had allegedly accepted money to sign for a French rugby union club. The matter was discussed at rugby union's International Board meeting in Cardiff on Friday, 13 March. Given the code's supposedly amateur status, as well as the terms of the protocol, which banned the movement of internationals from one code to the other, it appeared unlikely that the former France and Pia centre could ever be permitted to play union. As the news spread across the rugby-playing world, Wigan and newly-created Fulham both showed interest in signing the star player, but he remained in Perpignan, suspended until the end of the season.

As they were entitled to do under the protocol, and after the intervention of the Ministry of Sport, the two presidents of the rival codes, Jean-Paul Verdaguer (who had since stepped into Mauriès' shoes) and Ferrasse, eventually came to an agreement allowing Bourret's transfer to go ahead. The centre had represented France eleven times and, at the age of 23, looked to have a long and glittering international career ahead of him. He would now be banned from representing his country at rugby union. Costals, who ended the season as second-highest points-scorer, went on to play for the France XIII once.

As in 1947-48, the major transgression was accompanied by numerous other infringements, though less sensational. Hervé Girette has pointed out that, when Bourret eventually appeared in a USAP jersey at the end of summer 1981, alongside him in the Perpignan XV were four players who would switch to rugby league, two with St Estève, one with Pia and one with Carcassonne. A year later, Guy Spanghero, the youngest of the well-known union-playing brothers, moved from US Carcassonne XV to Limoux XIII, after international winger Jean-Marc Gonzalez had headed in the opposite direction.[xi] And so, just as Gaston Roux had foreseen when drawing up the first protocol in 1947, the agreement would prove impossible to enforce.

Amid the controversy, and despite losing an outstanding player, the France team ended the 1980-81 season on a high note. After drawing the two-match series against New Zealand, the French beat Wales 23-5 at Narbonne, before meeting England at Headingley to decide the European championship. At 3,229, the crowd was one of the lowest seen at the ground for an international match, but France held up well to record a 5-1 victory. A José Moya penalty and the only try of the match, scored by Hervé Guiraud, with only a George Fairbairn drop goal in reply, gave France the title. Led by Villeneuve loose forward Joël Roosebrouck, France posted their first win against England on English soil since 1949 (although they had beaten Great Britain more recently, at Wigan in 1967). England coach Johnny Whiteley, the former test loose forward, singled out the France captain for praise: 'In Roosebrouck they have a world-class forward and leader,' he offered, adding, 'he is a well-built athlete, a player who allies weight and speed to his skills.'[xii] French referee Guy Cattaneo came in for strong criticism, however, for awarding France eleven penalties to England's two in the first half and allowing half-back Guiraud to feed the scrum to his own forwards' advantage. David Oxley took the unusual step of speaking to the referee at half-time, all of which threw the idea of having an exchange of referees (French referee in England, English referee in France) into question, particularly since in the previous season Billy Thompson had caused French protests when refusing a late try which would have swung the match in their favour.

All of that seemed part of the scenario of Anglo-French encounters. Far more harmful to the rugby league movement in France was what took place at the end of that 1980-81 season.

Two founder clubs, Villeneuve, the title-holders, who had finished fourth in the league, and XIII Catalan, second behind Pia, were due to meet in the Championship final for the first time. The weekend before, the Catalans had played Tonneins at Albi in a Cup semi-final littered with incidents. The following Tuesday, two XIII Catalan players, Jean-Jacques Cologni and Bernard Guasch, were dealt with by the disciplinary committee, following an alleged assault on a touch judge. Guasch maintained that a case of mistaken identity was at the root of the incident.[xiii] The disciplinary put off making a decision until the Thursday, so that further information could be given. Cologni and Guasch were then suspended, and would miss the Championship final. Furious, the XIII Catalan directors, who wanted the suspensions to apply to the following week's Cup final, threatened to pull their team out of the match. After two days of wrangling, and with the apparent assent of Villeneuve chairman Dr François Mourgues, mindful of the need for a share of the receipts,[xiv] the Federation backed down and reinstated the two players at 8.30 on the Saturday evening before the match. 'Blackmail' was the word on everyone's lips, from television presenters to the Federation's vice-president.[xv]

Interestingly, the threat issued by the Catalans had had a precedent in rugby union. The day before the rugby union Championship final of 1943, the Agen club told the FFR president that if one of their players, who had been suspended in the southern zone final, was not reinstated, they would boycott the final. But this was wartime in occupied France and the redoubtable Colonel Pascot issued a threat of his own to ensure that Agen fell back into line, which they did, and the final went ahead as planned.[xvi]

Sunday, 17 May 1981 at the Stadium de Toulouse. Some of

the players had not known whether the match was on or off until eleven o'clock on the Saturday evening, others as late as the Sunday morning.[xvii] Fans were even more in the dark; consequently the crowd numbered just 6,733 paying spectators.

The juniors of the same two clubs played their own Championship final as a curtain-raiser to the main event, XIII Catalan winning 31-5. 'The Perpignan juniors were better perhaps,' said Villeneuve juniors coach Jacques Balleroy. '[But] if we handed them the trophy, there was a reason for it .... In the first quarter of an hour it was like Dien Bien Phu,' he claimed.[xviii]

A delayed start to the main event made the atmosphere in the stadium even more tense. As a protest against the lifting of the sanctions against the Catalans and as a general statement about the threats regularly suffered by match officials, referee Cattaneo and his two assistants stood silently in the tunnel for several minutes. 'We don't feel protected,' he explained. 'Every Sunday referees are abused and the sanctions are not severe enough. We are protesting against the reinstatement of the Catalans.'[xix]

The two teams waited in the tunnel, some players provoking others verbally, before deciding to go out on to the pitch, with the referee following some minutes later. 'There was a climate of violence,' said Villeneuve stand-off Patrick Pedrazzani.[xx]

On seeing that the two Catalan players had been allowed to play (Cologni was named in the starting line-up, Guasch on the bench), Villeneuve supporters vented their anger on the Federation president. René Mauriès, after suffering insults and being pelted with bottles and cans, hot-footed it indignantly out of the stadium. A week earlier he had threatened to resign over a separate issue. This time it was for real.

When the match finally started, late tackles, high tackles came thick and fast. Villeneuve winger Pascal Laroche, kicking ahead, was taken out after the ball had gone. Two passes earlier, in the same sequence, full-back Martial Vrech was flattened off the ball. Daniel Gilbert kicked the penalty goal from 25 yards out and close to touch for a 2-0 lead. Which, after four minutes' play, is where the score remained. Soon after the restart, what the television cameras showed was Villeneuve's captain, Didier Hermet, tackling Catalan stand-off Jean-Jacques Vila waist-high from behind after Vila had already passed the ball. The tackle was little more than a shove, both players remaining on their feet. Hermet was in turn felled from behind by a blow from Catalan second rower Alain Perez. With the touch judge on the field, waving his flag above Hermet's prone body, Villeneuve loose forward Joël Roosebrouck was surrounded by several Catalans, leading to a full-scale brawl involving virtually all the players. Fists flew, boots went in. It was a street fight transferred to the pitch. Normally irreproachable players weighed in. Laroche, isolated from the rest, was being kicked on the ground. Coach Raymond Gruppi dragged him by his ankles to the touchline and was later heard to say 'I think I saved his life.'[xxi] Gruppi had seen enough and told his players to leave the field. The Villeneuve team trooped off, leaving the arena to the Catalans.

Heated exchanges between officials took place in the dressing-room area. With Mauriès gone, it was left to vice-president Jean-Paul Verdaguer to try to calm the situation and especially to bring Villeneuve back on to the field. 'I tried everything,' said Verdaguer, 'but without success.' The Villeneuve players would not go back on. 'There was real danger,' said Pedrazzani. Their chairman Dr Mourgues refused all attempts to persuade him to call his team back into action. 'Can you be serious? Haven't you seen what went on out there?' he was quoted as saying.[xxii] 'Rugby is not systematic violence.'[xxiii]

José Guasch, XIII Catalan's director of rugby and father of Bernard, countered: 'We fell into a trap. I am convinced that Villeneuve's leaving the field was premeditated well before the match. The public have been robbed and XIII Catalan, who were prepared to continue playing, are not responsible.'[xxiv]

'[What happened] was a result of all the tension before the match,' said XIII Catalan loose forward Guy Laforgue, 'but there have always been brawls, in both league and union.'[xxv]

But those other fights did not happen in a Championship

final abandoned after a few minutes in full view of the cameras. The violent scenes were condemned in the press, on radio and on television. One television journalist talked of the 'veritable blackmail' which had gone on in the days leading up to the final, and said that 'the players were pumped up to such an extent that the match could not have played out any other way.'[xxvi]

'Rarely in France have we seen such a brawl on a sports field,' it was also reported. 'Millions of viewers discovered a deplorable, repulsive sporting reality.'[xxvii]

The scenes inside the stadium dealt a severe blow to rugby league's reputation, as Verdaguer acknowledged in a television interview the next day. 'Yesterday was a black day for rugby league,' he said. 'I am truly in despair. I beg all those who love rugby league and sport in general to quickly forget this totally lamentable spectacle.'[xxviii]

Verdaguer's plea was in vain. The images of those two minutes of mayhem were shown far and wide. People who had hitherto little knowledge of rugby league now associated the game with uncontrolled violence. Rugby league's detractors – and they were many – exploited the scenes to paint a lasting negative picture of the game. Whenever a televised discussion about violence in sport took place – it was a hot topic with remarkable longevity – those clips reappeared. The harm done to a sport struggling for positive recognition could not have been greater.

The irony was, as Bernard Guasch later said, 'There were so many good players at that time, it would have made an exceptional final.'[xxix]

Exceptional it was, but in a different sense. 'A sport once glowing with health is now at death's door,' announced an opinion piece in *Midi-Olympique*.[xxx]

In *L'Equipe*, André Passamar, clearly sickened by the events and their significance for the game, wrote: 'Yesterday, in the Stadium, we felt ashamed. Ashamed of continuing, despite all the obstacles, to love the game of rugby league. Ashamed of what has been done to it and the eight thousand or so people who travelled to take part in a celebration and who were not even offered a semblance of a match.' Referring to the 'imbecilic' brawling, he described the final as 'the height of disgrace, scandal and, ultimately, of derision and ridicule.'[xxxi]

Nor was the news of the incident restricted to France. Under the headline 'Brawl threatens future', the *Yorkshire Post*, not known for hysterical reporting, stated: 'French rugby league was fighting for its life after an ugly mass brawl which ended the championship final in Toulouse on Sunday less than five minutes after the game started.'[xxxii] Equally sober, *The Times* carried the same report, adding that the Federation's acting president had been summoned by the Sports Ministry 'to give explanations and discuss the future of the game in France.'[xxxiii]

It was as serious as that. Passamar put the 'sad and debilitating incidents' into context. 'Moribund nine years ago, rugby league, propelled by a minor miracle of willpower and dynamism, had managed to turn around a situation which appeared for a long time irretrievably compromised.... Can we [now] imagine, even for a moment, that it will retain, in the opinion of the public, an ounce of respectability and esteem?'[xxxiv]

If the Federation had been responsible, in recent times, for reviving rugby league's fortunes, the blame for the present disaster was now also laid at the door of the governing body and its president, who was eight months into his third term of office. The *Midi-Olympique* match report concluded: 'The lack of firmness on the part of the Federation these past years has resulted in an event without precedent.'[xxxv]

As acting president initially, Verdaguer, a civil servant responsible for the computer systems of the regional Family Allowances unit, remained at the head of the governing body for three years until June 1984. His first task was to steady the Federation's boat, battered by one storm after another and on the point of capsizing.

After the catastrophe of the Championship final, the Federation took another unprecedented step by cancelling the Cup final, scheduled for a week later. In what would have been a reprise of the 1980 final, XIII Catalan had been due to defend their title against Carcassonne. The ASC had no opportunity to avenge that defeat and were furious, calling the decision 'a veritable scandal'.[xxxvi] The notion of sanctioning the Catalans was accepted, but Carcassonne saw themselves as the innocent victims.

The Federation drew up a full list of punishments for the transgressors. Both teams were banned from taking part in the Cup the following season, though it was regarded as not practicable to bar them from the Championship final, should they qualify. Several Catalan players and officials were suspended. The Villeneuve chairman and coach were also censured. For their part in the semi-final against Tonneins, it was proposed that Guasch be suspended for a year and Cologni sine die. The club, of course, appealed. Eventually, after much close-season haggling, most of the sanctions were either lifted or reduced.[xxxvii] The decision to bar Villeneuve and XIII Catalan from contesting the Lord Derby trophy in 1981-82 stood, but Guasch was back in action at the start of the season. Cologni was made to wait until February before being given back his licence.

It is interesting to note, incidentally, how many of the players involved in that final went on to play major roles in rugby league's future. On the XIII Catalan side, Bernard Guasch became chairman of Union Treiziste Catalane, which became the Catalan Dragons in Super League; Ivan Grésèque was later appointed France coach and Guy Laforgue France team director. Among the Villeneuve team, Carlos Zalduendo became chairman of Toulouse and then president of the Federation; Patrick Pedrazzani was appointed National Technical Director, Pascal Laroche became vice-president of the Federation and Jean-Pierre Sagnette took on the role of chairman of the Elite League and co-chairman of Villeneuve.

Just nine days after the final, the France team were due to set off on their first tour down under for seventeen years. Verdaguer had to give assurances to the Sports Minister that the tour of Australia, New Zealand and Papua-New Guinea would go ahead as planned. The tour party itself was also the centre of controversy. A week before the unfinished final, Mauriès had gone over the heads of the selectors and asked full-back Alain Touchagues, a prolific goal-kicker who, however, had not played all season, to join the tour squad. Tour captain Joël Roosebrouck and vice-captain Ivan Grésèque both condemned the selection and asked what the president was trying to do in undermining the cohesiveness of the squad and coaches. Coach Roger Garrigues threatened to resign, which drew a response from former France captain Didier Hermet, speaking for the tour squad: 'Roger has done so much for this team,' he said. 'If he doesn't go [on tour], I'll stay in Villeneuve.'[xxxviii] Heavily criticised for his meddling, Mauriès in turn threatened to step down, but was persuaded by other Federation committee members to stay. After that one fateful week, though, his tenure was over.

Garrigues withdrew his threat. Touchagues was left behind. Catalans (Guy Delaunay, Ivan Grésèque, Guy Laforgue, Jean-Jacques Vila) and Villeneuvois (Max Chantal, Philippe Fourquet, Didier Hermet, Christian Macalli, Joël Roosebrouck, Carlos Zalduendo) were obliged to put any lingering differences from the aborted final behind them.

And they did, but on the first leg of the tour, in New Zealand, they came up against an outstanding crop of Kiwis, including James Leuluai, Gary Prohm, Dane O'Hara, Graeme West, Shane Varley, Fred Ah Kuoi, Mark Graham, Kevin Tamati, Howie Tamati and Mark Broadhurst, almost all of whom were to make a reputation in England. France lost both tests, the first by 26-3, the second by 25-2.

In Australia, where they played just six matches, as opposed to 25 in 1964, France faced a team which would develop into the all-conquering Kangaroos of 1982 and beyond. The Aussies were keen to make up for the series loss of 1978, an upset they had not been prepared for. There were no slip-ups this time. Steve Rogers and Mick Cronin in the centres, Wally Lewis and Steve Mortimer at half-back, with Ray Price, Les Boyd and Craig Young in the forwards, would see to that. Watched by a crowd of 16,277 at the SCG – a far cry from the enormous attendances of 1951, 1955 and 1960 - Mortimer scored in the first minute and

Australia were 30-0 up at half-time. They eased off in the second period, when winger Hugues Ratier went over for France's only try, and satisfied themselves with a 43-3 scoreline. For the second and last test at Brisbane, where 14,000 attended, France welcomed back captain Joël Roosebrouck from injury and provided sterner opposition before going down 17-2. France managed just one win on the Australian leg, beating North Queensland 25-15 at Townsville. They ended the tour by drawing 13-all with PNG at Port Moresby.

Once back home, the XIII Catalan players found their future still in doubt. The club remained mired in discussion with the Federation. Perpignan was more divided than ever. Not only were there three elite clubs in the area, but for a few anxious days the senior club split into two as a result of a breakdown of negotiations. The situation became increasingly complicated as the XIII Catalan committee which had been elected by members was not recognised by the Federation, while a second administration, approved by the governing body, was led by a former chairman of rivals St Estève. A number of players found themselves preparing for the new season by training under the auspices of both committees, each of which had appointed its own coach.[xxxix] For the first time ever, the competition started without the name of XIII Catalan appearing on the fixture list. Finally, many strong words later, a kind of peace prevailed and the Catalans entered the fray on the fifth weekend. With Francis Mas as coach, XIII Catalan set about making up for lost time – to such effect that they won the Championship by beating neighbours St Estève 21-8 in the final.

The international season of 1981-82, in which France played just two tests against Great Britain, started badly with a tame display in the 37-0 defeat at Hull. Two weeks later at Marseille, in front of a 6,500 crowd and national television cameras – proving, incidentally, that the abandoned final did not put paid to TV coverage – the French proved that they were still capable of springing surprises. 'On a warm, sunny day there were even flashes of the champagne rugby which used to be the hallmark of their play,' noted the *Yorkshire Post* reporter.[xl] Roosebrouck carved out openings from loose forward, lively stand-off Michel Laville, also of Villeneuve, supplied some decisive passes and Tonneins winger Patrick Solal, who was to become the first French player to sign for a British club when he joined Hull, capitalised with two tries. France won 19-2, their biggest winning margin against Great Britain since test status was awarded in 1957.

It was no surprise that the 1982 Kangaroos should prove as invincible in France as they had been in Britain, though the test match scores of 15-4 at Avignon and 23-9 at Narbonne were more subdued than on that first, dazzling leg. But France's victories over the other three major nations were becoming rarer. Four defeats in a row by Great Britain prefaced the fiftieth anniversary of the launch of French rugby league.

To mark the occasion, a celebration match was organised between 'Oceania' (Australia, New Zealand, PNG) and Europe. The southern hemisphere authorities had sent some of their very best players – among them Wally Lewis, Mal Meninga, Ray Price, Wayne Pearce, Mark Graham and Hugh McGahan. The British seemed less enthusiastic, preoccupied as they were with the penultimate weekend of their domestic championship. It turned out to be not so much a celebration as an indictment. The venue of La Cipale, on the outskirts of Paris, had been chosen because it was closest to both Stade Pershing, the venue for the 1933 exhibition game, and Stade Buffalo, which hosted France's pre-war international matches. But La Cipale proved unsuitable, the pitch bare of grass, the facilities antiquated. A sparse crowd of fewer than 2,000 spectators took the trouble to turn up, providing a sorry background for the television cameras. The Oceania team, vastly superior, was not impressed either, and cantered to a 54-4 victory.

But in one corner of French rugby league they were happy. In the late seventies, XIII Catalan had appeared in two Championship finals, winning one, and had won the Lord Derby trophy in 1976, 1978 and 1980. They were not deflected from their private path of glory by the events of 1981. The Perpignan club had assembled a talented and dangerous team, most of whom had come through its own junior ranks. Scrum-half Ivan Grésèque, loose forward Guy Laforgue and his twin brother Francis in the centre, second row Jean-Jacques Cologni, full back Serge Pallarès, centre Guy Delaunay and wingers Jean-Pierre Siré and Patrick Nauroy were some of the key players coached successively by Francis Mas, Pierre Zamora and Yvon Gourbal. Together they dominated the Championship, winning it not only in 1982, the year they had to hastily regroup, but in the next three seasons as well.

In the last of those four finals, in 1985, XIII Catalan defeated a relative newcomer to the top level, US Le Pontet, who would provide a serious challenge to the Perpignan club up to the end of the decade. Le Pontet, on the northern outskirts of Avignon, had been one of the first clubs in Provence to take to rugby league, but did not reach the elite division until the 1980-81 season. The rise took place under the chairmanship of Alain Cortade, a Catalan, who became mayor of Le Pontet. In this prosperous industrial area, he was well placed to bring money into the club, which produced some of its own players but made some shrewd signings as well, such as international forwards Christian Macalli, Thierry Bernabé, Marc Palanques and José Giné. Between 1985 and 1989, Le Pontet appeared in every Championship final, the first four against XIII Catalan, and won twice. In the Cup they were finalists three times and twice took the Lord Derby trophy, beating St Estève on both occasions. They completed the Cup and Championship double in 1986 and 1988. Their impact was brilliant but brief. Proving that it wasn't only the Catalans who could shake the Federation to its core, Le Pontet's departure was even more dramatic than their arrival.

The decade ended as it had started, with a damagingly controversial Championship final. In the 1989 version, in which Le Pontet faced St Estève at Narbonne, play was held up midway through the second half, after St Estève centre Guy Delaunay scored from what looked like a forward pass. (The chairman of the Federation's refereeing committee later explained that the pass had initially gone backwards, then hit the ground and was blown forward by the wind, so that the decision to award the try was correct.) But the Le Pontet players, who, in the first half, had seen their winger Marcel Criottier refused a try for offside, on the intervention of a touch judge, protested violently to referee Francis Desplats, who was confronted and jostled. Team captain Marc Palanques was sent off, allegedly for assaulting the referee, but refused to leave the field. Under threat from several players, the referee headed for the changing-room instead. Just as he had done eight years earlier, Federation president Jean-Paul Verdaguer was obliged to deal with the crisis. After some ten minutes, he persuaded the referee to continue. Le Pontet, champions the previous season and league leaders, stronger on paper than their opponents, ended up losing 23-4 to a St Estève side that played better as a team and kept their heads. At the end, the defeated Le Pontet went off still complaining and threatening the referee. A week later they also lost in the final of the Lord Derby trophy, beaten 12-11 by Avignon.

The Federation's disciplinary committee handed Palanques a long suspension, though he was allowed to resume playing part-way through the following season. Two other players also received suspensions for their part in the chaos. Three directors, including Cortade, resigned before the Federation was able to pass judgement on them. The club as a whole was punished with fines amounting to 25,000 francs. But US Le Pontet refused to accept the sanction, vowed to have nothing more to do with rugby league and promptly switched to rugby union.[xli] It was an infantile and reprehensible move, though a number of players, including internationals Palanques, Bernabé and David Fraisse, remained in rugby league, signing for Carcassonne. As a footnote, almost thirty years later, Palanques would team up with St Estève's Mathieu Khedimi as the Federation's president and vice-president respectively.

Verdaguer told the Federation's management committee that 'the irresponsibility of the officials of Le Pontet almost led to

France's exclusion from the International Board when they refused to honour an agreement to play an international club match.'[xlii] He called their failing 'unforgivable'. St Estève, thinking their season had ended and with several players missing, stepped in to play the European Club Championship match against Widnes at distant Arles and were hammered 60-6.

In the middle of his second spell as president, Verdaguer had now twice been forced to deal with an explosive situation. After taking over from René Mauriès in 1981, continuing until 1984, he had returned to office in 1987 when Jacques Soppelsa was forced out amid another crisis, this time financial. Soppelsa had the most impressive academic background of any Federation president. Dean of the University of Paris 1, often referred to as the Sorbonne, he also showed a combative spirit in fighting to restore the name of *rugby à treize* instead of the nondescript label of *jeu à treize* which it had been required to use for the previous forty years. The principle of reverting to *rugby à treize* had first been taken up in 1968 and was proposed again at the Federation's AGM of 1985 at the Mediterranean resort of La Grande Motte.

'[For] forty years ... rugby league has been saddled with a derisory name which has had no other motive for its existence than the desire of Rugby Union Federation officials to eliminate a potentially rival sport,' stated the mouthpiece of the movement, Jean-Pierre Lefevre, chairman of Les Amis du Treize.

'... It is undeniable that a pejorative name for a sport like rugby league could only make its development more difficult. It is the logical and undeniable result of the injustice.'[xliii]

At the congress at La Grande Motte, delegates voted for the return to the original name, as used in all other parts of the rugby league-playing world. The decision outraged the French Rugby Union Federation and its president Albert Ferrasse, who vehemently attacked the move, claiming that people would be 'confused' if there were two sports called rugby.

Consequently the battle to regain the name of *rugby à treize*, necessary as it might seem, proved long and costly. At first the Minister of Sport, accepting the quinzistes' argument, asked the

Federation to revert to its previous title of Fédération Française de Jeu à XIII. But Soppelsa refused to back down. The Rugby Union Federation went to the High Court in Paris to protect what it regarded as its exclusive right. Soppelsa fired an angry response. 'The French Rugby Union Federation has sufficiently important means,' he argued, 'to exert unacceptable pressure on the public authorities without any respect for the general principles of French law.'[xliv]

The matter was batted back and forth between the two federations, the Ministry and the courts. In 1987 it was decided by the High Court that the term 'rugby' was a generic one and that the Rugby Union Federation should not have a monopoly of it. In 1991 the quinzistes took the case to the Court of Appeal, which finally found that they had no case. In 1994 the French Rugby League Federation was back on its original footing, but the affair, which had started with Soppelsa, continued through the presidencies of Jean-Paul Verdaguer in his second period of office, Gilbert Dautant and Jean-Paul Ferré. The *cause célèbre* had been a drain on the Federation's finances and energy. Following the Rugby League Federation's refusal to renew the protocol with the Rugby Union Federation, the quinzistes, themselves on the cusp of professionalism, declared open season on treiziste players, having already gleefully accepted Le Pontet into their third division.

It was Jacques Soppelsa who was also responsible for appointing France's first overseas coach. The Australian Tas Baitieri, a forward formerly with Penrith and Canterbury, had arrived in France in 1981 to play for Paris-Châtillon, alternating between French and Australian seasons. Baitieri was one of a growing number of foreign players – mainly English and Australian – who were recruited by French clubs from the mid-1980s.

Soon after his arrival, the Australian was given responsibility for coaching the Châtillon team – no easy task, given its location in the suburbs of the capital. It was immediately apparent that practices in Paris and Sydney were worlds apart.

Though two training sessions a week, without any physical preparation, were regarded as insufficient, wholesale changes were impracticable, as Baitieri realised, like many others who had been involved in rugby league in Paris over the decades.

'It's hard in a big city like Paris to demand the level of commitment that's needed,' said Baitieri. 'After work [players] have to take the *périphérique*, which often causes delays. Training sessions can't start till 8 p.m., whereas in Australia we train at three or six. And then the enthusiasm for rugby league is not the same as you find in the south, for example. What I did manage to change is the attitude. Before I arrived, Châtillon had never won away from home in group B [Elite 2]. I tried to make them understand the importance of winning away. In the first year, Châtillon succeeded in that. We started to do things more seriously.'[xlv] Under his coaching the club won promotion to the top level, at the same time as he began to develop the *école de rugby*.

With Soppelsa as the Federation's Paris-based president, Baitieri, at the age of 28, was put in charge of the national team at the start of the 1985-86 season. It was not a universally popular move. First because the previous coach, Villeneuve's Raymond Gruppi, who had overseen a record-equalling 50-4 defeat by Great Britain at Headingley in March, had succeeded in rallying his men to a 24-16 victory in Perpignan two weeks later, in which, incidentally, winger Didier Couston became the first Frenchman to score three tries against Great Britain. There were plenty who lamented the appointment of a foreign coach, as well as what was regarded as the imposition of Australian ways.

But Australia was at the forefront of innovation, and more than any other country France needed to be brought up to date. As Baitieri was careful to say, 'Each country must keep its own characteristics. I cannot impose Australian methods. We must continue to play in the French style, while training in the Australian way. Because up till now, I have seen the national team play well in patches, but never over the full 80 minutes.'[xlvi] Baitieri also admitted that little could be achieved in the short term.

Though there may have been others within the French game who were fully aware of its inadequacies, the views of an outsider, and especially an Australian, had greater currency. He was able to express himself freely on some contentious issues, such as discipline in training and in matches, the interpretation of the rules – which, he argued, led to more spectacular play in Australia – and the physical condition of players. In particular, Baitieri did not hold back when discussing discipline on the field.

'As far as violence is concerned,' he said, 'a lot of things I've seen in France would get a life ban in Australia. But here, the same people continue every weekend to commit dirty play. Who profits from it? Certainly not our sport, but the others.

'I attach part of the blame to French rugby league officials, who don't act decisively to give out effective sanctions.... Will that continue, or will it change? It has to if the greatest game of all is not to die. The international results speak for themselves. We're seeing the start of a new era, one of technology and new ideas. We must progress.'[xlvii]

Violence on the field appeared endemic. Lessons had not been learned. In January 1982, in the season following the abandoned final, referee Cattaneo walked off ten minutes from the end of a match between Lézignan and XIII Catalan as the game degenerated into a mass brawl in which spectators also became involved.[xlviii] Almost exactly five years later, in a match described as 'violent', Carcassonne centre Jean-François Daré died following a high tackle in a match against XIII Catalan.

Nor, of course, were brutalities the preserve of French rugby league. In Britain, stiff-arm tackles, late tackles and leading with the elbow, though illegal, had long been regarded as part of the game. Matches between British and Australian teams were often typically rough, to say the least. Examples abound, particularly when touring teams, either British or French, played country or representative teams, or when the Kangaroos played against English clubs. In 1954 fighting marred the match between Great Britain and New South Wales to such an extent that the referee abandoned the match after sixteen minutes of the second half. Similarly, in the 1970 World Cup final at Headingley, the brawling carried on after the referee had blown his whistle to end a spiteful televised match.[xlix]

French rugby union could be equally brutal. Rugby league had the Battle of Brisbane in 1932, or the Battle of Bradford in 1952; rugby union had the Battle of Durban, as Henri Garcia named it, in 1971. Following two particularly heavy tackles by a South African on French players, a fist-fight involving all sixteen forwards broke out 'such as had never been seen in an international match.' After this had been going on for a full minute, the matter was settled in what seems like a parody of gentlemanly behaviour as the two captains agreed to halt the fisticuffs and return to playing rugby.[l]

Another example is recounted by Garcia, this from the 1975 Championship semi-final between Narbonne and Brive, played at the same Stadium de Toulouse which hosted rugby league finals, including that of 1981. Extra time was played in an atmosphere of riot. In a rage, Narbonne supporters ripped out seats and fencing. As the referee was heading for the changing-rooms, he was hit on the head by a metal bar and had to be rushed to hospital, where he had seven stitches inserted. Narbonne suffered sanctions, but, wrote Garcia, 'it is doubtful whether these sanctions suffice to purify a worrying climate in which we see violence and bad behaviour rear their heads at every turn.'[li]

By that stage, observers were more likely to denounce violence, even in rugby union. It was time to speak out, argued a writer in *Midi-Olympique* after the two Stade Toulousain internationals, Jean-Pierre Rives and Gérald Martinez, both required stitches to the face to repair injuries sustained in a match against the same Narbonne in October 1978. Traditionally, claimed writer Henri Gatineau, all those involved , including those on the receiving end of the aggression, didn't mention such incidents.

'By tradition,' he wrote, 'all those concerned (players, club officials, the injured parties) stay silent over incidents such as those which marred the final of the Toulouse Challenge. They prefer to regard them as mistakes, unavoidable but without great consequence, since they are forgotten by the time of the post-match toasts, when it is regularly declared, "The only winner is rugby!"'

Gatineau quoted the scrum-half Martinez, who said, 'Events like those that we have experienced in our last two matches do considerable harm to rugby. They will discourage a lot of people who will be afraid either for their own safety or for their children. French rugby is going down the wrong road.'[lii]

For rugby league in France, however, the image left by the 1981 final was hard, if not impossible, to erase. As former international stand-off Michel Mazaré noted in 1987, speaking in his capacity as coach of Villeneuve and regional technical adviser, 'The problem is not specific to our sport but it is a significant problem for our movement because in the media our "reputation" is based on violence. At the slightest transgression, people point their finger at us and condemn us.'[liii]

France's international results did little for rugby league's reputation either. The World Cup was revived after an eight-year absence; each of the five nations (PNG was included for the first time) played one another home and away in a league system that took three years to complete. In February 1986, with Tas Baitieri and Guy Vigouroux in charge, France managed a 10-10 draw against Great Britain at Avignon. Full-back Gilles Dumas scored all his side's points with a try and three goals on his debut. The previous autumn they had lost to New Zealand 22-0 at Perpignan and went on to lose 52-0 to Australia at Carcassonne in December 1986 and 52-4 to Great Britain at Headingley the following month. When it came to playing the away fixtures in Australia, New Zealand and PNG, the French found themselves in further trouble.

In February 1987 at a meeting of the Federation at Toulouse, a vote of no confidence in Soppelsa, who had a year of his term of office still to run, was unanimously carried. Debts amounted to 900,000 francs. Verdaguer was again left to pick up the pieces. An immediate decision was taken to cancel the first tour down under since 1981. 'We have no money. No players. And the morale is no longer there,' said Federation secretary Pierre Rayssac.[liv]

The Tricolores' only international success in the rest of the decade was a 21-4 win over PNG on the Kumuls' first tour of Europe in November 1987. The three southern hemisphere nations were each awarded two points after France failed to fulfil fixtures there, which resulted in the French finishing bottom of the World Cup table.

The vultures, with distinctive XV-shaped markings, were circling. Two of Villeneuve's internationals, centre Eric Vergniol and second row Daniel Verdes, were signed by neighbouring union clubs. Vergniol went to Marmande and Verdes, who had long been a target, finally 'succumbed to the financial propositions put to him over several months by members of the management committee of the Rugby Union Federation and the Agen club', as Verdaguer put it. The signing had particular relevance because Agen was the club of FFR president Ferrasse.

Verdaguer believed that the quinzistes had specifically targeted Villeneuve and the France team and said so at a press conference on September 8, 1989 at Toulouse. 'Particularly repugnant', Verdaguer called the French Rugby Union's actions. To accept a club into their midst which had already been sanctioned by the FFRXIII, namely Le Pontet, he deemed 'contrary to morality'. Rugby League, he said, with RFL secretary-general David Oxley at his side, intended to fight 'this intolerable imperialism'. Since it was impossible, he argued, to have any confidence in those whose acts gave the lie to their words, treizistes would fight 'this unsavoury hypocrisy'.[lv]

Oxley, referring to the signing of rugby league players by union clubs in contradiction of its own laws, added in a later interview: '[The French Rugby Union] don't give a damn whether the players they poach become successful RU players. They are just pleased to have taken them away from rugby league and thereby weakened our game over there.

'They even jumped in to take Le Pontet, the French RL champions, en bloc after they had been suspended by the Rugby League for foul play. The fact they were quick to embrace a disgraced team says much about their approach.'[lvi]

These were strong words to bring down the curtain on the much-abused protocol, but the reality was that the far more powerful French Rugby Union Federation would do as it liked, unworried by those taints of professionalism which it had casually brushed aside for most of its existence.

Chapter 18

•

A Coup in Paris: 1989-97

IT HAD BEEN five years since France's last win against one of the major nations. That 24-16 victory over Great Britain at Perpignan in March 1985 had itself ended a four-year drought. Lack of strength in depth was one obvious problem, compared to what was available to the British, the Aussies or the Kiwis. Once more, following the two defeats to New Zealand which came eight months after that heart-lifting triumph against the British, questions were asked about where France was going wrong. For Kiwi coach Graham Lowe, the French were as unpredictable as ever, but lacked the physical and technical ability to make a virtue of their creative instincts. He particularly criticised the lack of urgency in the movement of the ball. 'It took a week for the ball to get out to the wing,' he commented.[i] That amounted to a condemnation of a rugby league nation whose players in the past had been universally admired for the speed of their passing.

Hubie Abbott, who, with Tas Baitieri, was one of the first Australians to feature in the French championship in the 1980s, believed that the play of the France team was simply a reflection of the domestic game: too much concentration on negative aspects such as slowing down the play-the-ball and offside. He maintained that the France team would not regain its place among the elite without a huge amount of physical and technical work. 'Obviously,' he said, 'that depends on having more demanding competitions.'[ii]

In the domestic championship, Jacques Jorda had led St Estève to four finals, winning two. The 1989-90 season was his third in charge of the France team. With Louis Bonnery and Robert Cousty alongside, the charismatic Jorda, always insisting on French values allied to defensive rigour, gave the team the confidence they needed. Twice they flirted with victory. At Carcassonne in November 1989, the Tricolores raced to a 14-0 lead against the touring Kiwis before going down 16-14. Though an injury-hit French side were defeated 34-0 in the World Cup-rated second test, they bounced back the following March against Great Britain at Perpignan. It was a match which France should have won. After Martin Offiah raced away for a long-range try only four minutes into the match, his opposite number Cyril Pons quickly hit back when he scooped up a huge cut-out pass from stand-off Gilles Dumas and went over. Dumas and David Fraisse missed five goal-kicking opportunities between them and second-half tries by Guy Delaunay and Hugues Ratier were disallowed by the New Zealand referee, resulting in an unimpressive 8-4 British win to extend their run of victories over the French to eight.

That sequence was finally shattered at Headingley on April 7, when France overturned predictions to triumph 25-18, a record score and their first away win against Great Britain since 1967. It hadn't looked that way when Britain, fielding five debutants, went 12-0 up after 22 minutes' play, but, as at Perpignan, the St Gaudens combination of Dumas and Pons produced France's first try, goaled from the touchline by stand-off and man of the match Dumas, to which Fraisse added a penalty for a 12-8 half-time score. Fraisse, who ended the match with five goals from five attempts, landed a second penalty before Pons broke along the touchline and prop Jean-Luc Rabot, running like a centre in support, went over. Dumas' kicking, which also included a drop goal, and scrum-half Patrick Entat's switches of direction kept Great Britain on the defensive. Second rower Dany Divet, put through by prop Thierry Buttignol, crossed for France's third, decisive try. So frustrated were the home side that stand-in captain Shaun Edwards was sin-binned for dissent towards the end. A late effort by Offiah could do nothing to deflect the French from claiming victory and winning the British Coal trophy on points aggregate over the two-match series. It was, wrote the *Yorkshire Post*'s Raymond Fletcher, 'the best result for international rugby since Great Britain beat Australia two years ago.'[iii]

'It was a surprise and yet it wasn't,' said Dumas. 'We should have won in France but lost 8-4, just as we should have beaten New Zealand, who won 16-14. So we felt we were very close to winning against Great Britain and travelled to Leeds with the intention of producing something. We were so well prepared. For the first time we used individualised videos of opposition players, so, for example, I knew all about Steadman and his side-step. It was a real advantage. We worked enormously hard.'[iv]

The French Federation, which had long regarded the national side as the 'shop window' of the game, had plenty to be happy about. The France XIII had lost its inferiority complex, along with its tendency to indiscipline, and had gained a promising new group of players who responded enthusiastically to Jorda's coaching style. Among them figured loose forward Jacques Moliner, hooker Thierry Valero, prop or second row Didier Cabestany, centre Pierre Chamorin, as well as Divet and Fraisse, and all were under 23 years old. Avignon's scrum-half Patrick Entat signed for Hull that summer, following in the footsteps of Patrick Solal. With Hull KR and Leeds also interested, Gilles Dumas and Jacques Moliner were targeted as well, though Dumas returned injured from the Australian tour and could not take up the offer he had received. Divet, who had grown up in Australia, and Fraisse would also sign for British clubs.

No one, however, was under any illusions about the size of the task awaiting them as they prepared to tour Australia, whose test team, Jorda admitted, was stronger in every position than his own. Compared to the great tours of the past, this was a low-key affair consisting of six matches, including one test. Neither Sydney nor Brisbane was on the itinerary, the sole test being moved out to Parkes, where 12,374 spectators saw France concede eight tries in losing 34-2. Three matches were won, at Perth, Cairns and Bathurst, but despite the promise shown by individual French players, it was abundantly obvious that the Australians were playing at a different level entirely. France's lack of strength in depth was also made clear. 'We only have one team,' said Jorda. 'But we knew that before we set off.'[v]

As in 1982 and 1986, the Kangaroos demonstrated their superiority on the 1990 European tour, though Great Britain closed the gap in a 2-1 series defeat, with all three matches closely contested. It was a different matter at Avignon, where the 60-4 scoreline against a weakened French side said it all. The following week at Perpignan a 34-10 reverse represented an improvement of sorts, but crowds of under 3,500 for each match showed that treizistes had no stomach for inevitable thrashings. Nor did France fare any better in the home and away fixtures against Great Britain in January and February 1991. The French returned to Perpignan and Headingley, where they had done so well the year before, but their performances did not come close. After the 45-10 defeat at Gilbert Brutus came the 60-4 hammering at Leeds with a side that lacked seven of the thirteen who had triumphed there the year before. After the first, team director Jean Panno was already saying that France had hit rock bottom. 'The [French] championship does not produce players comparable to our British opponents,' he said. 'It is up to the clubs to change this state of affairs.'[vi] The second made everyone wince. Coming just two months after an identical thrashing by the Australians, it was France's heaviest defeat to a British side, when only the year before they had celebrated their biggest win in England. Great Britain winger Martin Offiah scored a record five tries, beating Alex Murphy's four, set in 1959. Yet France were only 16-0 down at half-time. Jorda maintained that the 1990 France team would even have been ahead at that stage, 'but the new players weren't physically or mentally strong enough to compete for eighty minutes.'[vii]

The coach resigned and went back to leading his new club XIII Catalan, who had recently made what turned out to be an ill-advised foray into rugby union. The most high-profile recruit was Béziers' international flanker, 23-year old Alain Carminati, who, following his sending-off in the Scotland-France rugby union match, had been suspended for seven months. No longer could the French Rugby League Federation take the moral high ground, though it was clear from Carminati's performances that the gulf between the two codes in terms of athleticism was considerable, even if largely unappreciated by the general public. Rugby league might struggle for recognition, but it was obvious that the game had evolved to the extent that it was now a much less safe proposition to sign a rugby union player, even an international, than it had been thirty or even twenty years before.

Carminati admitted that he could have gained as much by signing for union clubs such as Toulon, Agen or Racing, but had always had a soft spot for rugby league, even if he had not been previously able to say so. He recalled that, on tour in Australia, the captain, Daniel Dubroca, had asked FFR president Albert Ferrasse if some of the team could go to a rugby league match in Sydney. According to Carminati, Ferrasse replied, 'Don't even think about it, with all the problems treizistes cause me in France!' Instead, the players stayed in their hotel rooms, watched the match on television and thoroughly enjoyed themselves.[viii]

The mood of optimism that had pervaded French rugby league in the first half of 1990 had now all but disappeared, and with it Jean-Paul Verdaguer's administration, ousted in May 1991 to be replaced by one headed by Gilbert Dautant. Fernand Soubie, chairman of double-winning St Gaudens, had actually polled the highest number of votes in the federal elections before turning down the role of president in favour of his club responsibilities. Dautant's first duty was to ensure that the scheduled tour of New Zealand and Papua-New Guinea went ahead. On taking office, the new president discovered 'to his horror'[ix] the Federation's financial predicament. Debts amounted to around £100,000 and their bank had put a stop on all cheques, a situation David Oxley described as 'little short of catastrophic'.[x] The French sought an interest-free loan of £50,000 from the RFL, to be repaid over two years, in order to ease what Oxley called 'a state of deep crisis'.

The tour did go ahead, with a hurriedly assembled team and management. National technical director Louis Bonnery teamed up with Carlos Zalduendo, the tour director, with Michel Mazaré, the regional technical adviser for Aquitaine, who stepped in as coach. The tour was badly planned, with the first test as second match in, even though several of the France team had not played in over a month, apart from in the opening defeat by the Kiwi Colts. Two test defeats duly followed at the hands of Kiwis who earned their living playing in Australia or England, by 60-6 at Auckland and 32-10 at Christchurch. The defeat at Auckland also meant that France had conceded sixty points three times in six months. After winning just one game out of six played in New Zealand, the Tricolores emerged with credit when, with a last-minute try and conversion by young hooker Patrick Torreilles, they beat PNG 20-18 in the cauldron of Goroka to snatch two valuable World Cup points. The victory was all the more satisfying given that Great Britain had failed by the same score at the same ground the year before.

When the French backed up with a 28-14 victory at Carcassonne the following November, they managed to end their World Cup campaign in fourth spot, ahead of the Kumuls, after losing 36-0 to Great Britain at Hull in a match which marked the return of Patrick Entat to the Boulevard. The French had earlier put up an encouraging display in a 30-12 defeat at Perpignan, but away from home their confidence evaporated. Though they defended manfully, a Tricolore side containing several newcomers put themselves under pressure with the old failing of not keeping the ball secure. Entat spoke of what he had learned during his season at Hull, then coached by the Australian Brian Smith. 'I would never have imagined I would make so much progress in so little time,' he said. 'In France I had the reputation of being a good defender. At Hull, I realised that that judgement was not based on anything serious. I re-learned everything, not only in defence, but in every other area as well. Physically, I had to follow a personalised weight-training programme... I already had vision, but the British competition forced me to think and make decisions faster. Defences move up quickly... A bad decision and you lose ten or twenty metres...'[xi]

However, France was to play a leading role in the development of rugby league in Russia, where the game had made its first appearance two years earlier. Drawing their players, as well as officials, from rugby union, the Russians paid a short visit to France in October 1991, playing against a President's XIII at Corbeil, on the outskirts of Paris, where the hosts won 60-10, before losing to France 26-6 at Lyon in what was the former Soviet Union's first-ever rugby league international match. In June the following year, France became the first country to tour the CIS, as the former USSR had become known, playing three matches and winning the international in Moscow by 28-8. The Russians returned to France in October, losing 38-4 at St Gaudens. A second tour followed in the summer of 1993, when four matches were staged at St Petersburg and Moscow, and Tiraspol and Kishinev in Moldova, with the French, as might be expected, winning all four games.

On the way back home from their 1995 tour of New Zealand, the French again fulfilled a development role. In French-speaking Montreal, a high-scoring exhibition match resulted in a 72-32 win for France against Canada. Fiji, with a much more significant rugby background, proved more troublesome, however. A match in Suva, played on the way home from the 1994 tour of Australia and PNG, ended in a 20-12 defeat.

If the French had lost hope of staying in touch with the top three nations, they expected to be at the head of the following peloton. But the Fijians, then Samoans and Tongans came along to dent French self-esteem. Not to mention Wales. When a number of high-profile recruits from Welsh rugby union came into the game, the Wales national team was resurrected and played their first match against France for eleven years. At Swansea in March 1992, a Wales team captained by Jonathan Davies and including half a dozen members of the Great Britain team beat the French in a 35-6 victory, watched by a crowd of over 10,000 at Swansea. Nine months later at Perpignan, a much closer match still ended in a defeat for France, who went down 19-18. Unluckily for the French, who did not deserve to lose, a single point also separated the two sides at Cardiff in March 1994, Wales winning 13-12 with a last-minute try. At Carcassonne in the same month, they were comparatively happy to have conceded defeat to Great Britain by the much reduced score of 12-4, their efforts giving heart for the future.

But the fact remained that France's international status had diminished after the high note of Headingley 1990, the last time they would defeat a major nation. Great Britain, Australia and New Zealand had all registered a sixty-point total in test matches against France with only single figures in reply. Just when it seemed it couldn't get any worse, it did. Only three years after their famous Leeds victory, the Tricolores returned to the same stadium and lost by the record score of 72-6 with a patched-up and hopelessly outclassed side. It was the highest score and widest margin in test match history. A year and a half later at Béziers, the Australians inflicted even greater damage with a 74-0 whitewash. 'We're back to square one,' said coach Jean-Christophe Vergeynst after Headingley, and added that a reformed domestic championship was a must if France was ever to get out of its predicament.[xii]

The shop window was looking bare. Its emptiness was not so much a condemnation of the Federation, now headed by former secretary-general Jean-Paul Ferré, who took over on the death of the respected Gilbert Dautant in 1993, as the result of a long decline which had been masked by occasional triumphs thanks to the efforts of a small group of players capable of standing comparison with the British, Australians or New Zealanders. In general terms, there were too few of them and far too many others lacked the individual technique and the physical condition to deal with the demands of test match rugby league. The forwards in particular lacked physical presence, which is why, from 1992, with the selection of the St Gaudens pair Richard Clarke and Theo Anast, Pia's Karl Jaavuo or Brian Coles of XIII Catalan, Australians who would not get near their national side began to turn up in the France XIII. An understandable inferiority complex on the part of French players completed the downward spiral. After the Béziers rout by Mal Meninga's men, there were plenty of officials to be found saying enough is enough. Ferré was one of those who wanted to promote alternative international competition more in line with France's capabilities.

Apart from their own failings on the field, a great deal seemed to conspire against their success. The summer tour of 1994 was misconceived, starting as it did in Papua-New Guinea. A number of players had declined selection, weakening the squad. Those problems were compounded by climatic conditions in PNG, where, after a first-up win against the Highlands, three defeats ensued, including a 29-22 reverse in the international match at Port Moresby. More than half the squad were on antibiotics after picking up infections, which was not ideal preparation for Australia. To start the tour in the tropical climate of PNG was, said tour director Carlos Zalduendo, 'a monumental error'.[xiii] After the 58-0 hammering by the Australians at Parramatta, then the defeat in Fiji, coach Vergeynst resigned. He claimed that the tour had been sabotaged from the start by the late withdrawal of key players at Catalan clubs.[xiv]

Vergeynst admitted that there had been more failures than triumphs in his three years in charge, but pointed to the last-minute defeat at Cardiff, where both sides scored one try, and the loss at Carcassonne in which Great Britain scored just two tries to one. It was some vindication but also looked like clutching at straws, which the French had long been in the habit of doing. It contrasted strongly with the hard-nosed attitude of the British, whose captain, Andy Platt, said before the Headingley débâcle that anything less than fifty points would have been seen as failure.

Into the midst of all this despondency rode a totally unexpected ally. Unthinkable perhaps, but Albert Ferrasse's one-time right-hand man, former vice-president of the FFR, ex-captain and coach of the France rugby union team, Jacques Fouroux, declared his ambitions for rugby league (and for himself). One of the most powerful as well as controversial figures in French rugby union, Fouroux was now being hailed as the saviour of rugby league. 'He alone is capable of dragging our movement out of its debilitating routine,' concluded an editorial in *Treize-Magazine*.[xv]

At a press conference in Paris on 7 November, 1994, Fouroux drew a media audience not seen in French rugby league for at least thirty years and presented his big-scale project. Flanked by Australian and British supremos Ken Arthurson and Maurice Lindsay and by FFRXIII president Jean-Paul Ferré, the man who had been the France XV's coach only four years earlier spoke of rugby league's great advantages over union, namely that it is spectacular and easily understood by all, and has a far higher effective game time. Arthurson and Lindsay, representing the International Board, talked of giving rugby league the global dimension they believed it should always have had. These men put their faith in the renegade because they believed he had the power to open the doors which had often been slammed in rugby league's face.

According to Louis Bonnery, Fouroux's initial contact was with Ferré in July 1994 on the rugby union man's home turf of Auch in the Gers before meeting Arthurson and Lindsay on the eve of the first test between Great Britain and Australia at Wembley.[xvi] At the Paris press conference in November, Fouroux launched a project to be known as France Rugby League. It was conceived as a summer competition between sixteen regional teams from all over France, accompanied by the kind of American-inspired razzamatazz that was commonplace in Australia and would become accepted in Britain too. *L'Equipe* called it 'Fouroux's incredible gamble'.[xvii] Some individuals even spoke of Fouroux as the new Jean Galia, though it was a facile comparison well wide of the mark.

A reminder of France's dire international status came in December with the massive rout by the Australians at Béziers. Coach Ivan Grésèque likened it to 'a race between a 2CV and a Porsche'.[xviii] Australian captain Mal Meninga, at the end of his international career, was one of half a dozen tourists who, according to Tas Baitieri, now back in France as a special envoy, would be interested in playing a couple of seasons in France. 'These players have an admiration for French rugby of the type played by Puig-Aubert, Brousse, Ponsinet, Aillères, Marsolan. They told me so quite clearly but they don't understand how this inventive style of rugby, which lit up the rugby league world, could have fallen so low. They would be happy and proud to take part in its revival.'[xix] It didn't happen because no clubs could have afforded to take on these world-class stars. But still the race to save French rugby league was on, played out against the background of a nascent Super League, confirmed in April of the following year.

When the France Rugby League competition took off in the summer of 1995, the number of teams was a more realistic eight, based on the regions where the game was played and where players and officials would be readily available. The teams were Avignon-Provence, Bordeaux-Aquitaine, Carcassonne-Aude-Languedoc, Lyon-Rhône-Alpes, Marseille-Méditerranée, Paris-Ile de France, Perpignan-Roussillon-Catalogne and Toulouse-Midi-Pyrénées.

But all of that was shoehorned into an already tightly-packed schedule. In May, the finals of Championship and Cup were contested by the same two Catalan teams. At Narbonne, watched by 13,200 spectators, Pia beat St Estève 12-10 in a thrilling match of high quality, the best by far for fifteen years, wrote André Passamar. He added: '[It was] a final, if not Australian-style, at least English-style, which is no mean compliment.'[xx] He believed it equalled the Lyon-XIII Catalan encounter of 1951 or the Villeneuve-Lézignan clash of 1959. He quoted two ex-internationals, Jean Audoubert and André Rives, as saying that if the France team had shown the same level of motivation and application against the Australians at Béziers the previous December, they would never have suffered such a hiding. A week later in the Cup final at Perpignan, seen by a crowd of 6,000, St Estève got their revenge, winning 28-8.

In June the Tricolores, with Ivan Grésèque as coach and Hervé Guiraud and Roger Palisses as co-directors, set off to New Zealand on a short tour, playing four matches, including two tests. In the first, at Auckland, the Kiwis were flattered by the 22-6 score. At Palmerston North in the second, France came back from being 16-8 down at half-time to earn a merited 16-all draw, with captain Patrick Entat and forwards Thierry Valero, Didier Cabestany and Patrick Torreilles outstanding. The performances were considered encouraging and for once France was able to look ahead more confidently to the Centenary World Cup due to start in England and Wales in October.

Jacques Fouroux's France Rugby League tournament kicked off with double-headers on six dates in August, matches taking place at Perpignan, Saintes, Narbonne, Mazamet, Villeneuve and Roanne. Apart from Perpignan and Villeneuve, these towns had not been home to a top division club for a long time, if ever. Fouroux had mobilised impressive support, attracted media attention in a way that the existing bodies could not, and signed up sponsors to cover the costs of staging the matches. In terms of back-up, many were those former players or officials who returned to the fold, as well as ex-quinzistes who had not taken too much persuading to follow, such was Fouroux's influence and the loyalty he inspired. He insisted on making each match a spectacle, bringing in rock bands as part of the occasion – a novelty in the pre-Super League era – and telling the teams to provide attacking play without neglecting the impact of defence. Each game was played in four quarters because of the heat, admission was free and the average attendance was around 5,000. The two-legged semi-finals took place at Auch and Villeurbanne and the final was scheduled for Béziers on 16 September.

The Stade de la Méditerranée at Béziers was hired, but the combination of Fouroux and rugby league was too much for the quinzistes to bear. The FFR got in touch with the mayor's office to say that it was unacceptable to stage a rugby league match there (even though France had met the Australians there the year before). They also made it clear that if the rugby league match went ahead, the planned game against the All Blacks two months later would be compromised. It was nothing less than blackmail, but the municipality gave in and the final was switched to Carcassonne. In a thrilling match, in front of a crowd of around 7,500, Toulouse-Midi-Pyrénées edged out Perpignan-Roussillon-Catalogne to win 16-14. The game was shown on the major subscription channel, Canal +, and was greeted as a revelation. Even *L'Equipe* was impressed, describing the event as 'superb' and 'an exceptional spectacle, intense and aggressive without being brutal'.[xxi]

The Federation was crossing its fingers in the hope that this new enthusiasm would translate to the regular domestic championship, which had begun just as the France Rugby League competition was finishing. The very least that could be said is that rugby league was never off the agenda at this period. In October the Centenary World Cup brought the largest-ever number of participating nations together – ten – in a tournament played over a three-week period. At Wembley in the opening game, 41,271 fans watched as England beat Australia 20-16. Returning to Wembley for the final, Australia beat England 16-8 in front of a crowd of 66,540, another figure which silenced doubters and made others take notice. In the group matches, France had the misfortune to be drawn in the same pool as Wales and Western Samoa. Against a talented and powerful Welsh side, the French went down 28-6 at Ninian Park, Cardiff in front of a 10,250 crowd, before taking a 56-10 hammering by the very physical Samoans at the same stadium three days later.

Like others before him, St Estève and France centre Pierre Chamorin, one of the most gifted players of his generation, put the blame on the domestic championship which did not ask enough of players on a regular basis. It had been unrealistic, he thought, to imagine that France would have got very far. The reason was 'an obvious lack of matches at this level. Against the Welsh, even though the score was heavy, we were competitive. But against the Samoans we cracked physically. We don't have the means to play two top-level matches in such a short space of time.'[xxii]

At that point, the most obvious sign that the rugby league world was being torn apart appeared in the composition of the Australian team which won the World Cup. The side had only been selected from around half the players available as a result of the battle over television rights, won at a high price by Rupert Murdoch's media empire. When the dust had settled from the crumbling of the Australian Rugby League's walls, the project presented in the northern hemisphere would in theory put French rugby league back on the map.

Already there had been talk, considerably premature, of the launch of global rugby league across continents. High-flying notions of a pan-European league were put forward, suggesting that the game might very soon be played in, say, Barcelona or Milan. What it boiled down to, for the start of the back-to-front 'summer' season of 1996, was the English first division, reduced to eleven clubs plus Paris, to be known as the European Super League. Once again, Fouroux showed his ability to open doors when he acquired the right to call the capital city's team Paris Saint-Germain, a name recognised the world over for its football club. For the first time a French club took part in an essentially British championship, although French teams had taken part in the Regal Trophy from 1992 until 1996, the year in which the competition ended. Carcassonne and XIII Catalan had been the first to be invited, the Catalans losing 32-16 at Rochdale and the ASC 52-0 at Wigan.

In November 1995, five months before the Super League competition got under way, Fouroux, the Paris chairman, and his chief executive, none other than Tas Baitieri, travelled to Los Angeles for a series of Super League meetings between Australian and British officials and Murdoch's representatives. The high level of professionalism, commented on by Baitieri, set against a background of serious money and the American 'matchday experience', appeared to put rugby league in Britain and France on an entirely new footing, as the £87 million deal agreed with Murdoch's company showed. 'The revolution is under way. It offers France a golden opportunity,'[xxiii] said Baitieri, who had returned to the country the year before, seconded, ironically, by the now increasingly isolated ARL and its chairman Ken Arthurson. Baitieri was not the first and would not be the last to assert that what New Zealand had gained from having a professional team like the Auckland Warriors playing in the Australian competition might also be achieved by Paris Saint-Germain in Super League.

The France Rugby League competition of the summer of 1995 had helped to promote the idea of rugby league's new era, but Paris Saint-Germain's appearance in Super League attracted far greater notice. When the team stepped out, wearing the famous red and blue vertical bands, into the Charléty stadium on that Friday evening of 29 March, 1996, in front of a crowd of 17,873 – one of the most quoted attendances in rugby league history – the game in France took on a different dimension. The atmosphere generated by the pre-match events in this modern stadium gave the impression of a sport that was bang up-to-the-minute, setting the pace in the capital city, hitherto relatively unconnected to rugby of either code. An appropriately cosmopolitan team, in which a Polish second rower and a Moldovan winger lined up alongside ten Frenchmen, three Aussies, a New Zealander and a Tongan, ran out to the sound of rock music and fireworks, relayed by the big screen, to face Sheffield Eagles, another team representing expansionist ideals, founded only twelve years earlier. Full-back Fred Banquet became Super League's first try scorer when he went over in the ninth minute but despite Mikhail Piskunov's try just before half-time, the two sides were locked on 10-all after forty minutes. Darren Adams and captain Pierre Chamorin both crossed before two tries in six minutes from winger Arnaud Cervello proved decisive. Patrick Torreilles' late penalty, adding to his two earlier conversions, extended a narrow margin. In an eleven try game, full of suspense, a 30-24 win for PSG signalled a wider victory. As RFL chief executive Maurice Lindsay famously declared, 'Some reporters came for a funeral and had to write about a party,' while Jacques Fouroux insisted, 'The rugby of tomorrow, that's what you have seen tonight.'[xxiv]

Charles Biétry, head of PSG Omnisports and director of Canal +, agreed that it had been the best possible start but sounded a note of caution, saying that the players had been fantastic but in sport you start all over again each week. 'There won't always be this huge crowd and not necessarily a victory every time,' he said.[xxv]

For the players, the opportunity to become fully professional and to compete against the British seemed like a dream come true. But it came at a price. Those who had played in England, like Entat, knew what was required, but in reality the French players had to make an even greater commitment than their British counterparts. They were supposed to be fully professional, but most of the French players still worked at their regular jobs, while during April and May many were involved in the final stages of the domestic competition with their French clubs, which meant constant shuttling back and forth to Paris.

'The majority of players were not professional at all,' said Chamorin. 'Depending when the match was, we would go up to Paris and train either on a Thursday or a Saturday. I worked the rest of the week in my company. [PSG] was a fine opportunity, but badly prepared.'[xxvi]

In terms of results on the field, the fairly modest objective was set at finishing eleventh out of twelve in order to avoid relegation. After four games PSG were well on course, with two wins, a draw and a defeat. But a run of eleven straight losses – five of them with fifty points or more against – showed that life in Super League was not so simple. Maurice Lindsay despatched John Kear from RFL HQ to help Michel Mazaré and David Ellis with the coaching. The defence improved, the scores were generally much closer and a crucial 24-18 home win over London meant that PSG had accrued enough league points – seven – to stay up and send Workington down. The run of defeats was given as a reason by Canal + for not televising live matches.

As Biétry had also predicted, attendances never reached the same level as on that first glorious night. But the crowd for the Leeds game in May came close, when 15,107 watched PSG's 40-14 defeat. The lowest point came towards the end of the season, when the figure for the match against St Helens was a mere 4,050, and yet the average attendance was over 8,000, which put the French club in the same bracket – astonishingly – as Leeds. There was only one snag. The vast majority of the crowd got in for free. It was claimed that the local authority and other bodies bought tickets which they distributed to local people, leaving only the visiting English fans paying money at the turnstiles. That meant that the club existed almost entirely on its share of the television rights from the BSkyB channel. Nor did the club have the appropriate structures for a professional set-up, relying instead on the indefatigable Tas Baitieri to do most of the leg-work.

The pressure on players was considerable. On 16 May, in a break with precedent, the final of the Coupe de France was played on a Thursday, Ascension Day, in order to accommodate PSG's match at Bradford three days later. For the first time in their history, Limoux took the Lord Derby trophy by beating Carcassonne 39-12, watched by a crowd of around 9,000. On Saturday, 25 May, 10,000 spectators travelled to Narbonne to see Villeneuve pip St Estève to the Championship title by 27-26. PSG winger Arnaud Cervello had both the distinction and misfortune to score four tries and kick three goals yet end up on the losing side, which also included Paris team-mates Pierre Chamorin and Todd Brown. Villeneuve, coached by PSG assistant David Ellis, had two Super League players, Fabien Devecchi and Régis Pastre-Courtine, on duty before the home match against Halifax two days after. A week and a half later, on the Wednesday evening of 5 June, international duty called. France's starting thirteen for the match against Wales at Carcassonne contained eight of those Paris players who had suffered a 52-10 thrashing at St Helens on the Sunday before. It was no surprise when the Tricolores lost 34-14.

The following Wednesday, June 12, after PSG had endured another 50-point defeat at the weekend, this time at home to Castleford, the France side were humiliated by England at Gateshead in a 73-6 rout. It was Patrick Entat's last of 36 appearances, which at the time was higher than any other French player had achieved since the 1960s. It was an unfortunate but sadly predictable finale. Already by the time of the Championship semi-finals, David Ellis was complaining that the twin demands of Super League and the domestic championship, let alone international matches, made life impossible.

In this context, the second France Rugby League summer programme, though it featured no PSG players, seemed superfluous and irrelevant. All the matches were played in rugby league strongholds or at least in places where the game had a presence: Carcassonne, Limoux, St Gaudens, Lyon, Tonneins, Arles and Mazamet. The final took place at Narbonne in front of 3,000 spectators and was won for the second year running by Toulouse-Midi-Pyrénées, who beat Marseille-Méditerranée 25-18.

By this stage the Fouroux project was over, and so was its founder's foray into rugby league. The instigator resigned as chairman of PSG on June 6, just ten weeks into the season, having had his proposal to become a European development officer turned down by the RFL. He returned to his home town rugby union club of Auch as chairman, leaving PSG Rugby League in the hands of Jacques Larrose, who had supported him in both projects from the start. Jean-Paul Ferré called him a 'visionary ... [who] showed rugby league people that it was possible to do something on a big scale. By making matches into an event he opened the game up to a new audience, and many people, including high-ranking figures in rugby union, took their inspiration from what he did.'[xxvii]

Super League's second season began with a very different-looking Paris team than in the inaugural year. Despite Ferré's presence, PSG became an RFL-run club, with Maurice Lindsay and Harry Jepson joining the board and two RFL employees – one of them, Rob Elstone, was to become Super League chief executive two decades later – overseeing the day-to-day running of the club. On the field too the team had changed. Australian Peter Mulholland, formerly of Perth Western Reds, was brought in as coach and with him came a whole roster of players from down under. Arriving on tourist visas only, the coach and players lived out of a hotel at Bougival in the Paris suburbs.

Before the start of the season, Ferré said that in the future the team should become 'more and more French' and in 1997 would aim for a place in the top four.[xxviii] In fact Pierre Chamorin was the only French player regularly on the team-sheet, his compatriots barely getting a look-in, which defeated the object of improving home-grown players. With a strictly limited budget and with a brief at least to avoid relegation, Mulholland used what he believed were tried and tested methods. But after one win in nine matches, he was replaced in May by former Wigan international second rower and ex-Oldham coach Andy Goodway. When Mulholland departed, so did Fouroux's stand-in chairman, Jacques Larrose, following tensions between the RFL and the French.

Goodway, the future Great Britain coach, oversaw notable victories against his two former clubs. The shock 30-28 win over Wigan at Charléty gave the club a great boost, while the victory over Oldham in the penultimate game of the season kept PSG up but condemned the Lancashire club.

Two matches were taken on the road in August, one to Narbonne, where a crowd of 7,000 paying spectators left PSG officials to ponder whether setting up the sole French Super League club in the south-west would have been a better bet. The other match, at the deserted former stronghold of Bayonne, produced a crowd of just 1,500.

The grand notion of establishing a Super League club in the French capital was matched by a full-scale World Club Championship, involving all the European clubs and their Australian and New Zealand counterparts. The outcome weighed heavily in favour of the southern hemisphere, but though PSG did not get as far as the quarter-finals, they racked up a surprising 24-0 win over Mulholland's former club, Perth Reds. To general dismay, the Western Australian outpost was disbanded at the end of the season. To even greater disappointment, given that it was the only French club playing at the top level, PSG also took a 'sabbatical' year, from which there proved to be no return.

It had been a fine idea, but in practical terms the club had been thrown together without appropriate structures in place, as Chamorin agreed. 'It all happened too soon,' he said. 'Paris had great commercial and economic potential but not enough preparation went into it. As players [in the first season], we should have been living and training in Paris. Everything was organised in a hurry.'[xxix] A costly exercise too, since it had virtually no income other than the Murdoch pay-out and was heavily in debt. Jean-Paul Ferré described the club as 'no more than an Australian [sic] franchise operating in Super League. When they left, the foreign officials left a [financial] hole which we had to fill.'[xxx]

Or, as he more imaginatively put it, 'Paris was like a beautiful woman, very seductive but making increasing demands the more time you spent with her.'[xxxi]

Chapter 19

•

Perpignan, Centre of the Universe: 1997-2018

IN THE AUTUMN of 1997 French rugby league looked very much as if it had been cast adrift from the mainstream of European competition. Paris Saint-Germain were on their way out of the so-called European Super League, even though their presence had provided the justification for the organisation's title.

Maurice Lindsay said he did not want to continue running the club, since clearly as RFL chief executive he had other preoccupations. He maintained that PSG could not, and should not, live on hand-outs and, after throwing the club into the deep waters of professionalism, now believed that it was better to let it mature slowly, even suggesting that two French clubs could join the English division below Super League and fight their way towards promotion. But for the top level, he insisted that there were neither the players nor the coaches to compete.[i] Promises of a restart in 1999 hardly appeared credible.

There were plenty who believed that the Paris project could have been made to work and that the opportunity for rugby league remained too good to pass up. The majority of Super

League clubs were thought to be in favour of retaining the club provided it could be made to pay its way. If the Paris business plan was unworkable, it was suggested that a French Super League club might be better placed in Toulouse, as had originally been suggested by some, or in another established rugby league city in the south-west with a ready fan base willing to pay to watch.

Not only did that not happen but France was now reduced to competing in a second-tier international competition, facing Ireland and Scotland, two teams made up of hardened English players mostly with a tenuous connection to the countries they were representing, plus a handful of native amateurs. In the wider scheme of things, it could hardly get more depressing than a draw against the Irish on a wet midweek night in Evry, miles away from the capital; or indeed a fortunate two-point win against the Scots in Glasgow. For the first time, South Africa played on French soil. A developing national team of former rugby union players were beaten 30-17 at Arles. In 1998, France faced Ireland again, this time at Dublin in front of a crowd given as 1,500. Against an Irish side full of Super League players, including Shaun Edwards, making his debut at the age of 32, the French pulled off a 24-22 win thanks to Fred Banquet's last-minute try which he converted himself. With Jean-Marc Garcia, formerly of Sheffield Eagles, Canberra-bound Jérôme Guisset and Castleford's Gaël Tallec, there was some substance to the side, which went on to beat Scotland 26-22 at Perpignan. In a format which later included Wales, these wins were seen as encouraging, though the authenticity of other teams was often questioned.

At club level, French teams remained in contact with their English counterparts through a new tournament known as Treize Tournoi. It involved France's top three, St Estève, who had done the double, Villeneuve and Limoux, up against Division One Grand Finalists Wakefield and Featherstone and Division Two Champions Lancashire Lynx, a club now defunct. But it was the Chorley-based side who showed the greatest enthusiasm for the tournament and reached the final, superbly staged at the Stadium de Toulouse and watched by a crowd of over 10,000. Their opponents, Villeneuve, led by Australian player-coach Grant Doorey, and with ex-Kangaroo forward Paul Sironen, future Catalan Dragons coach Laurent Frayssinous and ex-PSG stars Banquet and Fabien Devecchi in their ranks, were made to work hard for their 16-10 victory. What the game showed once again was the French appetite for matches against English clubs. Gradually the broadcast media were beginning to renew an interest in rugby league. The regional channel FR3 showed the final, while subscription channels Eurosport and AB Sports screened matches from the home championship and British and Australian games. But it was a Eurosport-scheduled match between Villeneuve and Toulouse which provoked yet another anti-rugby league move from rugby union, just when it had been thought that hostilities had ceased, union having joined the professionals, or, as they called it, non-amateurs, three years earlier. When the Villeneuve stadium lights were judged inadequate for the television cameras, the club directors agreed with Agen rugby union club to play the match there. Agen, however, held a special place in rugby union mythology, being the home club of former FFR president Albert Ferrasse, whose successor Bernard Lapasset faxed the Villeneuve chairman to put a block on the treizistes' use of the hallowed turf. In the end, the match was played at nearby Fumel, a rugby union club of lesser status.

At the turn of the millennium, Villeneuve were France's top team, a convincing blend of locally produced players like backs David Despin and Fabien Devecchi and forwards Laurent Carrasco and Pierre Sabatié, to which were added players from other French clubs such as Fred Banquet and Laurent Frayssinous, in addition to high-profile overseas recruits like former Kangaroo forward Paul Sironen or ex-Kiwi Quentin Pongia. Other foreign signings like forwards Cavill Heugh, Vincent Wulf and Artie Shead also played important roles in the club's success. The Leopards, to give them their new Super League-style nickname, contested every Championship final but one between 1996 and 2003, winning the Max Rousié shield on five occasions, and took the Lord Derby trophy four times in the same period. Coach David Ellis, who went on to become the France rugby union team's defence mentor, was succeeded by Aussie player-coach Doorey.

The Regal Trophy, in which French clubs had participated, was phased out in 1996, but cross-Channel clashes continued in the Challenge Cup between 2000 and 2013. Champions Villeneuve and runners-up St Gaudens were the first French clubs to be invited into the venerable English competition. As many as four French clubs took part each season between 2002 and 2005, with Russian clubs also invited from 2001. The experience could often be a chastening one, but early successes included Villeneuve's 2001 run, which took them through three rounds, all away from home, to reach a quarter-final tie at Super League club Warrington, where they went down 32-0. In 2004 the merged Perpignan club, Union Treiziste Catalane, travelled to National League One (second tier) club Hull KR and came away with a 23-22 victory before going out by 32-20 at Super League club Castleford in round four.

The Catalans defeated Super League aspirants Hull KR again the following season, this time by 32-18 in Perpignan, and then came close to causing an upset at Wigan, who pulled ahead in the last ten minutes to win by 16-10. Toulouse, coached by future Hull KR boss Justin Morgan and with Trent Robinson at loose forward, did even better, beating Super League club Widnes by 40-24 in the quarter-finals at the Stade des Minimes, before meeting Leeds at Huddersfield in a memorable semi-final. Facing the World Club Champions, Toulouse upset all the predictions in the first half, which ended with a spectacular 40-metre try by second row Sébastien Raguin to send them in at half-time with just a 22-18 deficit. Though they tired in the second period to go down 56-18, their performance gave the game in France a huge boost. 'There's no question that a lot of good things are going on in France,' said RFL executive chairman Richard Lewis in the year before the Catalans joined Super League, 'and this is a ... clear symbol of what is happening.'[ii]

Although Paris Saint-Germain Rugby League vacated the Charléty Stadium in 1997, the year of the club's demise, the ground was still regarded as the game's home in the capital. The desire to impress in Paris, to take the game to the metropolitan-based media, had still not gone away, despite all indications that it took something special to draw the crowds there. Since 1951, the Championship final had traditionally been played at Toulouse. Narbonne – without a rugby league club, but handily placed for the Catalan and Aude clubs – had more recently been favoured. But in 1999 the Federation decided, audaciously, to take the final to Paris for the first time in the game's history. Villeneuve beat St Gaudens there by 33 points to 20, watched by a crowd of 7,592, considerably fewer than the 12,000 who were estimated to have seen the previous year's final at Narbonne. The experiment was repeated in 2000 and, on the only occasion between 1996 and 2003 when Villeneuve did not take part, Toulouse edged out St Estève, who were appearing in their ninth final in twelve years, by 20-18. A crowd of around 6,500 at Charléty did not compare well with the 9,000 who saw the Cup final – traditionally regarded as the lesser event – at Narbonne, though the Federation were keen to persevere with Paris for a third year. In the face of a sort of mutiny by fans and clubs, who were tired of taking their season's highlight 500 miles north for, as they saw it, no good reason, the Federation backed down at short notice and the Max Rousié shield was contested in 2001 at Toulouse, where around 9,000 fans saw the local side lose 32-20 to Villeneuve.

When France hosted one of the four group stages of the 2000 World Cup, the opening double-header was staged at Charléty, though it brought the home team no luck as they lost 23-20 to an Adrian Lam-inspired PNG in front of 7,500 spectators, who also saw Tonga hammer South Africa. Coached by Gilles Dumas, the ex-test stand-off who had been man of the match at Headingley ten years earlier, the French redeemed themselves at Carcassonne, beating Tonga 28-8, watched by a crowd of 10,000. A 56-6 defeat of South Africa, seen by 8,000 at Albi, saw France through the group stage, in second place behind PNG. But in the quarter-final at Castleford, the French proved no match for New Zealand, whose scrum-half Robbie Paul scored a hat-trick in the 54-6 win.

The year before, in the autumn of 1999, France also took part in an international sideshow known as the Mediterranean Cup, a pre-World Cup tournament also contested by Italy, Lebanon and Morocco. Since the first two of those countries could barely exist on the rugby league stage without the participation of Australians, France was expected to win a competition which the Federation judged to be at their level. After a surprise defeat by Italy, the French came second on points difference behind Lebanon.

Still smarting from the record defeat by the Kangaroos in 1994, the Federation fought shy of having the national side meet the Aussies again, but were happy to give the go-ahead for a tour of the South Pacific in the summer of 2001. Though France lost the test at Auckland 36-0, they won their other three matches in New Zealand. They travelled on to Port Moresby, coming from behind to win the first test against PNG 27-16 before losing the second 34-24 in the heat and altitude of Goroka. Towards the end of the same calendar year, a couple of forty-point wins on a short tour of South Africa could not deflect the continuing disappointment of defeat by a similar margin against Great Britain and, worryingly, against Scotland, who recorded their first win against the French. The 42-12 reverse at the hands of Great Britain took place, incidentally, at the same Agen stadium where Villeneuve and Toulouse had been refused permission to play three years earlier. That in itself showed an easing of tensions between the two codes and the declining influence of the quinziste old guard.

Although a handful of French players had experience of playing in Super League in England – Jean-Marc Garcia (Sheffield), Sylvain Houlès (Huddersfield, London Broncos), Jérôme Guisset (Warrington) or Gaël Tallec (Wigan, Castleford) for example – it was evident that only regular participation in a professional competition would improve standards. There were regular calls for a European club competition and most of all for the return of a French club to Super League.

Between 1997, the year of Paris's demise, and 2003, the year when a decision would be made about the reappearance of a French club in Super League, Villeneuve set the pace. In those six seasons, the Leopards were champions four times; St Estève twice and Toulouse once. Off the field, Toulouse began to put structures in place befitting a big-city club with professional ambitions.

Necessity brought about a third contender. Fully a decade earlier, St Estève chairman René Durand had come to the conclusion that the only way ahead for the two major clubs in the Perpignan area was to merge. 'It's inevitable,' he said. There are too many of us. For the top clubs, it's a question of amalgamating or dying.'[iii] In the summer of 2000, it became clear that XIII Catalan, financially hard hit, would find it difficult to make the starting line-up. St Estève were not much better off. Maintaining that the gap between these two Catalan clubs and the pace-setters, Toulouse and Villeneuve, would have become impossible to bridge, former half-back Bernard Guasch took the bold step of proposing a merger of the two under the name of Union Treiziste Catalane. The son of the XIII Catalan hooker and *directeur sportif*, José Guasch, Bernard was not an official of either club at the time but famously brought together a host of ex-players and directors of both at his fortieth birthday party. There was an immediate consensus. Of course it would not have been Perpignan, and it would not have been rugby league, if there had not been dissenters. But most of those not initially won over changed their minds by the time UTC won the Lord Derby trophy in their first season, defeating Limoux 38-17, or when they appeared in their first Championship final, in the following year of 2002, though they still lagged behind Villeneuve, who won 17-0 in a dull game at Béziers. In that season, and the following season of 2002-3, Villeneuve maintained their stranglehold. The Leopards of Aquitaine did the Championship and Cup double, beating Pia back to back to take the Lord Derby trophy, to add to the victories over UTC and St Gaudens in the Championship final.

Under the direction of Richard Lewis, the RFL now decided that it was an appropriate time to recall a French club into

Super League. The main motivation was to try to give the best French players a professional pathway, keeping them in rugby league rather than letting them go off to rugby union, and to improve the performance of the national team. Toulouse, with the driving force of chairman Carlos Zalduendo behind it, was the club many thought best equipped to face the challenge. Villeneuve, the doyen club, had dominated the domestic competition. Perpignan, a city with an equally long tradition, was, since the merger, beginning to re-establish itself. After an exhaustive assessment of each of the three candidates, the Perpignan club got the nod, the RFL's visiting officers having been swayed by its potential to revive a rugby league hotbed. Sensibly, UTC were given three years to prepare, unlike PSG, which had had around six months without any existing structures to build on. In more enlightened times, the Perpignan bid was also given three years' security once up and running in Super League, meaning that the club could not be relegated in its first two seasons even if it finished bottom of the league.

France was continuing to struggle on the international front. The Federation, keen to play its part in international development, appeared content to see the national side operate at a secondary level of competition. The Mediterranean Cup was again contested for three years in a row from 2002 to 2004, bringing very mixed results. In 2002 in Tripoli, fifty miles north of Beirut, the French suffered an embarrassing 36-6 defeat at the hands of the Lebanese, two of whom were recruited from the NRL and the rest from the Metro Cup, and thus were accustomed to more rigorous competition than the French league provided. A second defeat ensued in 2003, after the French had delivered a thrashing to the two fledgling nations, Morocco, who were hammered 72-0 and Serbia-Montenegro, who suffered a 120-0 rout, centre Fabrice Estebanez scoring ten tries. France's participation in that year's Mediterranean Cup brought about divisions in the Federation. President Jean-Paul Ferré insisted that the France team go to Lebanon as a priority over meeting Australia. An unsatisfactory compromise was reached when half the first-choice national team headed off for a 26-18 loss in Tripoli, while the other half, called a French Selection, met Australia at Carcassonne on the same weekend and lost 34-10, though it could have been much worse. Lebanon won again in 2004, when, with Nicolas Larrat as newly-elected president, France entered their Espoirs team. This competition and the ongoing European Nations tournament showed that France was wedged between two levels: too good for the newcomers, unless they were stuffed with Aussies, but too weak to offer serious resistance to the three major nations. That was proved once more when the 2002 Kiwis, at the end of their Great Britain tour, in which they halved the series, won 36-10 at Perpignan.

The European Nations Cup, in which France was the one constant, allowed the French to compete on more or less equal terms with Ireland, Scotland and Wales, but not England, even when the English team was composed of emerging young international players. Such was the case in 2003, when France beat Ireland 26-18 in Dublin and lost 8-6 to Scotland at Narbonne before an under-strength side was thumped 68-6 by England at Warrington.

France could take satisfaction from their matches against New Zealand and Australia, which were fitted around those countries' involvement in the Tri-Nations in the autumn of 2004. A new coach, Mick Aldous, who had a background in development in his native Australia, had arrived six weeks earlier on a short contract after being recommended by Tas Baitieri. He succeeded in infusing the French side – in which no foreign-born player figured - with the self-belief that had so often been lacking and encouraged them to play to their spontaneous best. At Carcassonne, France were leading 20-18 after stand-off Maxime Grésèque had opened the scoring with a sixth-minute try and gone on to kick four goals from four attempts. Only an Ali Lauitiiti try three minutes from full time saved the Kiwis from their first defeat in France since 1980.

French officials might have been wary of taking on the Australians for the first time since the 74-0 defeat ten years earlier, and understandably so since even Great Britain had slipped to a record 64-point defeat in Sydney just two years before and, despite beating the Aussies 24-12 in the lead-up, were to endure a 44-4 lashing in the Tri-Nations final a week later. But ten days after facing the Kiwis, France came close to causing a huge upset against Darren Lockyer's Kangaroos at Toulouse. With explosive second rower Jamal Fakir spearheading a pack of forwards who would all feature in the Catalans' Super League team and with half-backs Maxime Grésèque and Julien Rinaldi presenting their opponents with all manner of problems, France scored six tries and trailed by just 34-30 with six minutes remaining. Three late converted tries gave the Australians a flattering 52-30 victory, but France's performance was judged as giving the whole game 'a shot in the arm', as Baitieri put it.[iv] Their uplifting display also drew rare praise from Kangaroo coach Wayne Bennett. 'They were wonderful, they were very spirited,' he said.[v]

Of that team, only Wakefield's Olivier Elima was playing in Super League. Hopes were high, therefore, that when the UTC players who made up the majority of the side were operating regularly at the same level in eighteen months' time, France's national team would see the benefit. After all, that was a major reason why a French club was taken into Super League. The announcement of the appointment of the RFL's performance director David Waite as the Catalans' director of rugby was hailed as another important step along that road. But it was clear that many difficulties lay ahead, not least of which was the high profile of rugby union in a city of around 120,000 population. The average attendance of the USAP club, which dominated the area's sporting life, stood at 11,000, whereas UTC's best crowds were in the region of 3,000 in an Elite competition which averaged about 1,200. Like many other union clubs, USAP had benefited from the arrival of professionalism in the 15-a-side game a decade earlier as well as the increasing interest of television companies.

There had also been divisions within the Federation, widened by the debate over the international calendar of the autumn of 2003, when president Jean-Paul Ferré had insisted that the Mediterranean Cup take precedence over facing Australia. Ferré decided not to stand for re-election in 2004 after serving for more than ten years, during which time the national team's record – despite avoiding Australia and a full-strength Great Britain – was a dismal one. His position was filled by Nicolas Larrat, whose father had been an official of the Carcassonne club and later became mayor of that city. A Toulouse-based lawyer who had the support of the British and Australian governing bodies, Larrat set himself the arduous task of modernising the Federation.

'We have written some of the great pages in the history of French sport,' he said. 'But we haven't really understood what has been happening over the past thirty years. We need to restore the game's image and what it stands for, and to do that we have to restructure the Federation at all levels ... My vision of French rugby league is perhaps idealistic, but I want it to rediscover the identity it used to have and which should never have been lost. I want all the national teams – not just the senior France team – to catch up on the major rugby league-playing countries. It will be a very long and very hard battle.'[vi]

On Larrat's wish-list was an Elite division of twelve or thirteen clubs, which would ideally include Marseille, a Paris representative (Paris-Châtillon were relegated without a win the previous season), Bordeaux, Lyon (who were already there), and Albi, as well as those he regarded as 'institutions', such as Lézignan, Limoux and Villeneuve. He cited four examples of clubs which had appropriate infrastructures: Carcassonne, Perpignan, Toulouse and St Gaudens. But two months after Larrat's election, Villeneuve went into voluntary liquidation. The leading club had lost its bid to join Super League and as a result also lost four key players – Romain Gagliazzo, Julien Rinaldi, Laurent Frayssinous and Jamal Fakir – to UTC, who, on the Federation's say-so, did not pay a transfer fee. With a change of name from US Villeneuve to Villeneuve Rugby League, the club was quickly revived. Lézignan found itself in financial difficulties too. In fact the majority of Elite clubs had suffered or were to suffer a similar fate. Even *Treize-Magazine*, the organ of the Federation and a vital means of communication and promotion of the game, was brought to a close in June 2004, deemed too expensive to run, although rugby league reappeared in a very limited way in the pages of *Midi-Olympique* after an absence of over two decades.

Yet the two finals of 2004 gave the impression of a game in good heart. As expected, UTC beat Carcassonne in a spectacular game at Albert Domec stadium, winning the Cup by 39-24 in front of a 10,500 crowd. But in the Championship final, second-placed St Gaudens caused a shock by beating league leaders UTC 14-10 at the Aimé Giral stadium. Centre Claude Sirvent scored two first-half tries, full back Adam Innes went over with ten minutes left and pulled off a try-saving tackle, showing to the 9,000 crowd that other French clubs could still have their day, even in the middle of July.

The following season of 2004-5 began in December, as the Federation briefly and pointlessly experimented with aligning its calendar with the British – a consequence of the Catalans joining Super League. In their last campaign in the French competition, UTC asserted their supremacy by racking up the highest-ever Championship final score when they defeated Toulouse, who were no doubt feeling flat after their Challenge Cup semi-final against Leeds, by 66-16. As might have been foreseen for a final played in the first week in August, a comparatively small crowd of 5,000 turned up to see it. The Catalans took double honours, having already beaten Limoux 31-12 to lift the Lord Derby trophy in May in front of 9,500 at Carcassonne. As for Toulouse, as coach and former player Justin Morgan headed off for Hull KR, another ex-player, 30-year old Trent Robinson, who had retired early from the game with a serious bicep injury, began his own exceptional coaching career.

The Catalan Dragons, as they were to be known, had finally been accepted into Super League in May 2004, when the British clubs voted them in by seven votes to five. What made those clubs sit up and take notice of the newcomers was Bernard Guasch's coup in recruiting one of the world's best players and all-time Kiwi great Stacey Jones from New Zealand Warriors. The 28-year old scrum-half had won 34 caps for his country and had been a Golden Boot winner in 2002. Since the Catalans were expected to model themselves on the Warriors, Jones's signing seemed timely in all respects.

The Federation also made the headlines when it was announced in July 2005 that John Monie, best known for a record-breaking spell at Wigan before joining New Zealand Warriors and then London, was to take charge of the national side. Said Nicolas Larrat: 'We were looking for a big name with a natural authority.'[vii]

Monie had an easy initiation – an 80-0 whipping of Russia at Arles – before getting down to the more serious business of facing England at Leeds. Though the England team was again a second-string side, France showed that their defence had improved considerably as they went down 22-12. After beating fledglings Georgia 60-0 in Tbilisi, a match in which Maxime Grésèque scored more than half his side's points with three tries and ten goals, France went on to beat Wales in the European Nations final at Carcassonne. The 38-16 victory was taken as further proof of improvement under the new coach. But Australia, wary of unpleasant surprises such as France had had in store for them the year before, went to a straightforward 44-12 win in Perpignan. At Toulouse a week later, the other Tri-Nations finalists and eventual winners, New Zealand, were less convincing. They trailed France by 22-16 before the French folded once more in the last ten minutes, the Kiwis running in three late tries to win 38-22.

The profitability of international matches partly accounted for the Federation's surplus of 84,000 euros (£60,000) in the year to June 2005, as opposed to a deficit of 285,000 euros (£200,000) the year before. 'French Rugby League has demonstrated that it can make money,' said Larrat.[viii]

The 2005-6 season began with an expanded twelve-team competition at Elite level. Marseille returned to the top division after a thirty-year absence, in line with Larrat's policy of taking rugby league back to the big cities. When Carpentras also stepped up after a lapse of three seasons, the game in the south-east corner was given a fillip. This was also the first season without a major team from Perpignan, although the Dragons agreed to field their reserve side in the Elite division, while Pia also represented the Catalan area. But in mid-season, when their financial backing failed to materialise, Marseille dropped out, just as Avignon had done six years earlier, causing a major dent in Larrat's expansion hopes. The Federation was having difficulty enough in going beyond an existing small core of teams. The unevenness of the Elite division was demonstrated when Pia demolished Carpentras by 126 points to 4, Grésèque helping himself to 54 points from four tries and nineteen goals. Earlier Pia had beaten Carpentras 92-12 away. Toulouse had also hammered the Provence club by 120-3. The previous highest total recorded came in 2003, when Villeneuve thrashed Paris-Châtillon 130-10.

When the Catalan Dragons made their bow in Super League on 11 February 2006, they did so without coach Steve Deakin, who had been with the club since 2003 and had guided them to two Lord Derby trophy wins and a Championship victory. David Waite took temporary charge and, at USAP's Aimé Giral stadium, saw his charges defeat Wigan, tipped as one of the title favourites, by 38-30. An 11,122 crowd plus 85 journalists watched as the Catalans, masterminded by captain Stacey Jones, marked France's return to Super League with an exciting performance in which stand-off Sean Rudder, prop Chris Beattie, and second rowers Jérôme Guisset and Jamal Fakir stood out. Jones, one of eight overseas players in the 17, said, 'It was fantastic to be a part of history for the club and for the Catalans. I'll remember this for the rest of my life.'[ix]

But at Salford in the very next match, Jones broke his arm, causing chairman Guasch to seriously doubt whether his club would win another game. Only days later, ex-St George full-back and former Bradford assistant coach Mick Potter was brought in as the club's first permanent head coach and Australian scrum-half Michael Dobson was signed as a replacement for Jones. By the end of that 2006 season, in which matches had also been staged at Carcassonne, Narbonne and Canet, the Dragons had won eight of their 28 matches, with winger Justin Murphy ending as Super League's top try scorer. It wasn't enough to stop the club from finishing last, but as they were exempted from relegation for two seasons Castleford took the drop in their place.

In the championship the Catalans had left behind, Pia and Lézignan took it in turns to fill the void in the next six seasons. Pia lifted the Max Rousié shield in 2006 and 2007 and were twice runners-up to Lézignan. The FCL took the title in every season from 2008 to 2011 after being runners-up in 2007 to Pia. Only Limoux threatened to overthrow these two teams' dominance, losing twice in the final. It was those two clashes with Lézignan which attracted the largest Championship final attendances of that period, both of them over 11,000.

It was a similar story in the Cup, won by Pia in 2006 and 2007. Lézignan were victorious in 2010 and 2011. Only Limoux, when they narrowly won the trophy in 2008 by defeating promoted club Albi, and Carcassonne, by beating Limoux in 2009, also by a slim margin, broke up the pattern. It was not what Larrat had in mind: Pia, a village team of some 8,000 souls, and Lézignan, scarcely much bigger at around 10,000, dominating a purportedly national competition.

Larrat was soon pressing for a second French Super League team, which would almost certainly have been Toulouse, possibly in 2009 or 2010. 'My strategy is clear,' he said. 'The French championship will never be professional, given the state of the clubs and their slowness to put structures in place. The idea of a fully professional championship is a pipedream. We play against England, Australia and New Zealand, which are professional countries. To beat them we also have to be professionals. The French team playing in Super League is essentially the France team. It's obvious that a second French team would allow us to have a reservoir of around fifty professional players, which would allow us to compete with the best countries in the world.'[x]

The Catalan Dragons players selected for the France team had the unusual experience of facing the autumn internationals at the end of their playing season, rather than the start, which had always been the case for those operating in the domestic championship. It brought only partial success. Along with

England, Samoa and Tonga, the French were competing in a new tournament called the Federation Shield. At Headingley, France lost to another young England side by 26-10 in a performance which John Monie labelled 'disappointing'. 'We were very poor with the fundamentals of the game.'[xi] France improved as Jamal Fakir touched down twice in the 28-6 win over Samoa at Colomiers, but with eight non-Super League players in the side, they were crushed 48-10 in the third and last match by a physically powerful Tonga, many of whose players came from the NRL.

In their second season, the Catalans returned to the recently renovated Gilbert Brutus stadium. The reopening of their spiritual home was marked by a last-minute defeat by Wigan amid a deluge. It was in the Challenge Cup that the Dragons made history. Thomas Bosc kicked a club record eleven goals – equalled later by himself and Scott Dureau – and scored a record 26 points in the 70-12 rout of National League Two side Featherstone before a sterner test at League One club Whitehaven and a win by 24-14. A 26-23 quarter-final victory at Hull, one place above the Dragons in Super League, led to a semi-final against 17-time Cup winners Wigan at Warrington. In a scintillating first quarter, the Dragons went 22-0 up following tries by Casey McGuire, John Wilson, Adam Mogg and Vincent Duport, with three conversions from Stacey Jones, whose out-of-hand kicking was also an important feature in establishing the Dragons' dominance. Up front, props Jérôme Guisset and Alex Chan, and second rowers Jason Croker and Sébastien Raguin set the opposition back on their heels while at the back Clint Greenshields shone in both attack and defence. When Duport crossed for his second and Jones added the conversion and then a drop goal, the Catalans had built an unassailable lead. Wigan hit back hard but it was not enough and Croker's late try gave victory by 37-24. Certainly the Dragons' overseas players had taken a major role in this historic victory, but they did not outnumber Wigan's foreign contingent, which also stood at eight out of the 17.

If the Catalan Dragons' appearance at Wembley was not epoch-making, it was at least unprecedented. As the Challenge

Cup final was staged for the first time at the new Wembley Stadium, the Catalans became the first French club in history to play in the Cup final, where they were watched by a crowd of 84,241, the biggest ever to see a French rugby team of either code in action. Winger Younes Khattabi became the first Frenchman, the first player of Moroccan origin and the first Muslim to score a try in a Wembley Cup final.

The Dragons had beaten their Cup final opponents, World Club champions St Helens, in the league by 21-0 only a fortnight earlier, but it was a different scenario at Wembley. St Helens led 12-4 at half-time, their defence clamping any Catalan attack. Justin Murphy went over for the second Catalan try just before the hour but by then the trophy belonged to Saints, who won 30-8. The Dragons' obvious disappointment was, however, mitigated by the huge media interest created by their appearance and the boost given to French rugby league after just two years of having a full-time professional team.

In the June before the August Cup final, *les Bleus*, as they tended to be referred to rather than Tricolores, met Great Britain at Headingley and lost 42-14. Nine of the 17 were non-Super League players, four of them from Toulouse, whose chairman Carlos Zalduendo submitted a business plan and presentation to the RFL, aimed at getting his club into the British competition. 'It was a massive blow to us when we were turned down in 2003, but since then we have worked hard to put together this new application,' he said.[xii]

It was too early to tell whether the Catalans' professionalism was having an effect on the France team, but the remainder of the 2007 international programme produced encouraging results. At Gilbert Brutus, a confident France side dominated Scotland by 46-16 before defeating PNG, on their first visit to Europe since 2000, by 38-26 at Avignon and by 22-16 at Bègles, with Grésèque as ever a key player. Against New Zealand at Stade Jean Bouin in Paris, France showed every sign of beating their opponents for the first time in 27 years. With only seven Catalans in the side, they led 14-10 with eight minutes left, but, as in 2004 and 2005, late tries saw the Kiwis home; they were relieved to emerge with a flattering 22-14 victory.

Strangely, at a time when the Dragons, in their third season, climbed from tenth place to third in 2008, the France team failed to live up to the promise of the year before. It was as if the performance of the national team was measured in inverse proportion to that of the Super League team.

The Dragons, with the likes of homegrown players such as Thomas Bosc, Jérôme Guisset, Olivier Elima, Greg Mounis and Sébastien Raguin playing alongside overseas signings like Alex Chan, Dane Carlaw, Jason Croker, Clint Greenshields, Adam Mogg and Casey McGuire, had exceeded expectations, reaching the play-offs and beating Warrington before losing in the elimination semi-final to Wigan.

The France team, on the other hand, were back to square one, suffering an embarrassing defeat at Toulouse in mid-season, when England hammered them 56-8. Without four first-choice players, France unravelled in the second half, conceding forty unanswered points. The timing of the game also did not help the French cause, as the Dragons' players had two Super League matches that week and those from the French championship had not played for between four and eight weeks, with little chance to practise as a team. Calls for a second French team in Super League intensified. A month later, Toulouse's application was rejected for the second time in five years. The idea of their joining League One surfaced, but was questioned by club chairman Carlos Zalduendo, who asked: 'Is this some kind of consolation? League One doesn't have the same impact. From a media and financial point of view, there is no comparison. It could be interesting from a playing point of view, but you don't have the revenue from gate receipts or television rights.'[xiii]

It was part of Larrat's plan, according to which the future of French clubs appeared to depend on integration into the British competitions. He expressed a wish to have three French clubs in Super League by 2015 and two in League One, which he deemed 'necessary for the development of our sport.'[xiv]

Before John Monie's appointment, Larrat had identified the France team's objective as a semi-final place in the 2008 World Cup in Australia. They fell a long way short. In the pool games, France opened with a 36-18 win over Scotland. Against Fiji in their second match, though expected to win, they failed to compete, their game falling apart under pressure from the powerful opposition forwards and strong-running backs. Following that 42-6 defeat, the French sank to bottom of their group on points difference and were left to face Samoa for a play-off to determine ninth and tenth place. In an error-strewn performance, France once again could not match their opponents' enthusiasm and energy and were left stranded at the foot of the ten-nation competition after losing 42-10. Questions were raised about the commitment of some of the squad and, not for the last time, it was suggested that the Catalan Dragons, who provided ten of the seventeen players involved in the defeats, were tired both mentally and physically. Monie, who had guided the France team towards a more rigorous approach, was not retained. As *les Bleus* looked towards participation in the following autumn's Four Nations tournament, expanded from three to accommodate another team, Larrat selected ex-Great Britain half-back Bobbie Goulding, despite his limited coaching experience, to take over.

In 2009 the Dragons, well led by Greg Bird and Adam Mogg, reached the qualifying semi-final in which they came close to winning at Leeds but went down 27-20. They were successful in attracting 18,150 fans to the first-ever Super League game to be played in Spain when they faced Warrington at Barcelona's Olympic Stadium. That match took place a week after France had suffered another midsummer mauling at the hands of England, who, in Goulding's first match in charge, racked up 44 first-half points before easing off to win 66-12 at Stade Jean Bouin, Paris. France showed more of a competitive edge in the autumn series but, as expected, lost their three matches against England (34-12) at Doncaster, New Zealand (62-12) at Toulouse and Australia (42-4) at Charléty.

A pattern was becoming established. In three consecutive

years France were hammered by England in mid-season, until it was decided that the contest was too one-sided and the concept was abandoned. Against Ireland, Scotland and Wales, the French showed themselves usually capable of beating two of those teams in any given season before possibly losing narrowly to the third, as happened, for example, in 2010, when Wales unexpectedly triumphed 12-11 at Albi to earn a place in the Four Nations tournament.

In that same year, the Catalan Dragons, without Bird and Mogg, slumped to last in Super League, but managed to retrieve their season with a Challenge Cup semi-final appearance, losing to the eventual winners, Warrington. In the domestic championship, Lézignan, in their run of four consecutive titles from 2008 on, achieved back-to-back Cup and Championship doubles in 2010 and 2011. The FCL therefore became the third club, after Villeneuve and Pia, to do the double in successive seasons. It is significant that those feats, the only three in the history of the game in France, happened between 2003 and 2011. Not even Carcassonne at the height of their powers had managed that, revealing that it had become easier for a single club, even a small-town club, to dominate the competition.

Of course the departure of the Catalans had lessened the league, as did the decision by the Federation to put Toulouse into the British second tier between 2009 and 2011. The three-year experiment proved inconclusive. Gilles Dumas' men secured some notable wins and no doubt learned a good deal about playing against British teams. But in an eleven-team competition, they finished tenth, eighth and tenth again. Getting the best out of a semi-professional team, where most of the players had a regular job to fit in around the training and travelling, did not prove easy. It was hard to discern what the point of it had been, particularly when the French domestic competition was not at its strongest.

In the autumn of 2011 at Avignon, *les Bleus* achieved their best performance against England for five years. They scored two late tries in a 32-18 defeat and made up for a weak display against an emerging England team, the Knights, the previous week at Leigh. That match had prompted Goulding to resign, claiming that a lack of cooperation between the Federation and Catalan Dragons had resulted in his never being able to field the strongest side, although thirteen of the team were from the Perpignan club and their Francophile coach Trent Robinson had tried to ensure that his players should be readily available to the national team. Goulding was persuaded to stay on but his contract was not renewed at the end of the year.

The attendance of almost 17,000 at Avignon came after a crowd of 14,500 the year before at the same Parc des Sports for the match against Ireland, 10,000 at Albi for the 2010 European Cup decider against Wales, and 10,000 at Perpignan in 2011 for the match against Scotland. Many of the tickets at those matches were given away, but it was still regarded as a marketing success to attract so many spectators, whether for free or not.

Robinson, who arrived at Perpignan in 2010, taking over from Kevin Walters, was named Super League Coach of the Year in 2011, while the Dragons were voted Club of the Year. Bottom in 2010, they rose to sixth the following season, reaching the preliminary semi-final as players such as David Ferriol, asserting an old-fashioned presence at prop, and veteran ex-Kangaroo back-rower Steve Menzies, with his exemplary standards, led the way. After acquiring a reputation, like other French teams in the past, of being poor travellers, the Dragons had a run of seven games undefeated, which included wins in consecutive weeks at Warrington and Wigan, the latter by 47-28. In 2012, finishing fourth, they also reached the preliminary semi-final before their young coach headed back to the NRL and Sydney Roosters, leading them to the title in his first year. His assistant and former Catalans stand-off, Laurent Frayssinous, took over, becoming the first French Super League coach.

Earlier there had been speculation that Robinson might combine his role at the Catalans with that of head coach of the France team, though he resisted any such call. The Lézignan coach, Aurélien Cologni, was given the job temporarily and oversaw two victories over Wales and two defeats in England. After success in June at Wrexham, the French staged the return in October in the north-eastern town of Lens, where, inspired by stand-off Thomas Bosc, they won 20-6 in front of an 11,628 crowd. Most of those spectators, again benefiting from free tickets, had turned up out of curiosity since rugby league was practically an unknown sport in this round-ball territory. The venue had been chosen as an experiment in a wider scheme known as the Dayan plan, named after a sports management consultant who had been given a brief to expand rugby league into new areas. The idea was to graft rugby league teams on to football clubs in cities such as Bordeaux or even uncharted territory like Strasbourg. That unrealistic notion was bound to fail and was mothballed as soon as Carlos Zalduendo took over as Federation president from Nicolas Larrat in November 2012.

As the 2013 World Cup approached, Wakefield and former Hull coach Richard Agar was appointed to guide the France team. In the first of three games at the group stage, the French edged out the Kumuls by 9-8 at Craven Park, Hull, thanks to a William Barthau drop goal from 40 metres and their opponents' failure to land a 79th minute penalty. For the match against New Zealand, an enthusiastic Avignon public once again turned out in force. The sell-out crowd of 17,518, who all paid, was a record for the stadium and the highest for a rugby league match in France since the Tricolores beat New Zealand in 1972. They watched in awe as the Kiwis proved far too powerful and experienced for the French, who lost 48-0. Outgunned for a second time, *les Bleus* went down 22-6 to Samoa at Perpignan, but qualified on points difference to meet England in the quarter-final at Wigan, seen by 22,276. There proved to be a world of difference in the official rankings between third-placed England and fourth-placed France, who went out of the tournament, losing 34-6.

In the domestic championship of 2013-14, the Elite 1 division of eight teams was the smallest ever. Though Toulouse Olympique had returned from the British second tier in 2011, two village teams dropped out. Lescure, near Albi, returned to Elite 2, but a far bigger gap was left by Pia. The champion club, who had won the title three times since 2006, had been hit by a 10,000 euro fine by the Federation and their chairman banned. The sanction had been imposed after Pia had allegedly threatened to boycott the 2012 Cup final against Carcassonne. Two days before the event, Pia protested against the choice of referee, who, they claimed, had unfairly ruled against them when acting as video referee in the previous week's Championship final, also against Carcassonne. The Federation, facing the potential embarrassment of having to cancel a televised final two days before it was due to happen, reluctantly yielded, but came down hard on the club afterwards. Carcassonne achieved their first double since 1967, but resentful Pia, faced also with a reduction in grant from the local council, withdrew from the competition at the end of the following season, when, ironically, they won the Championship, beating St Estève-XIII Catalan 33-26. 'It's unthinkable that the champion club will not compete in 2013-14,' said Zalduendo.[xv] Though different in detail, there were echoes of 1981 or 1989. The unthinkable happened.

When Toulouse reappeared in Elite 1 in 2011 after a three-year absence, their aim, said chairman Zalduendo, was to dominate the domestic championship. They did not do that until the 2013-14 season, after Zalduendo had become Federation president and his place as club chairman was taken by Bernard Sarrazain, who appointed their recently retired captain, Sylvain Houlès, as head coach. Toulouse won successive Championship titles, beating Lézignan, then Carcassonne, and did the double in 2014 by overwhelming Carcassonne 46-10 in the Cup final. After which, it was decided that there was nothing left to prove and the club headed for the British competition – not Super League, not even the second tier, but the third level, known as League 1. After the RFL had restructured its competitions and reduced Super League to twelve clubs, it was no longer possible for an outside club to be catapulted straight into either of the two higher divisions and so France's champion club ended up in the third division. They dominated it from start to finish, were unbeaten in the regular part of that 2016 season, scored 990 points in 21 matches, and duly earned promotion, for which Houlès was named coach of the year. In the Challenge Cup too, they made waves, winning 10-8 against Championship side Leigh, who earned promotion to Super League, and put on a brave, uninhibited performance in the 40-22 defeat at Super League club Wakefield.

In 2014, the year after the World Cup, the national side reverted to its familiar model of losing a key game in the four-team European Cup. A failure in Ireland in the first game, despite victories against Wales and Scotland in the other two fixtures, resulted in France finishing second on points difference to Scotland, who thus claimed fourth spot in the Four Nations tournament, due to take place in two years' time. The following season's edition of the European competition therefore had no such prize attached, but it would have made no difference. France travelled the same route, winning two and losing to the winners, Wales. Far more consequential was the match against England at Leigh, a warm-up for the English, who were set to face New Zealand in the Test series. A dozen players pulled out of the France team, some very late, some with more legitimate reasons than others, so that it was a very inexperienced France team which stepped out on the Sports Village pitch. Needless to say, it showed, even against an England side with four debutants. France conceded three tries in the opening eight minutes, fifteen in all, and fifty points in the second half. 'Catastrophe' was the word on many French lips but even that did not adequately express the nature of the record 84-4 defeat. Coach Agar, rueing the withdrawals, called the game a 'mismatch' and thought it should not have been played.

A year later, France's performance against England was much improved, but still ended in a 40-6 loss. The French could be satisfied, however, with another sizeable crowd at Avignon, where 14,267 saw a test match which was essentially another run-out for England ahead of the Four Nations. Under new coach Aurélien Cologni, now appointed on a permanent basis by new president Marc Palanques, *les Bleus* showed greater commitment.

Former international captain Palanques, a central figure in the inglorious 1989 final, had been out of rugby league for over two decades before returning to Carcassonne as a club director and then, supported by Catalan Dragons chairman Bernard Guasch, opposed Zalduendo in the 2016 elections and won. There had been concerns in Carcassonne and elsewhere that once-great clubs like ASC had been overlooked as attention was thought to focus on Perpignan and Toulouse, both playing in British competitions.

The future of the Elite 1 competition gave rise to serious worries, operating as it had with eight teams following the departure of Toulouse and Pia, then nine, although, in the close season before Zalduendo's departure, the league was restored to ten with the return of St Gaudens. The decline in crowds and the difficulty in attracting sponsors in a harsh economic climate were two of the main issues. That decline was mirrored in the attendances for the Championship and Cup finals, which nevertheless continued to produce some thrilling matches: Avignon's 38-37 Cup win over Limoux in 2013, or Lézignan's 27-25 victory over St Estève-XIII Catalan in 2015 in the same event, for example. The fall in attendances went back well beyond Zalduendo's administration. The last five-figure crowd in the Cup final was registered in 2005. In the Championship final, only two occasions produced a five-figure attendance since 2001, both of them Lézignan-Limoux clashes. But in both 2015 and 2016, the combined attendance of Championship final and Cup final fell short of 10,000. The two Championship finals, the first held at Colomiers, the second at Albi, were contested by Carcassonne. The great ASC, the club with more trophies than any other, had held sway in the city as long as anyone could remember. But in recent years, their sporting monopoly was threatened by the rugby union team, who, on being promoted to the professional second division had claimed much of the media attention as well as local money, not to mention a following based not so much on interest in what happened on the field as a perception of being involved in something nationally meaningful.

St Estève-XIII Catalan, the reserve team of the Catalan Dragons, took part in the Cup finals of 2015, 2016 and 2018, winning the last two. Their presence in what used to be regarded as a showpiece event gave the impression that the Lord Derby trophy counted for less than it used to, just as Toulouse's departure for England further diminished the French championship.

The Dragons' average attendance at Gilbert Brutus in 2015 was 8,635; in 2016 it rose to 9,348. At the same time, they had become recognised as Super League's most successful club in business terms: a huge triumph, and one on which Bernard Guasch and his men were rightly congratulated, but also one which cast France's domestic competitions into the shade. It was said, over and over, by one Federation president after another, that the France team was rugby league's shop window. That was no longer true. The Dragons had taken over the mantle, with everything that implied. Further proof was provided in 2018 when, within one short period, the Catalans registered a home attendance of over 10,000 for a regular Super League match and Toulouse had more than 5,000 for their first 'on-the-road' match at Albi. Neither the Lord Derby final at Perpignan, nor the Championship final at Albi produced more than 3,500, which showed starkly where fans' interests lay.

The 2017-18 season provided another reminder of the precarious state of domestic rugby league. The Elite 1 season began in December (January 2018 had initially been proposed) with a Championship final on 1 July. The partial alignment with the Super League calendar had been tried before, a dozen years earlier, with no notable benefit, though the present administration appeared unaware, announcing, 'We have to change or we're dead.'[xvi] It had an air of desperation about it. Played in sweltering conditions, the Championship final was nevertheless exciting and full of suspense till the final hooter, but, as has been said many times before, the quality of play deserved a bigger audience. Avignon claimed their first-ever title by beating Limoux 34-28 in a match which was streamed live on the Federation's own set-up, but, for the first time in years, was not broadcast on a television channel. It was not without controversy. Avignon had only qualified after appealing against their victors in the semi-final, St Estève-XIII Catalan, who had won 23-16 but had fielded two 'ineligible' players from their Super League roster. The pair had played fewer matches than was necessary to be selected for the final and should not have appeared on the team-sheet, according to a new regulation. However, a post-match counter-appeal by the Catalans was successful: the rule had only been introduced after the start of the season and should not have been implemented, it was declared. The Catalans decided to take the matter no further 'in the wider interests of rugby league and a concern to preserve the image of our sport.'[xvii] Which was a step forward.

In the 2017 British Championship, Toulouse continued with their inventive, free-flowing style to occupy second place for most of the campaign before just failing to make the top four and ensure a place in the so-called 'middle eight', in which they would have faced four Super League clubs, including the Catalans Dragons (who had added an ungrammatical 's' to their name). Toulouse had the consolation of winning the Championship Shield, contested by the remainder of the clubs in the division. It was the first British trophy – if a minor one - lifted by a French club. In 2018, at the second attempt, they achieved their short-term aim of qualifying for the middle eight, in which they met the previous season's Super League champions, Leeds. At Headingley they trailed by only four points at one stage in the second half before succumbing to superior experience, going down by 48-22. By the last game of the season they had come close to the play-offs for a coveted place in the top division but, despite beating two Super League clubs, ended in sixth spot out of eight.

The 2017 World Cup saw France drawn in the same group as Australia, England and Lebanon, with three of the four going through to the quarter-finals. In their first game, the French met their bête noire, Lebanon, at Canberra in a match which would effectively determine which side would accompany the two favourites into the quarter-finals. The 72nd minute of that match proved to be the turning-point of France's World Cup, as coach Cologni pointed out. That was when the Lebanon stand-off, the young Parramatta star Mitchell Moses, landed a drop-goal that set the French back on their heels, and then waltzed through for a self-converted try that won the game by 29-18. France went on to lose to the eventual winners, Australia, by 52-6 and the Aussies' opponents in the final, England, by 36-6.

The French players made plenty of mistakes, but no one could question their commitment. It was true that their preparation for the tournament had been disrupted by the Dragons' extended season. For three years, the Catalans had been marking time in mid-table. But in an uninspired 2017 campaign they ended up in the middle eight Qualifiers. Frayssinous made way for ex-England head coach Steve McNamara, whose immediate task was to avoid relegation. The Catalans' poor form continued, such that they found themselves having to travel to Leigh, promoted the year before, to decide, in the so-called 'Million Pound Game', which club would stay up. In a convincing display that left everyone wondering why they had left it so worryingly late, the Dragons took full advantage of an imploding Leigh and won 26-10.

The consequences of failure would have been awful to contemplate. As Sylvain Houlès commented, it would have been a disaster if Toulouse and the Catalans had met, not in Super League, but in the Championship.[xviii] The victory at Leigh on 30 September 2017, said chairman Bernard Guasch, 'saved French rugby league.'[xix] It was a big claim, but no one disagreed.

The Dragons' poor form continued through the first part of the 2018 season, relieved by an extended run in the Challenge Cup. They made a shaky start at League 1 club York, avoiding a major upset with a 34-22 win before brushing aside Whitehaven, also from the third tier, by 56-10 at Gilbert Brutus. A 20-6 quarter-final victory at Super League rivals Huddersfield pitched the Dragons into a semi-final clash with their 2007 Cup final victors and overwhelming favourites, St Helens. By then the Dragons' place in the Super 8 was secure, but they faced opponents who were the runaway league leaders after losing only two matches all season. Just as they had done eleven years earlier in the semi against Wigan, the Catalans produced a stunning display. This time their success was based on their forwards' dominance, with front-rowers Mickaël Simon and Sam Moa, backed by a third prop, captain Rémi Casty, named at loose forward in place of the suspended Greg Bird, much in evidence. Ex-Wigan hooker Michael McIlorum and second rowers Benjamin Garcia and Benjamin Jullien, supported off the bench by Julian Bousquet, Louis Anderson, Jason Baitieri and Kenny Edwards, completed a formidable set of forwards. In the first half, winger Lewis Tierney crossed first, Garcia touched down twice, and full-back Tony Gigot went over for a fourth as well as kicking a drop goal, to which scrum-half Josh Drinkwater added five goals for an astonishing and wholly unpredicted 27-0 half-time lead. Moa crashed through for a fifth try and Drinkwater landed two more goals as the Dragons went to a comprehensive 35-16 victory. 'They bullied us off the park,' said St Helens coach Justin Holbrook. 'They did to us what we've been doing to a lot of teams.'

As the Catalans headed for a Wembley final against Warrington, four places above them in the league and Challenge Cup-winners three times in the previous nine years, few expected McNamara's men to be capable of repeating their semi-final display. But, whereas in 2007 they gave the impression of simply being happy to have reached the final, eleven years on they had come with the firm intention of winning. In the media build-up to the event, much was made about the adversity French rugby league had had to overcome just to survive. What was also evident was that 'neutral' fans tended to align themselves with the Catalans, showing the extent to which British rugby league had embraced the French club.

On Saturday 25 August 2018, the Catalans took their first step towards a historic success as, in only the second minute, centre David Mead handed on to Jullien, who slipped the ball for Tierney to squeeze in at the corner, Drinkwater converting from near touch. They never lost that early lead. After Drinkwater had added a penalty, Warrington pulled back to 8-6 before Garcia tunnelled through a bunch of defenders from dummy half and his scrum-half kicked a simpler goal to put his side 14-6 ahead at the end of a remarkable, error-free first half. It would not be enough, but Gigot's fine 40/20 kick set up the position for centre Brayden Wiliame to slice through and Drinkwater to land his fourth goal. The remaining 34 minutes were played out amid increasingly unbearable tension as Warrington put the Dragons under severe pressure. The intensity led to crucial mistakes on both sides. Warrington drew ever closer with a try and two goals, but the Catalans' defence was a triumph of willpower over weariness. Not only the forwards, but the backs also brought off try-saving tackles with perfect timing. Tierney produced one of them, as did Mead, who, with stand-off Samisoni Langi, made almost as many tackles as the front five of the pack. In the dying minutes, Warrington threw all their power at the Dragons' line but it refused to yield. The 20-14 victory had the *sang et or* colours waving madly as Gigot was announced as the first Frenchman to earn the Lance Todd Trophy and captain Rémi Casty, the only survivor from the 2007 side, raised the 122-year old trophy before escorting it beyond British shores for the first time. A French team had won at Wembley before, the Tricolores having famously beaten England there in 1949, but it was hard to escape the conclusion that this was the greatest performance by a French club in the history of the game, one which was ripe with significance for its future.

Postscript

•

IT HAS PROVIDED some of the finest-ever expressions of rugby of either code. Those dazzling, innovative achievements of the early fifties figure among the greatest exploits in the history of French team sports, feats which shattered the Australians' usually unshakeable self-belief, making them tear up their coaching manual and start again.

Twenty years later, in a publication called *Essais et Tenus*, the question was being asked, as it had already been asked for over a decade: why was French rugby league in decline?[i] The question provoked a variety of articulate responses.

One reader argued that the 1951 tourists returned from Australia with a power style of play in their baggage which did not suit the French temperament, while at the same time the Aussies did everything possible to rival the French in terms of finesse and improvisation. This kind of imported 'trench warfare', it was claimed, went hand-in-hand with dirty play, which put the public off. Since this decline in interest coincided with a similar disaffection among football spectators, the French public opted for the national sport which seemed to be doing best, namely rugby union, well served on television by Roger Couderc. So the accepted story goes. As we know, the fortunes of league and union are intertwined.

The dual problem of violence and the play-the-ball rule was a common theme, though dirty play was not confined either to rugby league or to France. Nor were issues associated with the play-the-ball specifically French, as rugby league administrators, especially in Britain, wrestled with the rule for decades.

All respondents accepted rugby league's diminishing 'zone of influence'. The idea of rugby league as a by-product of union, which the name of *jeu à treize* appeared to confirm, as if union had patented the term 'rugby', led to another conception – that of league as an unimportant regional sport. In England rugby league had never quite managed to escape the perception of being a northern game. It had also had to face, from the late fifties onwards, exactly the kind of problems prevalent across the Channel, including financial difficulties, which continued at least until the dawn of Super League and its massive cash injection. 'Rugby league is dying' had become an all too familiar refrain. But England was better equipped to cope with such hardships. It certainly suffered discrimination of various kinds, but in Wigan or Widnes, Hull or Huddersfield, Whitehaven or Workington, the game had popular support which union simply could not match. That might also have been true in Lézignan or Villeneuve-sur-Lot, but in general rugby league in France was continually struggling against a more powerful rival.

The question is why rugby union should have had the upper hand when rugby league, at a point in its early history, left the other code trailing in its wake, having the undoubted advantage of being better suited to the French disposition.

Rugby union had, and still has its own advantages, none of them to do with its attractiveness on the field of play. Whereas, in 1944, the Ligue Française de Rugby à XIII had to start all over again, the FFR emerged from the war with its club base more or less intact. Because of the iniquitous measures enacted by Vichy, who, as befitted that reactionary regime, turned the clock back and forced all treizistes to play union, rugby league could not compete on anything like equal terms in the postwar era. With the complicity of the powerful Home Unions, who, despite their harrumphing about the French championship, knew from their experience of the 1930s what exclusion would mean, the France XV found itself back on the international rugby union scene.

Friends in high places… When Carlos Zalduendo, as president of the Federation, accompanied the President of the French Republic, François Hollande, on an official trip to Australia in 2014, it was the exception which confirmed the rule. Even then, his inclusion came about at the instigation of the Aussies. On the other hand, it shows the diversity and reach of rugby union that figures as disparate as Che Guevara, Idi Amin of Uganda and Benito Mussolini all had involvement with rugby union. Not only President de Gaulle, but subsequent heads of state, from Georges Pompidou to Nicolas Sarkozy, have found it appropriate to be associated with the 15-a-side code. Was it not Sarkozy who, soon after winning the presidential election of 2007, addressed the France XV before union's World Cup, telling them, 'I am a winner and so must you be'? If only the 1951 tourists had found similar recognition at the highest level of the French state.

Treizistes envy those priceless connections, but their envy turns to anger when those relations are misused in order to boost union and deflate, even try to kill off, rugby league. For sixty years and more, many of the dilemmas confronting rugby league bore the fingerprints of rugby union. If, as was claimed by Dr Raphaël Joué, chairman of XIII Catalan and president of the Federation from 1964 to 1967, the media bore a heavy responsibility in the demise of rugby league, evidence from one of his successors, 25 years later, showed how the media and other parties might be influenced by quinziste pressure.[ii]

In February 1990, Jean-Paul Verdaguer wrote to all International Board member countries asking for assistance in fending off the predatory FFR and its president. Not only had Ferrasse and his men not accepted the court ruling that the term 'rugby' could also apply to league, he was taking the Rugby League Federation back to court. It was obvious that the longer the case went on, the more rugby league would be drained of its resources.

'It is important to note,' wrote Verdaguer, 'that this continual harassment has led to numerous players switching codes and provoked the loss of numerous potential sponsors for our Australian tour. (The Rugby Union is touring Australia at the same time.)'

As for media pressure, Verdaguer gives a very clear example: 'Our three-year TV deal with TVSport France (Screensport England) was put into jeopardy by Mr Ferrasse, who proposed [to] this satellite network, rights to his RU fixtures, if they dropped ... the league.'[iii]

TVSport rejected Ferrasse's overtures. Other media might have been more acquiescent. David Oxley saw the FFR president's attacks as part of an 'all-out war' whose aim was to 'kill off rugby league'.[iv] Only after union itself became 'non-amateur' in 1995 did that kind of interference gradually wane. By then the quinzistes must have felt that league was no longer a threat.

Back in 1944, many rugby union sympathisers must have been thoroughly sickened to see the return of the rival they thought they had got rid of. The comeback was truly remarkable: this sport that had been unknown in France just over a decade earlier, and had been wiped out for four years, sprang back to life. But though the Vichy regime came to an end in 1944, the structures for sport which it had put in place remained largely untouched post-war. It was not until 1998, with the publication of the government enquiry into sport during the Vichy era, that some sort of light was shone on what actually had gone on. Even then, no one was held to account. Rugby union, alongside other favoured team sports, had continued to benefit from the measures taken between 1940 and 1944, crucial among which was the placing of these sports on the school curriculum.

Rugby league was not afforded that opportunity, with the consequence that its development has suffered enormously. The signing of an apparently important agreement between the Federation and the Ministry of Education was supposed to allow the game to have an official place on the curriculum, some eighty years after the sport had been introduced to France. It was not quite so straightforward and in any case it came late, very late. And that, according to such an experienced analyst as Robert Fassolette, is the main reason for rugby league's ultimate decline.

Accurate historical figures relating to rugby league are hard to come by. Precise comparisons with rugby union are therefore difficult to make, but in the 15-a-side code the number of clubs tripled between 1955 and 1984, jumping from 575 to 1,723. In 1980, there were 172,000 players, counting all age groups.[v] By 2016 official figures showed 435,000 participants, including those taking part in short introductory courses. In rugby league, the lack of records does not allow any kind of progression to be measured, but in 2011, the Federation was claiming 40,000 participants, taking into account children taking part in *mini-treize* tournaments and other projects aiming to introduce youngsters to the game.[vi] In other words, roughly one-tenth of rugby union's numbers. Figures provided in May 2010 by a Federation official, Laurent Roldos, showed 153 clubs, though up to a third of those did not have senior sections. Regular players of all age groups were counted as 7,474, of which 2,291 were open-age players, plus around 2,500 officials. That compares with the 16,200 open-age players registered with BARLA at that same time.[vii] The areas with the highest concentration of clubs were Languedoc (including Perpignan and the Aude), Midi-Pyrénées (Toulouse, Albi, St Gaudens) and Provence (Avignon, Carpentras).

As the researcher Jean Larronde was fond of saying, '*Sans élite, pas de masse; sans masse, pas d'élite.*'[viii] But when there was a strong elite in the fifties, the development of players who would eventually take their place was restricted because of lack of instruction at the lower levels. It was left to those clubs which had an *école de rugby* or local leagues to do the developmental work, which was not enough, whereas rugby union, helped enormously by Vichy's schools programme, and with its greater number of clubs, already had the structures in place to continue to produce players. Development became a major task undertaken by the Federation in the 1970s when the protocol put a brake on signings from rugby union. (The 15-a-side code, meanwhile, still claimed the right to be regarded as an amateur sport, while paying or giving other inducements to players, whom it restricted, via the protocol, from turning to a legitimately open sport.) Even so, the lack of access to schools was a serious impediment, meaning that rugby league was continually playing up the slope.

Nor can damage from within be overlooked. The self-harm committed by the final of 1981, with its unbridled violence, served to confirm the public's worst ideas about the game. It might all have been avoided if the Federation had acted more decisively. In the aftermath of the final of 1989, the Federation did indeed act more resolutely, though it could also be argued that such firmness needed to be applied more regularly at a time when brutality was rife.

Those who disavow the effects of Vichy, citing a victim culture, put forward the 1981 final in particular as an example of the game's failure to deal with internal issues which treizistes themselves brought about. Undoubtedly so, but Vichy is impossible to ignore as a cause of rugby league's later malaise. Before the war, the Ligue's clubs were on the increase, the quinzistes' in apparently inexorable decline. After the war, with international relations restored, it was simply a matter of time before the quinzistes made up the ground they had never quite lost, and the treizistes were left like hares chased by Ferrasse's dogs. This is the conclusion reached by the writer J-L Gonzalez in *Midi-Olympique,* who maintained, 'Without the helping hand of history and Vichy, rugby league would no doubt have supplanted rugby union in the long term; all historians are in agreement on that.'[ix]

As for the French game's present and future, former Federation president Nicolas Larrat appeared justified in believing that, at the top level which sets the example, it was essentially bound to the British competition, full professionalism being beyond the reach of the French domestic set-up. The declining interest of the national and regional media, with certain exceptions, made the task of revitalising the game harder. The closure of the Paris office, carried out for financial reasons in June 2018, simply sent out a message that this was a provincial sport, based not even in a big city like Toulouse, but in Carcassonne, much smaller and therefore less economically significant.

Professionalism is inescapable in popular modern sport. For decades in rugby league, Australia has provided the template. Its pursuit of progress, as it sees it, is never-ending. The Wales and one-time France coach John Kear noted at the 2017 World Cup, after seeing for himself how much things had moved on: '[The Australians] not only have a greater player pool but I also believe they have a better development and performance path at the elite end... Results are showing just how good the southern hemisphere teams really are.'[x]

By becoming France's first fully professional rugby league club when they entered Super League in 2006 (unless we count the Aussie-filled Paris Saint-Germain of 1997), the Catalan Dragons have led the way, providing the vital pathway for young players, giving supporters the chance to see a French team compete with the best in the northern hemisphere and showing that France plays a part in the professional future of the game.

Their Challenge Cup victory of 2018 gave French rugby league its biggest boost in many years, reinvigorating all those connected with the game. It was, however, based on qualities we would be hard pushed to identify as typically French. The Catalan fans clamour for bold, expansive play. Sometimes they get what they wish for. But in general the Dragons' style of play is not significantly different from other Super League clubs'. It was their defence, above all else, which won them the Cup.

The idea of 'French flair' is a cliché which once applied to both codes but for a long time has been no more obvious in France than any other country. Thirty years after his finest hour in Brisbane, Jean Dop could insist: 'The French style is improvisation based on well-mastered technique... The risk must be calculated but it is the very expression of talent *à la française*.'[xi] In the Dragons' team – half French, half foreign – the equivalent of those improvised one-arm lobs of Jean Dop which were part of the French way are the huge cut-out passes delivered, as likely as not, by an Australian.

The Catalans' Wembley triumph was achieved in a different way from the France team's style of '51 or '55, since sport, like everything else, adapts and evolves. But in the long history of the Challenge Cup, this team's victory was as great if not greater than any other. In the face of the forces which had tried to stifle French rugby league's very existence, it was the ultimate act of defiance.

Appendix I

•

How Rugby League was Banned

DUAL-INTERNATIONAL ANTOINE BLAIN, secretary-general of the French Rugby League Federation and manager of the first four tours to Australia and New Zealand, describes, in a *Midi-Olympique* article of 15 November 1955, how he first discovered the plot to ban rugby league:

'August 1940. On a visit to Mauléon,[i] I met one of my friends from Côte Basque XIII, who, returning from a clandestine trip to Bayonne,[ii] told me of the rumours circulating between Nive and Adour[iii] about an approach made by rugby union officials to an important Basque politician, a Minister of State, in order to obtain what was referred to as the reunification of French rugby by, in effect, the elimination of rugby league.

'I could not imagine such an underhand act, unworthy of sportsmen. A few days later I was forced to face the facts. Jean Ybarnegaray, Minister for the Family and Youth, declared on a visit to Pau, "The fate of rugby league is clear. Its life is over. It is purely and simply deleted from French sport."

'It only remained for the Commissariat Général des Sports[iv] to carry out the order issued by the Minister. No time was lost. Dr Ginesty, president of the FFR, was summoned to Vichy on 15 September and the Sports Department, run by ex-rugby [union] players, made haste so that less than a month later one could read in the press of the unoccupied zone: "It's over. Rugby league is no more. From Sunday 20 October all teams will have to play rugby union…'

Blain went on to make the analogy with a criminal case. He suggested that the investigator looking for the murderer always asks the question 'Who profits by the crime?' Among his own archives, he stated that he had numerous documents with quotations from leading rugby union officials of major clubs or regional committees:

'But the main exhibit in the trial was provided by the Official Journal of the French State, dated 11 June 1942,' Blain continued, 'relating to appointments on the management council of the French Federation of Basque Pelota on the one hand and the French Rugby Federation on the other…

'On the list of persons charged with administering rugby, of which most are still in office, one finds, in the position of honorary vice-president, the vice-president of the Federation of Basque Pelota.

'That would be nothing in itself if the president-designate of the Federation of Basque Pelota was not Ybarnegaray, the executioner of rugby league, and if one did not find him surrounded by the pride of Basque rugby officials who might well be, barring a truly unfortunate coincidence, the ones who inspired their president and Minister for the Family and Youth in the execution of his act against our sport.'

Blain recalled how the case against rugby league was prepared, with 'evidence' provided by leading rugby union officials. He quoted the chairman of the Ile-de-France committee, who declared: 'The rugby league experiment has not been a happy one. It showed the excesses of a sport which generally did not have officials who were sufficiently competent.' Blain's riposte was to say that: '...the excesses of rugby league were, in 1939, after only five years' existence, to have rallied the elite of French rugby to its cause, to have beaten the English in England[v] and to have won the international tournament for the first time in the history of French rugby.'

Those beginnings of the move against rugby league which Blain first heard about in the Basque country in August 1940 were seen through to their conclusion at Vichy. The department responsible, the Commissariat Général des Sports, was headed by another well-known Basque, Jean Borotra, operating within the Ministry led by his friend Ybarnegaray. As Blain notes, the department was run by ex-rugby union players, including Colonel Joseph Pascot, the former USAP player who took over from Borotra in 1942. It is widely held that Pascot was responsible for overseeing the suppression of rugby league. It is for these reasons that it has been said that the process of banning rugby league began at one end of the Pyrenees – Bayonne – and ended at the other – Perpignan, the city of Pascot's home club.

The effect was that all rugby league players, if they were to continue to play rugby at all, must play the 15-a-side code, while all the Ligue's assets were seized by the Comité National des Sports and have never been recovered.

Appendix II

•

Championship finals (Max Rousié Shield)

1935 Villeneuve *on points*
1936 XIII Catalan 25 Bordeaux 14
1937 Bordeaux 23 XIII Catalan 10
1938 Albi 8 Villeneuve 5
1939 Roanne 9 Villeneuve 0
1940 XIII Catalan 20 Pau 16
(*wartime championship*)
1945 Carcassonne 13 Toulouse 12
1946 Carcassonne 12 Toulouse 0
1947 Roanne 19 Carcassonne 0
1948 Roanne 3 Carcassonne 2
1949 Marseille 12 Carcassonne 5
1950 Carcassonne 21 Marseille 7
1951 Lyon 15 XIII Catalan 10
1952 Carcassonne 18 Marseille 6
1953 Carcassonne 19 Lyon 12
1954 Bordeaux 7 Marseille 4
1955 Lyon 7 Carcassonne 6
1956 Albi 13 Carcassonne 5
1957 XIII Catalan 14 Avignon 9
1958 Albi 8 Carcassonne 6
1959 Villeneuve 24 Lézignan 16
1960 Roanne 31 Albi 24
1961 Lézignan 7 Roanne 4
1962 Albi 14 Villeneuve 7
1963 Lézignan 20 St Gaudens 13
1964 Villeneuve 4 Toulouse 3
1965 Toulouse 47 Villeneuve 15
1966 Carcassonne 45 St Gaudens 20
1967 Carcassonne 39 St Gaudens 15
1968 Limoux 13 Carcassonne 12
1969 XIII Catalan 12 St Gaudens 11
1970 St Gaudens 32 XIII Catalan 10
1971 St Estève 13 St Gaudens 4
1972 Carcassonne 21 St Gaudens 9
1973 Toulouse 18 Marseille 0
1974 St Gaudens 21 Villeneuve 8
1975 Toulouse 10 St Estève 9
1976 Carcassonne 14 Lézignan 6
1977 Albi 19 Carcassonne 10
1978 Lézignan 3 XIII Catalan 0
1979 XIII Catalan 17 Carcassonne 2
1980 Villeneuve 12 St Estève 7
1981 Villeneuve v XIII Catalan
match abandoned
1982 XIII Catalan 21 St Estève 8
1983 XIII Catalan 10 Villeneuve 8
1984 XIII Catalan 30 Villeneuve 6
1985 XIII Catalan 26 Le Pontet 6
1986 Le Pontet 19 XIII Catalan 6
1987 XIII Catalan 11 Le Pontet 3
1988 Le Pontet 14 XIII Catalan 2
1989 St Estève 23 Le Pontet 4
1990 St Estève 24 Carcassonne 23
1991 St Gaudens 10 Villeneuve 8
1992 Carcassonne 11 St Estève 10
1993 St Estève 9 XIII Catalan 8
1994 XIII Catalan 6 Pia 4
1995 Pia 12 St Estève 10
1996 Villeneuve 27 St Estève 26

1997 St Estève 28 Villeneuve 24
1998 St Estève 15 Villeneuve 8
1999 Villeneuve 33 St Gaudens 20
2000 Toulouse 20 St Estève 18
2001 Villeneuve 32 Toulouse 20
2002 Villeneuve 17
Union Treiziste Catalane 0
2003 Villeneuve 31 St Gaudens 18
2004 St Gaudens 14
Union Treiziste Catalane 10
2005 UTC 66 Toulouse 16
2006 Pia 21 Toulouse 18
2007 Pia 20 Lézignan 16
2008 Lézignan 26 Pia 16
2009 Lézignan 40 Limoux 32
2010 Lézignan 32 Pia 22
2011 Lézignan 17 Limoux 12
2012 Carcassonne 26 Pia 20
2013 Pia 33 St Estève-XIII Catalan 26
2014 Toulouse 38 Lézignan 12
2015 Toulouse 20 Carcassonne 12
2016 Limoux 26 Carcassonne 24
2017 Limoux 24 Lézignan 22
2018 Avignon 34 Limoux 28

Cup finals (Lord Derby Trophy)

1935 Lyon 22 XIII Catalan 7
1936 Côte Basque 15 Villeneuve 8
1937 Villeneuve 12 XIII Catalan 6
1938 Roanne 36 Villeneuve 12
1939 XIII Catalan 7 Toulouse 3
1940 *not played*
1945 XIII Catalan 27 Carcassonne 18
1946 Carcassonne 27 XIII Catalan 7
1947 Carcassonne 24 Avignon 5
1948 Marseille 5 Carcassonne 4
1949 Marseille 12 Carcassonne 9
1950 XIII Catalan 12 Lyon 5
1951 Carcassonne 22 Lyon 10
1952 Carcassonne 28 XIII Catalan 9
1953 Lyon 9 Villeneuve 8
1954 Lyon 17 XIII Catalan 15
1955 Avignon 18 Marseille 10
1956 Avignon 25 Bordeaux 15
1957 Marseille 11 XIII Catalan 0
1958 Villeneuve 20 Avignon 8
1959 XIII Catalan 7 Avignon 0
1960 Lézignan 7 Carcassonne 4
1961 Carcassonne 5 Lézignan 2
1962 Roanne 16 Toulouse 10
1963 Carcassonne 5 Toulouse 0
1964 Villeneuve 10 Toulouse 2
1965 Marseille 13 Carcassonne 8
1966 Lézignan 22 Villeneuve 7
1967 Carcassonne 10 XIII Catalan 4
1968 Carcassonne 9 Toulouse 2
1969 XIII Catalan 15 Villeneuve 8
1970 Lézignan 14 Villeneuve 8
1971 Marseille 17 Lézignan 2
1972 St Estève 12 Villeneuve 5
1973 St Gaudens 22 Carcassonne 8
1974 Albi 21 Lézignan 11
1975 Pia 9 Marseille 4
1976 XIII Catalan 23 Toulouse 8
1977 Carcassonne 21 XIII Catalan 16
1978 XIII Catalan 18 Lézignan 7
1979 Villeneuve 15 Carcassonne 5
1980 XIII Catalan 18 Carcassonne 8
1981 *not played*
1982 Avignon 18 Carcassonne 12
1983 Carcassonne 10 XIII Catalan 3
1984 Villeneuve 18 Limoux 7
1985 XIII Catalan 24 Limoux 7
1986 Le Pontet 35 St Estève 10
1987 St Estève 20 XIII Catalan 10
1988 Le Pontet 5 St Estève 2
1989 Avignon 12 Le Pontet 11
1990 Carcassonne 22 St Estève 8

1991 St Gaudens 30 Pia 4
1992 St Gaudens 22 Carpentras 10
1993 St Estève 12 XIII Catalan 10
1994 St Estève 14 XIII Catalan 12
1995 St Estève 28 Pia 8
1996 Limoux 39 Carcassonne 12
1997 XIII Catalan 25 Limoux 24
1998 St Estève 38 Avignon 0
1999 Villeneuve 20 Lézignan 5
2000 Villeneuve 34 XIII Catalan 14
2001 Union Treiziste Catalane 38 Limoux 17
2002 Villeneuve 27 Pia 18
2003 Villeneuve 16 Pia 14
2004 Union Treiziste Catalane 39 Carcassonne 24
2005 Union Treiziste Catalane 31 Limoux 12
2006 Pia 36 Lézignan 20
2007 Pia 30 Carcassonne 14
2008 Limoux 17 Albi 14
2009 Carcassonne 18 Limoux 16
2010 Lézignan 18 Limoux 14
2011 Lézignan 27 Pia 18
2012 Carcassonne 14 Pia 12
2013 Avignon 38 Limoux 37
2014 Toulouse 46 Carcassonne 10
2015 Lézignan 27 St Estève-XIII Catalan 25
2016 St Estève-XIII Catalan 33 Limoux 16
2017 Carcassonne 30 Lézignan 24
2018 St Estève-XIII Catalan 30 Limoux 26

Endnotes

•

Chapter 1

[i] Paul Voivenel, *Mon Beau Rugby*, Paris, La Table Ronde, 2007, pp 337-8, first published by Editions de l'Héraklès, 1942
[ii] *La Petite Gironde*, 9 May 1944
[iii] Albert Camus, *La Chute* (translated into English as *The Fall*), Paris, Editions Gallimard, 1956
[iv] Henri Garcia, *La Fabuleuse Histoire du rugby*, Paris, Editions de la Martinière, 2011 (revised edition), p 345
[v] J-L Gay-Lescot, *La Politique sportive de Vichy*, in Jean-Pierre Rioux (ed.) *La Vie culturelle sous Vichy*, Brussels, Editions Complexe, 1990, pp 101-7
[vi] Figures taken from J-P Augustin and A Garrigou, *Le Rugby démêlé*, Bordeaux, Le Mascaret, 1985, p 81
[vii] Figure provided by Jean Larronde, who has calculated that in 1939 there were 14 professional clubs, 132 amateur clubs and 79 school or university clubs.
[viii] See Appendix 1: How Rugby League Was Banned
[ix] See Mike Rylance, *The Forbidden Game*, Brighouse, League Publications, 1999, pp 121-157
[x] For Voivenel report, see ibid., pp 132-4
[xi] Conversation with Raymond Roussennac, Albi, 7 June 2017, and subsequent e-mail 2 September 2017
[xii] The attack is recorded in Yves Benazech, *Les Terroristes de l'Espérance, Chronique de la Résistance dans le Tarn*, Puygouzon, Imprimerie Siep France, 2006; and in *Graulhet : Arc-en-ciel*, no. 109, Comité culturel, Autumn 2007
[xiii] Conversation with Madame Berthomieu, Albi, October 2008
[xiv] Conversation with René Rouanet, Albi, October 2008
[xv] Marcel Ruby, *La Résistance et la Contre-Résistance à Lyon et en Rhône-Alpes*, Lyon, Editions Horvath, 1995, pp 269-270; and letter to author from Réné Barnoud, 26 April 1994
[xvi] Taken from a hand-written statement by Louis Chauvin dated 10 June 1944 and two unidentified newspaper articles, one from May 1945, possibly from *La Voix du Peuple*, the other dated 10 June 1946, possibly from *Le Dauphiné Libéré*; provided by Madame Marcelle Mathon
[xvii] Lucien Maury, *La Résistance audoise*, vol. I, Comité d'Histoire de la Résistance du Département de l'Aude, 1980, p. 387
[xviii] Archives départementales de l'Aude, biographical note to personal collection 79J.
[xix] Maury, op. cit., vol. II, p. 225
[xx] Information provided by Pierre Rayssac, who interviewed Jean Escourrou, a relative of Mazon by marriage.
[xxi] Robert Barran, *Du Rugby et des Hommes*, Paris, Albin Michel, 1971, p 34
[xxii] Bernard Busson, *Héros du Sport, Héros de France*, Paris, Editions d'Art Athos, 1947
[xxiii] André Amila, *Le Rugby, des hommes, un club et sa légende*, Lézignan, Imprimerie Lézignanaise, 2001, p.106
[xxiv] Lucien Maury, op. cit., vol. II, p. 396
[xxv] Conversation with Madame Berthomieu, Albi, October 2008
[xxvi] *Le Tarn Libre*, 21 August 1944

[xxvii] Antony Beevor and Artemis Cooper, *Paris After the Liberation*, revised edition, Penguin, 2007, p 97
[xxviii] *Le Tarn Libre*, 23 September 1944 and *Midi Libre*, 26 Sept 1944
[xxix] Interview with Irénée Carrère, Perpignan, 18 July 2008
[xxx] *Midi Libre*, 25 September 1944
[xxxi] See Mike Rylance, op.cit. p149 & ff
[xxxii] *La Dépêche du Midi*, 17 October 1940
[xxxiii] 'Le Commissaire-Soleil' in the text: 'Commissaire' was Pascot's title as head of the department of general and sports education. 'Soleil' is evidently a reference to the all-powerful Roi-Soleil, Louis XIV
[xxxiv] Emmanuel Gambardella in *Midi-Libre*, 4 October 1944
[xxxv] Rugby union was endorsed by the Italian fascist régime under Mussolini
[xxxvi] *Midi-Libre*, 6 October 1944
[xxxvii] André Amila, *Le Rugby, des hommes, un club et sa légende*, 2001, p.103
[xxxviii] Information from Pierre Rayssac
[xxxix] Information provided by Jean Roques
[xl] Quoted in *Toulouse Olympique XIII - 73 years of rugby*, L'Amicale des anciens du TO, Toulouse, 2009
[xli] *But*, 8 October 1946
[xlii] Information provided by Jean Larronde
[xliii] *Midi-Libre*, 14 May 1945
[xliv] *Midi-Libre*, 27 May 1945.
[xlv] See Jean-Pierre Bodis, *Histoire mondiale du rugby*, Toulouse, Editions Privat, 1987, p 217
[xlvi] Conversation with Jean and Jeannine Cabrol (née Bergèse), Carcassonne, 22 October 2014
[xlvii] Bernard Pratviel, *Immortel Pipette*, Toulouse, Editions Empreinte, 2004, pp 41 and 150
[xlviii] Bernard Pratviel, ibid., pp 43-9
[xlix] *Les Deux Rugbys dans l'Aude, des origines à 1980*, Carcassonne, Archives départementales de l'Aude, 1998, p 80

Chapter 2

[i] RFL Council minutes, 21 March 1945
[ii] *Sud-Ouest*, 19 November 1945. The following March, Huddersfield travelled to face Toulouse and XIII Catalan, winning both matches, while in the same month Broughton Rangers beat the Catalans but lost at Carcassonne.
[iii] Newspaper cutting, probably *Sunday Dispatch*, 18(?) December 1960
[iv] Lucien Maury, *La Résistance audoise*, vol. 1, p 287
[v] Ibid., p 359
[vi] Marianne Amar, *Nés pour courir*, Grenoble, Presses Universitaires de Grenoble, p 31
[vii] Antony Beevor and Artemis Cooper, *Paris after the Liberation*, p 99
[viii] Some sources give Barrière's rank in the Resistance as captain; others, such as here, as lieutenant
[ix] *Midi Libre*, 14 October 1944
[x] Robert Fassolette, *Histoire politique du conflit des deux rugby en France*, Diplôme de l'INSEP, Paris, 1996
[xi] In fact, Borotra was first imprisoned at Fresnes, Paris, before being transferred to Sachsenhausen, where he spent six months, and, on the intervention of the King of Sweden, saw the war out at Itter in Austria, in the company of notables including Paul Reynard, the ex-Prime Minister of France, and several generals
[xii] Quoted in Sir John Smyth, *Jean Borotra, The Bounding Basque*, London, Stanley Paul, 1974, p. 165
[xiii] J-T Fieschi, *Histoire du sport français de 1870 à nos jours*, Paris, PAC, 1983, p. 100
[xiv] Quoted in J-L Gay-Lescot, *Sport et Education sous Vichy*, Lyon, Presses universitaires de Lyon, 1991, p. 194
[xv] *La Vie de la FSGT*, December 1945, quoted in Marianne Amar, *Nés pour courir*, p. 30
[xvi] *Procès Jep Pascot*, quoted in Amar, ibid.
[xvii] Amar, p. 48
[xviii] Theodore Zeldin, *Histoire des passions françaises*, Paris, Seuil, 1980-81, quoted in J-L Gay-Lescot, *Sport et Education sous Vichy*
[xix] Figures for basketball, volleyball and rugby union given in J-L Gay-Lescot, *Sport et Education sous Vichy*, p 170
[xx] Augustin et Garrigou, *Le Rugby démêlé*, Bordeaux, Le Mascaret, 1985, p. 81
[xxi] *Midi Libre*, 19 September 1945

[xxii] Adolphe Jauréguy, *Qui veut jouer au rugby avec moi?*, Editions Correa, 1939
[xxiii] Georges Poggi, *Le Patriote du Sud-ouest*, 20(?) October 1944
[xxiv] *Midi Libre*, 18 December 1945
[xxv] *Rugby Treize*, November 1946
[xxvi] Fancello, Poggi et Odoul, *Le Stade Vélodrome 1937-98*, Editions Européennes de Marseille-Provence, n.d.
[xxvii] Ibid.
[xxviii] Serge Darboit in *Sport-Digest*, 1951
[xxix] *Midi Libre*, 21 September 1946
[xxx] See Jean-Michel Guiraud, *Marseille, cité-refuge des écrivains et des artistes* in *La Vie culturelle sous Vichy*, ed. J-P Rioux, Brussels, Editions Complexe, 1990
[xxxi] Marius Servant, *Midi-Olympique*, 20 July 1948
[xxxii] Ibid.
[xxxiii] Alex Bélias, *Midi-Olympique*, 20 January 1948

Chapter 3

[i] RFL Council minutes
[ii] Unidentified newspaper cutting, 7 January 1946
[iii] *Midi Libre*, 7 January 1946
[iv] *Yorkshire Post*, 25 February 1946
[v] RFL Council minutes, 30 June 1946
[vi] *Yorkshire Post*, 20 January 1947
[vii] *Yorkshire Post*, 27 October, 1947
[viii] *La Dépêche du Midi*, 24 November 1947
[ix] *Miroir Sprint*, 25 November 1947
[x] *Yorkshire Post*, 29 November 1948
[xi] Gaston Comes, interviewed in *Treize-Magazine*, November 1986
[xii] *L'Equipe*, 24 January 1949
[xiii] *Treize-Magazine*, November 1986
[xiv] Paul Déjean, interviewed in *Treize-Magazine*, November 1986
[xv] *Yorkshire Post*, 14 March 1949
[xvi] *But*, 14 March 1949
[xvii] Pierre About in *La Guerre des Deux Rugby*, Paris, Croisades Sportives, 1938
[xviii] *L'Equipe*, 14 March 1949
[xix] *But*, ibid.

Chapter 4

[i] Henri Garcia, *La Fabuleuse Histoire du rugby*, p 356
[ii] RC Albi XIII review 1960-61
[iii] AFP, 10 October 1944
[iv] *L'Equipe*, 18 September 1947, quoted in RC Albi XIII review 1960-61
[v] RFL archives
[vi] Robert Barran, *Du rugby et des hommes*, Paris, Albin Michel, 1971, p 37
[vii] Antoine Blain, *Midi Libre*, 30 January 1947
[viii] RC Albi XIII review 1960-61
[ix] *L'Equipe*, 18 September 1947
[x] RC Albi XIII review 1960-61
[xi] Match programme: Wales v England, 6 December 1947
[xii] *Le BEC*, sports journal of the Bordeaux Etudiants Club, 21 November 1947
[xiii] *La Dépêche du Midi*, 25 November 1947
[xiv] Ibid.
[xv] François Estrade, *La Dépêche du Midi*, 26 November 1947
[xvi] *La Dépêche du Midi*, 5 December 1947
[xvii] RFL archives
[xviii] *Vaincre*, 30 October 1944. Bergougnan's first and only appearance of the season for TO was also recorded in *La Liberté*, *L'Espoir* and *Le Patriote du Sud-Ouest*
[xix] *La Liberté*, 16 November 1944
[xx] *La Dépêche du Midi*, 2 January 1948
[xxi] *La Dépêche du Midi*, 7 January 1948
[xxii] Match programme: Wales v England, 6 December 1947
[xxiii] Lucien Remplon, *Bergougnan un génie du rugby*, Toulouse, Editions Farem, 2008, pp 114-5
[xxiv] In such publications as *Miroir-Sprint*, *But et Club*, and *Actualité Sportive*
[xxv] Lucien Remplon, op.cit.
[xxvi] *Midi-Olympique*, 20 January 1948
[xxvii] *La Dépêche du Midi*, 26 January 1948
[xxviii] *La Dépêche du Midi*, 8 January 1948
[xxix] Robert Fassolette, *Histoire politique du conflit des deux rugby en France*, p. 358
[xxx] *Rugby Treize*, June-July-August 1948, quoted in Bonnery, *Le Rugby à XIII, le plus français du monde*, p. 126
[xxxi] Marcel Oger, *L'Equipe*, 29 October 1948, quoted in Louis Bonnery, ibid., p.127.
[xxxii] Marcel Oger, ibid.
[xxxiii] Antoine Blain, *Midi Libre*, 30 January 1947

[xxxiv] Robert Fassolette, *ibid.*, p. 361
[xxxv] *Le Patriote Villeneuvois*, 18 November 1944
[xxxvi] *Midi-Olympique*, 20 January 1948

Chapter 5

[i] *Midi-Olympique*, 28 December 1948
[ii] *Midi-Olympique*, 25 January 1949
[iii] *Midi-Olympique*, 23 January 1951
[iv] Lucien Pelofi, *AS Carcassonne XIII – 50 ans en jaune et noir*, Carcassonne, 1988
[v] *Midi-Olympique*, 30 August 1949
[vi] Information provided by Bernard Vizier, June 2014
[vii] *Midi Libre*, 24 September 1949
[viii] *Le Patriote Villeneuvois*, 21 October 1944
[ix] *Rugby Treize*, March 1947
[x] *Rugby Treize*, November 1946, quoted in Fassolette, *Histoire politique du conflit des deux rugby en France*, 1996, p 365
[xi] *Midi-Olympique*, 27 June 1950
[xii] Ibid.
[xiii] *Toulouse Olympique XIII: 73 ans 1937-2009*, publ. by L'Amicale des anciens du TO XIII, Toulouse, 2010
[xiv] *Midi-Olympique*, 9 May 1950
[xv] *Midi-Olympique*, 6 February 1951
[xvi] Henri Garcia, *La Fabuleuse Histoire du Rugby*, p 381
[xvii] Ibid., p 382
[xviii] *Midi-Olympique*, 2 January 1951
[xix] Garcia, p 386
[xx] *Midi-Olympique*, 15 May 1951
[xxi] André Passamar, *L'Encyclopédie de Treize-Magazine*, Toulouse, 1984
[xxii] Marcel de Laborderie, *But et Club*, 14 November 1949
[xxiii] *Yorkshire Post*, 13 November 1950
[xxiv] JK Sharp, Report on Conference with French officials, Swansea, 21 October 1948 re tour of Australia by French team in 1949. I am indebted to Tony Collins for bringing this document to my attention.
[xxv] *Midi-Olympique*, 12 December 1950
[xxvi] Ibid.
[xxvii] *Paris-Presse*, 3 May 1951

Chapter 6

[i] *L'Equipe*, 14 January 1949
[ii] Henri Garcia, *Rugby Champagne*, Paris, Editions de la Table ronde, 1961, p 59
[iii] *L'Equipe*, March 1949
[iv] Interview by Didier Beaune, unidentified cutting
[v] Journal of Jo Crespo, unpubl.
[vi] Gaston Comes in *L'Indépendant*, 27 September 1951
[vii] George Crawford of *Sydney Morning Telegraph* in *Rugby League Review*, 7 June 1951
[viii] Ibid.
[ix] *Le Provençal*, 24 May, 1951
[x] George Crawford, ibid.
[xi] Gaston Comes in *L'Indépendant*, 27 September 1951
[xii] George Crawford, *Rugby League Review*, 21 June 1951
[xiii] Jim Mathers, *Sydney Truth*, 3 June 1951
[xiv] Ibid.
[xv] Gaston Comes in *L'Indépendant*, 1 October 1951
[xvi] Ibid.
[xvii] Tom Goodman, *Sydney Sunday Herald*, 12 June 1951
[xviii] Ibid.
[xix] *Sydney Sunday Telegraph*, 12 June 1951
[xx] George Crawford, *Sydney Morning Telegraph*, 12 June 1951
[xxi] Jim Mathers, *Sydney Truth*, 12 June 1951
[xxii] All quotes from *Sydney Sunday Herald*, 12 June 1951
[xxiii] Tom Goodman, *Sydney Sunday Herald*, 12 June 1951
[xxiv] Unidentified French newspaper clipping
[xxv] Gaston Comes in *L'Indépendant*, 3 October 1951
[xxvi] Interview with Elie Brousse, 19 May 2015
[xxvii] For example in *Le Provençal*, 27 June 1951
[xxviii] Journal of Jo Crespo
[xxix] Bernard Pratviel, *Immortel Pipette*, Toulouse, Editions Empreinte, 2004, p 97
[xxx] *Les Cahiers de l'Equipe*, 1959, reproduced in Pratviel, pp 30-31
[xxxi] Unidentified article with the byline of Didier Beaune
[xxxii] *L'Indépendant*, 21 June 1951
[xxxiii] *L'Indépendant*, 27 June 1951
[xxxiv] *Sydney Sunday Herald*, 1 July 1951

[xxxv] *Sydney Sunday Telegraph*, I July 1951
[xxxvi] Journal of Jo Crespo
[xxxvii] *Sydney Sunday Telegraph*, I July 1951
[xxxviii] Ibid.
[xxxix] Journal of Elie Brousse
[xl] *Sydney Sunday Telegraph*, I July 1951
[xli] Journal of Jo Crespo
[xlii] Unidentified clipping from French newspaper, 7 July 1951
[xliii] Unidentified clipping from French newspaper
[xliv] Unidentified clipping from French newspaper, 11 July 1951
[xlv] Unidentified clipping from French newspaper, 18 July 1951
[xlvi] Journal of Jo Crespo
[xlvii] *Midi-Olympique*, 17 July 1951
[xlviii] George Crawford, *Sydney Sunday Telegraph*, 22 July 1951
[xlix] *Sydney Sunday Herald*, 22 July 1951
[l] *Sydney Sunday Telegraph*, 22 July 1951
[li] *Sydney Truth*, 22 July 1951
[lii] Quoted in *Rugby League Review*, 9 August 1951
[liii] *Sydney Sunday Telegraph*, 22 July 1951
[liv] *Sydney Sunday Herald*, 22 July 1951
[lv] Jack Reardon, *Brisbane Courier-Mail*, 23 July 1951
[lvi] Ibid.
[lvii] Quoted in *Rugby League Review*, 9 August 1951
[lviii] Rylance, *The Forbidden Game*, pp 29-30

Chapter 7

[i] Journal of Jo Crespo
[ii] John Coffey in Trevor Delaney, *International Grounds of Rugby League*, Keighley, self-publ., 1995
[iii] Retranslated from an undated article in *L'Indépendant*
[iv] Journal of Jo Crespo
[v] Ibid.
[vi] Retranslated from an undated cutting from *L'Indépendant*
[vii] *Le Provençal*, undated cutting
[viii] Unidentified cutting from Gaston Calixte archive
[ix] *Le Provençal*, undated cutting
[x] George Crawford, *Rugby League Review*, Sept 1951
[xi] *Sydney Sunday Telegraph*, 22 July 1951
[xii] Henri Garcia, *Rugby-Champagne*, p 122. This achievement does not appear to have been recorded in the Australian press at the time.
[xiii] *Rugby League Review*, 25 October 1951
[xiv] Interview with Didier Beaune from unidentified cutting.
[xv] Ibid.
[xvi] Undated clipping from *L'Indépendant*
[xvii] Interview with Didier Beaune
[xviii] *Midi-Olympique*, 31 July 1951
[xix] Interview with Didier Beaune
[xx] *Le Provençal*, 20 September 1951
[xxi] *Midi-Olympique*, 7 August 1951
[xxii] *Midi-Olympique*, 3 July 1951
[xxiii] Figures taken from an unidentified newspaper article, written by Tom Goodman, 17 August 1951. It is not clear whether the figures refer to Australian or British pounds.
[xxiv] Conversation with Jacques Merquey, Souillac, 11 June 2014
[xxv] Conversation with Elie Brousse, Le Coteau, 19 May 2015
[xxvi] *Midi-Olympique*, 11 September 1951
[xxvii] *Midi-Olympique*, 28 August 1951
[xxviii] *Midi-Olympique*, 11 September 1951
[xxix] Ibid.
[xxx] *Midi-Olympique*, 29 May 1951
[xxxi] Alcide Carrière, *Midi-Olympique*, 21 August 1951
[xxxii] F Cousteaux, *Midi-Olympique*, 18 September 1951

Chapter 8

[i] Jean Dumas in *Miroir-Sprint*, autumn 1949, quoted in Pratviel, *Immortel Pipette*, p 98
[ii] G Pagès, *Le Livre d'Or de Limoux XIII 1951-1993*, Limoux, Cano et Franck, 1993
[iii] J-P Souyri, *Un Demi-siècle de rugby à 13 à Villefranche de Rouergue*, Villefranche de Rouergue, Amicale treiziste villefranchoise, 2000
[iv] Marcel de Laborderie, *But et Club*, 26 November 1951
[v] Alfred Drewry, *Yorkshire Post*, 3 November 1951
[vi] Raoul Raynal, *Midi-Olympique*, 6 November 1951

[vii] *Yorkshire Post*, 5 November 1951
[viii] Conversation with Jacques Merquey, Souillac, 11 June 2014
[ix] *Yorkshire Post*, 26 November 1951
[x] Gaston Bénac, *But et Club*, 26 November 1951
[xi] *But et Club*, 24 December 1951
[xii] Ibid.
[xiii] *But et Club*, 31 December 1951
[xiv] *Midi-Olympique*, 11 December 1951
[xv] *Midi-Olympique*, 29 July 1952
[xvi] *Midi-Olympique*, 2 September 1952
[xvii] Ibid.
[xviii] Pelofi, *50 Ans en jaune et noir*, p 38
[xix] *Miroir-Sprint*, 15 September 1952
[xx] *Midi-Olympique*, 31 March 1953
[xxi] *Midi-Olympique*, 30 September 1952
[xxii] *Midi-Olympique*, 7 April 1953
[xxiii] Ibid.
[xxiv] *Midi-Olympique*, 28 October 1952
[xxv] Robert Gate, *The Struggle for the Ashes II*, self-publ., 1996
[xxvi] *Midi-Olympique*, 30 December 1952
[xxvii] *Midi-Olymique*, 13 January 1953
[xxviii] *Miroir-Sprint*, 28 January 1953
[xxix] Pelofi, *50 Ans en jaune et noir*, p 39

Chapter 9

[i] Robert Barran, *Le Rugby des Villages*, Paris, Les Editeurs français réunis, 1974, p 116
[ii] This chapter is based on an nterview with Elie Brousse, Le Coteau, 19 May 2015, and subsequent telephone conversations

Chapter 10

[i] *Midi-Olympique*, 9 June 1953
[ii] *Midi-Olympique*, 23 June 1953
[iii] *Midi-Olympique*, 4 August 1953
[iv] *Midi-Olympique*, 6 July 1953
[v] *Sunday Sun & Guardian*, 29 March 1953
[vi] *Miroir-Sprint*, 15 September 1952
[vii] *Midi-Olympique*, 18 May 1954
[viii] André Passamar, *L'Encyclopédie de Treize-Magazine*, 1984
[ix] *Midi-Olympique*, 18 May 1954
[x] *Midi-Olympique*, 10 August 1954
[xi] *Midi-Olympique*, 22 June 1954
[xii] *Midi-Olympique*, 6 July 1954
[xiii] *Midi-Olympique*, 13 July 1954
[xiv] *Midi-Olympique*, 10 November 1953
[xv] Unidentified newspaper cutting, 3 January 1954
[xvi] Newspaper cuttings dated 13 and 21 November 1934
[xvii] Bill Fallowfield, Official programme, World Cup Series 1960
[xviii] Ibid.
[xix] Ibid.
[xx] *Midi-Olympique*, 2 November 1954
[xxi] Joe Humphreys, *Daily Mirror*, in Rugby League World Cup Series, Official Souvenir
[xxii] Alfred Drewry, *Yorkshire Post*, 5 November 1954
[xxiii] Alfred Drewry, *Yorkshire Post*, 6 November 1954
[xxiv] *Yorkshire Evening Post*, 6 November 1954
[xxv] *Yorkshire Post*, 8 November 1954
[xxvi] Bill Fallowfield, Official programme, World Cup Series 1960
[xxvii] See for example Jean Boudey, *Midi-Olympique*, 16 November 1954
[xxviii] Ibid.

Chapter 11

[i] *Midi-Olympique*, 1 February 1955.
[ii] *Midi-Olympique*, 1 June 1954
[iii] *Midi-Olympique*, 21 September 1954
[iv] Bonnery, *Le Rugby à XIII le plus français du monde*, p 312
[v] *La Dépêche du Midi*, Aude edition, 17 June, 1985, quoted in Bonnery, ibid.
[vi] *Midi-Olympique*, 28 June 1955
[vii] Ibid.
[viii] RC Albi Calendrier-revue 1955-56
[ix] The various accounts of the match do not all concur. Jean Duhau, the coach, and Jacky Merquey, the captain, both agree on the crucial role played in all three tries by Jean Dop. Antoine Jimenez, who did not play, credits Maurice Voron with an interception which led to Roger Rey's second try and does not mention Dop's role. Merquey, in a telephone conversation of 16 December 2015, stressed that Dop was at the basis of the attacks which led to the three late tries.

[x] Telephone conversation, 16 December 2015
[xi] *Midi Libre*, 2 July 1955
[xii] François Montrucolis recalled that it was Voron who scored, not Vanel.
[xiii] ABC Sporting Service, French Rugby League tour booklet, 1955
[xiv] *Rugby Leaguer*, undated cutting – August-September 1955
[xv] *Midi-Olympique*, 2 August 1955
[xvi] *Midi-Olympique*, 30 Augusr 1955

Chapter 12

[i] All of this chapter is based on a conversation with Jacky Merquey and Antoine Jimenez on
7 July 2015 at Souillac and a previous conversation on 11 June 2014 at the same place
[ii] Jean-Pierre Bodis, *Histoire mondiale du rugby*, Toulouse, Privat, 1987

Chapter 13

[i] Jean-Pierre Bodis, *Histoire mondiale du rugby*, p 294
[ii] Ibid.
[iii] Communication from Robert Fassolette, 16 January 2018
[iv] Robert Fassolette, *Rugby League Football in France 1934-54: The Decisive Years and their Long-term Consequences*, Routledge, Sport in History, Vol 27, No. 3, Sept 2007, pp 380-398
[v] J-L Gay-Lescot, *Sport et Education sous Vichy*, p 158
[vi] Fassolette, ibid.
[vii] Quoted in RC Albi Calendrier-revue, 1954-55
[viii] *Midi-Olympique*, 21 June 1955
[ix] Tony Collins, *Rugby League in Twentieth-Century Britain*, p 109
[x] International Board minutes, 28 October 1954, quoted in Collins, ibid.
[xi] Allan Cave, *Daily Herald*, 12 December 1955
[xii] *Midi-Olympique*, 24 January 1956
[xiii] *Midi-Olympique*, 28 February 1956
[xiv] *Paris-Match*, 4 February 1956, quoted in Pratviel, *Immortel Pipette*, p 86
[xv] Derek Marshall in unidentified clipping, 27 or 28 January 1957
[xvi] I am indebted to Robert Gate for this official information. It should also be pointed out that Allan Cave, in his *Daily Herald* match report, records the France-GB match of 11 December 1955 in Paris as the first test match between the two countries.
[xvii] I am indebted to Harry Edgar for pointing out this fact.
[xviii] Bodis, pp 306-7
[xix] Henri Garcia, *La Fabuleuse Histoire du Rugby*, p 458
[xx] *Miroir-Sprint*, 12 December 1955
[xxi] Augustin et Garrigou, *Le Rugby démêlé*, p 338
[xxii] Ibid., p 337
[xxiii] *Cent ans de XV de France*, Toulouse, Editions Midi-Olympique, 2005, p 80
[xxiv] Unidentified clipping, 23 November 1958
[xxv] RC Albi Calendrier-revue 1955-56
[xxvi] *Midi-Olympique*, 8 August 1955
[xxvii] *Midi-Olympique*, 31 July 1956
[xxviii] Robert Barran, *Miroir Sprint*,
13 October 1958, reproduced in *Du Rugby et des Hommes*, p 151
[xxix] André Passamar, *L'Encyclopédie de Treize-Magazine*

Chapter 14

[i] Conversation with Honoré Conti, Puycelsi, 20 June 2014
[ii] Louis Bonnery, p 314
[iii] Jean Roques, *La Guerre des deux rugby à Albi* in *Mémoires Albigeoises*, ed. Robert Fabre, Pau, Editions Cairn, 2013
[iv] Conversation with Jean-Marie Bez, Albi, 28 March 2008
[v] Jean Roques, ibid.
[vi] Robert Fabre, *La Revue du Tarn*, no. 201, Spring 2006
[vii] Conversation with Gilbert Verdié, Albi, 30 May 2007
[viii] Conversation with Honoré Conti, Puycelsi, 20 June 2014
[ix] André Passamar, *L'Encyclopédie de Treize-magazine*, 1984
[x] *Midi-Olympique*, 26 June 1956
[xi] *Miroir-Sprint*, 2 June 1958
[xii] Harold Mathers, *Manchester Guardian*, 7 March 1960

[xiii] Jean Marquet, *L'Equipe*, 7 March 1960
[xiv] *Midi-Olympique*, 17 July 1956
[xv] *Midi-Olympique*, 24 July 1956
[xvi] *Midi-Olympique*, July 1958
[xvii] Ibid.
[xviii] *Midi-Olympique*, 17 August 1955
[xix] Ibid.
[xx] *Midi-Olympique*, 12 June 1956
[xxi] André Amila, *Le Rugby, des hommes, un club et sa légende*, p 144
[xxii] RC Roanne, *80 Ans de rugby à XIII à Roanne*, 2015
[xxiii] Information provided by Jean-Louis Toulouse, February 2016
[xxiv] *Un Demi-siècle de rugby à XIII à Villefranche-de-Rouergue*, Amicale treiziste Villefranchoise, 2000
[xxv] G Pagès, *Livre d'or de Limoux XIII 1951-1993*, Limoux, 1993
[xxvi] *Midi-Olympique*, July 1958

Chapter 15

[i] Henri Garcia, *L'Equipe*, 17 July 1960
[ii] *Midi-Olympique*, 19 July 1960
[iii] Jean Boudey, *Midi-Olympique*, 27 September 1960
[iv] Henri Garcia, *L'Equipe*, 25 September 1960
[v] Jean Boudey, *Midi-Olympique*, 4 October 1960
[vi] Unidentified clipping: probably Harry Sunderland, *Sunday Dispatch*, 18 December 1960
[vii] Crowd figures from R Fassolette in T Delaney, *The International Grounds of Rugby League*, 1995
[viii] Henri Garcia, *La Fabuleuse Histoire du rugby*, p 481
[ix] Laurent Roldos in Louis Bonnery, *Rugby à Treize France-Australie 1933-86*, Limoux, 1986, p 102
[x] André Passamar, unidentified clipping, 1964
[xi] Harold Mather, *Manchester Guardian*, 7 December 1964.
[xii] Jack Nott, unidentified clipping, 24 January 1965
[xiii] Unidentified clipping, 24 January 1965
[xiv] Conversation with Georges Aillères, Toulouse, 30 October 2017
[xv] Coincidentally, one significant mass demonstration took place at the Charléty stadium, which was to be associated with Paris Saint Germain almost thirty years later.
[xvi] Rod Kedward, *La Vie en bleu, France and the French since 1900*, London, Penguin, 2005, p 422
[xvii] Conversation with André Ferren, 11 August 2017.

Chapter 16

[i] André Passamar, *L'Equipe*, 11 May 1970, reproduced in *Album-Souvenir 1989-90, Le Racing Club Saint-Gaudinois à 30 ans*
[ii] Report by Jean Barrès to Federation Congress, 1970, FFRXIII archives.
[iii] Louis Bonnery, *Le Rugby à treize le plus français du monde*, p 249
[iv] Paul Tancrède, *Le XIII*, no. 18, 15 December 1976, quoted in Bonnery, ibid.
[v] *Rugby-Treize*, October-November 1972
[vi] Ibid.
[vii] Ibid.
[viii] *Treize-Magazine*, no. 3, November 1978, quoted in Bonnery, *Le Rugby à XIII le plus français du monde*, p 173
[ix] *Treize-Magazine* no. 215, April 2000
[x] Conversation with Carlos Zalduendo, 31 January 2018
[xi] *Treize-Magazine*, no. 4, December 1978.
[xii] André Passamar, *Encyclopédie de Treize-Magazine*
[xiii] See Hervé Girette, *Une Histoire du rugby à XIII en Roussillon*, p 49 & ff
[xiv] André Passamar, *L'aventure treiziste* in *Les Joies du rugby*, Paris, Hachette, 1971
[xv] Conversation with André Ferren, 11 August 2017

Chapter 17

[i] *Midi-Olympique*, 8 December 1980
[ii] 'The house opposite', i.e. rugby union.
[iii] *Midi-Olympique*, 15 December 1980
[iv] Ibid.
[v] *Midi-Olympique*, 17 November 1980
[vi] Conversation with Serge Costals, 6 February 2018
[vii] *Midi-Olympique*, 15 December 1980, quoting a previous statement by Ferrasse

[viii] Ibid.
[ix] Conversation with Jean-Marc Bourret, 8 March 2018
[x] Ibid.
[xi] Hervé Girette, *Une Histoire du rugby à treize en Roussillon*, Perpignan, Editions Mare Nostrum, 2007, p 47
[xii] *Yorkshire Post*, 21 February 1981
[xiii] Conversation with Bernard Guasch, 2 October 2018
[xiv] René Verdier, *Sports villeneuvois 1880-2005 et l'épopée du 13 vert*, Editions Le Luy de France, 2005, p 124
[xv] Jean-Paul Verdaguer, interviewed on TF1, 18 May 1981
[xvi] Henri Garcia, *La Fabuleuse Histoire du Rugby*, pp 347-8
[xvii] Information provided by Guy Laforgue (XIII Catalan), Patrick Pedrazzani and Carlos Zalduendo (both Villeneuve)
[xviii] Refers to the final battle of the First Indochina War in 1954, involving France and the Viet Minh; a precursor to the Vietnam War fought by the USA.
[xix] *Midi-Olympique*, 29 May 2006
[xx] Conversation with Patrick Pedrazzani, 17 March 2018
[xxi] Ibid.
[xxii] Verdier, *Sports villeneuvois*, p 124
[xxiii] *L'Equipe*, 18 May 1981
[xxiv] Ibid.
[xxv] Conversation with Guy Laforgue, 3 April 2018
[xxvi] Antenne 2, 18 May 1981
[xxvii] Ibid.
[xxviii] TF1, 18 May 1981
[xxix] Conversation with Bernard Guasch, 2 October 2018
[xxx] *Midi-Olympique*, 18 May 1981
[xxxi] *L'Equipe*, 18 May 1981
[xxxii] *Yorkshire Post*, 20 May 1981
[xxxiii] *The Times*, 20 May 1981
[xxxiv] *L'Equipe*, 18 May 1981
[xxxv] *Midi-Olympique*, 18 May 1981
[xxxvi] Lucien Pelofi, *50 ans en jaune et noir*, p 80.
[xxxvii] See Hervé Girette, *Une histoire du rugby à XIII en Roussillon*, pp 61-62
[xxxviii] *Midi-Olympique*, 11 May 1981
[xxxix] See Hervé Girette, ibid.
[xl] Raymond Fletcher, *Yorkshire Post*, 21 December 1981
[xli] FFRXIII minutes, 15 June 1989
[xlii] FFR XIII minutes, 15 June 1989
[xliii] Quoted in Bonnery, *Le Rugby à Treize le plus français du monde*, pp 128-9
[xliv] Quoted in Bonnery, p 130. Bonnery gives a detailed account of the battle to give rugby league back its original name, pp 125-134
[xlv] *Treize-Magazine*, October 1985
[xlvi] Ibid.
[xlvii] *Treize-Magazine*, December 1984
[xlviii] Girette, p 64
[xlix] See, for example, Tony Collins, *Rugby League in Twentieth Century Britain*, p 117
[l] Henri Garcia, *La Fabuleuse Histoire du rugby*, pp 538-9
[li] Garcia, pp 572-3
[lii] *Midi-Olympique*, 16 October 1978
[liii] *Treize-Magazine*, March 1987
[liv] *Treize-Magazine*, May 1987
[lv] *Treize-Magazine*, September 1989
[lvi] *Yorkshire Post*, 29 September 1989

Chapter 18

[i] *Treize-Magazine*, January 1986
[ii] Ibid.
[iii] *Yorkshire Post*, 9 April 1990
[iv] Conversation with Gilles Dumas, 16 May 2018
[v] *Treize-Magazine*, September 1990
[vi] *Treize-Magazine*, February 1991
[vii] Tony Pocock, ed., *The Rugby League Yearbook 1991-92*, London, Kingswood Press, 1991, p 175
[viii] *Treize-Magazine*, June 1990
[ix] David Oxley, Notes from a meeting with G Dautant and C Zalduendo, Leeds, 15 May 1991, RFL archives
[x] Ibid.
[xi] *Treize-Magazine*, March 1992
[xii] *Treize-Magazine*, May 1993
[xiii] *Treize-Magazine*, September 1994
[xiv] *Treize-Magazine*, October 1994
[xv] *Treize-Magazine*, December 1994
[xvi] Bonnery, *Le Rugby à XIII le plus français du monde*, p137
[xvii] *L'Equipe*, 8 November 1994
[xviii] *Treize-Magazine*, December 1994

[xix] *Treize-Magazine*, January 1995
[xx] *Treize-Magazine*, June 1995
[xxi] *L'Equipe*, 19 September 1995, quoted in *Treize-Magazine*, October 1995
[xxii] *Treize-Magazine*, November 1995
[xxiii] *Treize-Magazine*, December 1995
[xxiv] *Treize-Magazine*, April 1996
[xxv] Ibid.
[xxvi] Conversation with Pierre Chamorin, 29 May 2018
[xxvii] *League Express*, 19 December 2005
[xxviii] *Treize-Magazine*, March 1997
[xxix] Conversation with Pierre Chamorin, 29 May 2018
[xxx] *Treize-Magazine*, June-July 2004
[xxxi] Mike Rylance, *Fouroux the Bell Tolls* in Tony Hannan, ed., *Seasons in the Sun*, Halifax, Impress Sport, 2005, p64

Chapter 19

[i] Maurice Lindsay interview with Mike Rylance, *Treize-Magazine*, October 1997
[ii] *League Express*, 1 August 2005
[iii] *Treize-Magazine*, February 1992
[iv] *League Express*, 29 November 2004
[v] *League Express*, 22 November 2004
[vi] Nicolas Larrat interview with Mike Rylance, *League Express*, 2 August 2004
[vii] *League Express*, 4 July 2005
[viii] *League Express*, 19 December 2005
[ix] *League Express*, 13 February 2006
[x] Nicolas Larrat interview with Mike Rylance, *League Express*, 9 October 2006
[xi] *League Express*, 23 October 2006
[xii] Carlos Zalduendo interview with Mike Rylance, *League Express*, 6 August 2007
[xiii] Carlos Zalduendo interview with Mike Rylance, *League Express*, 28 July 2008
[xiv] *League Express*, 20 October 2008
[xv] *League Express*, 9 June 2013
[xvi] Mathieu Khedimi interview with Mike Rylance, *League Express*, 2 April 2017
[xvii] Communiqué from Catalans Dragons
[xviii] Sylvain Houlès interview with Mike Rylance, F*orty20*, October 2017
[xix] *League Express*, 2 October 2017

Postscript

[i] *Essais et Tenus*, Revue de l'amicale d'enseignants 'Les amis du rugby à XIII', no. 11, Carcassonne, n.d. (1970 ?)
[ii] XIII Catalan, *Cinquante ans d'épopée*, 1984, p 84
[iii] Letter dated 7 February 1990 (RFL archives)
[iv] *Yorkshire Post*, 29 September 1989
[v] Augustin et Garrigou, pp 86-7
[vi] *League Express*, 23 May 2011
[vii] *Rugby League World*, July 2010.
[viii] 'No elite, no mass; no mass, no elite.'
[ix] *Midi-Olympique*, 18 May 1992, quoted in Girette, *Une Histoire du rugby à treize en Roussillon*, p 21
[x] BBC Sport website, 8 November 2017
[xi] *Treize-Magazine*, October 1985

Appendix I

[i] Situated between Bayonne and Pau
[ii] In the German-occupied zone
[iii] These two rivers meet at Bayonne
[iv] The government department which oversaw the running of all sport, and which came under the aegis of Ybarnegaray's ministry
[v] Blain was a member of the France team which beat England 12-9 at St Helens on 25 February 1939